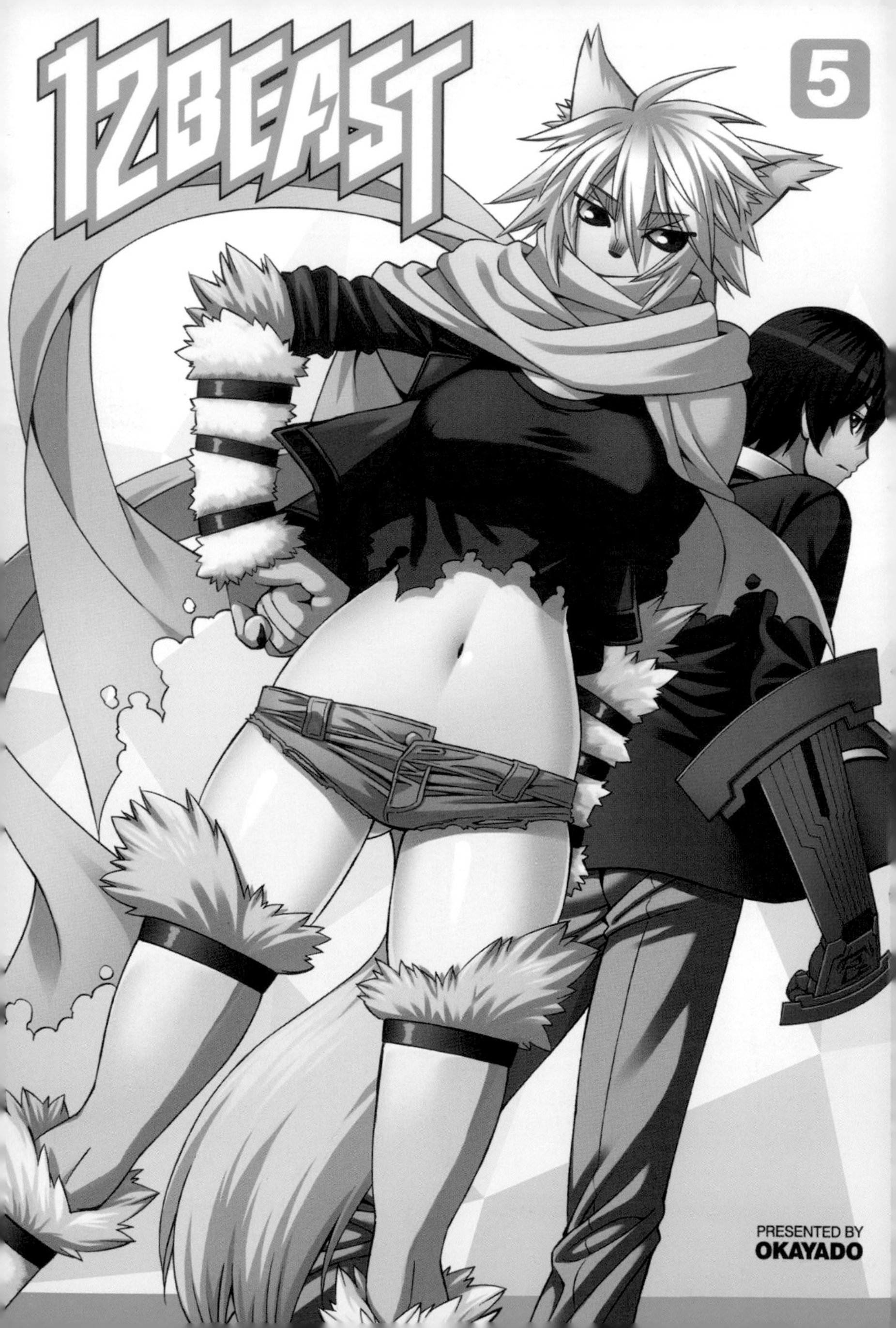
12BEAST
5
PRESENTED BY
OKAYADO

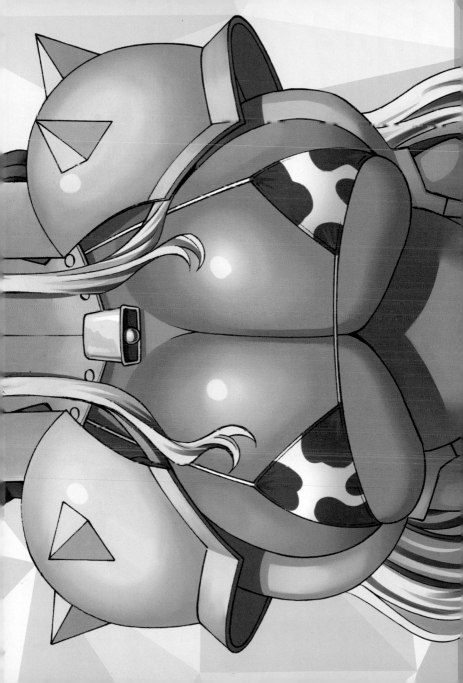

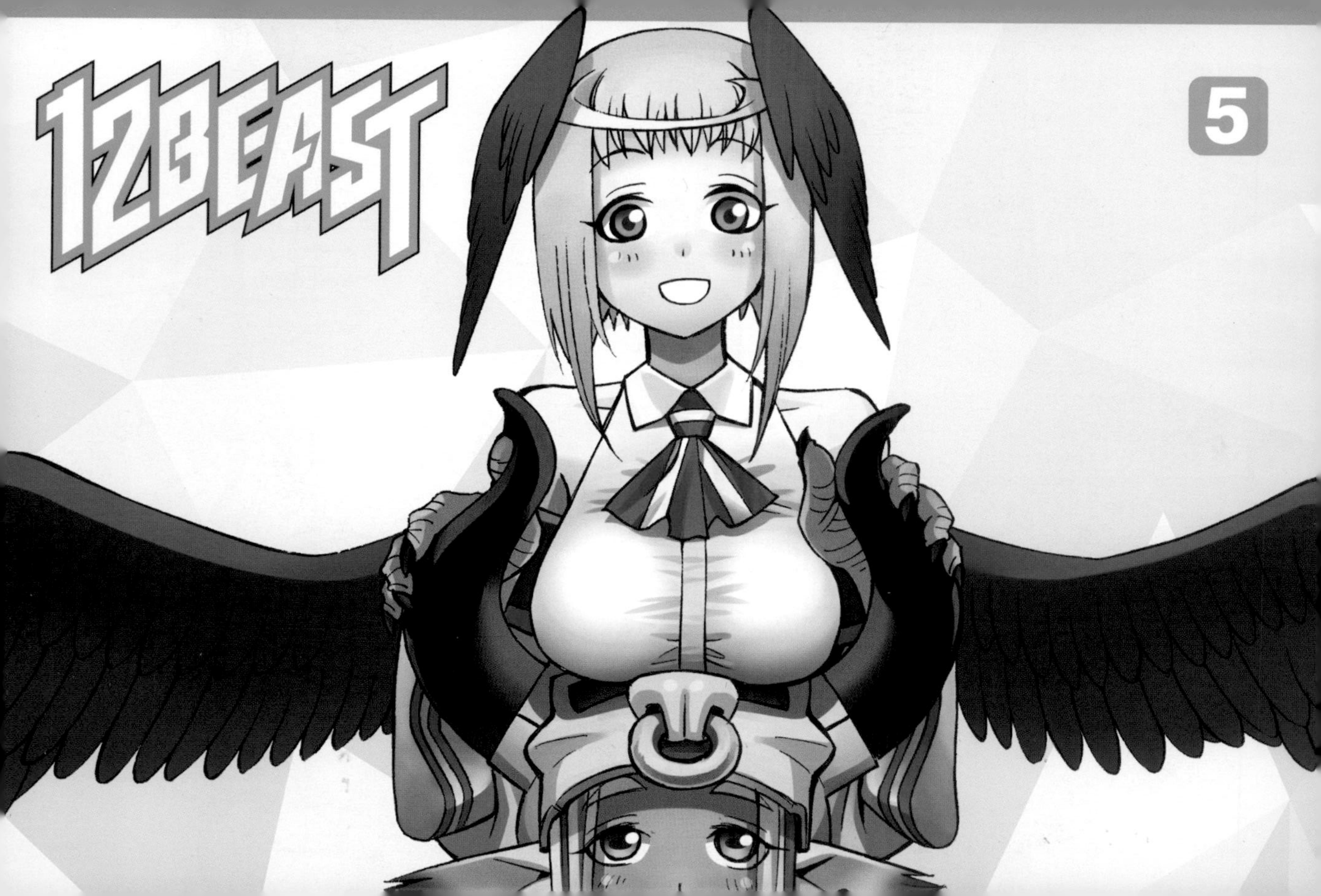
12BEAST
5

12 BEAST

PRESENTED BY **OKAYADO**

5

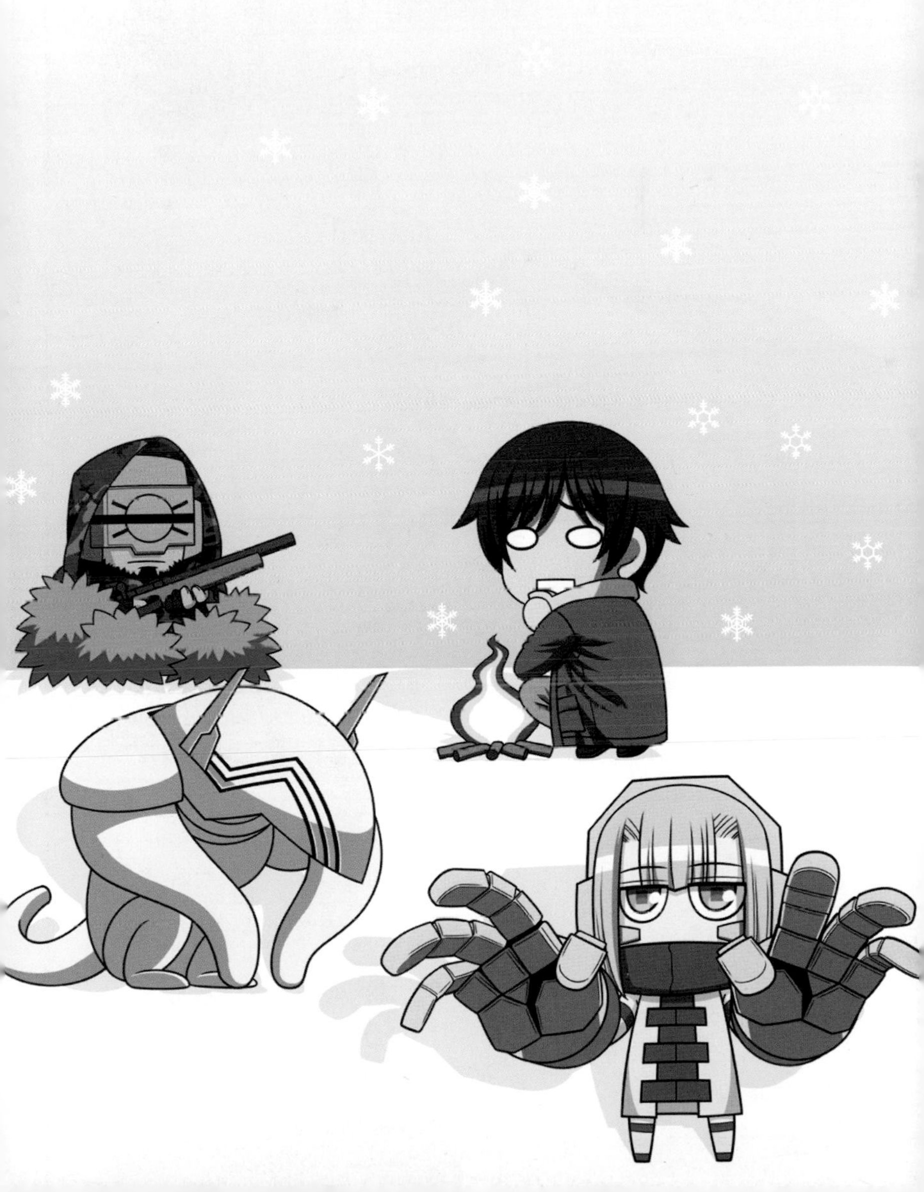

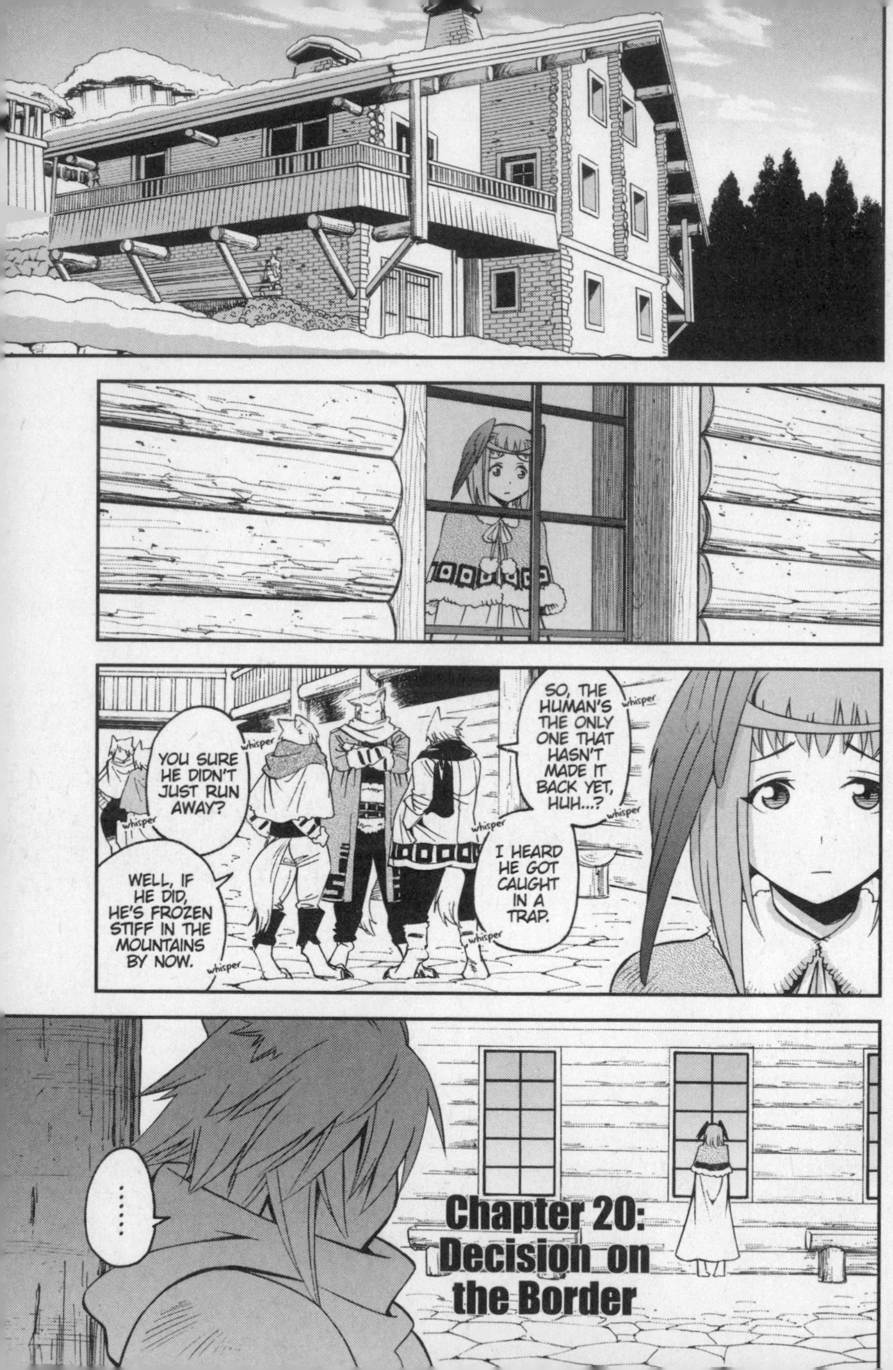
SO, THE HUMAN'S THE ONLY ONE THAT HASN'T MADE IT BACK YET, HUH...?
whisper
whisper
I HEARD HE GOT CAUGHT IN A TRAP.
whisper
YOU SURE HE DIDN'T JUST RUN AWAY?
whisper
whisper
WELL, IF HE DID, HE'S FROZEN STIFF IN THE MOUNTAINS BY NOW.
whisper
whisper
Chapter 20: Decision on the Border
......

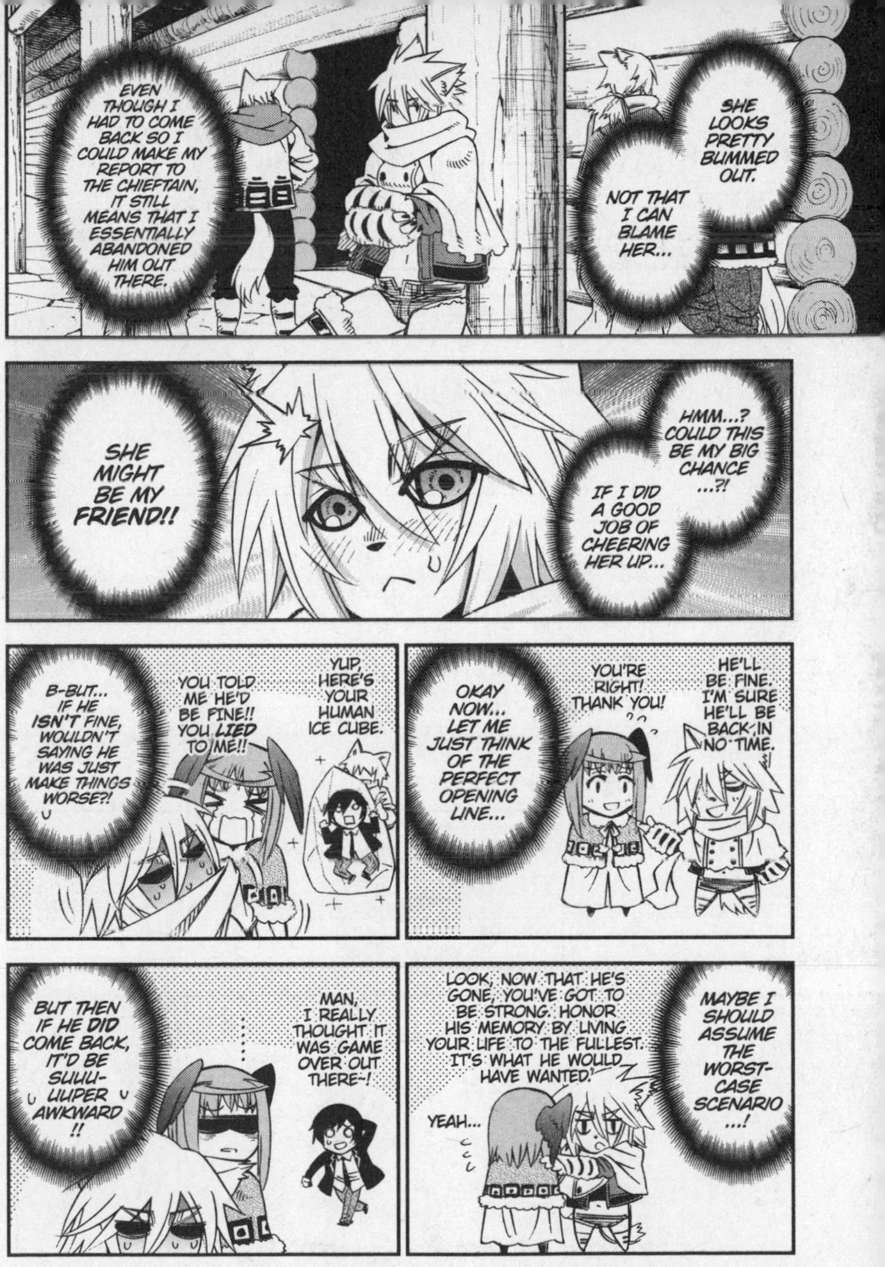
SHE LOOKS PRETTY BUMMED OUT.
NOT THAT I CAN BLAME HER...
EVEN THOUGH I HAD TO COME BACK SO I COULD MAKE MY REPORT TO THE CHIEFTAIN, IT STILL MEANS THAT I ESSENTIALLY ABANDONED HIM OUT THERE.
HMM...? COULD THIS BE MY BIG CHANCE ...?!
IF I DID A GOOD JOB OF CHEERING HER UP...
SHE MIGHT BE MY FRIEND!!
HE'LL BE FINE. I'M SURE HE'LL BE BACK IN NO TIME.
YOU'RE RIGHT! THANK YOU!
OKAY NOW... LET ME JUST THINK OF THE PERFECT OPENING LINE...
YUP, HERE'S YOUR HUMAN ICE CUBE.
YOU TOLD ME HE'D BE FINE!! YOU LIED TO ME!!
B-BUT... IF HE ISN'T FINE, WOULDN'T SAYING HE WAS JUST MAKE THINGS WORSE?!
MAYBE I SHOULD ASSUME THE WORST-CASE SCENARIO ...!
LOOK, NOW THAT HE'S GONE, YOU'VE GOT TO BE STRONG. HONOR HIS MEMORY BY LIVING YOUR LIFE TO THE FULLEST. IT'S WHAT HE WOULD HAVE WANTED.
YEAH...
MAN, I REALLY THOUGHT IT WAS GAME OVER OUT THERE~!
......
BUT THEN IF HE DID COME BACK, IT'D BE SUUU-UUPER AWKWARD !!

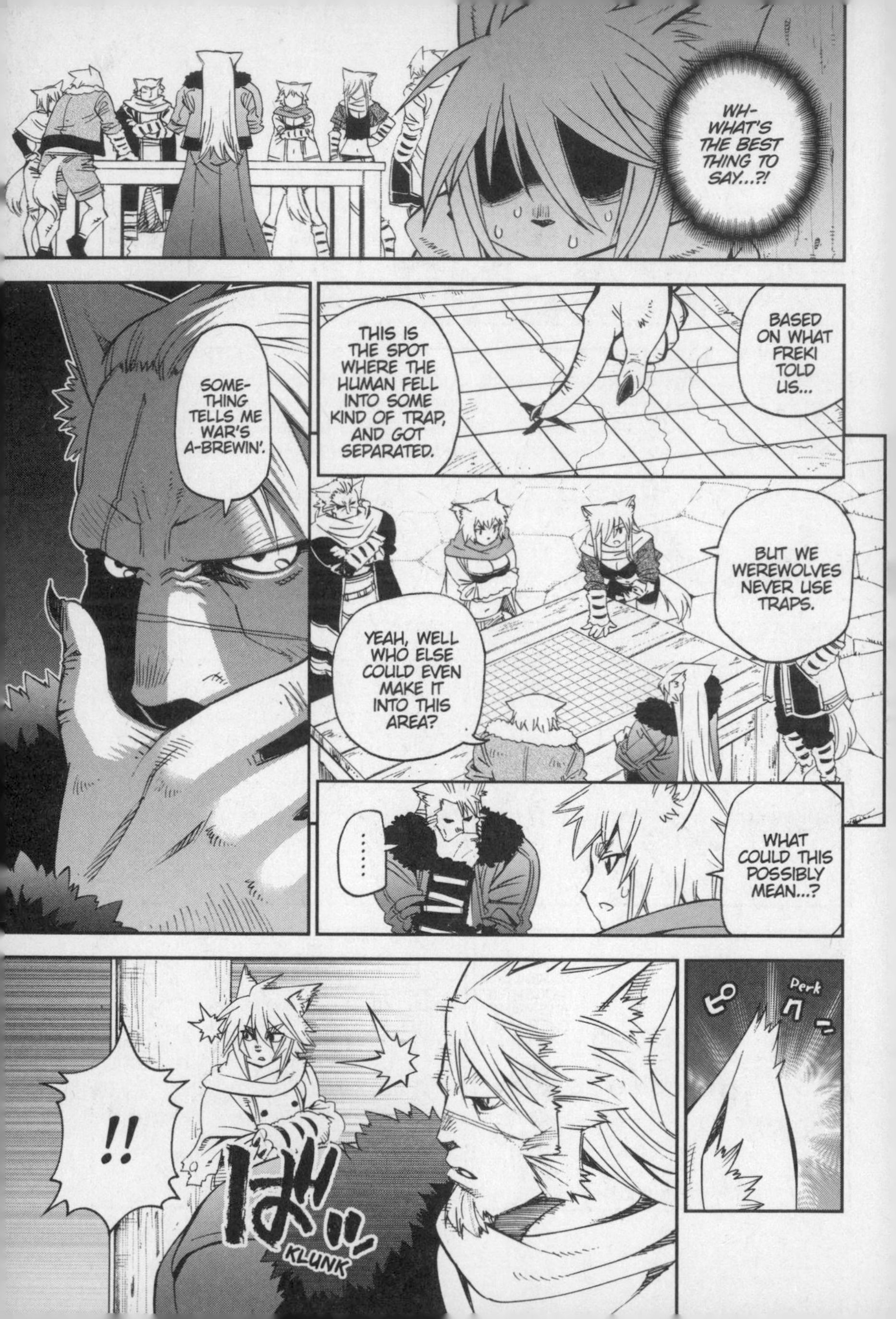
WH- WHAT'S THE BEST THING TO SAY...?!
BASED ON WHAT FREKI TOLD US...
THIS IS THE SPOT WHERE THE HUMAN FELL INTO SOME KIND OF TRAP, AND GOT SEPARATED.
BUT WE WEREWOLVES NEVER USE TRAPS.
YEAH, WELL WHO ELSE COULD EVEN MAKE IT INTO THIS AREA?
WHAT COULD THIS POSSIBLY MEAN...?
......
SOME-THING TELLS ME WAR'S A-BREWIN'.
Perk
!!
KLUNK

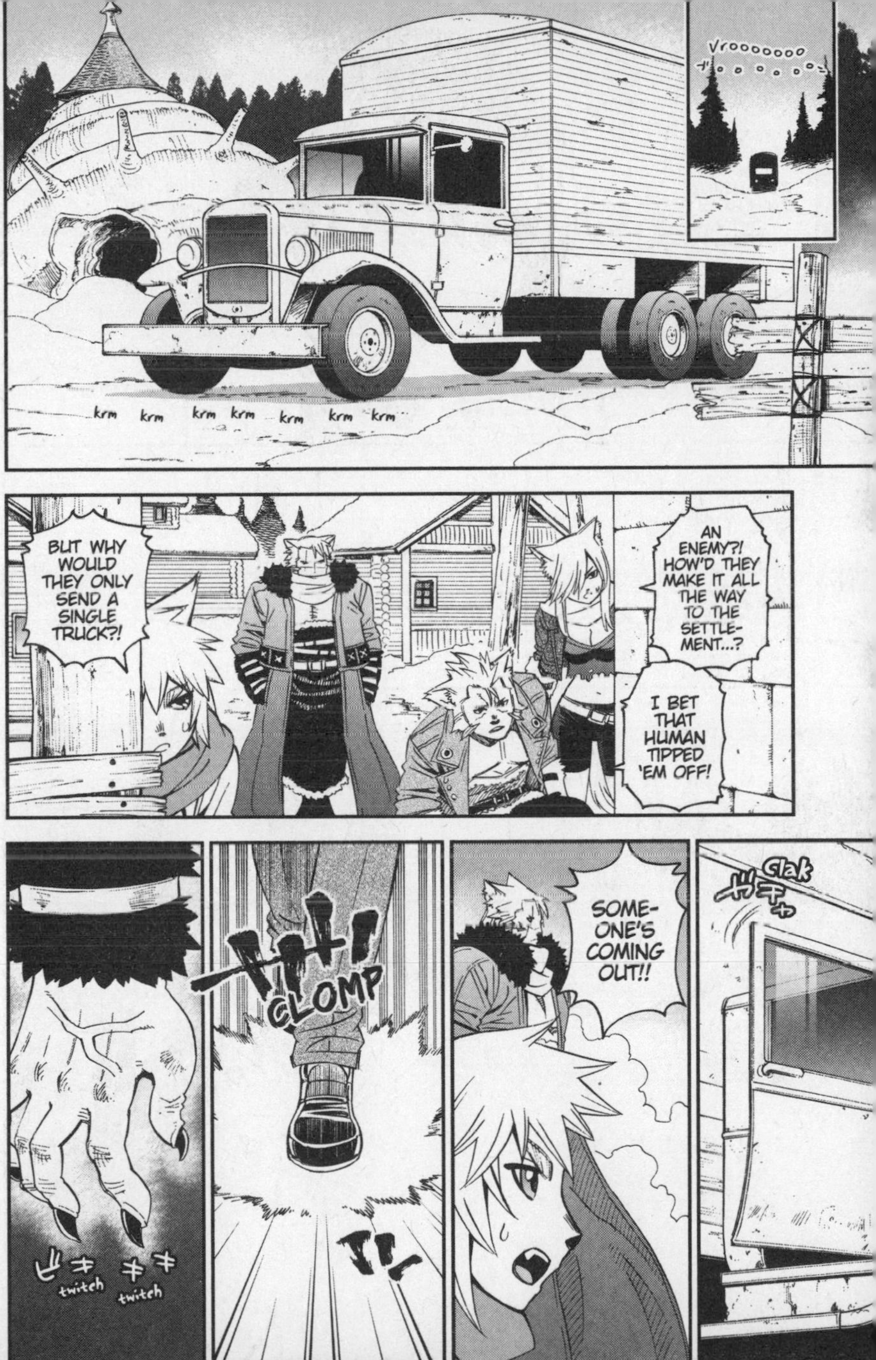
Vrooooooo
krm krm krm krm krm krm krm
AN ENEMY?! HOW'D THEY MAKE IT ALL THE WAY TO THE SETTLE-MENT...?
I BET THAT HUMAN TIPPED 'EM OFF!
BUT WHY WOULD THEY ONLY SEND A SINGLE TRUCK?!
Clak
SOME-ONE'S COMING OUT!!
CLOMP
twitch twitch

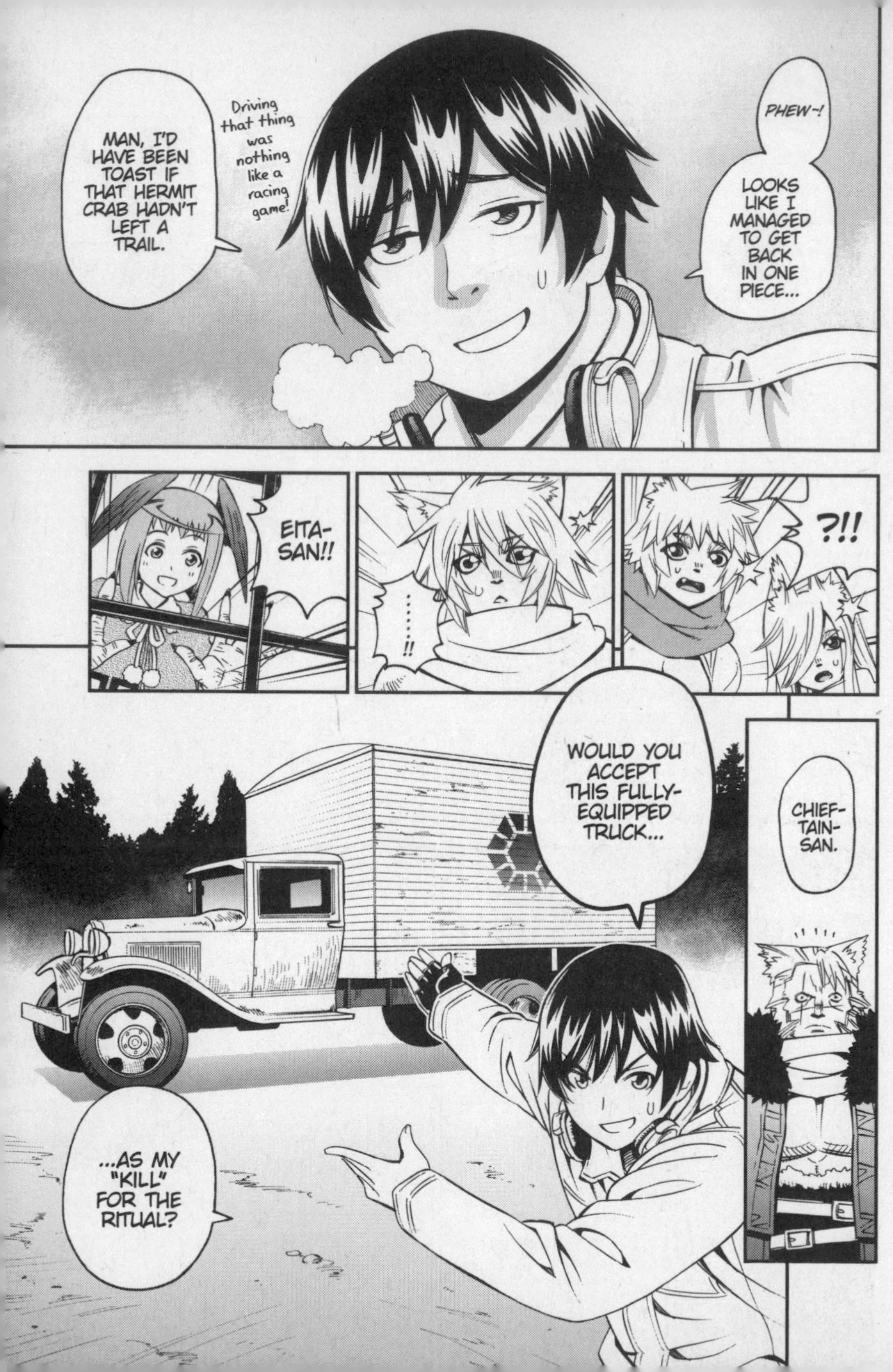
PHEW~!
LOOKS LIKE I MANAGED TO GET BACK IN ONE PIECE...
Driving that thing was nothing like a racing game!
MAN, I'D HAVE BEEN TOAST IF THAT HERMIT CRAB HADN'T LEFT A TRAIL.
?!!
......!!
EITA-SAN!!
CHIEF-TAIN-SAN.
WOULD YOU ACCEPT THIS FULLY-EQUIPPED TRUCK...
...AS MY "KILL" FOR THE RITUAL?

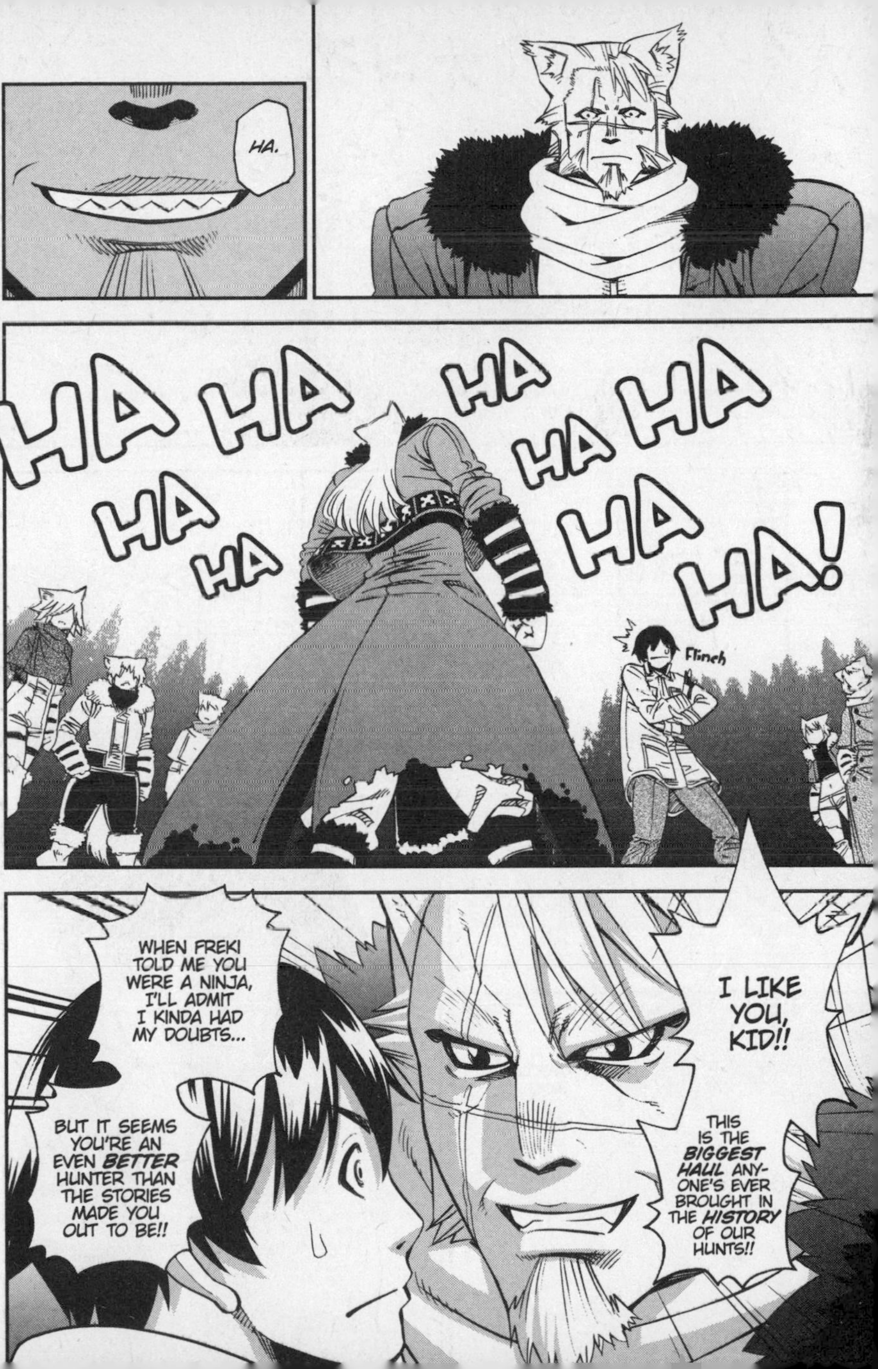
HA.
HA HA HA HA HA HA HA HA HA HA!
Flinch
WHEN FREKI TOLD ME YOU WERE A NINJA, I'LL ADMIT I KINDA HAD MY DOUBTS...
BUT IT SEEMS YOU'RE AN EVEN BETTER HUNTER THAN THE STORIES MADE YOU OUT TO BE!!
I LIKE YOU, KID!!
THIS IS THE BIGGEST HAUL ANYONE'S EVER BROUGHT IN THE HISTORY OF OUR HUNTS!!

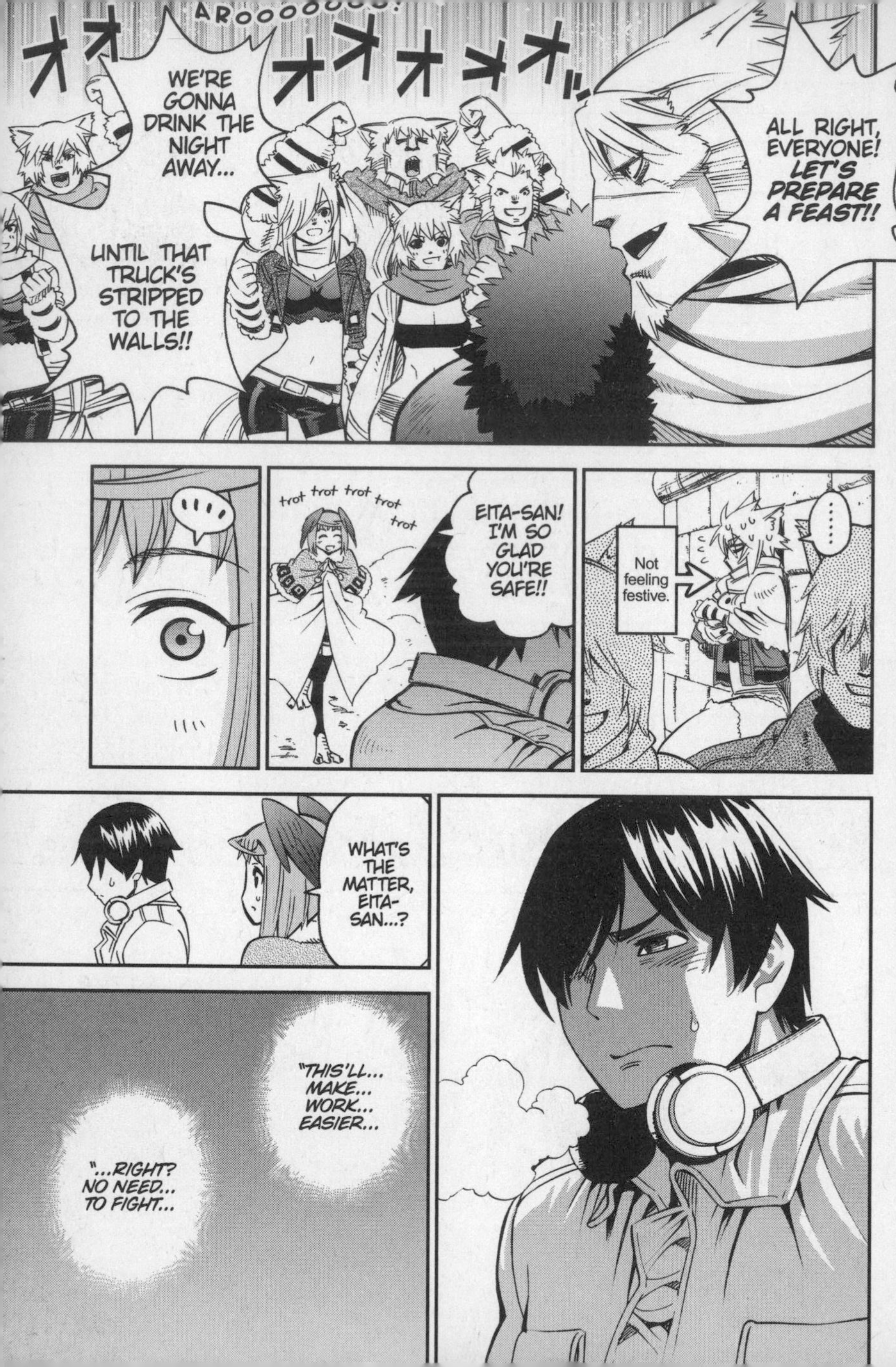
ALL RIGHT, EVERYONE! LET'S PREPARE A FEAST!!
オオオオオオッ
AROOOOOOO!
WE'RE GONNA DRINK THE NIGHT AWAY...
UNTIL THAT TRUCK'S STRIPPED TO THE WALLS!!
......
Not feeling festive.
EITA-SAN! I'M SO GLAD YOU'RE SAFE!!
trot trot trot trot trot
WHAT'S THE MATTER, EITA-SAN...?
"THIS'LL... MAKE... WORK... EASIER...
"...RIGHT? NO NEED... TO FIGHT...

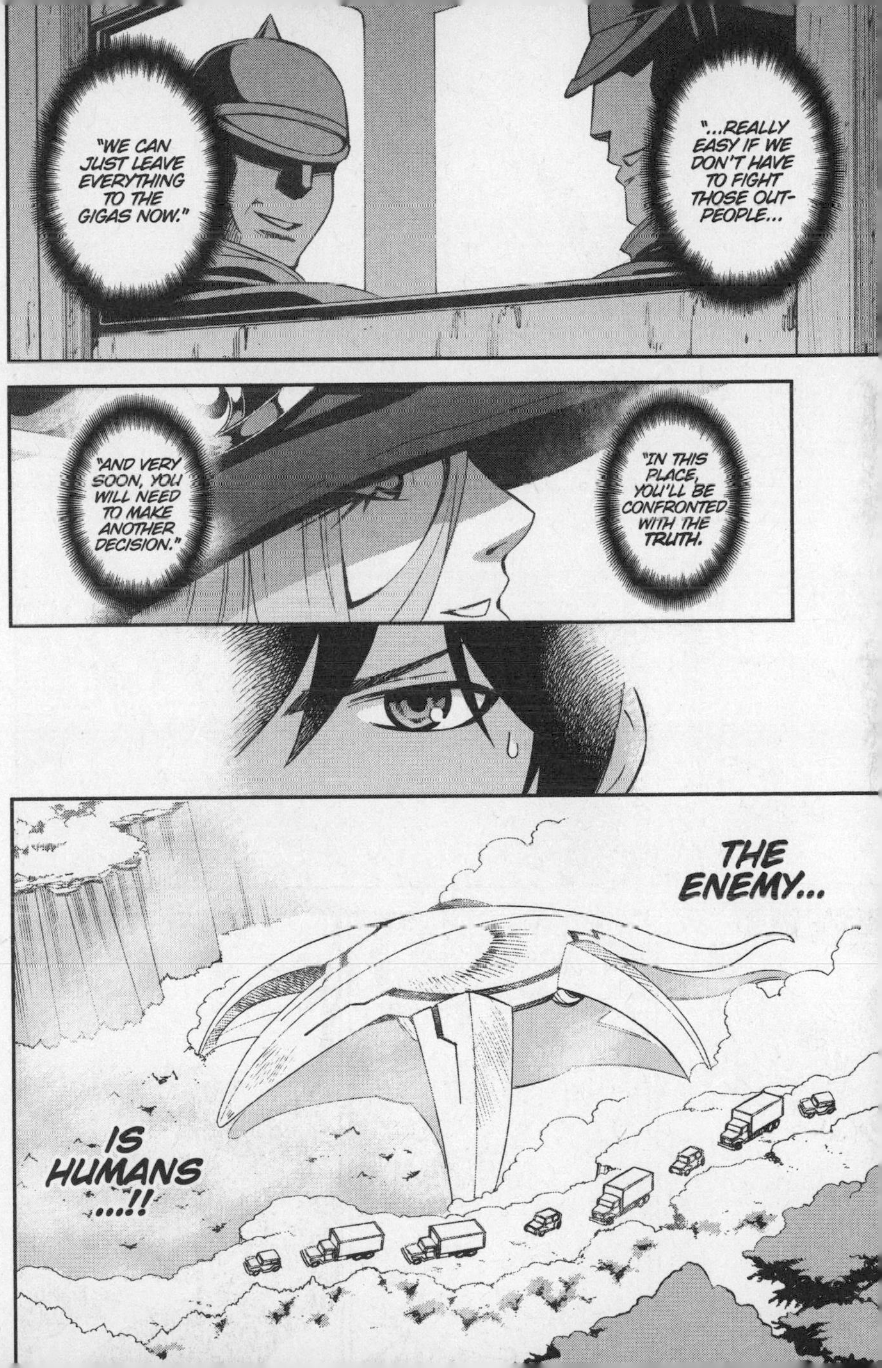
"...REALLY EASY IF WE DON'T HAVE TO FIGHT THOSE OUT-PEOPLE...
"WE CAN JUST LEAVE EVERYTHING TO THE GIGAS NOW."
"IN THIS PLACE, YOU'LL BE CONFRONTED WITH THE TRUTH.
"AND VERY SOON, YOU WILL NEED TO MAKE ANOTHER DECISION."
THE ENEMY...
IS HUMANS ...!!

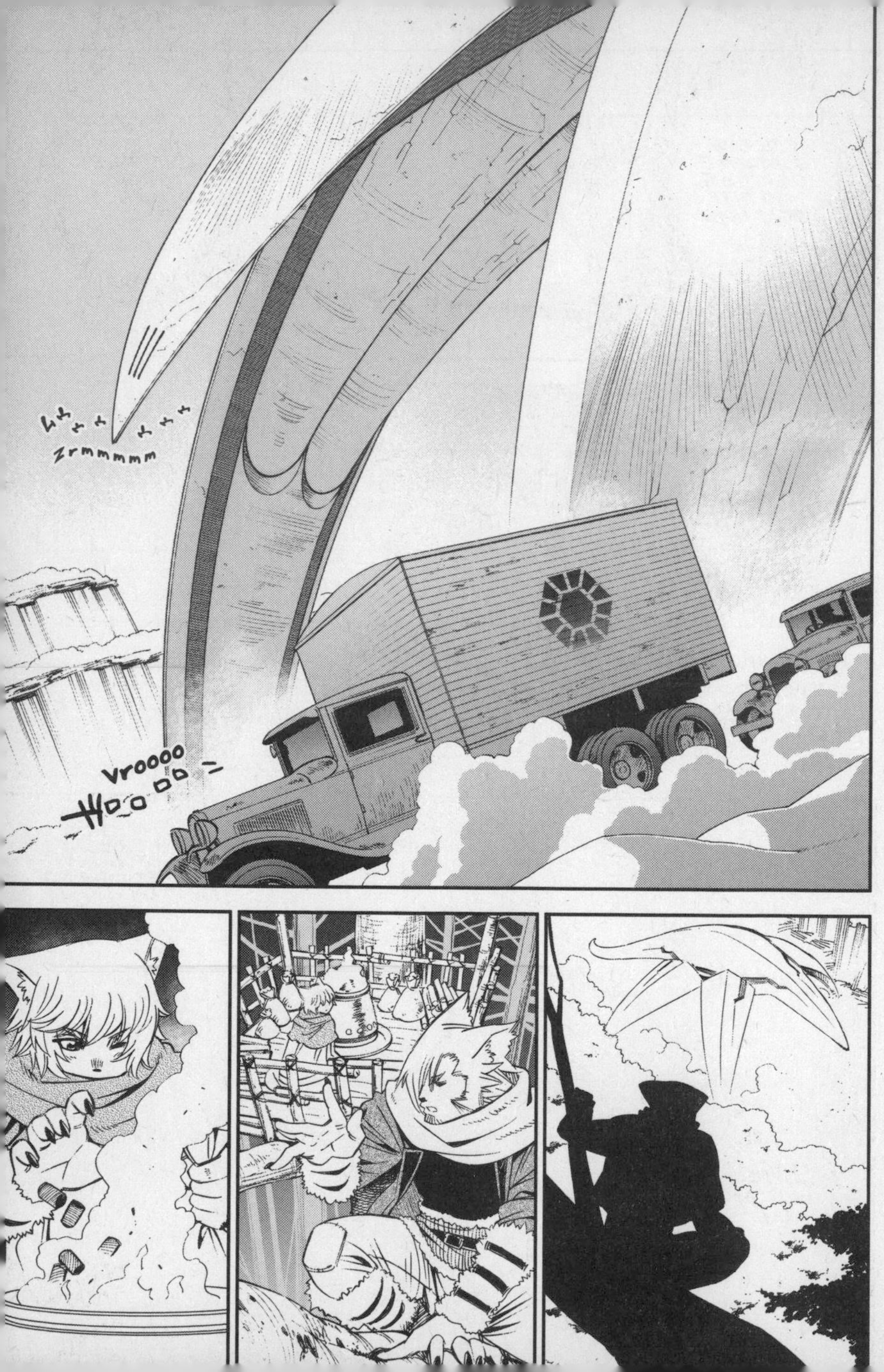
Zrmmmmm
Vroooo

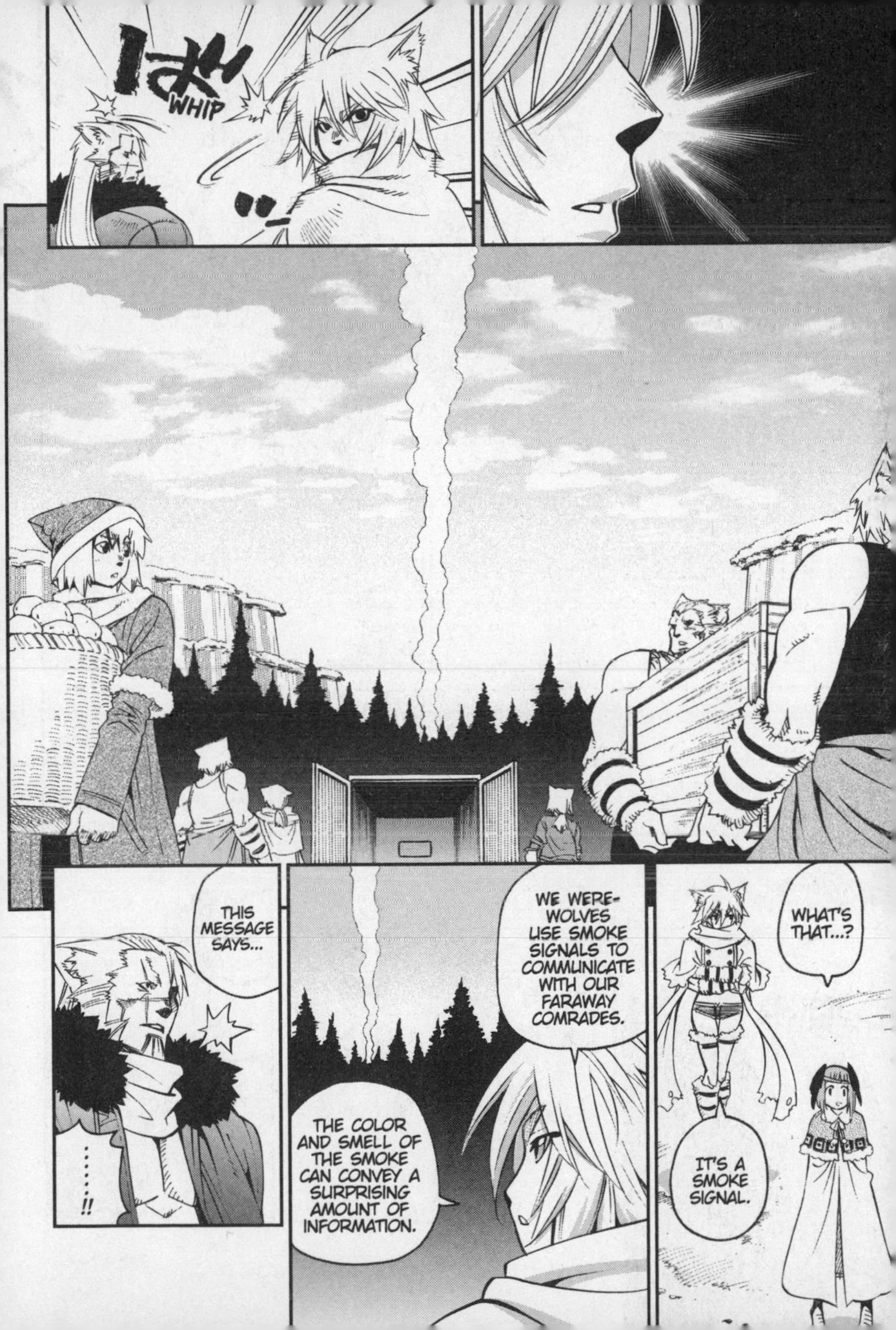
はっ
WHIP
WHAT'S THAT...?
IT'S A SMOKE SIGNAL.
WE WERE-WOLVES USE SMOKE SIGNALS TO COMMUNICATE WITH OUR FARAWAY COMRADES.
THE COLOR AND SMELL OF THE SMOKE CAN CONVEY A SURPRISING AMOUNT OF INFORMATION.
THIS MESSAGE SAYS...
......!!

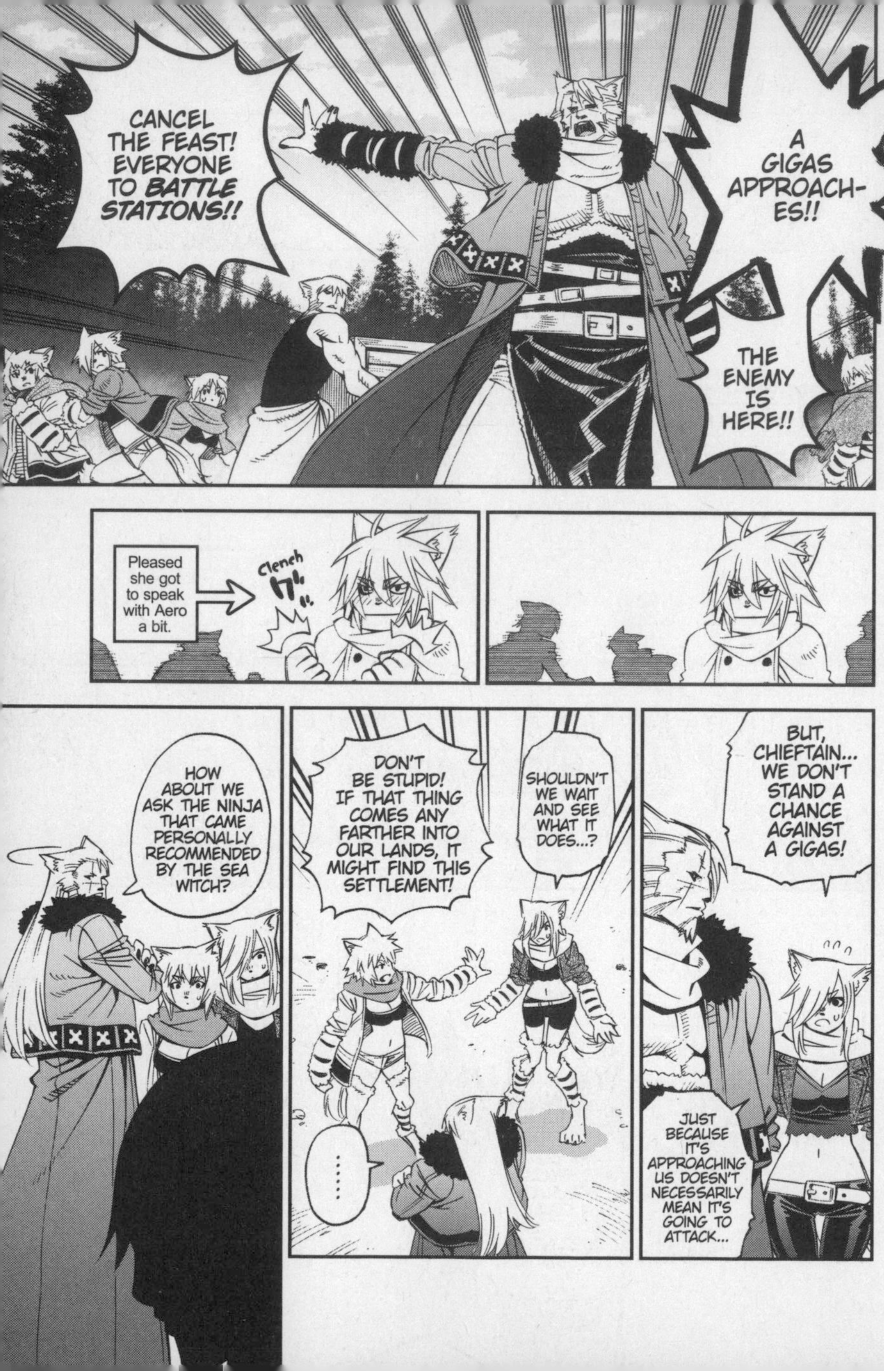
A GIGAS APPROACH-ES!!
THE ENEMY IS HERE!!
CANCEL THE FEAST! EVERYONE TO *BATTLE STATIONS!!*
Pleased she got to speak with Aero a bit.
Clench
BUT, CHIEFTAIN... WE DON'T STAND A CHANCE AGAINST A GIGAS!
JUST BECAUSE IT'S APPROACHING US DOESN'T NECESSARILY MEAN IT'S GOING TO ATTACK...
SHOULDN'T WE WAIT AND SEE WHAT IT DOES...?
DON'T BE STUPID! IF THAT THING COMES ANY FARTHER INTO OUR LANDS, IT MIGHT FIND THIS SETTLEMENT!
......
HOW ABOUT WE ASK THE NINJA THAT CAME PERSONALLY RECOMMENDED BY THE SEA WITCH?

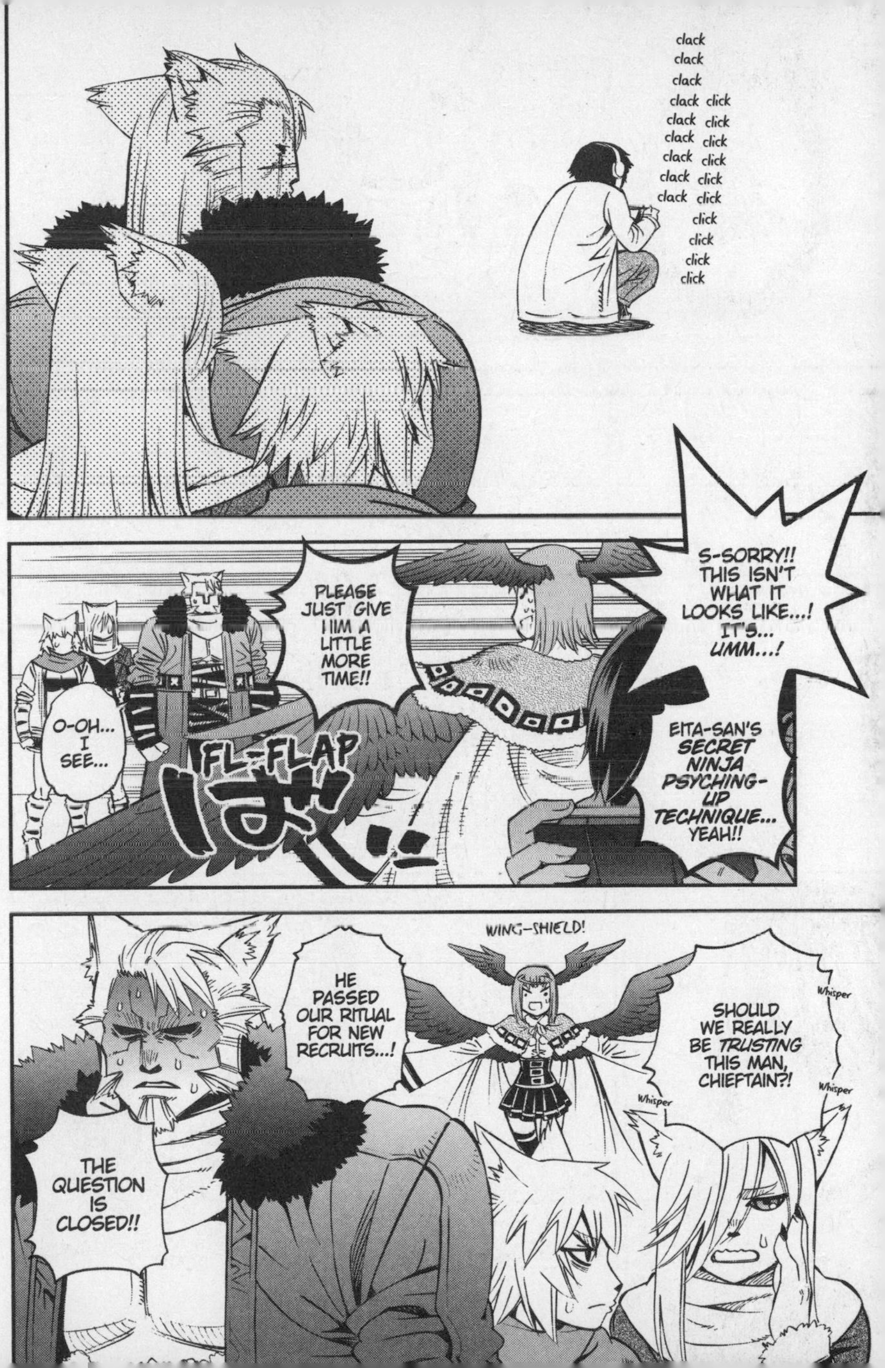
clack
clack
clack
clack click
clack click
clack click
clack click
clack click
clack click
click
click
click
click
S-SORRY!! THIS ISN'T WHAT IT LOOKS LIKE...! IT'S... UMM...!
EITA-SAN'S SECRET NINJA PSYCHING-UP TECHNIQUE... YEAH!!
PLEASE JUST GIVE HIM A LITTLE MORE TIME!!
FL-FLAP
O-OH... I SEE...
Whisper
Whisper
SHOULD WE REALLY BE TRUSTING THIS MAN, CHIEFTAIN?!
Whisper
WING-SHIELD!
HE PASSED OUR RITUAL FOR NEW RECRUITS...!
THE QUESTION IS CLOSED!!

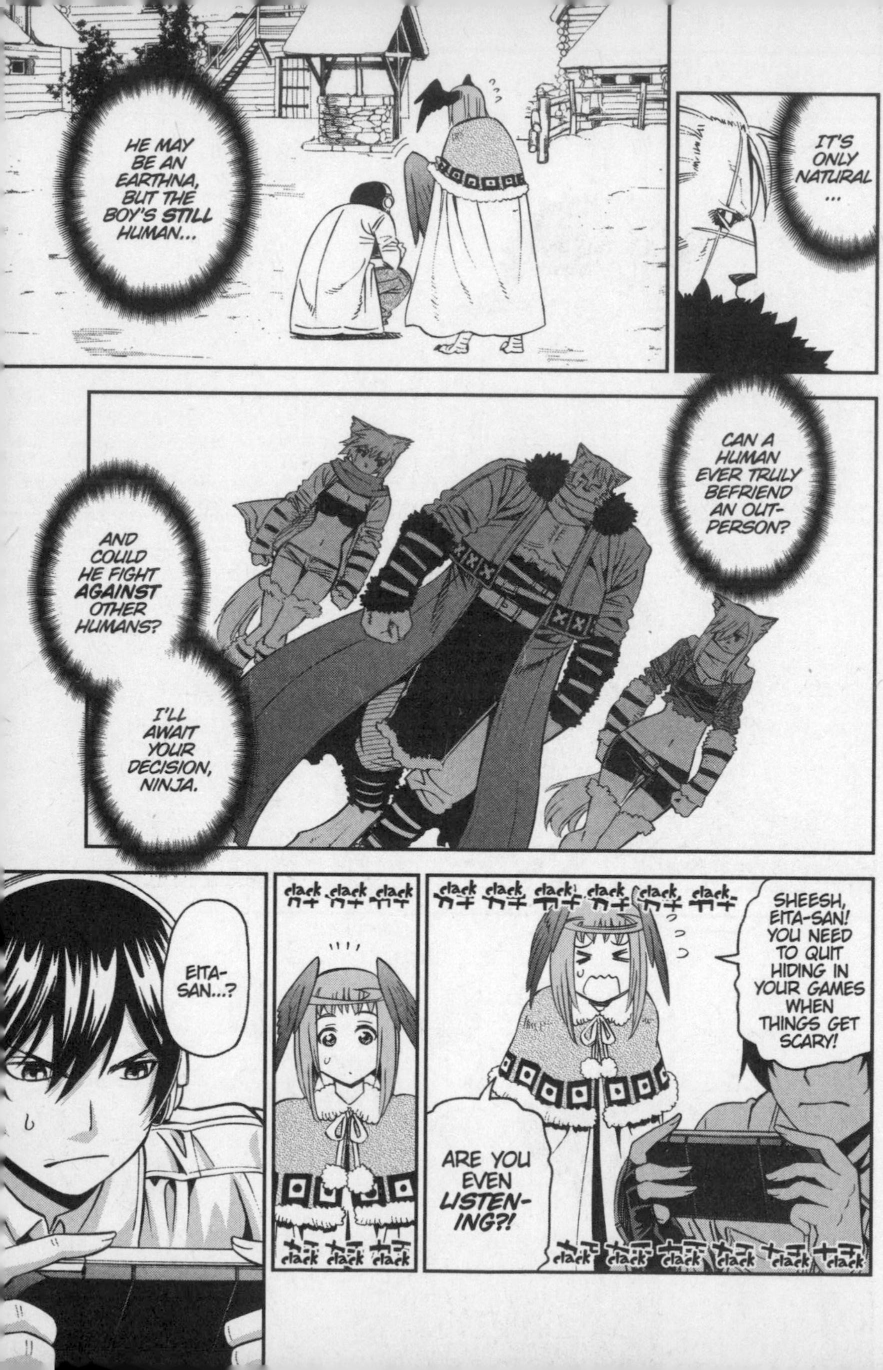
IT'S ONLY NATURAL...
HE MAY BE AN EARTHNA, BUT THE BOY'S STILL HUMAN...
CAN A HUMAN EVER TRULY BEFRIEND AN OUT-PERSON?
AND COULD HE FIGHT AGAINST OTHER HUMANS?
I'LL AWAIT YOUR DECISION, NINJA.
clack clack clack clack clack clack
SHEESH, EITA-SAN! YOU NEED TO QUIT HIDING IN YOUR GAMES WHEN THINGS GET SCARY!
ARE YOU EVEN LISTENING?!
clack clack clack clack clack clack
clack clack clack
clack clack clack
EITA-SAN...?

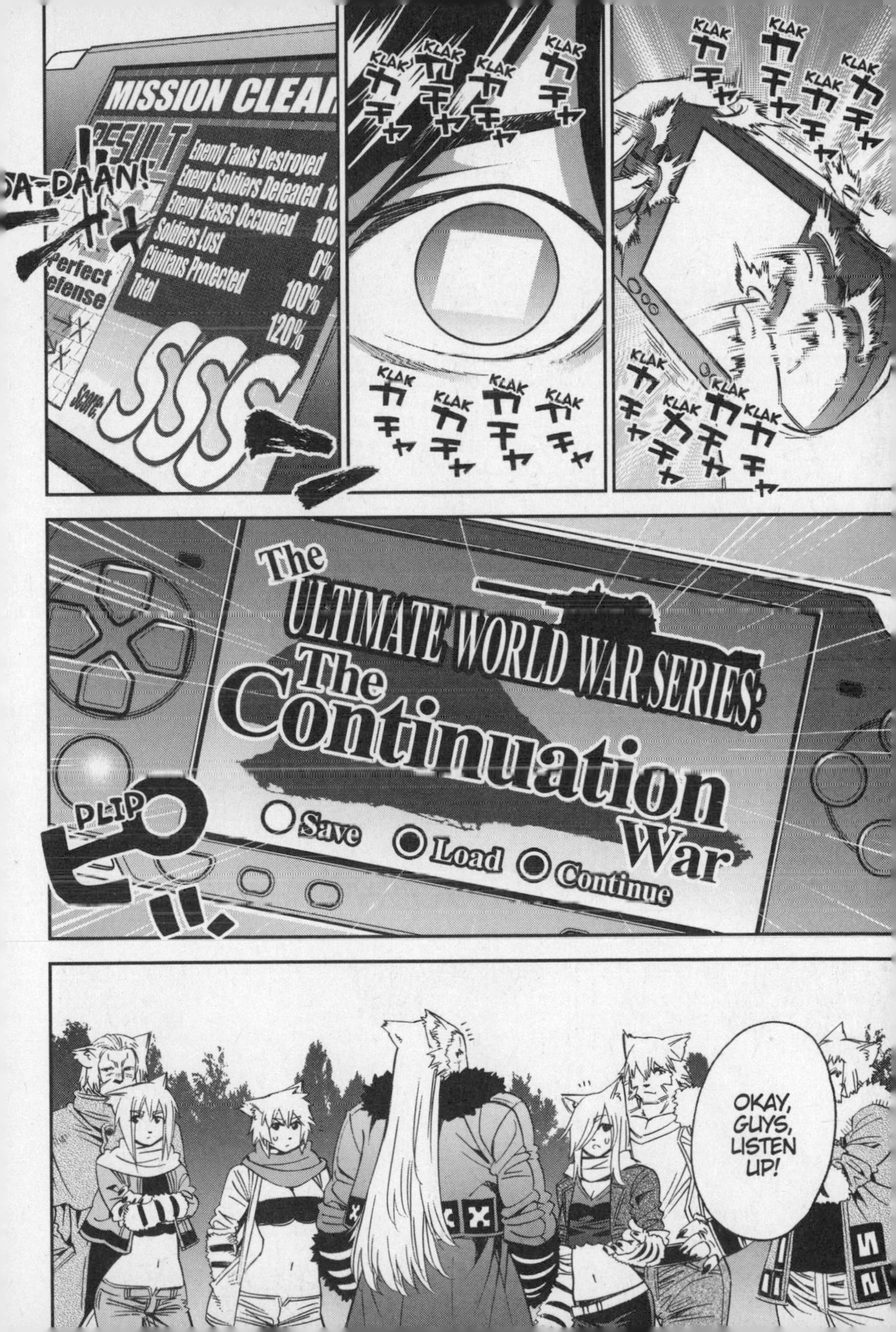
KLAK カチャ
KLAK カチャ
KLAK カチャ
KLAK カチャ
KLAK カチャ
KLAK カチャ
KLAK カチャ
KLAK カチャ
KLAK カチャ
KLAK カチャ
KLAK カチャ
KLAK カチャ
KLAK カチャ
KLAK カチャ
KLAK カチャ
KLAK カチャ
MISSION CLEA
RESULT
Enemy Tanks Destroyed
Enemy Soldiers Defeated 10
Enemy Bases Occupied 100
Soldiers Lost 0%
Civilians Protected 100%
Total 120%
Perfect Defense
Score: SSS
SA-DAAN!
The ULTIMATE WORLD WAR SERIES: The Continuation War
Save
Load
Continue
PLIP
OKAY, GUYS, LISTEN UP!

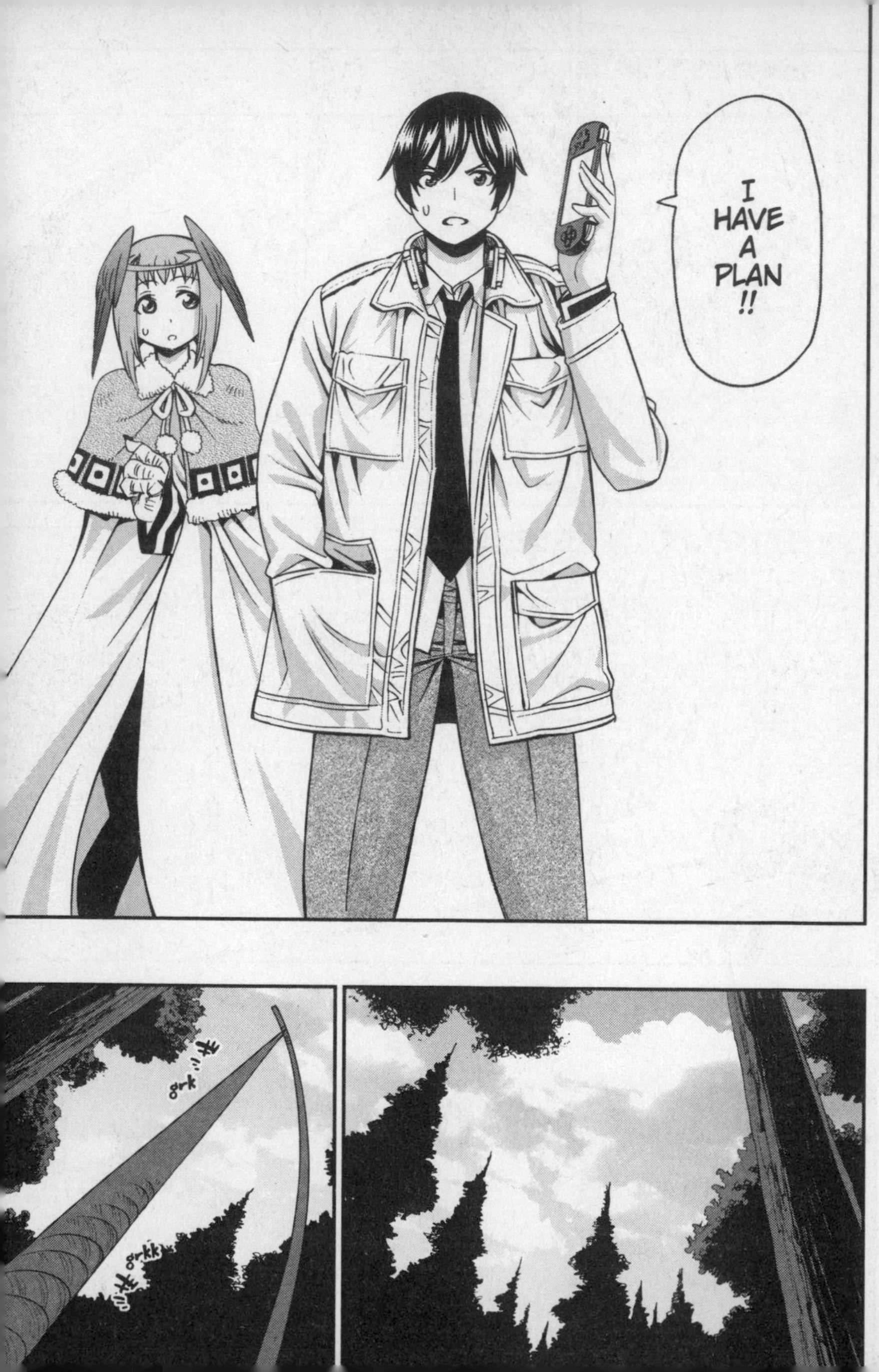
I HAVE A PLAN !!
grk
grkk

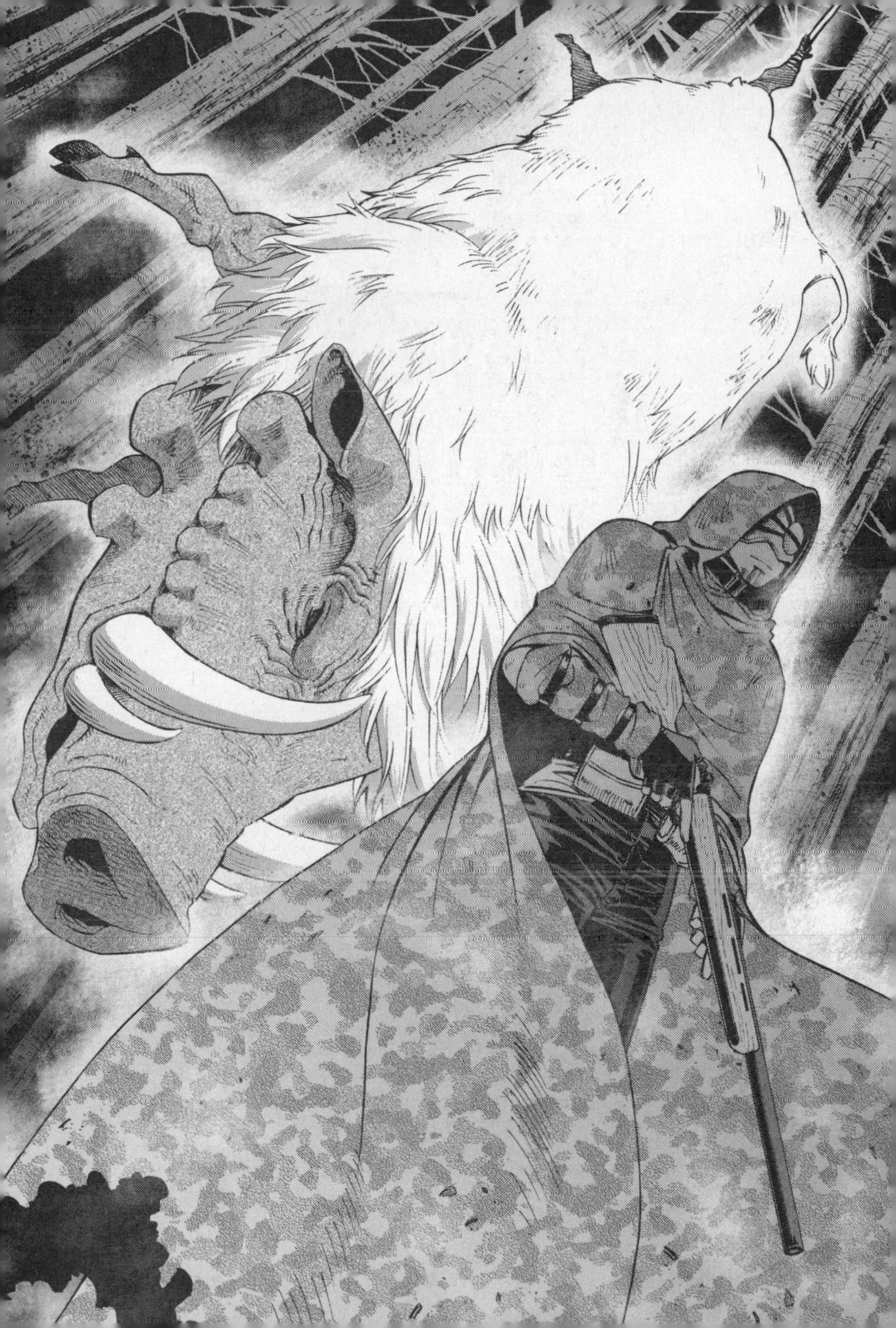

Carl Gustaf Emil Mannerheim

Commander-in-chief: Rank SS Level: 94

Leadership: 15
Charisma: 15
Tank Cmd.: 14
Naval Vessel
Command: 13
aft Cmd.: 14

Strateg
Charge!

Comrade General Secretary!
The Army Weapons Agency

With this, we can topple puny
of Finland in one fell swoop!

Introduction

• Focus on mass-producing MBTs!
• have development commit a mm
le the engineering

The ULTIMATE WORLD WAR SERIES: The Continuation War

Level UP

SERGEANT MAJOR → MAJ
Accuracy Up 3 Points
Movement Up 1 Point
Up 2 Points!

Soviet soldier
Тураааааа
ааааа

You successfull
confiscated a Soviet BT-7!

Ambush
SUCCESSFUL

5

2

5

2

7

**The Ultimate World War Series:
The Continuation War**

The eighth installment of the *Ultimate World War* series, held in
extremely high regard by a handful of passionate fans.
The sequel to the previous game, *The Winter War.*
Players can choose to play as either Finland or the Soviet Union.
This high-difficulty game is not at all friendly to casual players
and has caused many gamers to give up in frustration.

As a result of its relentless difficulty, its sales were disappointing.

Chapter 21: Tactics on the Snowfield

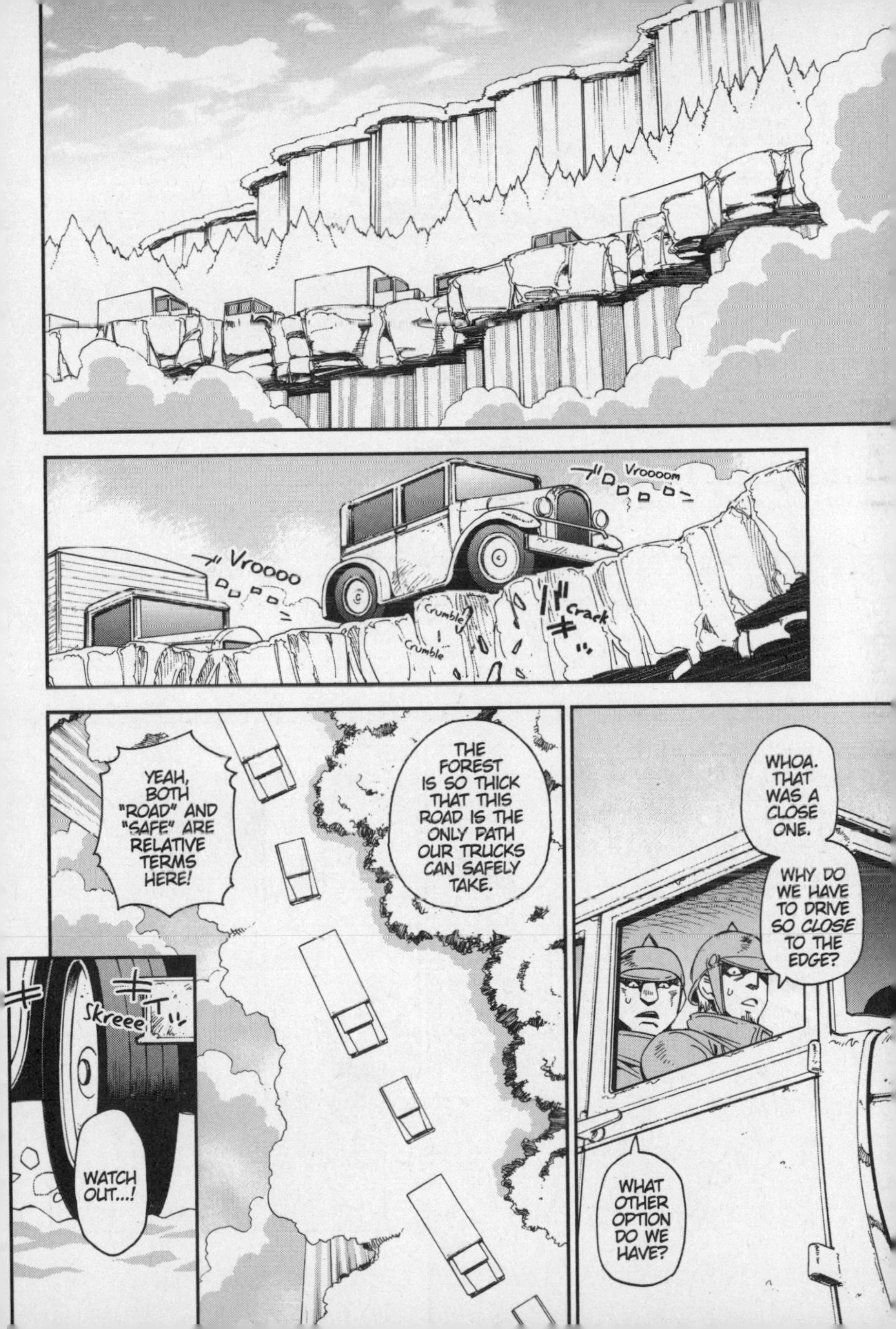
Vroooom
Crack
Vroooo
Crumble
Crumble
WHOA. THAT WAS A CLOSE ONE.
WHY DO WE HAVE TO DRIVE SO CLOSE TO THE EDGE?
WHAT OTHER OPTION DO WE HAVE?
THE FOREST IS SO THICK THAT THIS ROAD IS THE ONLY PATH OUR TRUCKS CAN SAFELY TAKE.
YEAH, BOTH "ROAD" AND "SAFE" ARE RELATIVE TERMS HERE!
Skreee
WATCH OUT...!

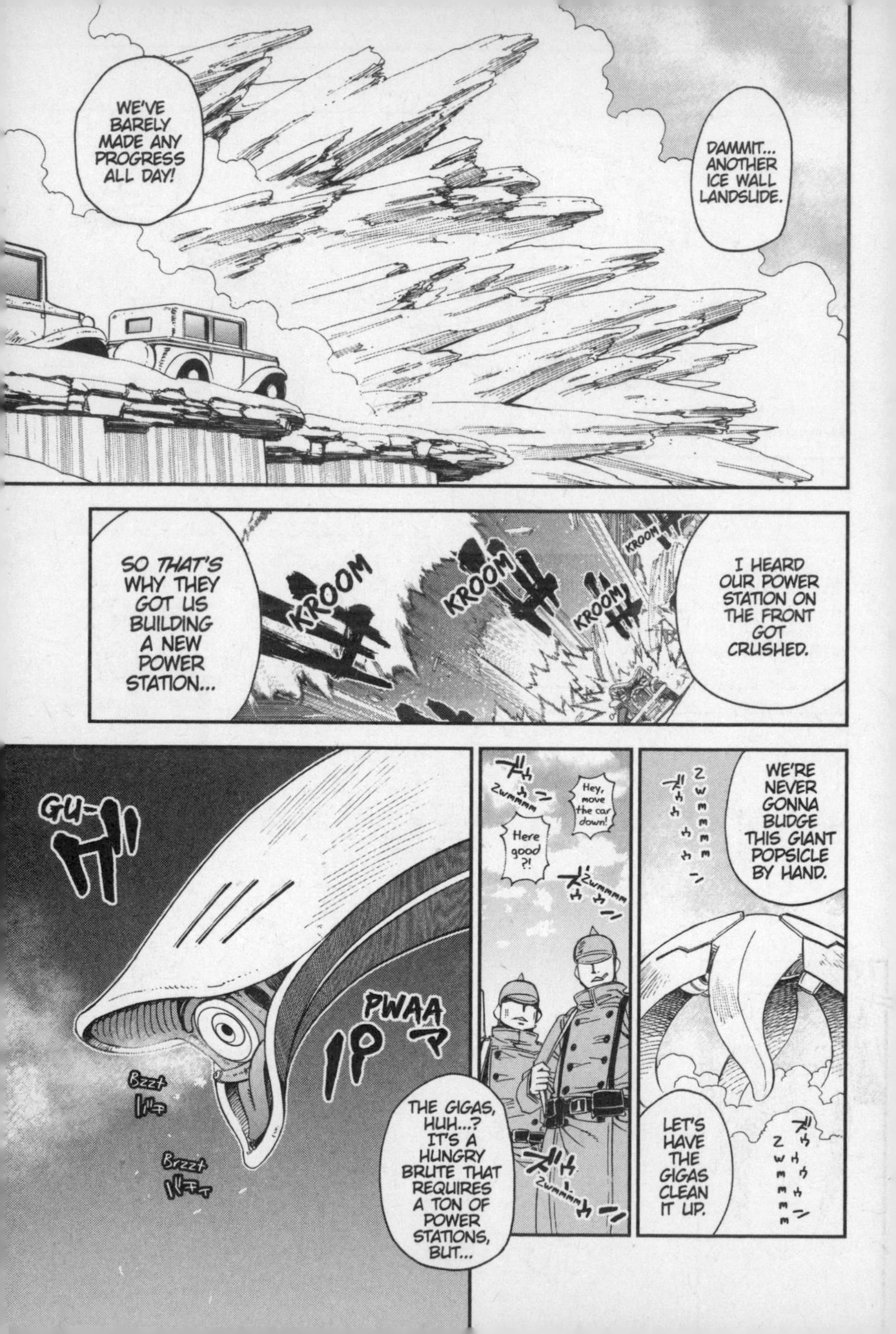
DAMMIT... ANOTHER ICE WALL LANDSLIDE.
WE'VE BARELY MADE ANY PROGRESS ALL DAY!
I HEARD OUR POWER STATION ON THE FRONT GOT CRUSHED.
KROOM
KROOM
KROOM
KROOM
SO THAT'S WHY THEY GOT US BUILDING A NEW POWER STATION...
WE'RE NEVER GONNA BUDGE THIS GIANT POPSICLE BY HAND.
Zwmmmm
LET'S HAVE THE GIGAS CLEAN IT UP.
Zwmmmm
Zwmmmm
Hey, move the car down!
Here good?!
Zwmmmm
Zwmmmm
THE GIGAS, HUH...? IT'S A HUNGRY BRUTE THAT REQUIRES A TON OF POWER STATIONS, BUT...
GU-
PWAA
Bzzt
Brzzt

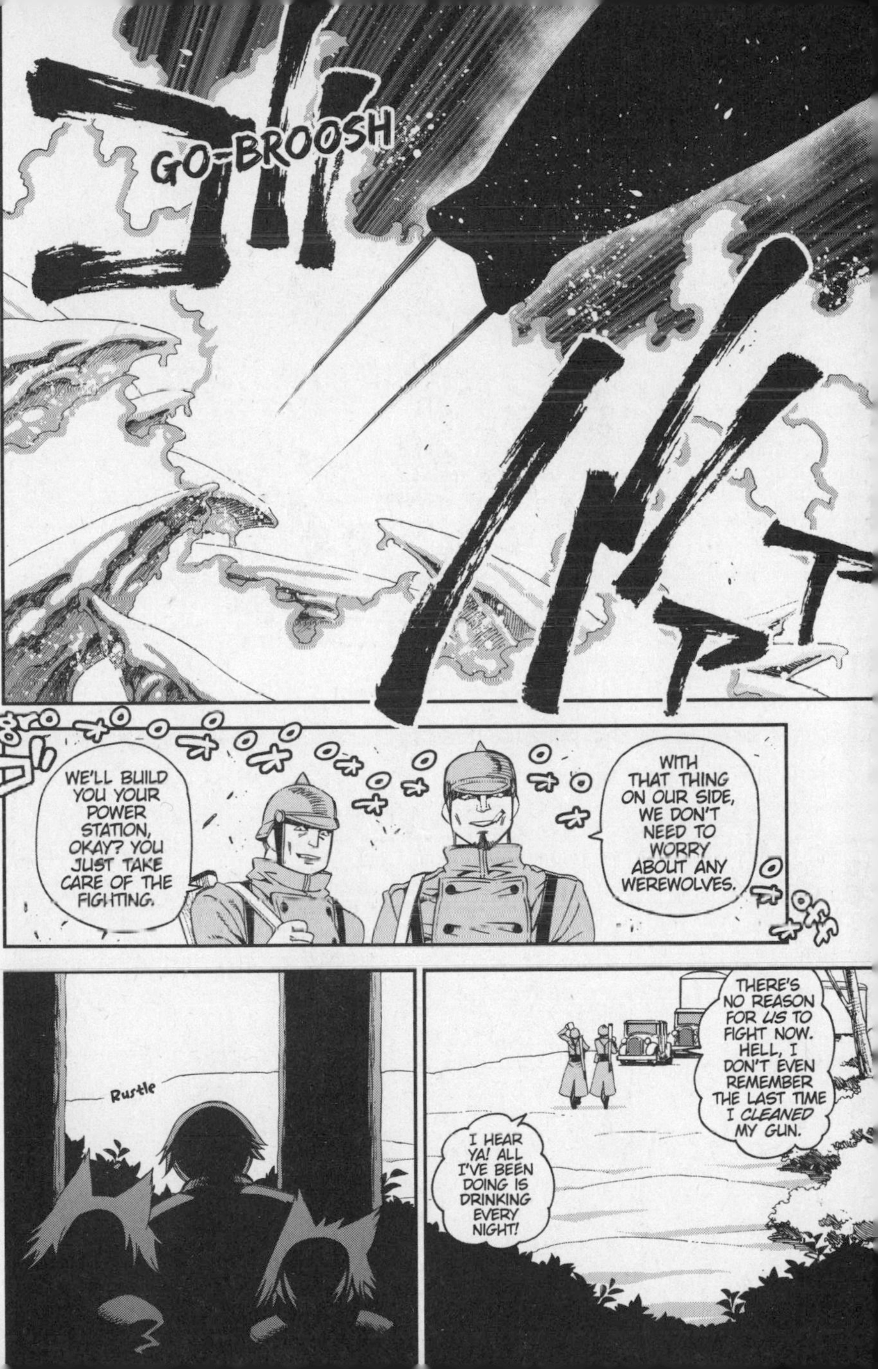
GO-BROOSH
WITH THAT THING ON OUR SIDE, WE DON'T NEED TO WORRY ABOUT ANY WEREWOLVES.
WE'LL BUILD YOU YOUR POWER STATION, OKAY? YOU JUST TAKE CARE OF THE FIGHTING.
THERE'S NO REASON FOR *US* TO FIGHT NOW. HELL, I DON'T EVEN REMEMBER THE LAST TIME I *CLEANED* MY GUN.
I HEAR YA! ALL I'VE BEEN DOING IS DRINKING EVERY NIGHT!
Rustle

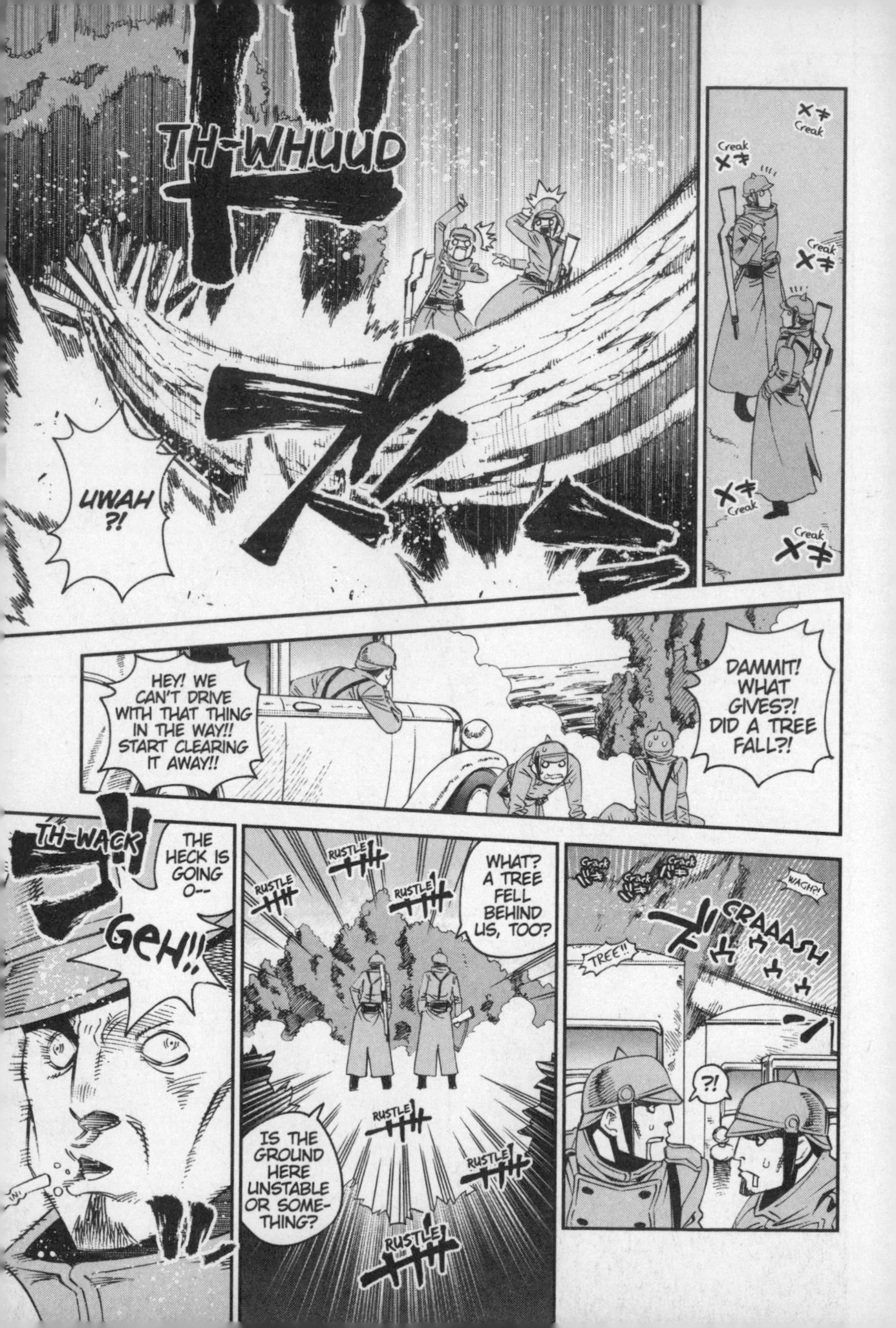
メキ
Creak
Creak
メキ
Creak
メキ
メキ
Creak
Creak
メキ
TH-WHUUD
UWAH ?!
DAMMIT! WHAT GIVES?! DID A TREE FALL?!
HEY! WE CAN'T DRIVE WITH THAT THING IN THE WAY!! START CLEARING IT AWAY!!
Crack
Crack
Crack
WAGH?!
CRAAASH
TREE!!
?!
RUSTLE
RUSTLE
RUSTLE
WHAT? A TREE FELL BEHIND US, TOO?
RUSTLE
IS THE GROUND HERE UNSTABLE OR SOME-THING?
RUSTLE
RUSTLE
TH-WACK
THE HECK IS GOING O--
GEH!!

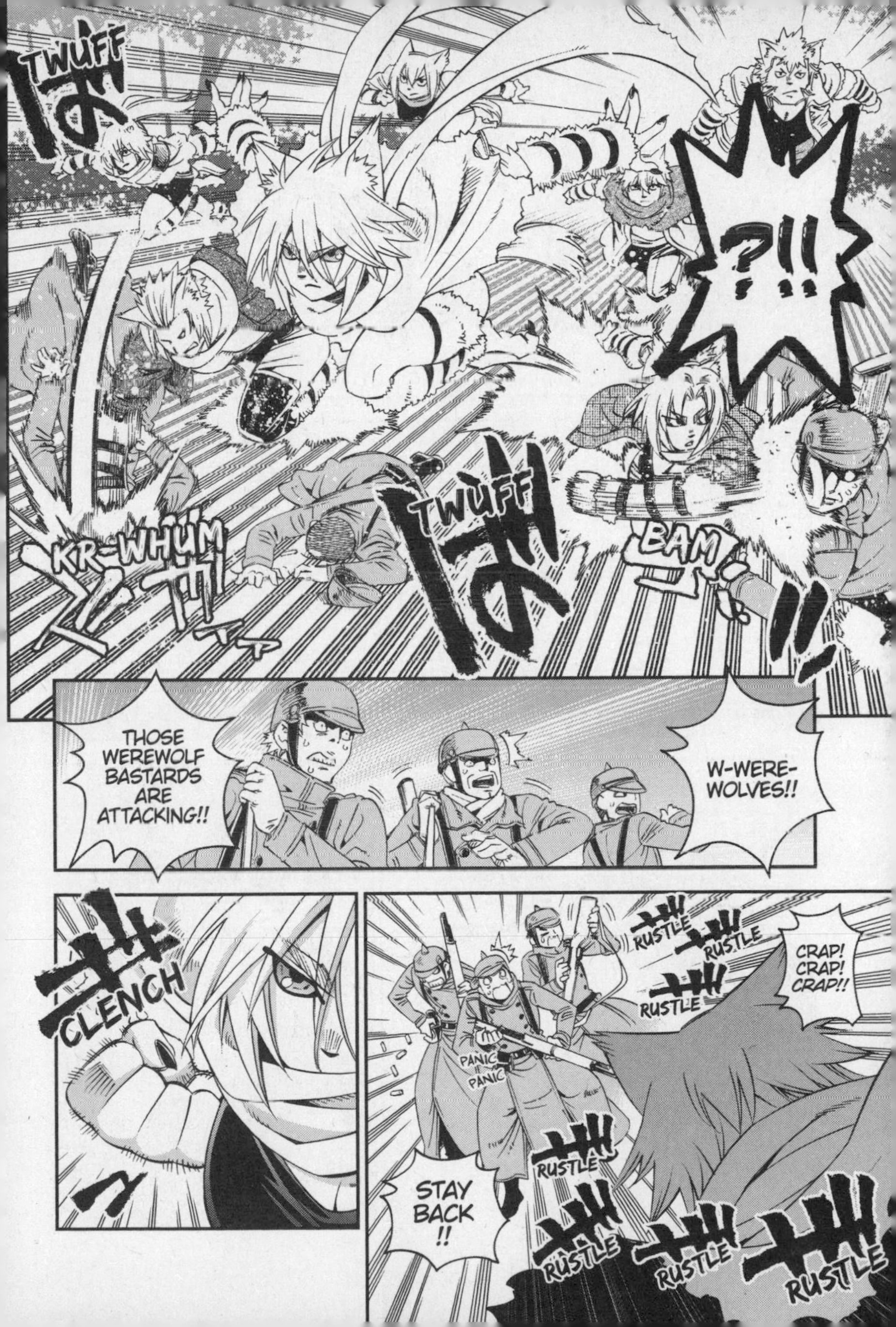
?!!
TWUFF
BAM!!
TWUFF
KR-WHUM
W-WERE-WOLVES!!
THOSE WEREWOLF BASTARDS ARE ATTACKING!!
CRAP! CRAP! CRAP!!
RUSTLE
RUSTLE
RUSTLE
PANIC PANIC
RUSTLE
STAY BACK!!
RUSTLE
RUSTLE
RUSTLE
CLENCH

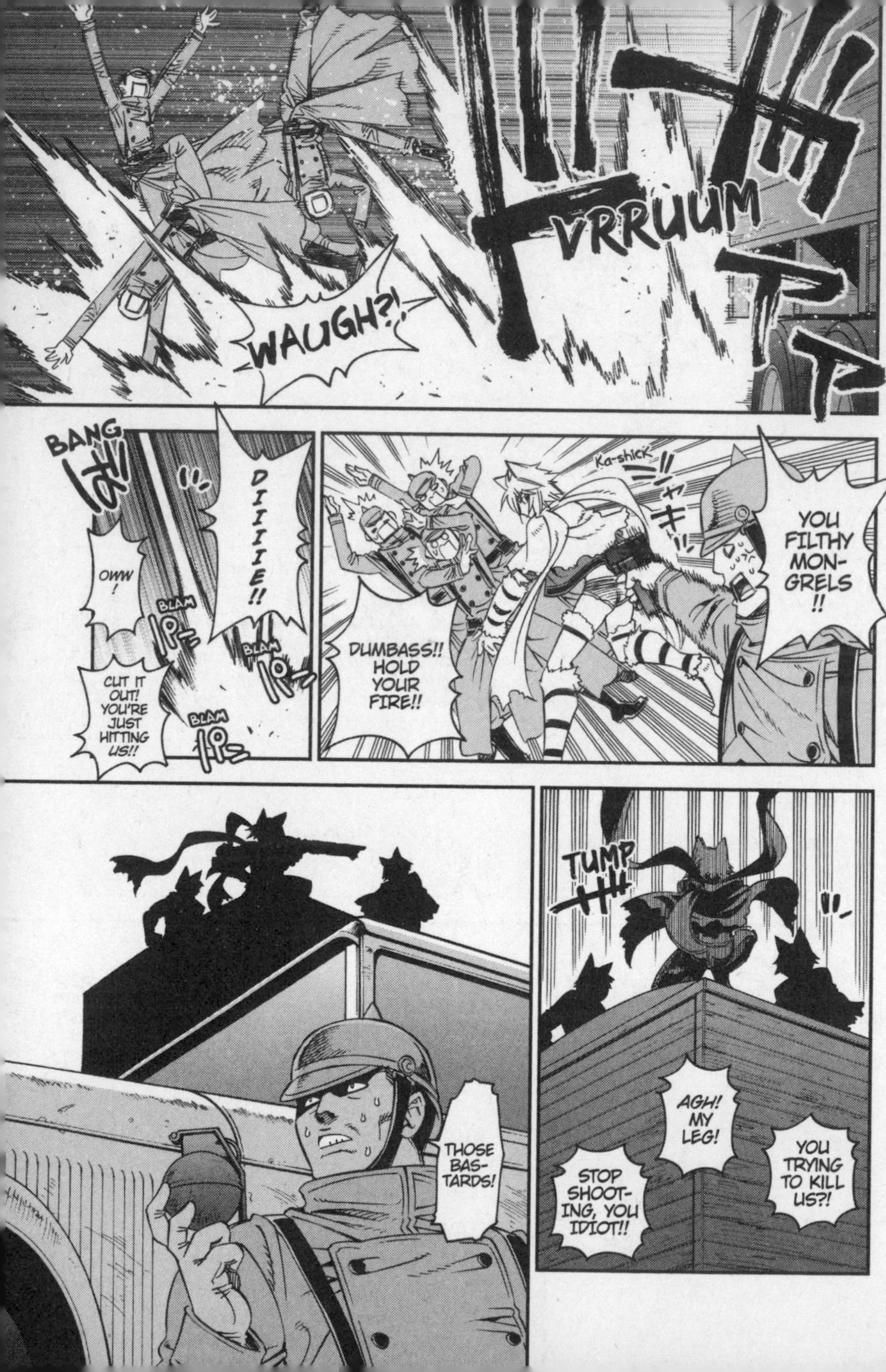
VRRUUM
WAUGH?!
Ka-shick
YOU FILTHY MON-GRELS!!
DUMBASS!! HOLD YOUR FIRE!!
BANG
DIIIIIE!!
OWW!
BLAM
BLAM
CUT IT OUT! YOU'RE JUST HITTING US!!
BLAM
TUMP
AGH! MY LEG!
YOU TRYING TO KILL US?!
STOP SHOOT-ING, YOU IDIOT!!
THOSE BAS-TARDS!

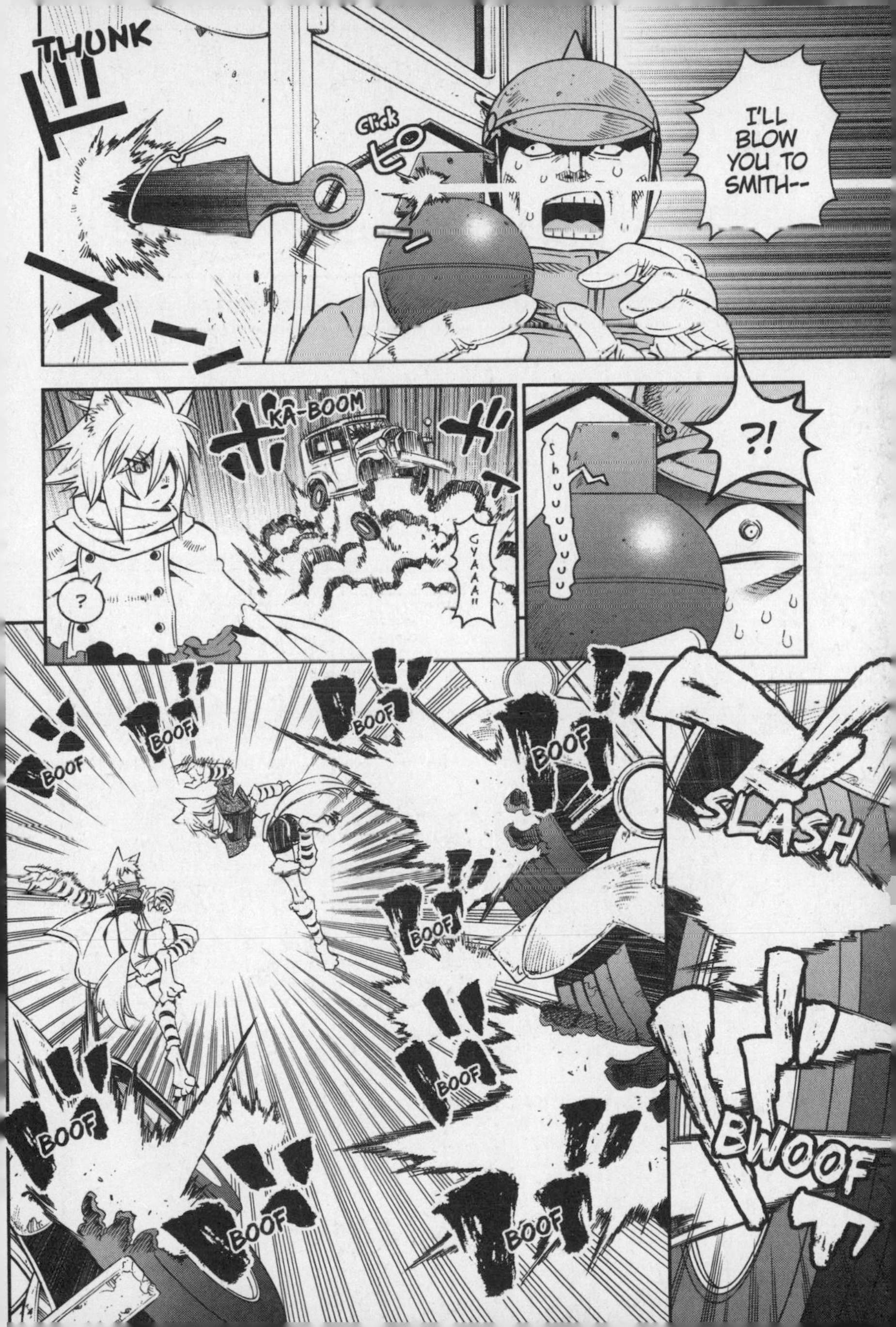
I'LL BLOW YOU TO SMITH--
Click
THUNK
?!
Shuuuuuuu
KA-BOOM
GYAAAA!!
?
SLASH
BWOOF
BOOF
BOOF
BOOF
BOOF
BOOF
BOOF
BOOF
BOOF
BOOF

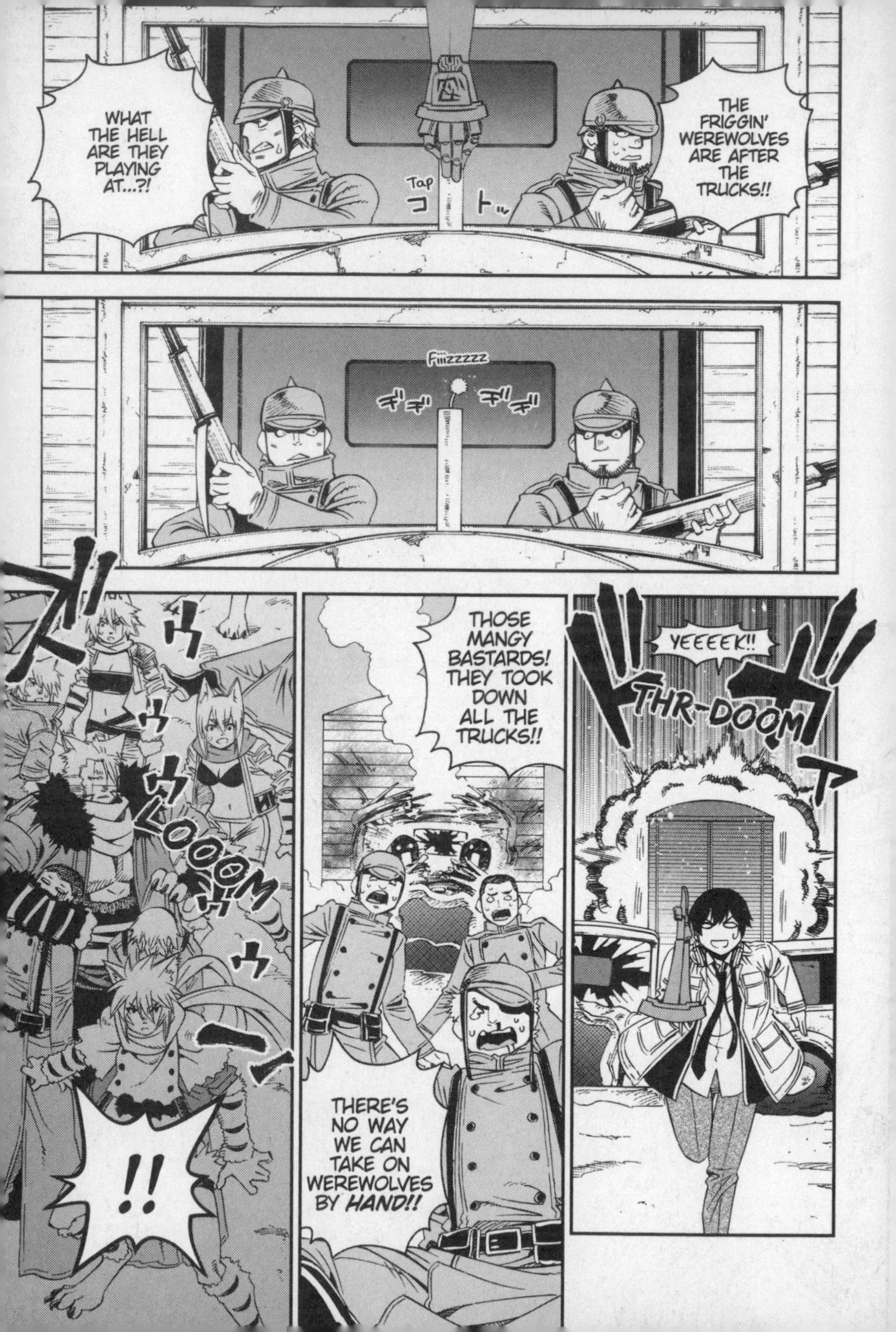

THE FRIGGIN' WEREWOLVES ARE AFTER THE TRUCKS!!
WHAT THE HELL ARE THEY PLAYING AT...?!
Tap
Fiiizzzzz
YEEEEK!!
THR-DOOM
THOSE MANGY BASTARDS! THEY TOOK DOWN ALL THE TRUCKS!!
THERE'S NO WAY WE CAN TAKE ON WEREWOLVES BY HAND!!
LOOOOM
!!

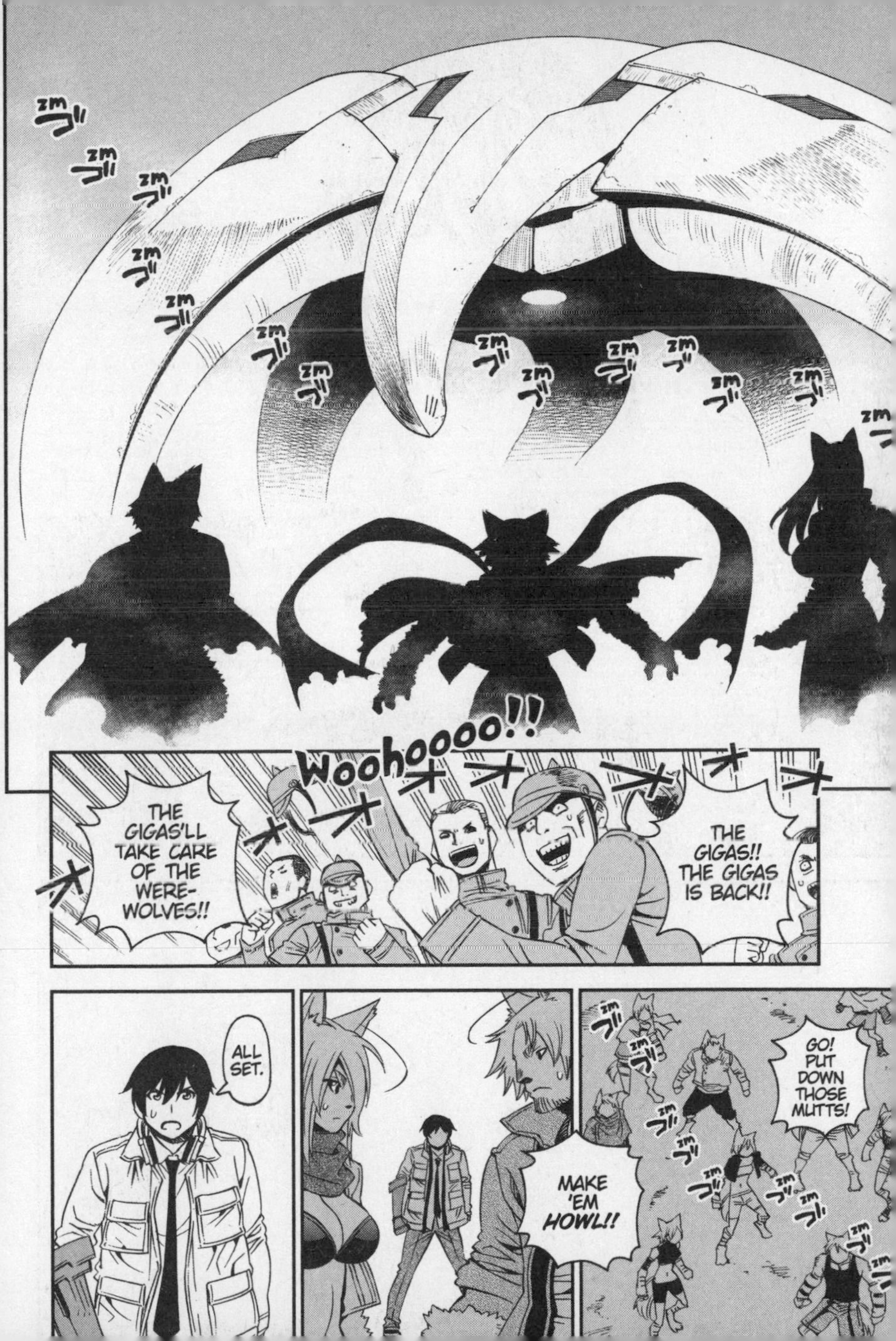
zm ゴ
zm ゴ
zm ゴ
zm ゴ
zm ゴ
zm ゴ
zm ゴ
Woohoooo!!
THE GIGAS!! THE GIGAS IS BACK!!
THE GIGAS'LL TAKE CARE OF THE WERE-WOLVES!!
GO! PUT DOWN THOSE MUTTS!
MAKE 'EM HOWL!!
ALL SET.

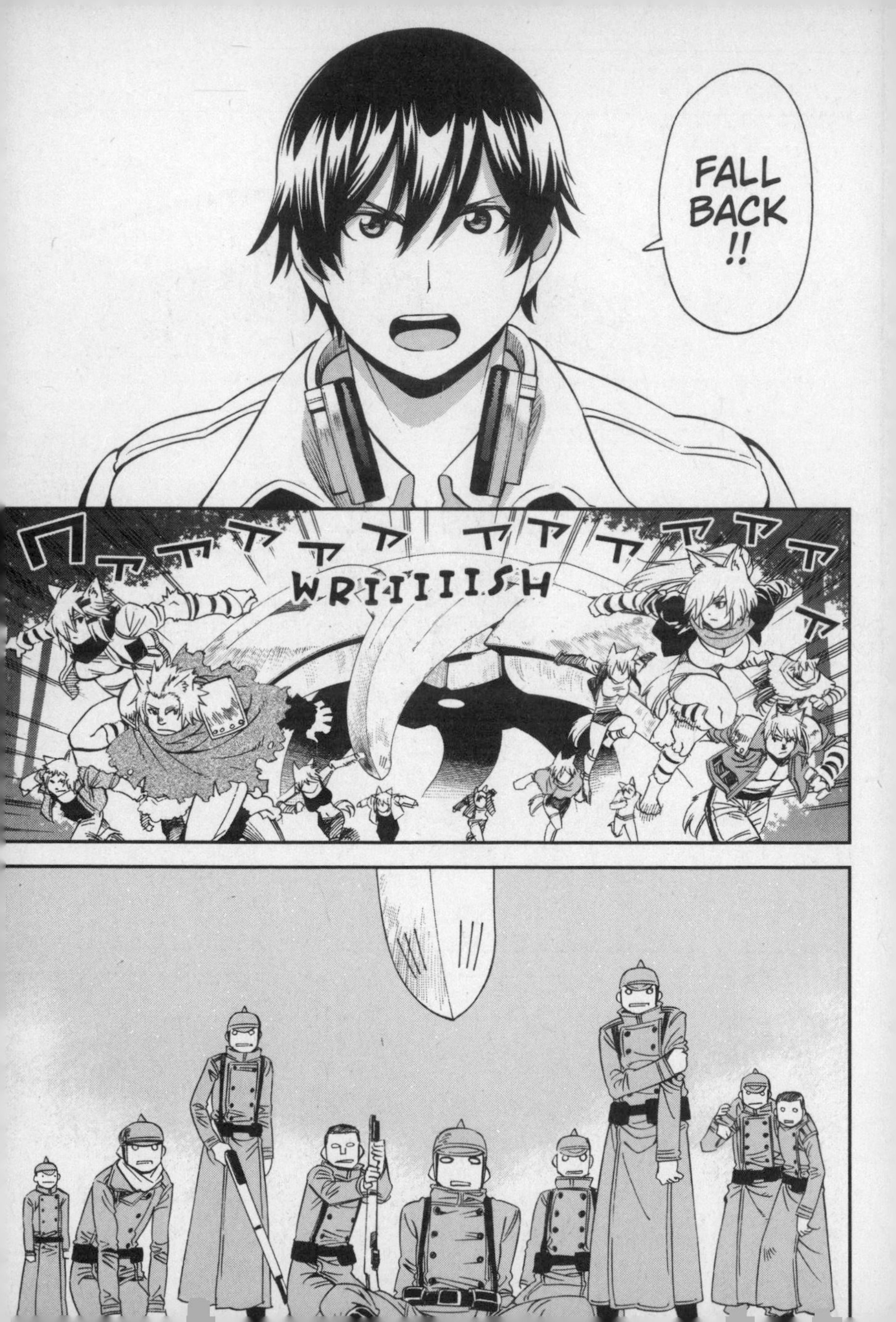
FALL BACK !!
WRIIIIISH

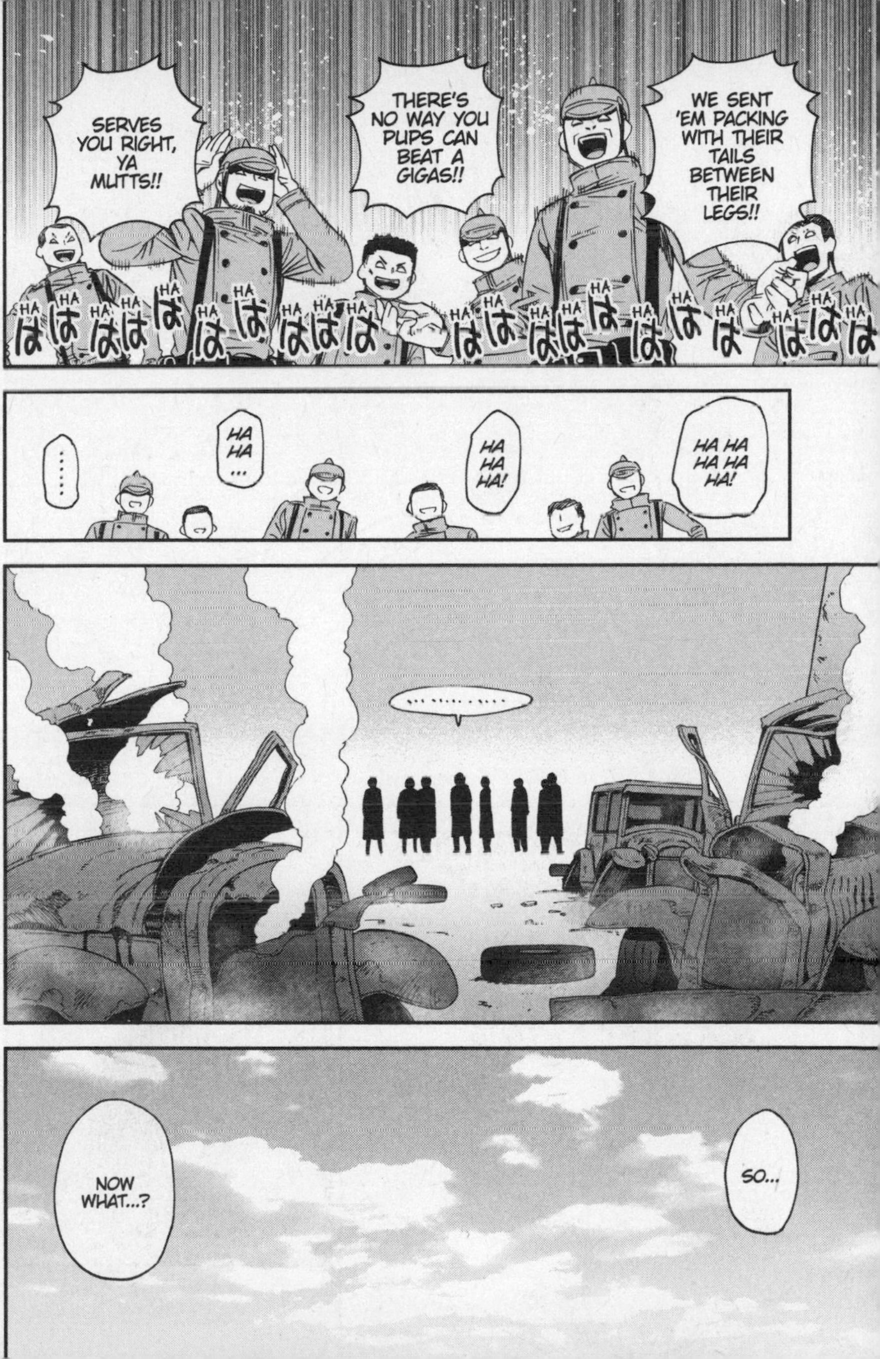

WE SENT 'EM PACKING WITH THEIR TAILS BETWEEN THEIR LEGS!!
THERE'S NO WAY YOU PUPS CAN BEAT A GIGAS!!
SERVES YOU RIGHT, YA MUTTS!!
HA HA HA HA HA HA HA HA HA HA HA HA HA HA HA HA HA HA HA HA
HA HA HA HA HA!
HA HA HA!
HA HA ...
......
SO...
NOW WHAT...?

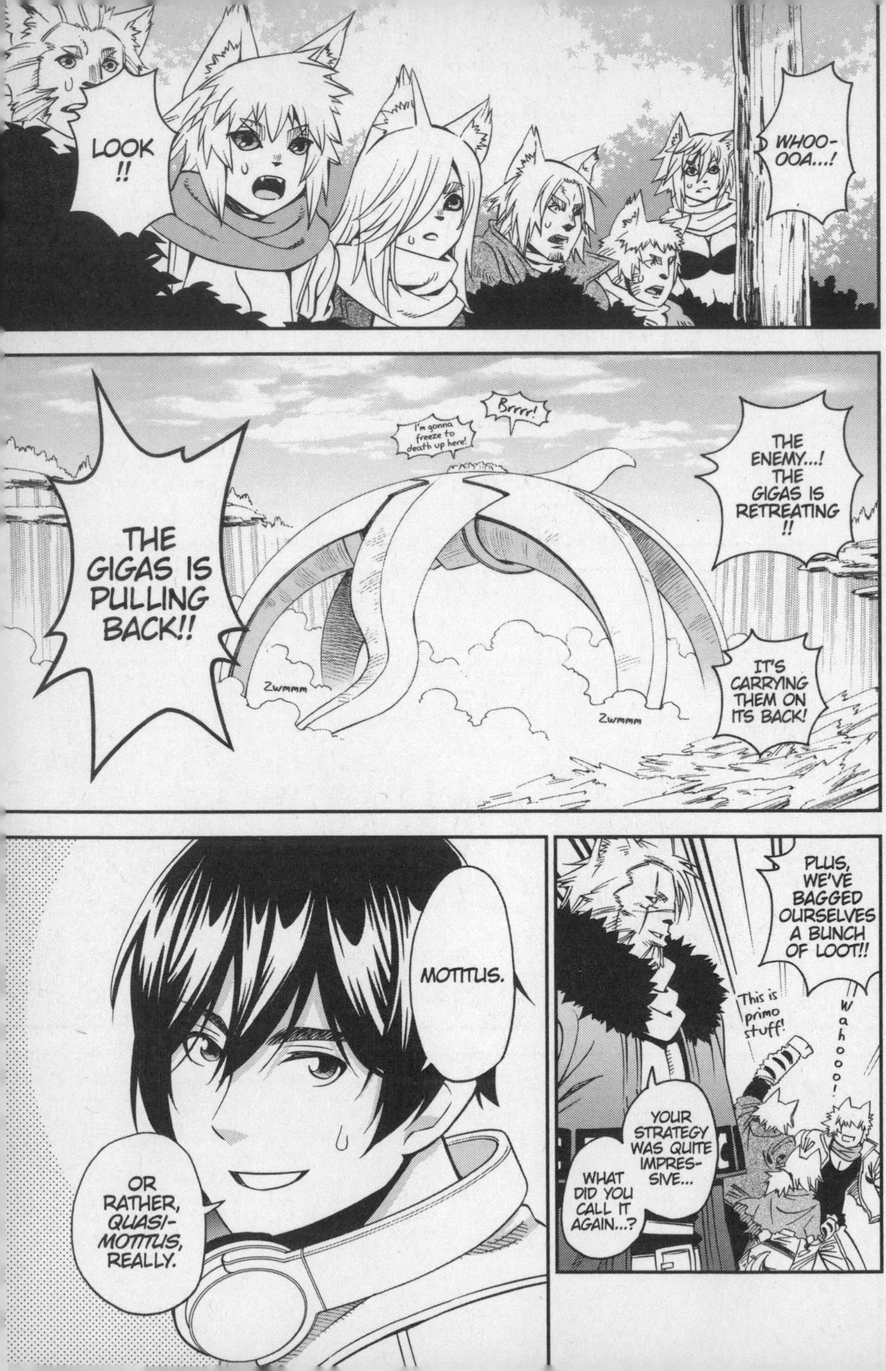
WHOOO-OOA...!
LOOK!!
THE ENEMY...! THE GIGAS IS RETREATING!!
Brrrr!
I'm gonna freeze to death up here!
IT'S CARRYING THEM ON ITS BACK!
Zwmmm
THE GIGAS IS PULLING BACK!!
Zwmmm
PLUS, WE'VE BAGGED OURSELVES A BUNCH OF LOOT!!
Wahoooo!
This is primo stuff!
YOUR STRATEGY WAS QUITE IMPRESSIVE...
WHAT DID YOU CALL IT AGAIN...?
MOTITUS.
OR RATHER, QUASI-MOTITUS, REALLY.

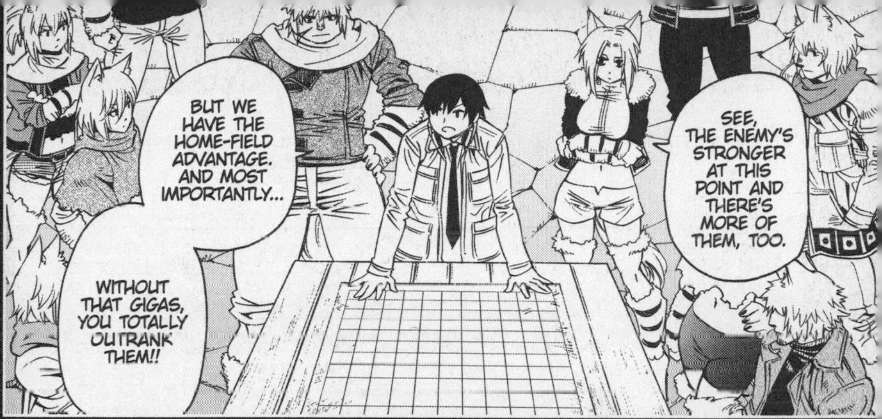
SEE, THE ENEMY'S STRONGER AT THIS POINT AND THERE'S MORE OF THEM, TOO.
BUT WE HAVE THE HOME-FIELD ADVANTAGE. AND MOST IMPORTANTLY...
WITHOUT THAT GIGAS, YOU TOTALLY OUTRANK THEM!!

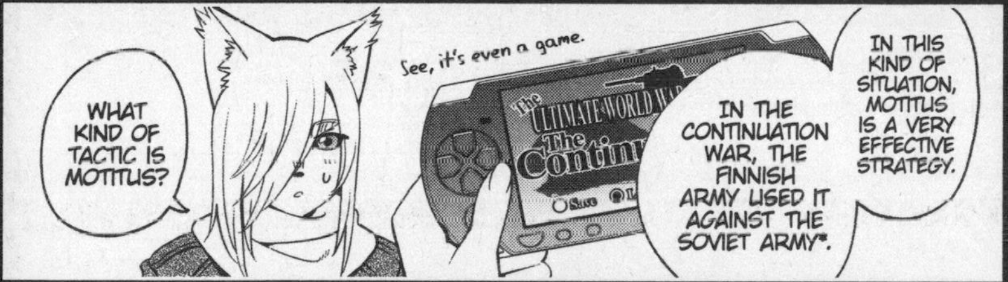
IN THIS KIND OF SITUATION, MOTITUS IS A VERY EFFECTIVE STRATEGY.
IN THE CONTINUATION WAR, THE FINNISH ARMY USED IT AGAINST THE SOVIET ARMY*.
See, it's even a game.
WHAT KIND OF TACTIC IS MOTITUS?

*The Continuation War was fought between Finland and the Soviet Union during World War II. It lasted from 1941-1944.

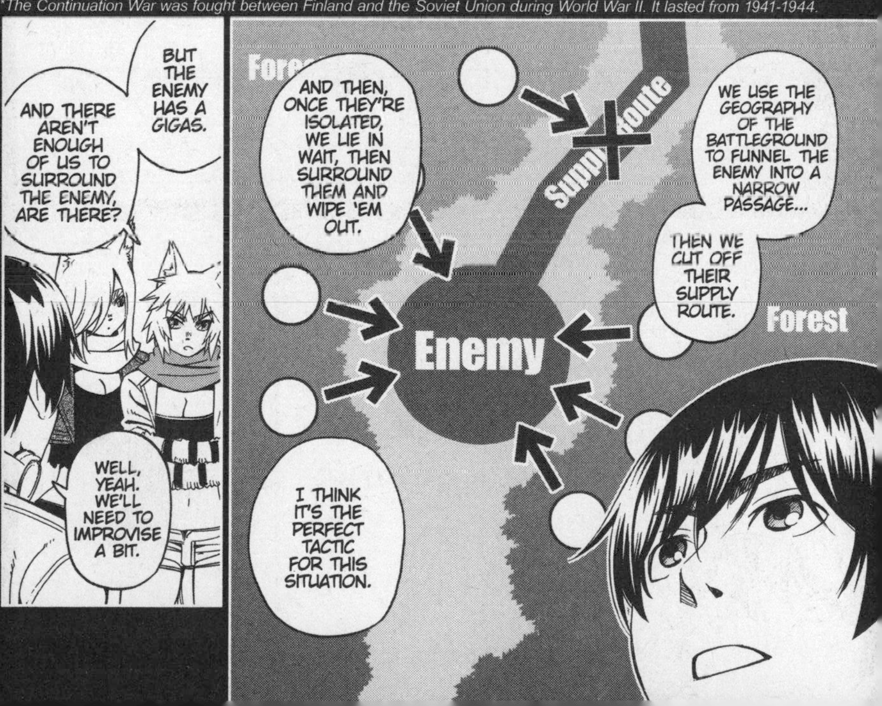
WE USE THE GEOGRAPHY OF THE BATTLEGROUND TO FUNNEL THE ENEMY INTO A NARROW PASSAGE...
THEN WE CUT OFF THEIR SUPPLY ROUTE.
AND THEN, ONCE THEY'RE ISOLATED, WE LIE IN WAIT, THEN SURROUND THEM AND WIPE 'EM OUT.
Forest
Enemy
I THINK IT'S THE PERFECT TACTIC FOR THIS SITUATION.
BUT THE ENEMY HAS A GIGAS.
AND THERE AREN'T ENOUGH OF US TO SURROUND THE ENEMY, ARE THERE?
WELL, YEAH. WE'LL NEED TO IMPROVISE A BIT.

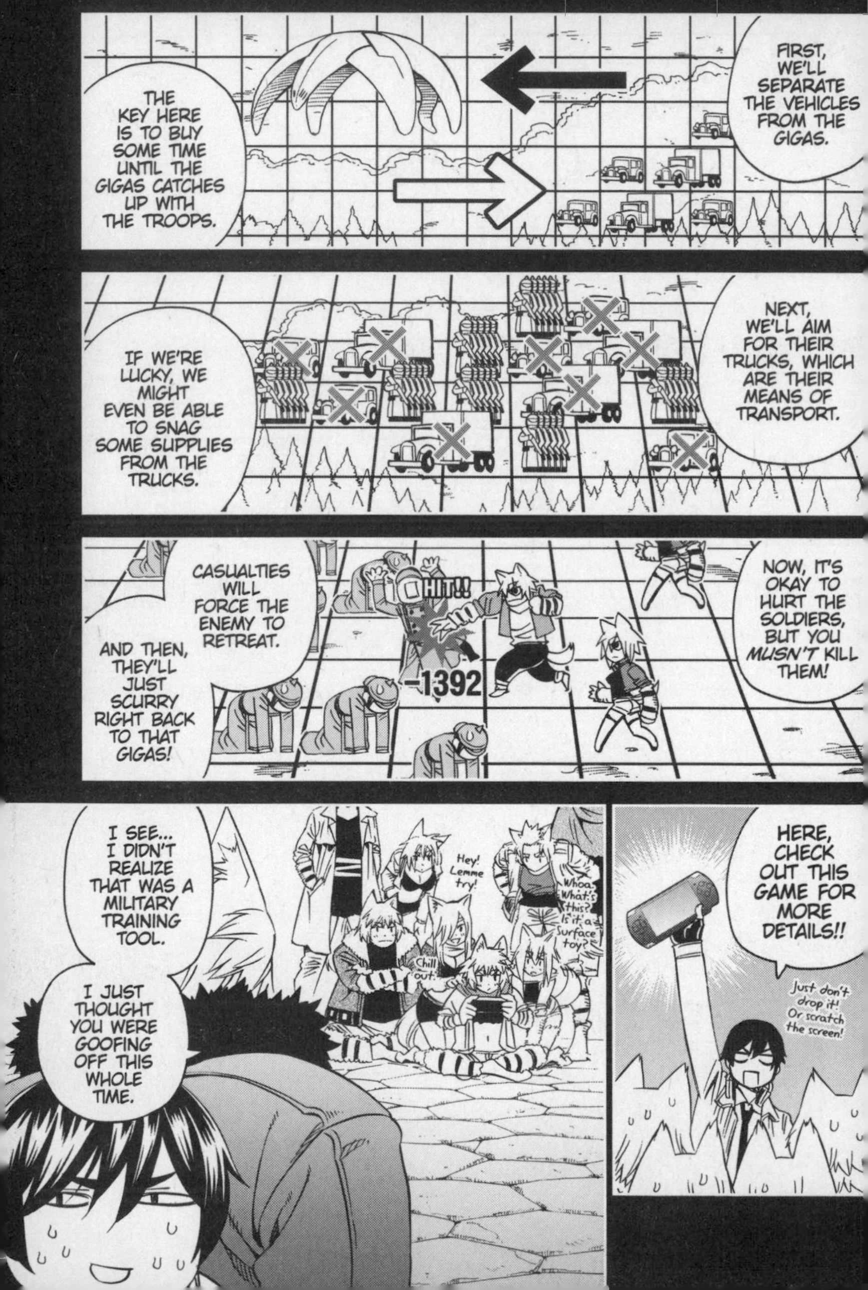
FIRST, WE'LL SEPARATE THE VEHICLES FROM THE GIGAS.
THE KEY HERE IS TO BUY SOME TIME UNTIL THE GIGAS CATCHES UP WITH THE TROOPS.
NEXT, WE'LL AIM FOR THEIR TRUCKS, WHICH ARE THEIR MEANS OF TRANSPORT.
IF WE'RE LUCKY, WE MIGHT EVEN BE ABLE TO SNAG SOME SUPPLIES FROM THE TRUCKS.
NOW, IT'S OKAY TO HURT THE SOLDIERS, BUT YOU *MUSN'T* KILL THEM!
HIT!!
-1392
CASUALTIES WILL FORCE THE ENEMY TO RETREAT.
AND THEN, THEY'LL JUST SCURRY RIGHT BACK TO THAT GIGAS!
HERE, CHECK OUT THIS GAME FOR MORE DETAILS!!
Just don't drop it! Or scratch the screen!
I SEE... I DIDN'T REALIZE THAT WAS A MILITARY TRAINING TOOL.
Whoa. What's this? Is it a Surface toy?
Hey! Lemme try!
Chill out.
I JUST THOUGHT YOU WERE GOOFING OFF THIS WHOLE TIME.

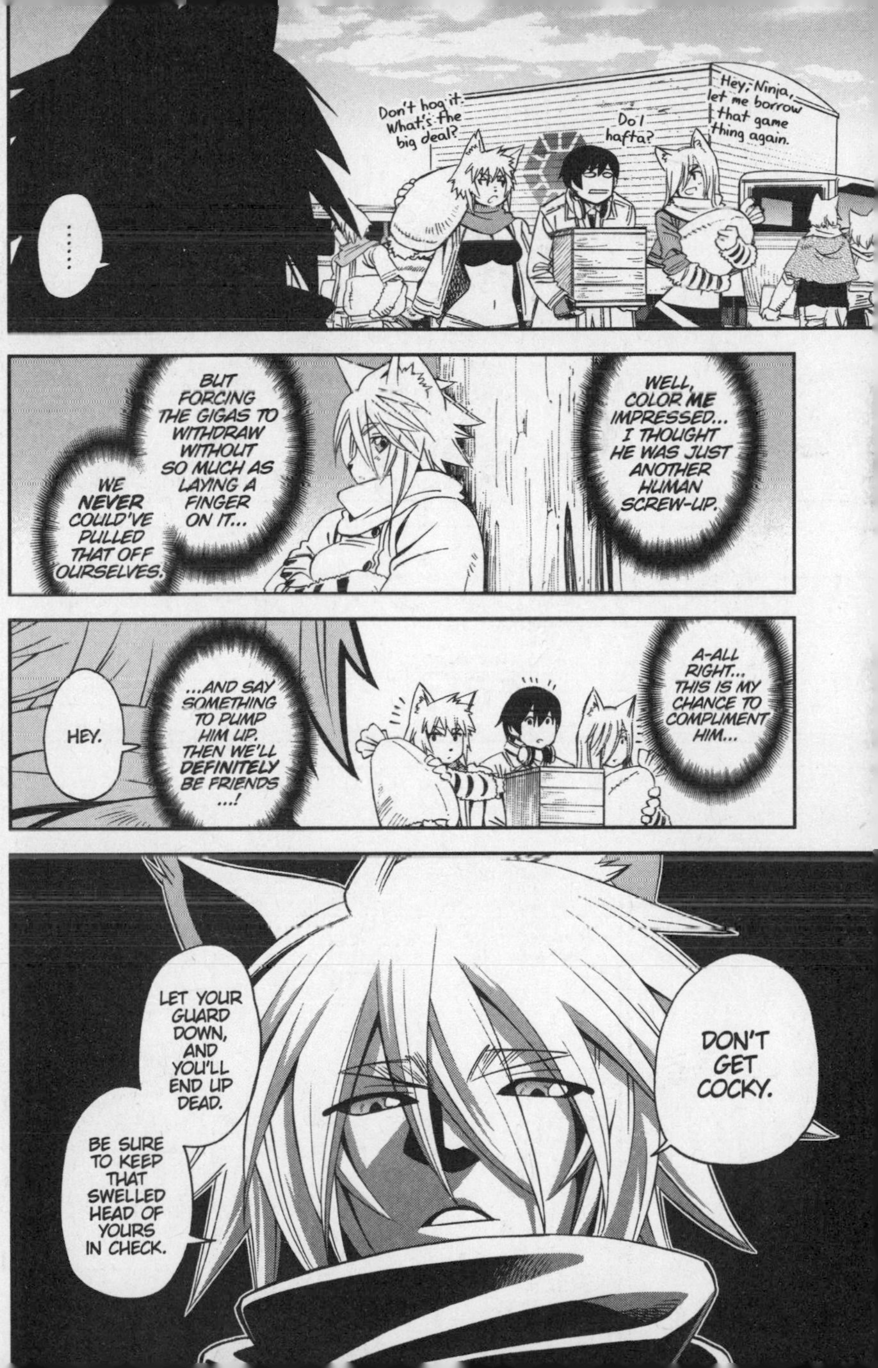
Hey, Ninja, let me borrow that game thing again.
Do I hafta?
Don't hog it. What's the big deal?
......
WELL, COLOR ME IMPRESSED... I THOUGHT HE WAS JUST ANOTHER HUMAN SCREW-UP.
BUT FORCING THE GIGAS TO WITHDRAW WITHOUT SO MUCH AS LAYING A FINGER ON IT...
WE NEVER COULD'VE PULLED THAT OFF OURSELVES.
A-ALL RIGHT... THIS IS MY CHANCE TO COMPLIMENT HIM...
...AND SAY SOMETHING TO PUMP HIM UP. THEN WE'LL DEFINITELY BE FRIENDS...!
HEY.
DON'T GET COCKY.
LET YOUR GUARD DOWN, AND YOU'LL END UP DEAD.
BE SURE TO KEEP THAT SWELLED HEAD OF YOURS IN CHECK.

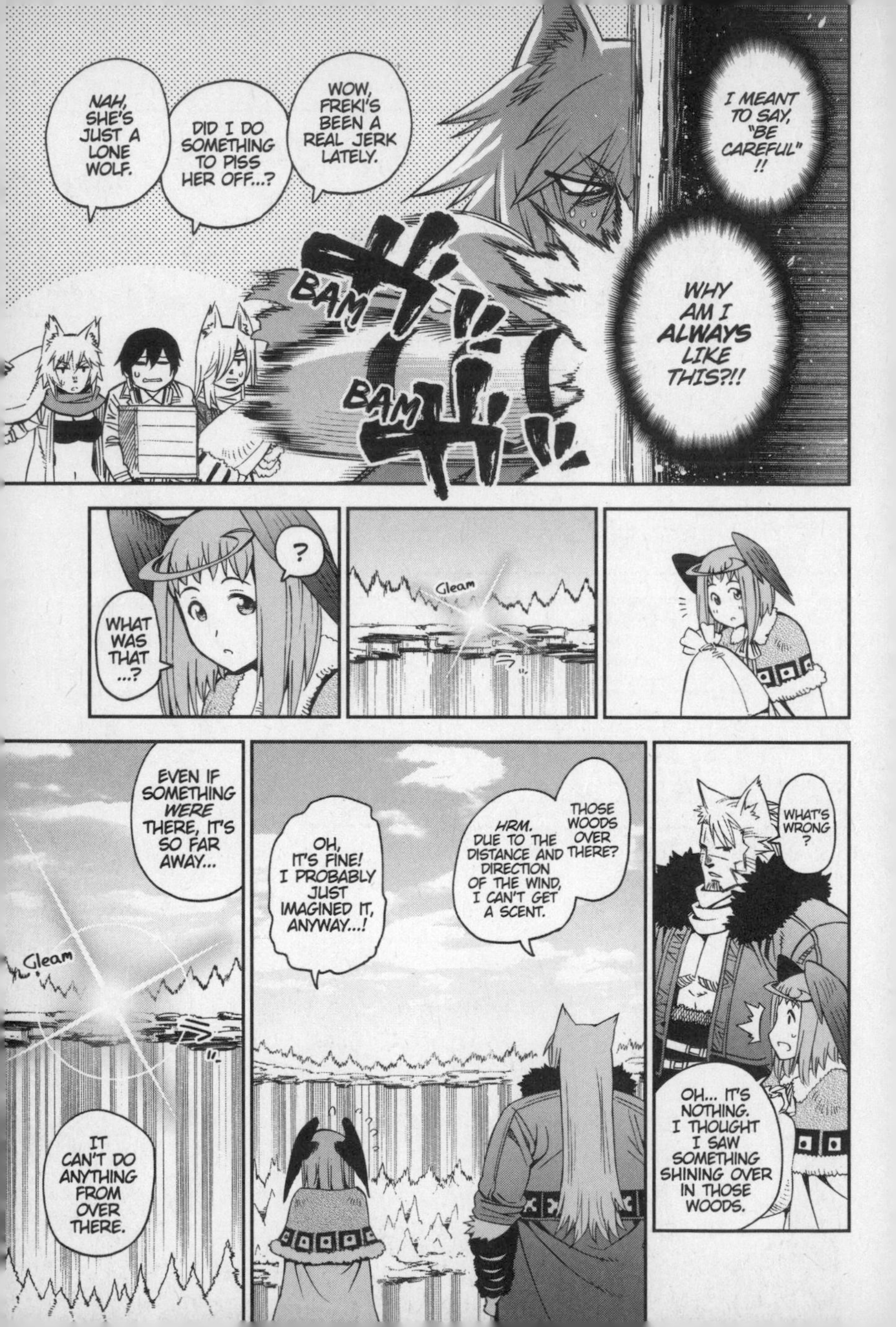
I MEANT TO SAY, "BE CAREFUL"!!
WHY AM I ALWAYS LIKE THIS?!!
WOW, FREKI'S BEEN A REAL JERK LATELY.
DID I DO SOMETHING TO PISS HER OFF...?
NAH, SHE'S JUST A LONE WOLF.
BAM
BAM
Gleam
?
WHAT WAS THAT...?
WHAT'S WRONG?
OH... IT'S NOTHING. I THOUGHT I SAW SOMETHING SHINING OVER IN THOSE WOODS.
THOSE WOODS OVER THERE?
HRM. DUE TO THE DISTANCE AND DIRECTION OF THE WIND, I CAN'T GET A SCENT.
OH, IT'S FINE! I PROBABLY JUST IMAGINED IT, ANYWAY...!
EVEN IF SOMETHING WERE THERE, IT'S SO FAR AWAY...
Gleam
IT CAN'T DO ANYTHING FROM OVER THERE.

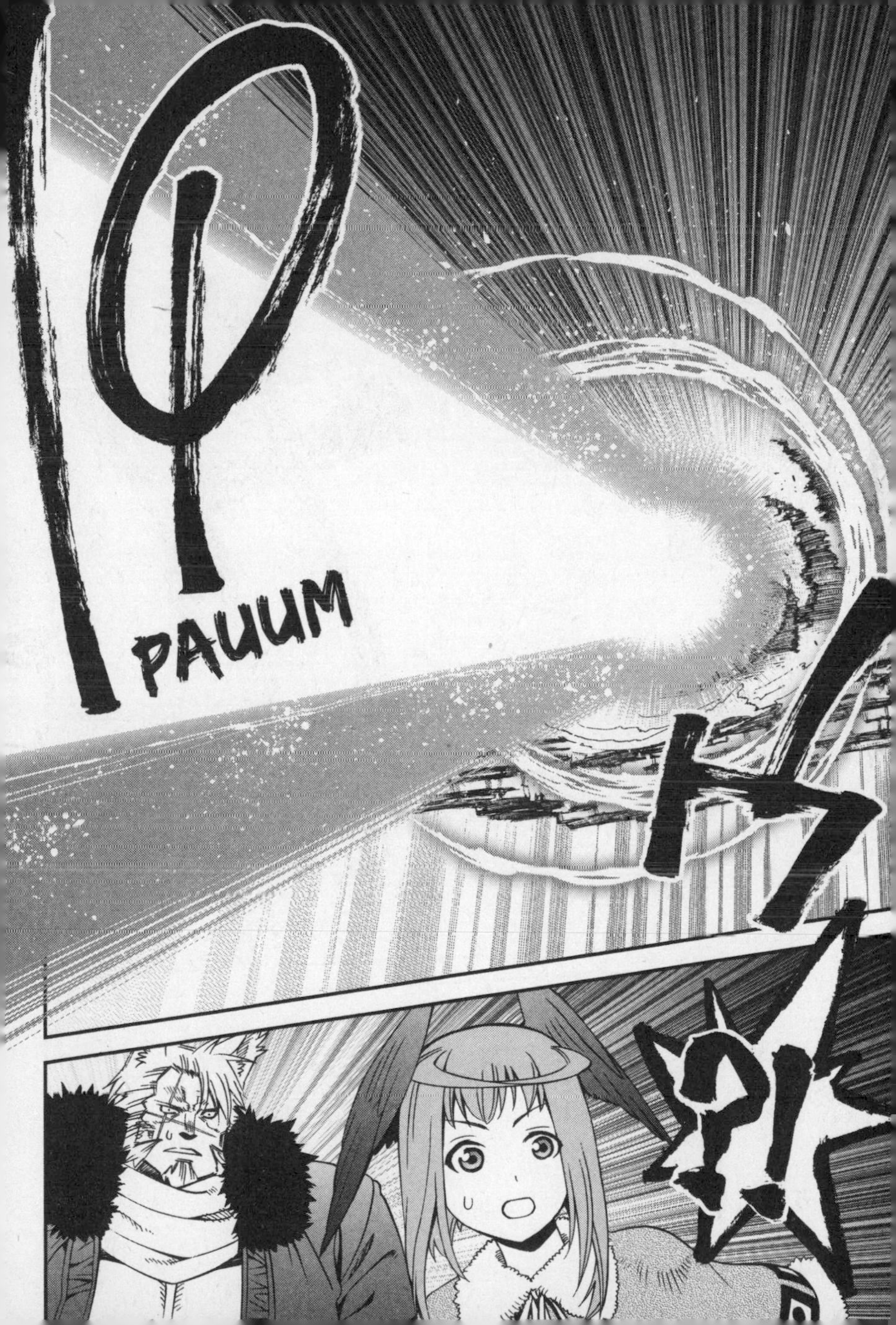
PAUUM
?!

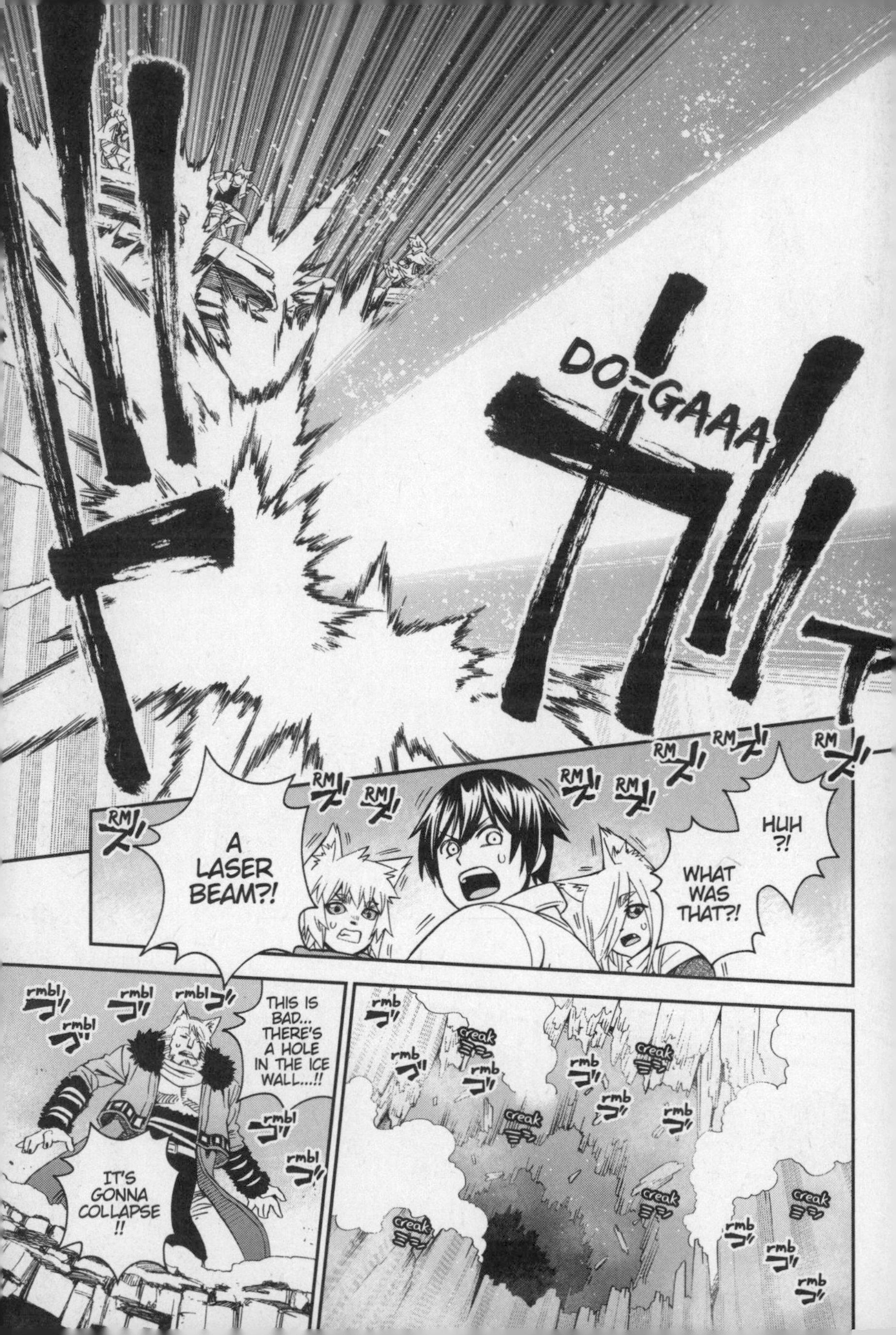
DO-GAAA
RM
RM
RM
RM
RM
RM
RM
RM
HUH ?!
WHAT WAS THAT?!
A LASER BEAM?!
rmb
creak
rmb
creak
rmb
rmb
creak
rmb
rmb
creak
creak
creak
rmb
rmb
rmb
rmbl
rmbl
rmbl
rmbl
THIS IS BAD... THERE'S A HOLE IN THE ICE WALL...!!
rmbl
rmbl
IT'S GONNA COLLAPSE !!

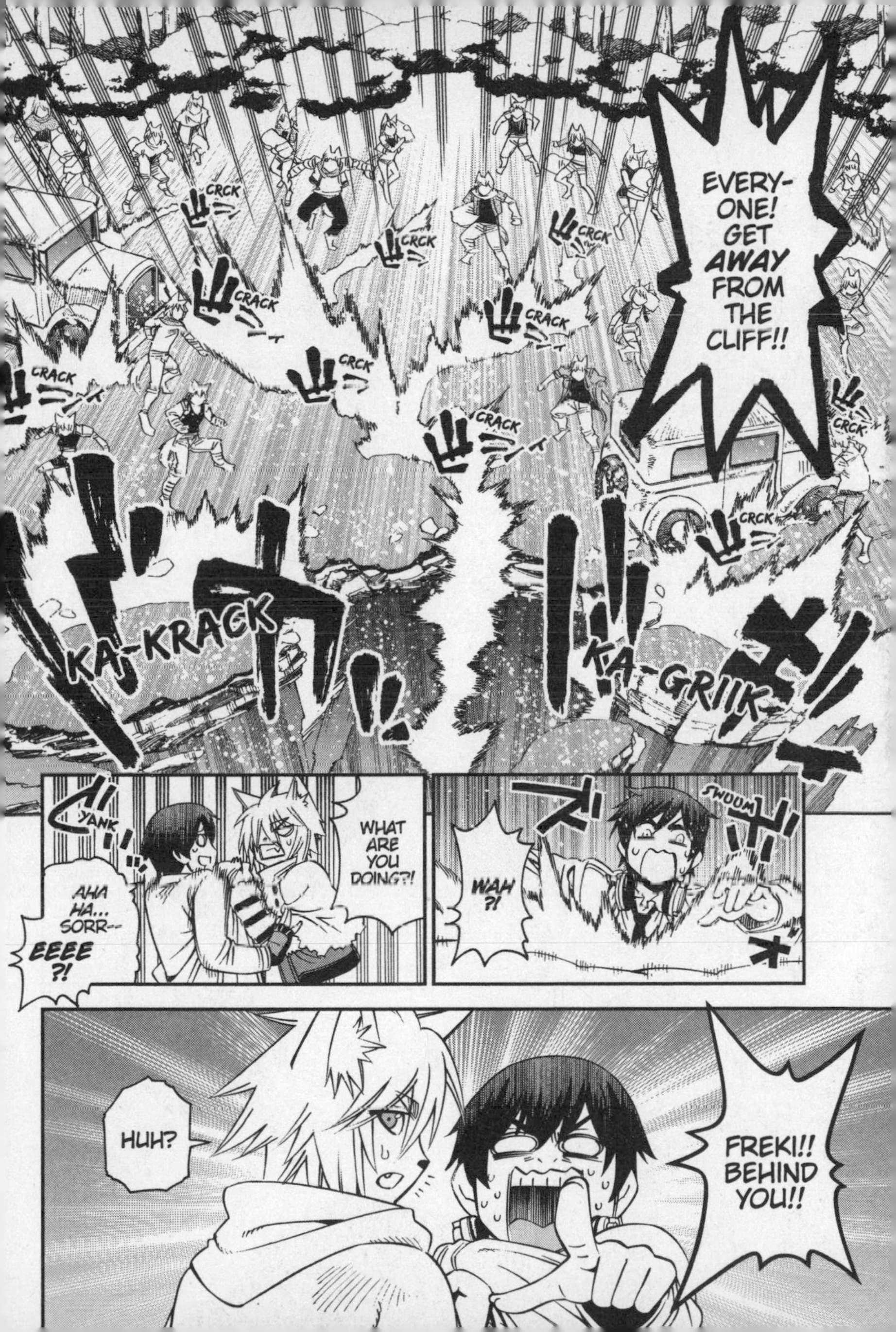
EVERY-ONE! GET AWAY FROM THE CLIFF!!
CRCK
CRCK
CRCK
CRACK
CRACK
CRCK
CRACK
CRACK
CRCK
CRCK
KA-GRIIK
KA-KRACK
SWUUM
WAH?!
YANK
WHAT ARE YOU DOING?!
AHA HA... SORR-- EEEE?!
FREKI!! BEHIND YOU!!
HUH?

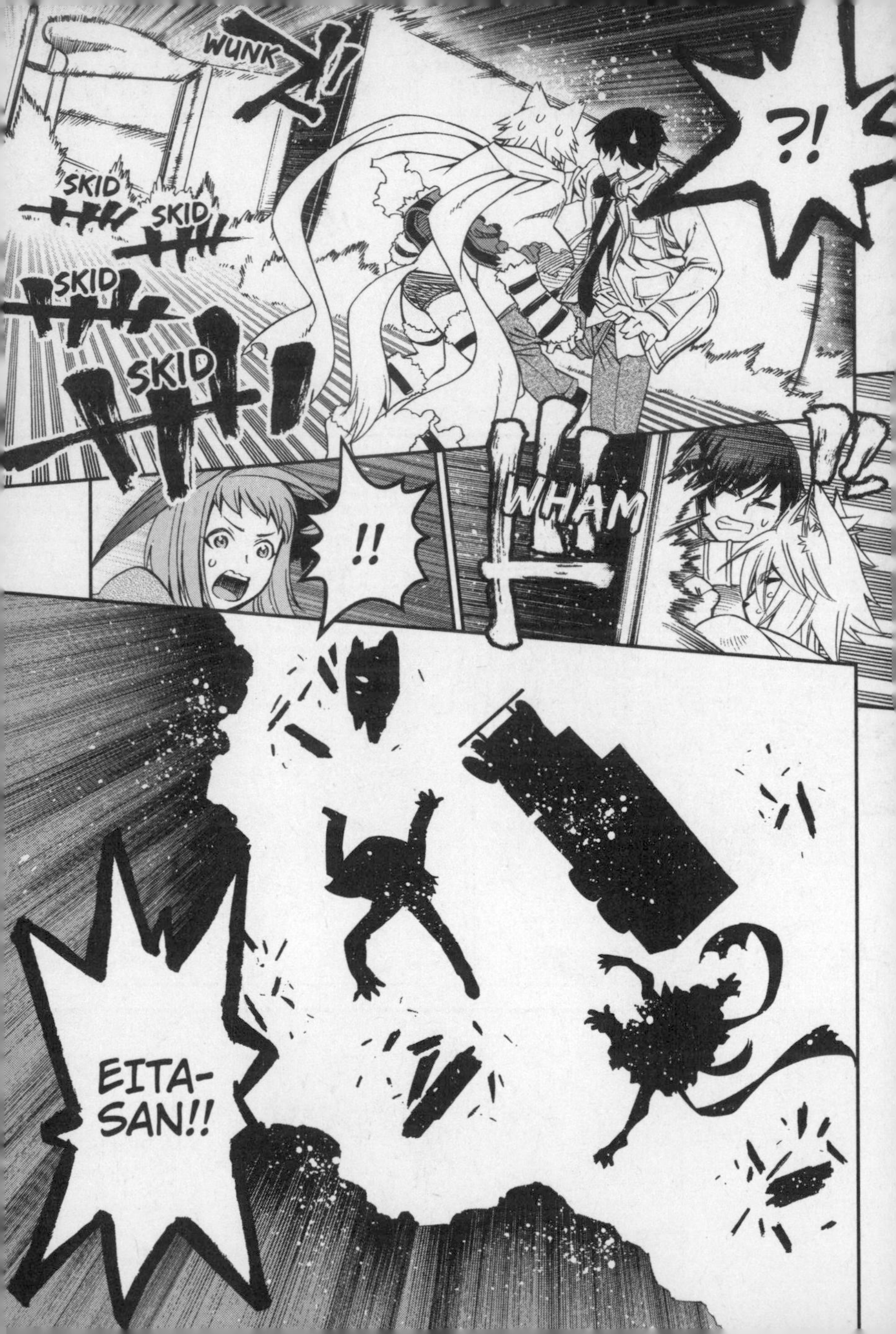
?!
WUNK
SKID
SKID
SKID
SKID
WHAM
!!
EITA-
SAN!!

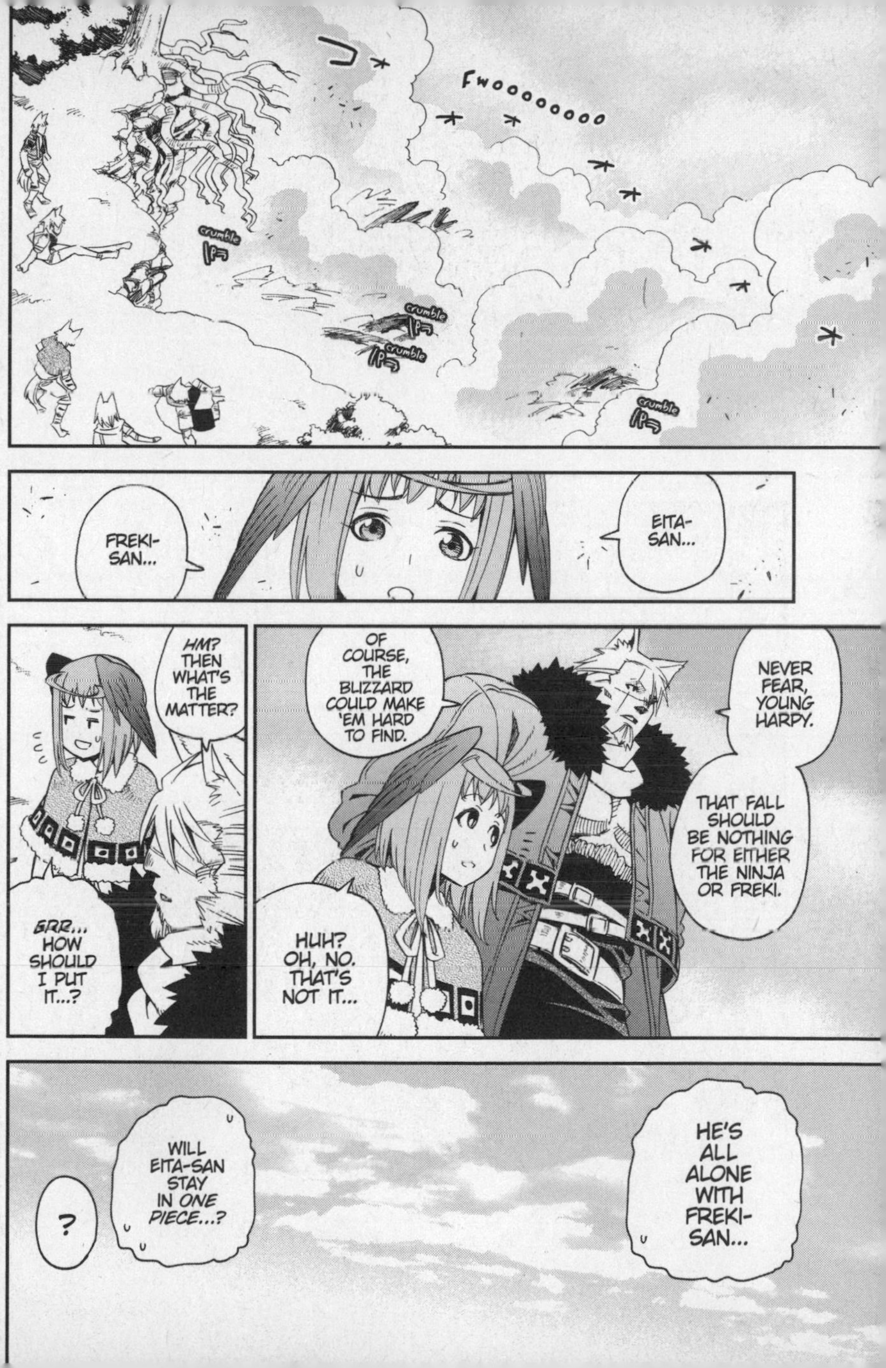

Fwoooooooo
crumble
crumble
crumble
crumble
EITA-SAN...
FREKI-SAN...
NEVER FEAR, YOUNG HARPY.
THAT FALL SHOULD BE NOTHING FOR EITHER THE NINJA OR FREKI.
OF COURSE, THE BLIZZARD COULD MAKE 'EM HARD TO FIND.
HUH? OH, NO. THAT'S NOT IT...
HM? THEN WHAT'S THE MATTER?
GRR... HOW SHOULD I PUT IT...?
HE'S ALL ALONE WITH FREKI-SAN...
WILL EITA-SAN STAY IN *ONE PIECE*...?
?

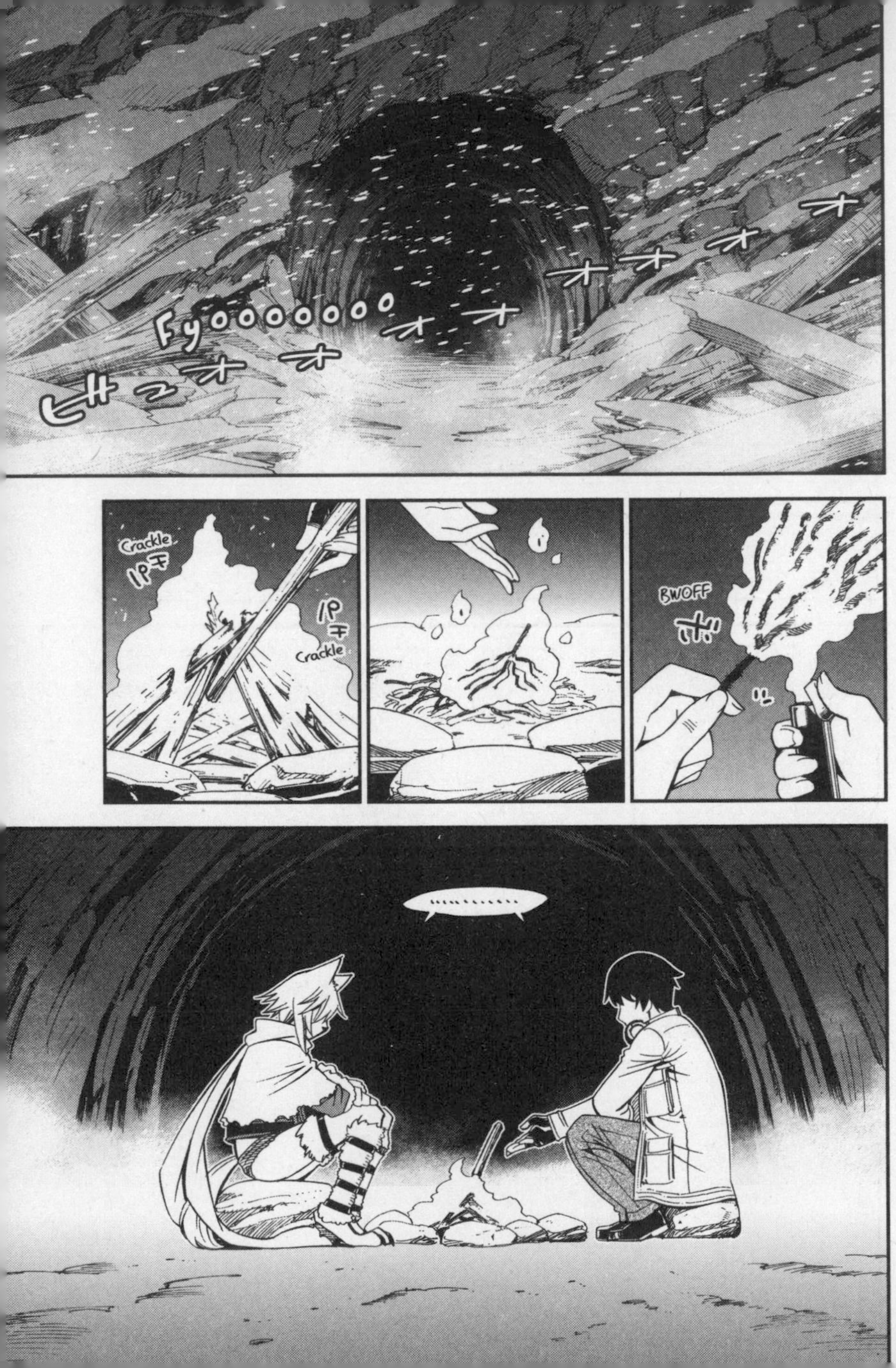

Fyooooooo
ヒュオオオオオオオオ
BWOFF
ボッ
Crackle
パチ
パチ
Crackle
......

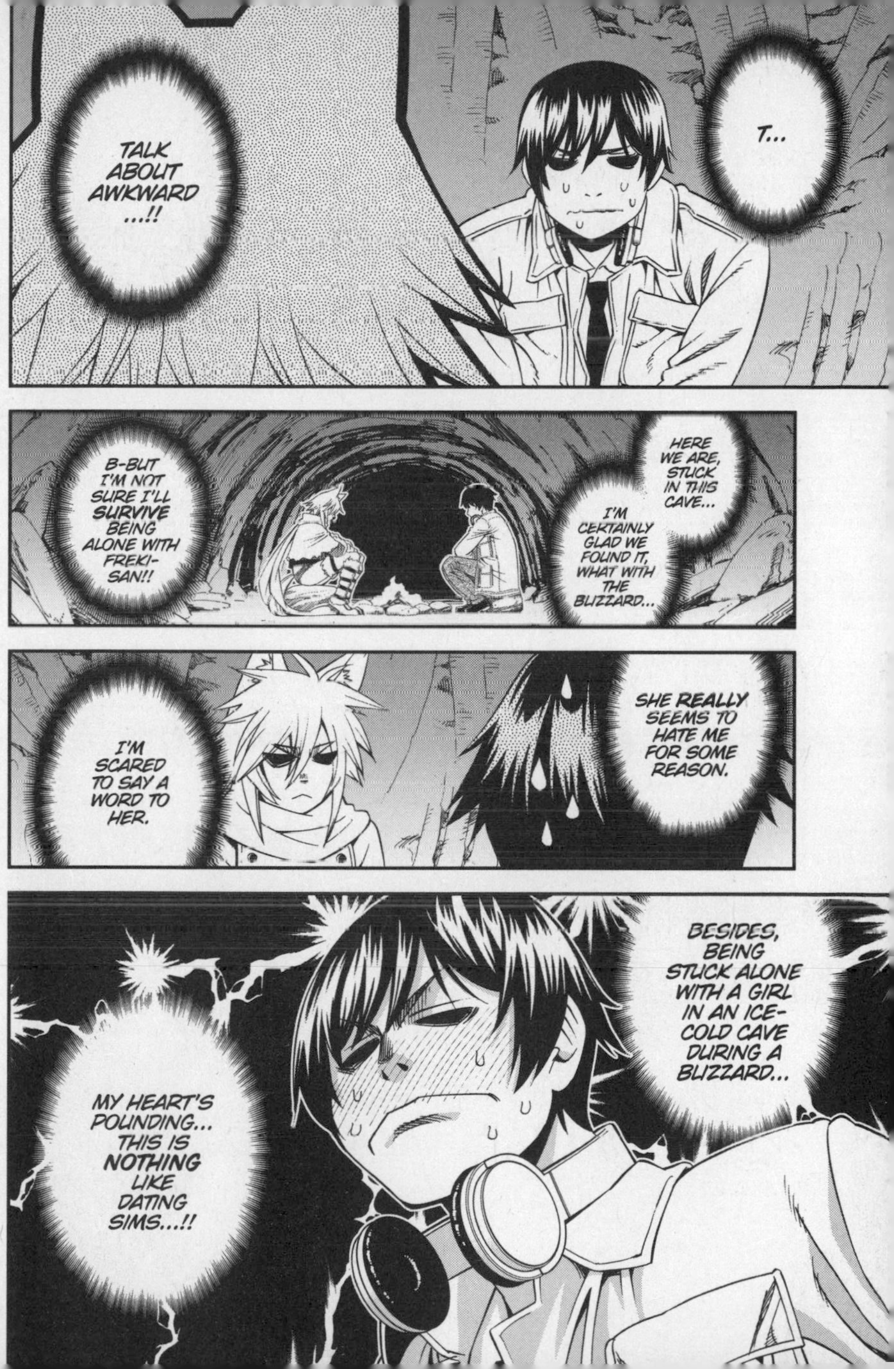
T...
TALK ABOUT AWKWARD ...!!
HERE WE ARE, STUCK IN THIS CAVE...
I'M CERTAINLY GLAD WE FOUND IT, WHAT WITH THE BLIZZARD...
B-BUT I'M NOT SURE I'LL **SURVIVE** BEING ALONE WITH FREKI-SAN!!
SHE **REALLY** SEEMS TO HATE ME FOR SOME REASON.
I'M SCARED TO SAY A WORD TO HER.
BESIDES, BEING STUCK ALONE WITH A GIRL IN AN ICE-COLD CAVE DURING A BLIZZARD...
MY HEART'S POUNDING... THIS IS **NOTHING** LIKE DATING SIMS...!!

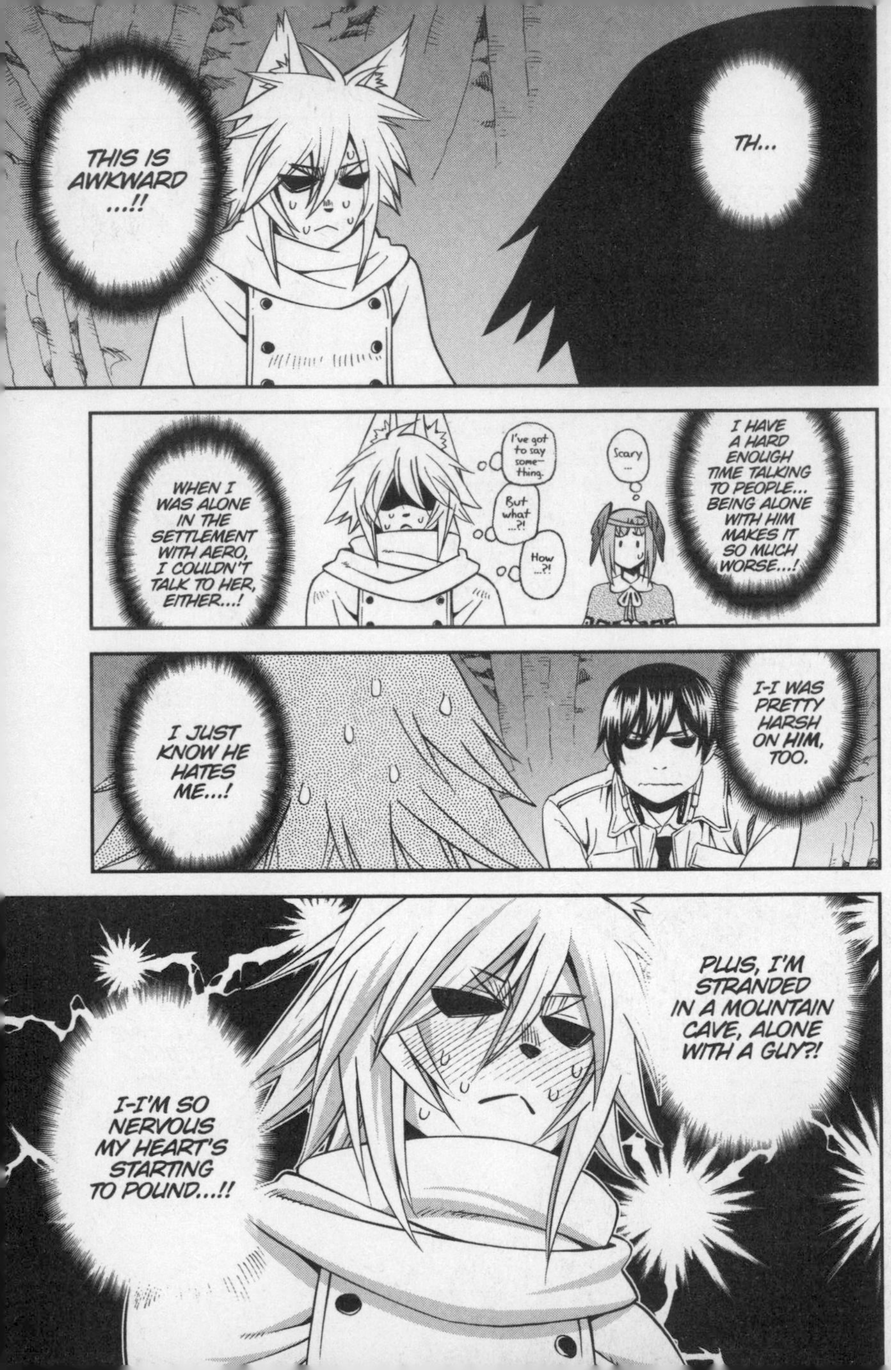
TH...
THIS IS AWKWARD ...!!
I HAVE A HARD ENOUGH TIME TALKING TO PEOPLE... BEING ALONE WITH HIM MAKES IT SO MUCH WORSE...!
Scary ...
I've got to say something.
But what ...?!
How ...?!
WHEN I WAS ALONE IN THE SETTLEMENT WITH AERO, I COULDN'T TALK TO HER, EITHER...!
I-I WAS PRETTY HARSH ON HIM, TOO.
I JUST KNOW HE HATES ME...!
PLUS, I'M STRANDED IN A MOUNTAIN CAVE, ALONE WITH A GUY?!
I-I'M SO NERVOUS MY HEART'S STARTING TO POUND...!!

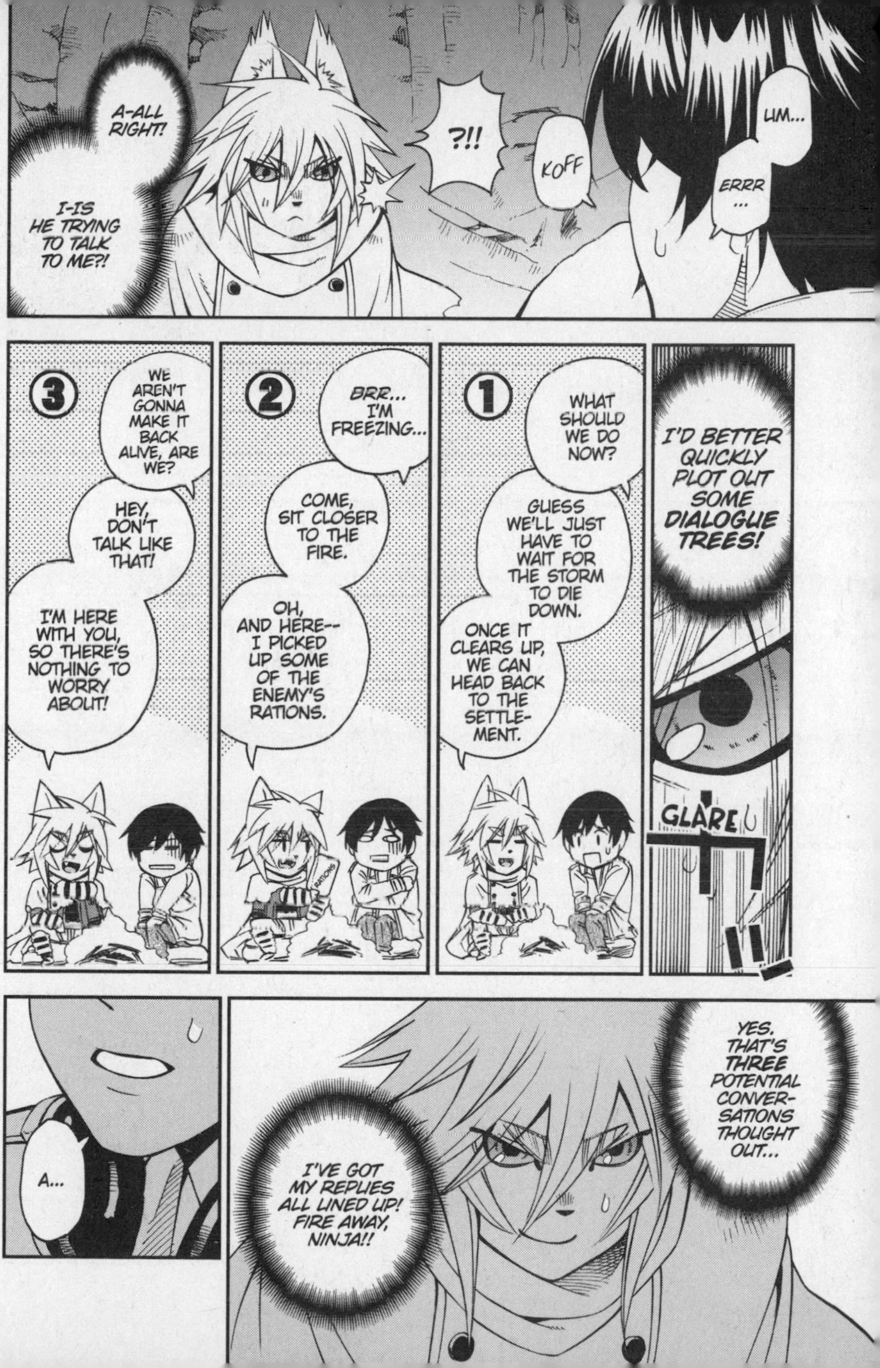
UM...
ERRR ...
KOFF
?!!
A-ALL RIGHT!
I-IS HE TRYING TO TALK TO ME?!
I'D BETTER QUICKLY PLOT OUT SOME DIALOGUE TREES!
GLARE
1
WHAT SHOULD WE DO NOW?
GUESS WE'LL JUST HAVE TO WAIT FOR THE STORM TO DIE DOWN.
ONCE IT CLEARS UP, WE CAN HEAD BACK TO THE SETTLE-MENT.
2
BRR... I'M FREEZING...
COME, SIT CLOSER TO THE FIRE.
OH, AND HERE-- I PICKED UP SOME OF THE ENEMY'S RATIONS.
RATIONS
3
WE AREN'T GONNA MAKE IT BACK ALIVE, ARE WE?
HEY, DON'T TALK LIKE THAT!
I'M HERE WITH YOU, SO THERE'S NOTHING TO WORRY ABOUT!
YES. THAT'S THREE POTENTIAL CONVER-SATIONS THOUGHT OUT...
I'VE GOT MY REPLIES ALL LINED UP! FIRE AWAY, NINJA!!
A...

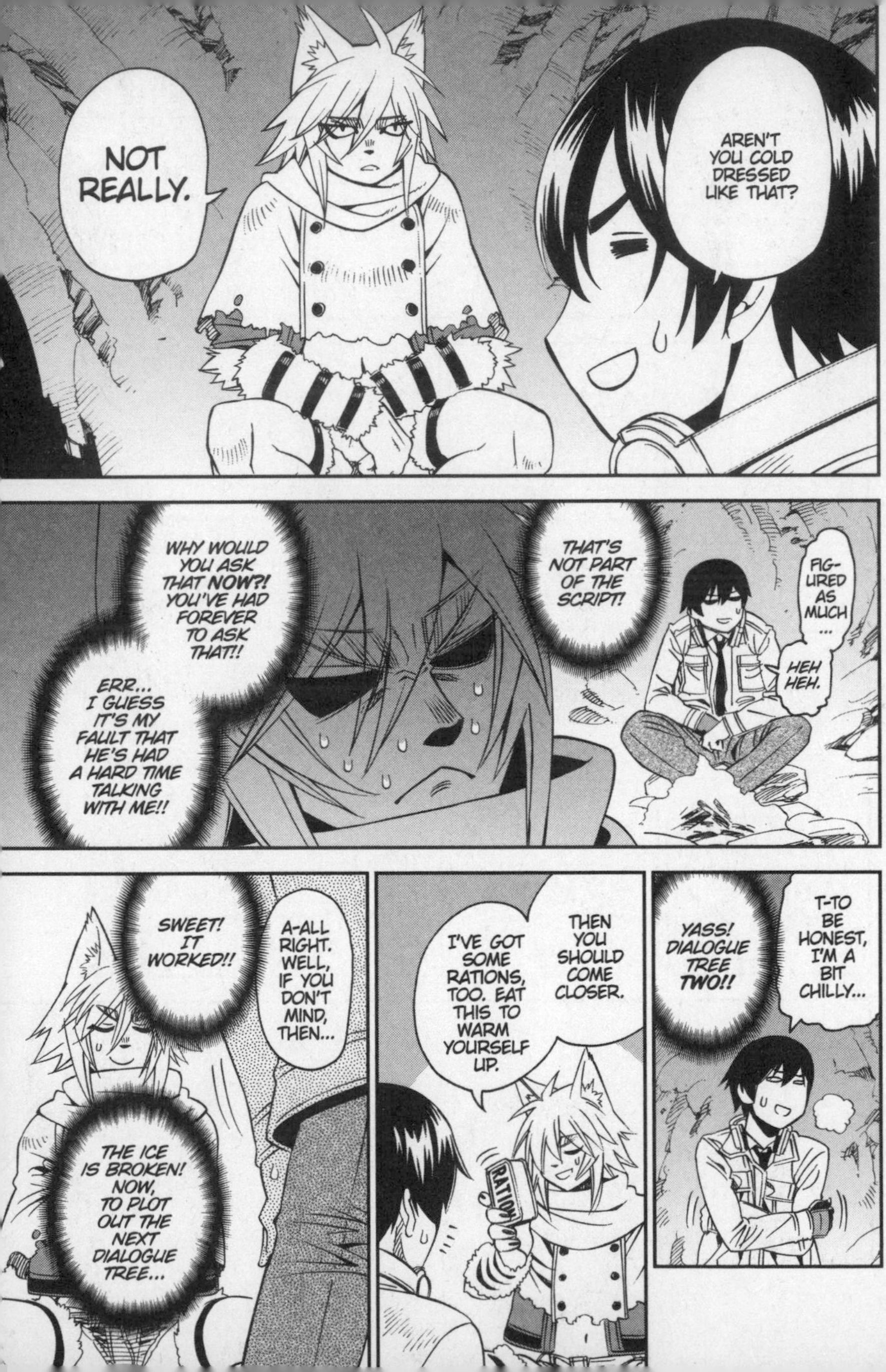
AREN'T YOU COLD DRESSED LIKE THAT?
NOT REALLY.
FIG-URED AS MUCH...
HEH HEH.
THAT'S NOT PART OF THE SCRIPT!
WHY WOULD YOU ASK THAT NOW?! YOU'VE HAD FOREVER TO ASK THAT!!
ERR... I GUESS IT'S MY FAULT THAT HE'S HAD A HARD TIME TALKING WITH ME!!
T-TO BE HONEST, I'M A BIT CHILLY...
YASS! DIALOGUE TREE TWO!!
THEN YOU SHOULD COME CLOSER.
I'VE GOT SOME RATIONS, TOO. EAT THIS TO WARM YOURSELF UP.
RATION
A-ALL RIGHT. WELL, IF YOU DON'T MIND, THEN...
SWEET! IT WORKED!!
THE ICE IS BROKEN! NOW, TO PLOT OUT THE NEXT DIALOGUE TREE...

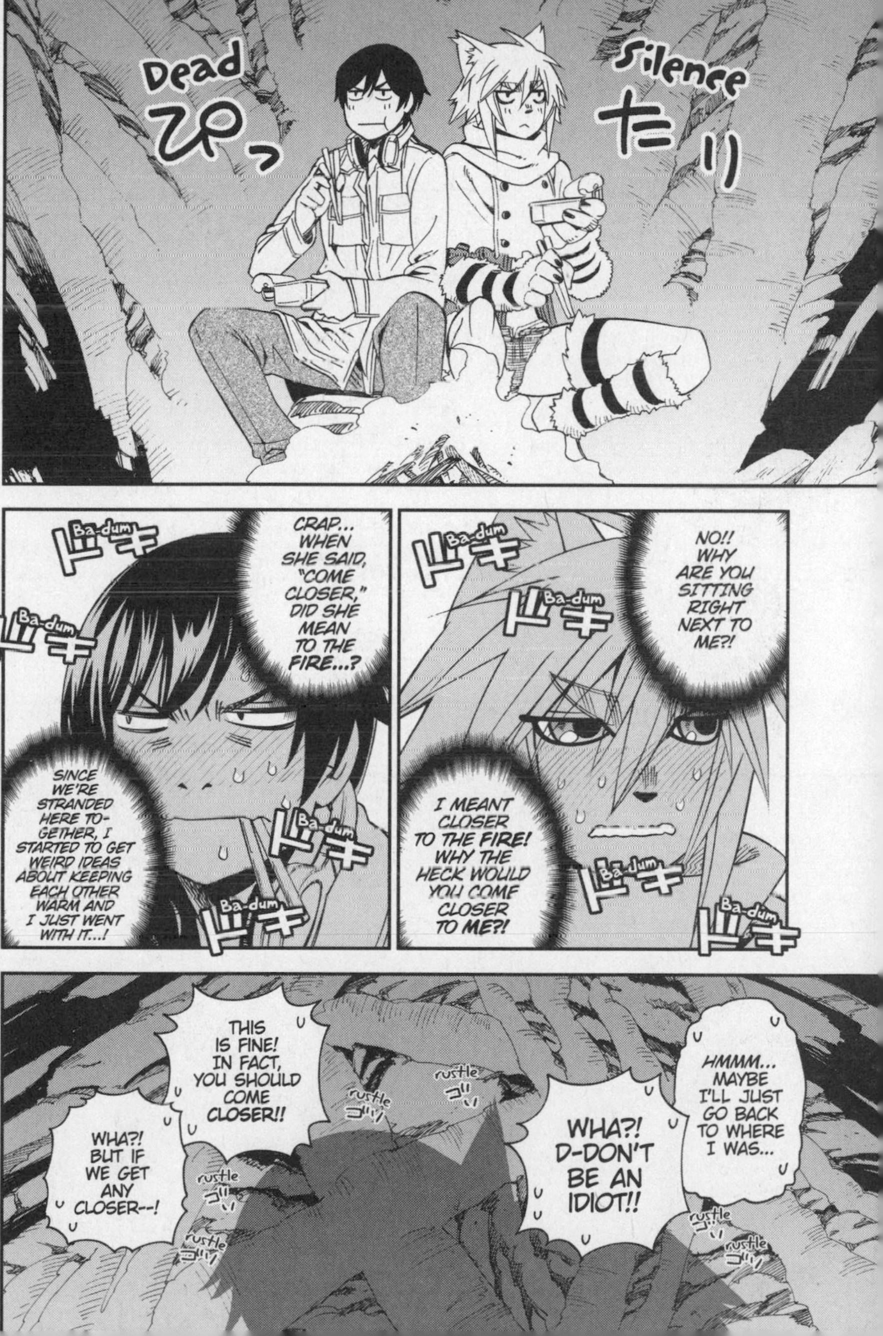
Dead ぴっ Silence たり
Ba-dum ドキ
Ba-dum ドキ
NO!! WHY ARE YOU SITTING RIGHT NEXT TO ME?!
I MEANT CLOSER TO THE FIRE! WHY THE HECK WOULD YOU COME CLOSER TO ME?!
Ba-dum ドキ
Ba-dum ドキ
Ba-dum ドキ
CRAP... WHEN SHE SAID, "COME CLOSER," DID SHE MEAN TO THE FIRE...?
Ba-dum ドキ
SINCE WE'RE STRANDED HERE TO-GETHER, I STARTED TO GET WEIRD IDEAS ABOUT KEEPING EACH OTHER WARM AND I JUST WENT WITH IT...!
Ba-dum ドキ
Ba-dum ドキ
HMMM... MAYBE I'LL JUST GO BACK TO WHERE I WAS...
WHA?! D-DON'T BE AN IDIOT!!
rustle
rustle
rustle
THIS IS FINE! IN FACT, YOU SHOULD COME CLOSER!!
rustle
WHA?! BUT IF WE GET ANY CLOSER--!
rustle
rustle

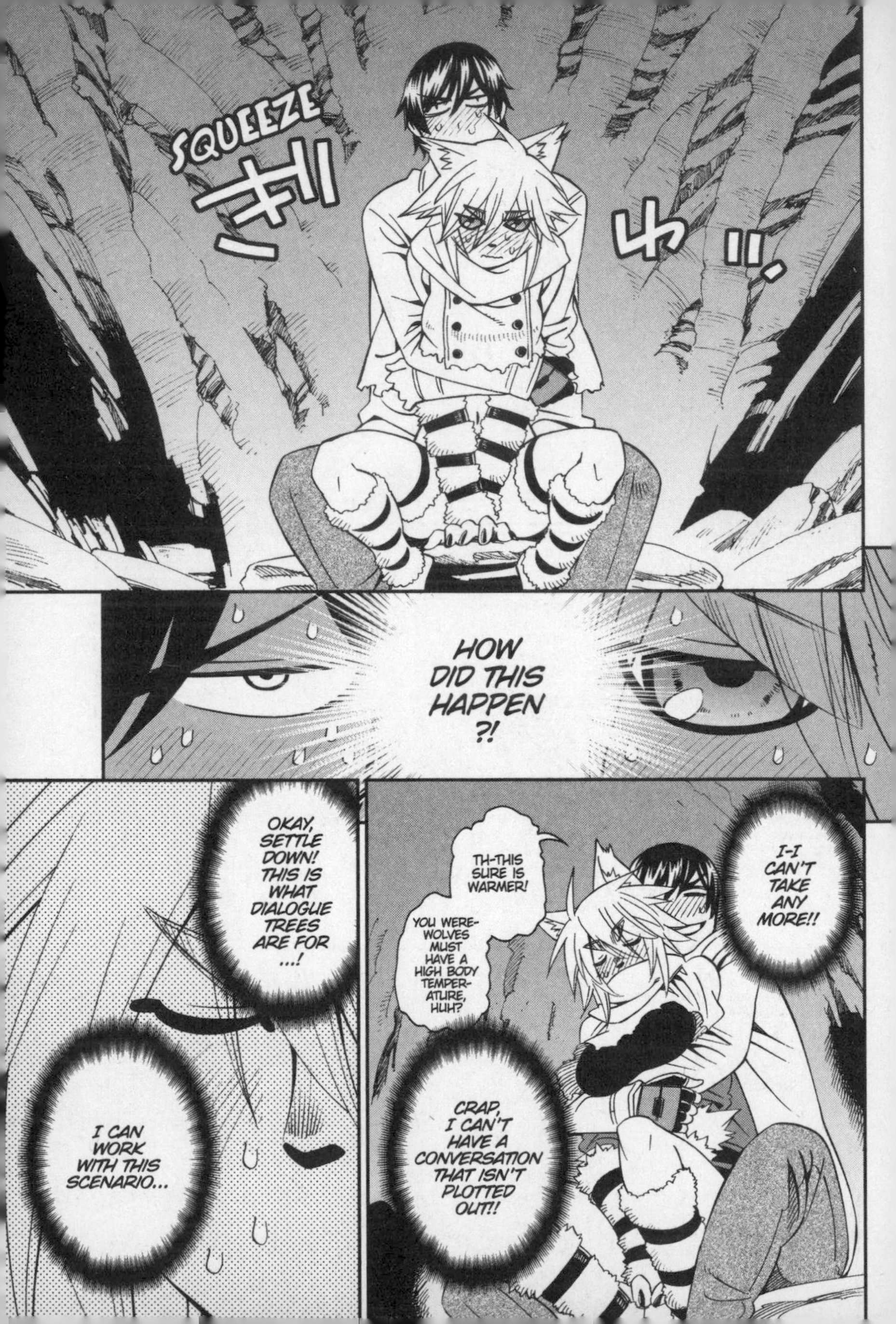
SQUEEZE
HOW DID THIS HAPPEN?!
I-I CAN'T TAKE ANY MORE!!
TH-THIS SURE IS WARMER!
YOU WEREWOLVES MUST HAVE A HIGH BODY TEMPERATURE, HUH?
CRAP, I CAN'T HAVE A CONVERSATION THAT ISN'T PLOTTED OUT!!
OKAY, SETTLE DOWN! THIS IS WHAT DIALOGUE TREES ARE FOR...!
I CAN WORK WITH THIS SCENARIO...

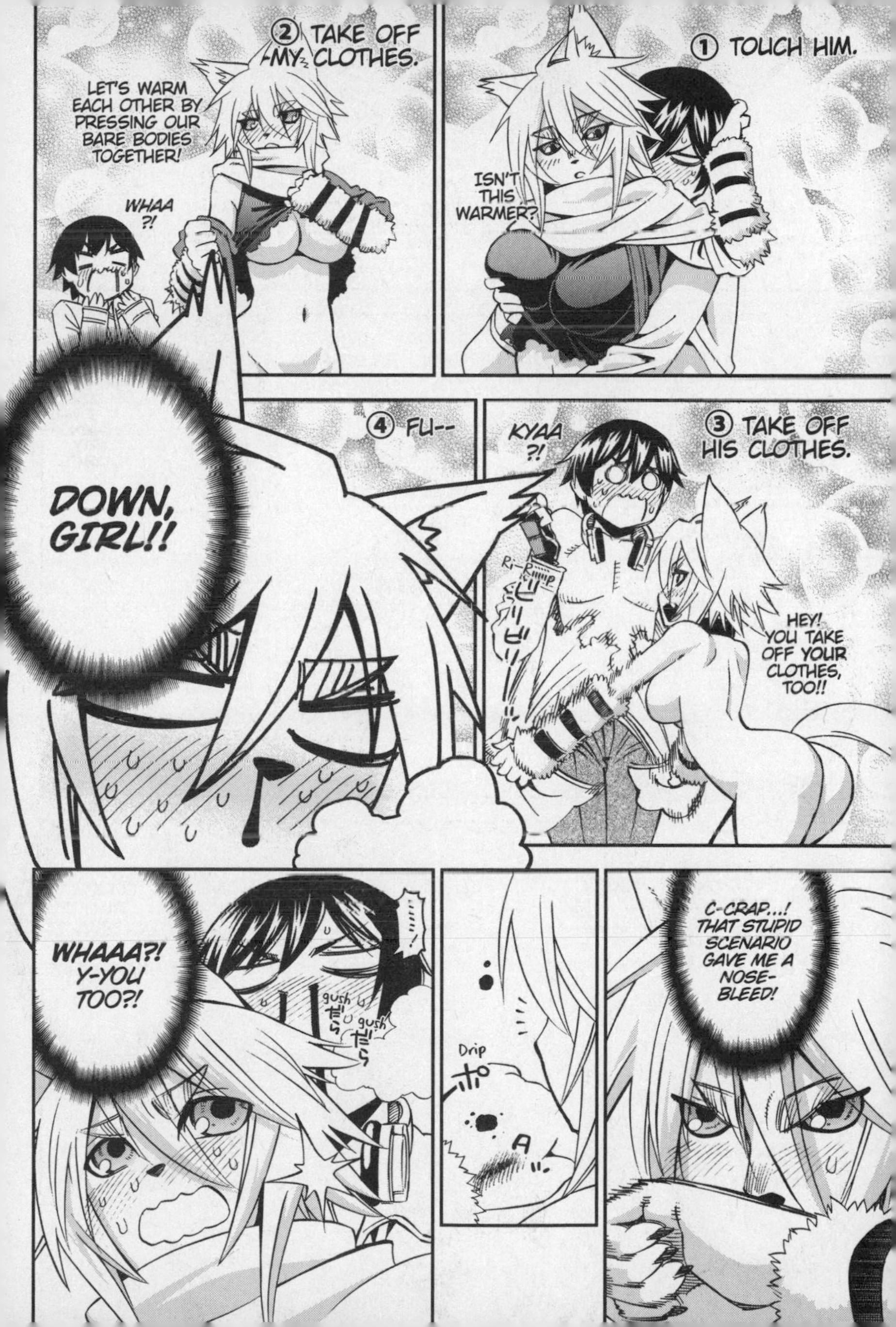
① TOUCH HIM.
ISN'T THIS WARMER?
② TAKE OFF MY CLOTHES.
LET'S WARM EACH OTHER BY PRESSING OUR BARE BODIES TOGETHER!
WHAA ?!
③ TAKE OFF HIS CLOTHES.
KYAA ?!
Ri-Riiip
HEY! YOU TAKE OFF YOUR CLOTHES, TOO!!
④ FU--
DOWN, GIRL!!
C-CRAP...! THAT STUPID SCENARIO GAVE ME A NOSE-BLEED!
Drip
WHAAA?! Y-YOU TOO?!
gush
gush

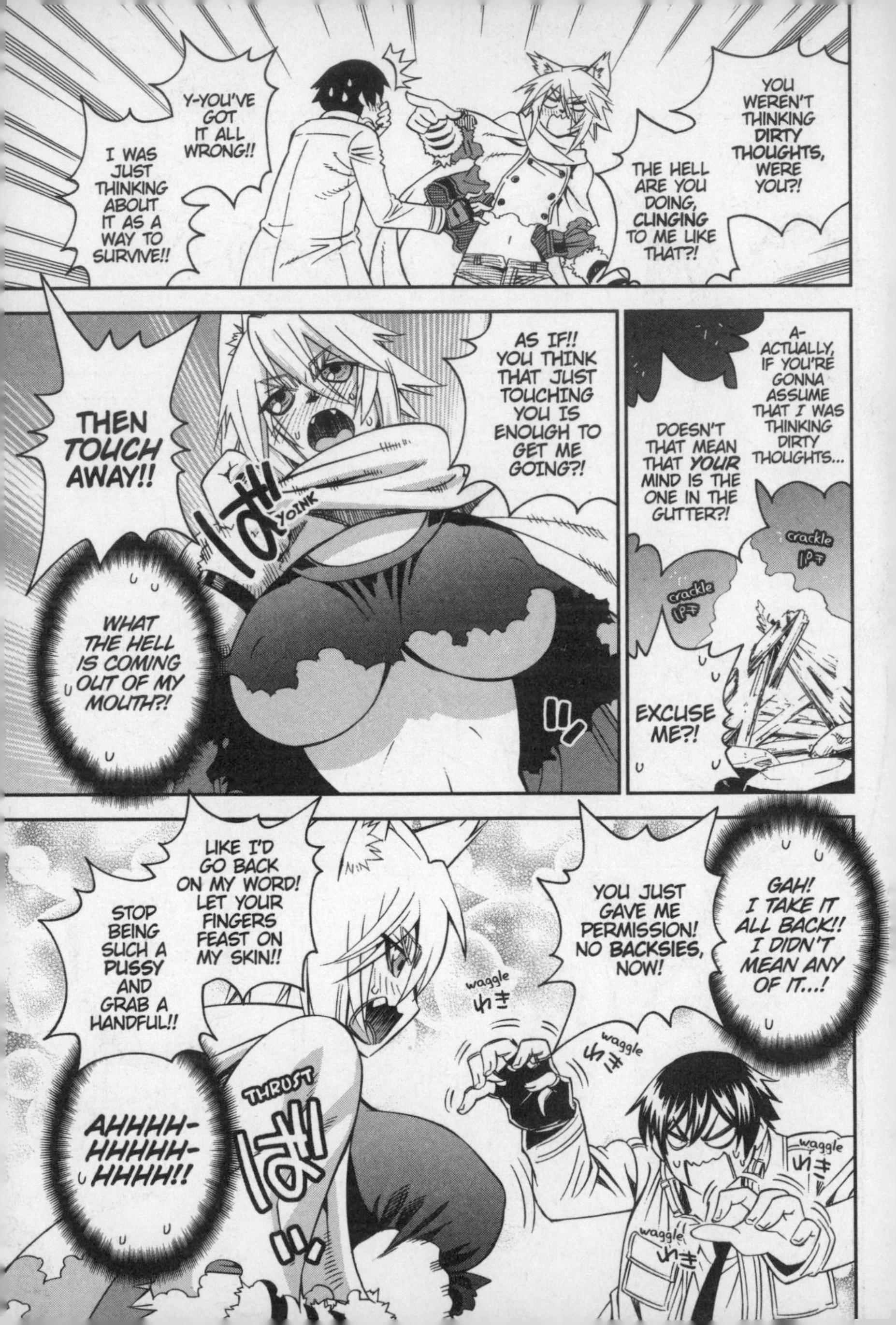
YOU WEREN'T THINKING DIRTY THOUGHTS, WERE YOU?!
THE HELL ARE YOU DOING, CLINGING TO ME LIKE THAT?!
Y-YOU'VE GOT IT ALL WRONG!!
I WAS JUST THINKING ABOUT IT AS A WAY TO SURVIVE!!
A-ACTUALLY, IF YOU'RE GONNA ASSUME THAT I WAS THINKING DIRTY THOUGHTS...
DOESN'T THAT MEAN THAT YOUR MIND IS THE ONE IN THE GUTTER?!
crackle パチ
crackle パチ
EXCUSE ME?!
AS IF!! YOU THINK THAT JUST TOUCHING YOU IS ENOUGH TO GET ME GOING?!
THEN TOUCH AWAY!!
YOINK ばっ
WHAT THE HELL IS COMING OUT OF MY MOUTH?!
GAH! I TAKE IT ALL BACK!! I DIDN'T MEAN ANY OF IT...!
YOU JUST GAVE ME PERMISSION! NO BACKSIES, NOW!
waggle わき
waggle わき
waggle わき
waggle わき
LIKE I'D GO BACK ON MY WORD! LET YOUR FINGERS FEAST ON MY SKIN!!
STOP BEING SUCH A PUSSY AND GRAB A HANDFUL!!
THRUST ばっ
AHHHH-HHHHHH-HHHH!!

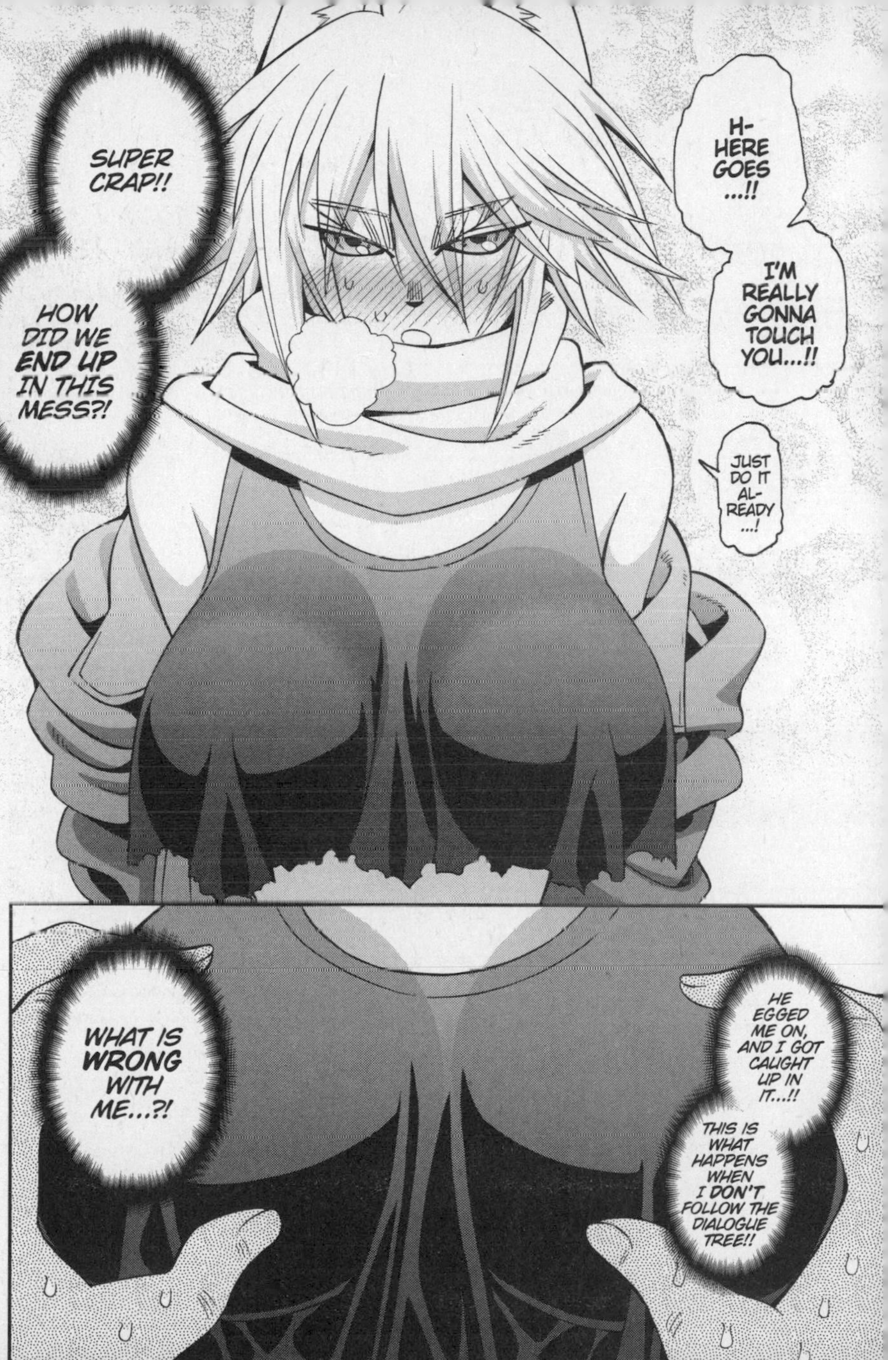
H-HERE GOES...!!
I'M REALLY GONNA TOUCH YOU...!!
JUST DO IT AL-READY...!
SUPER CRAP!!
HOW DID WE END UP IN THIS MESS?!
HE EGGED ME ON, AND I GOT CAUGHT UP IN IT...!!
THIS IS WHAT HAPPENS WHEN I DON'T FOLLOW THE DIALOGUE TREE!!
WHAT IS WRONG WITH ME...?!

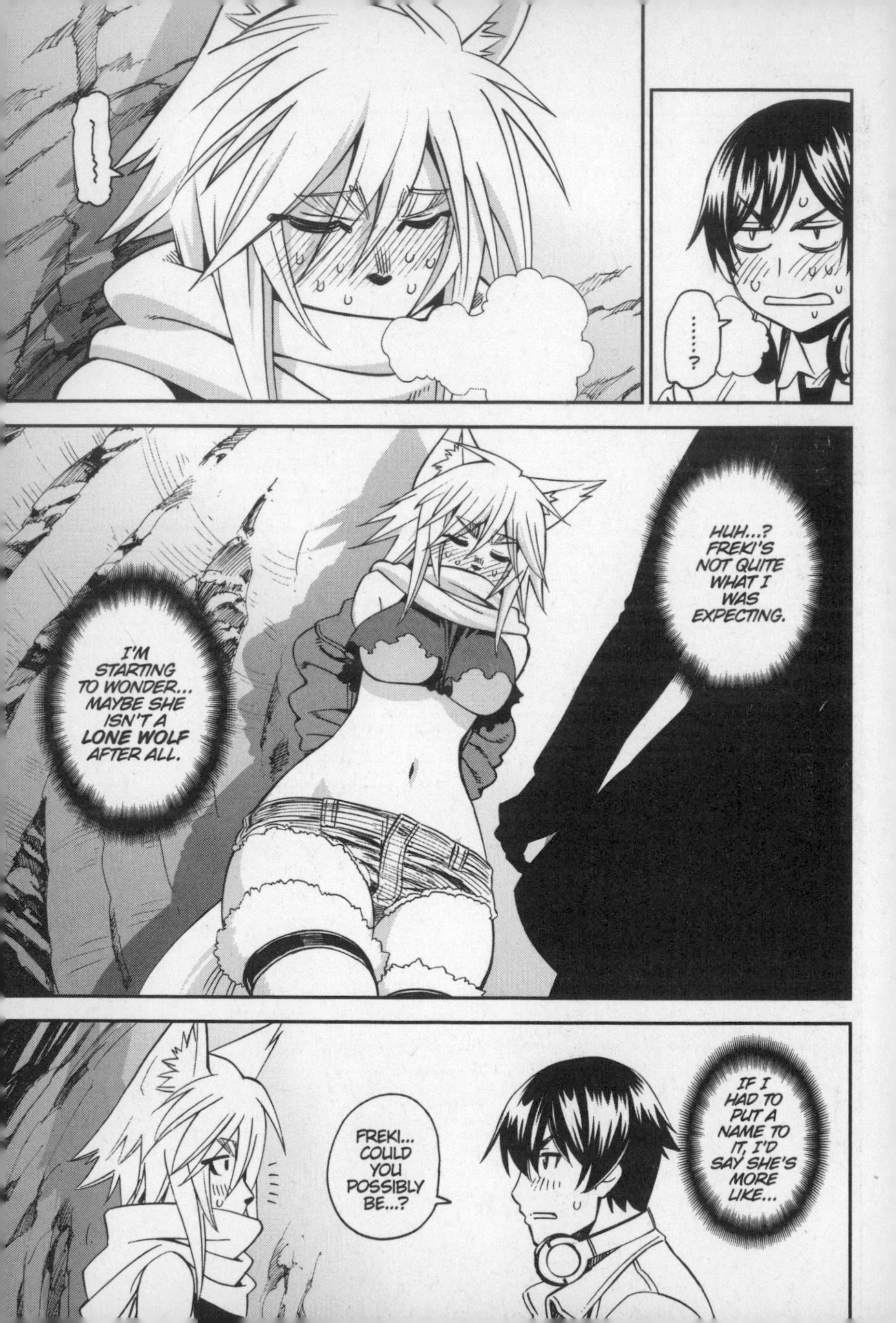
......?
HUH...? FREKI'S NOT QUITE WHAT I WAS EXPECTING.
I'M STARTING TO WONDER... MAYBE SHE ISN'T A **LONE WOLF** AFTER ALL.
IF I HAD TO PUT A NAME TO IT, I'D SAY SHE'S MORE LIKE...
FREKI... COULD YOU POSSIBLY BE...?

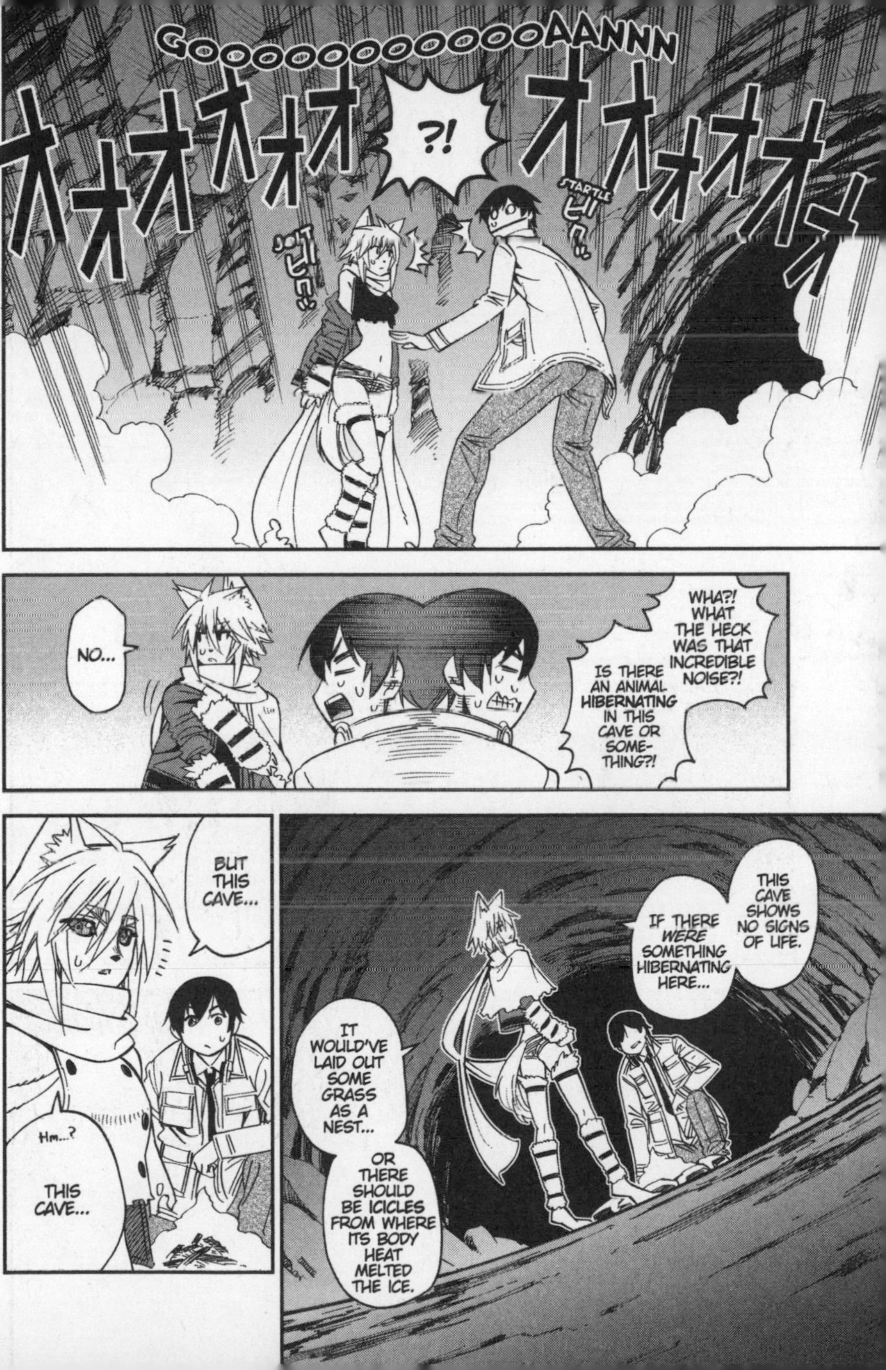
GOOOOOOOOOOOOOAANNN
?!
STARTLE
JOLT
WHA?! WHAT THE HECK WAS THAT INCREDIBLE NOISE?!
IS THERE AN ANIMAL HIBERNATING IN THIS CAVE OR SOME-THING?!
NO...
THIS CAVE SHOWS NO SIGNS OF LIFE.
IF THERE *WERE* SOMETHING HIBERNATING HERE...
IT WOULD'VE LAID OUT SOME GRASS AS A NEST...
OR THERE SHOULD BE ICICLES FROM WHERE ITS BODY HEAT MELTED THE ICE.
BUT THIS CAVE...
Hm...?
THIS CAVE...

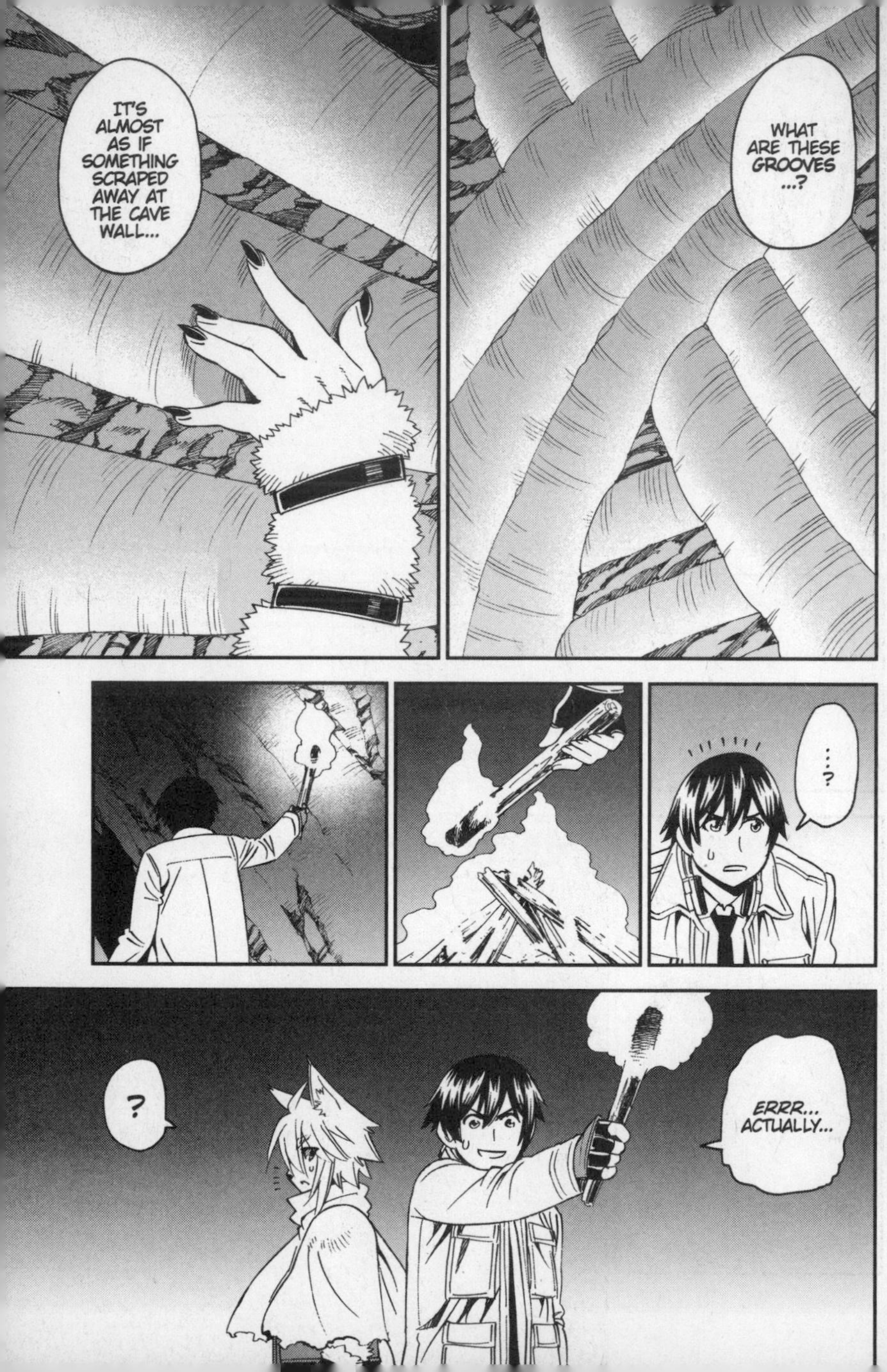
WHAT ARE THESE GROOVES ...?
IT'S ALMOST AS IF SOMETHING SCRAPED AWAY AT THE CAVE WALL...
...?
ERRR... ACTUALLY...
?

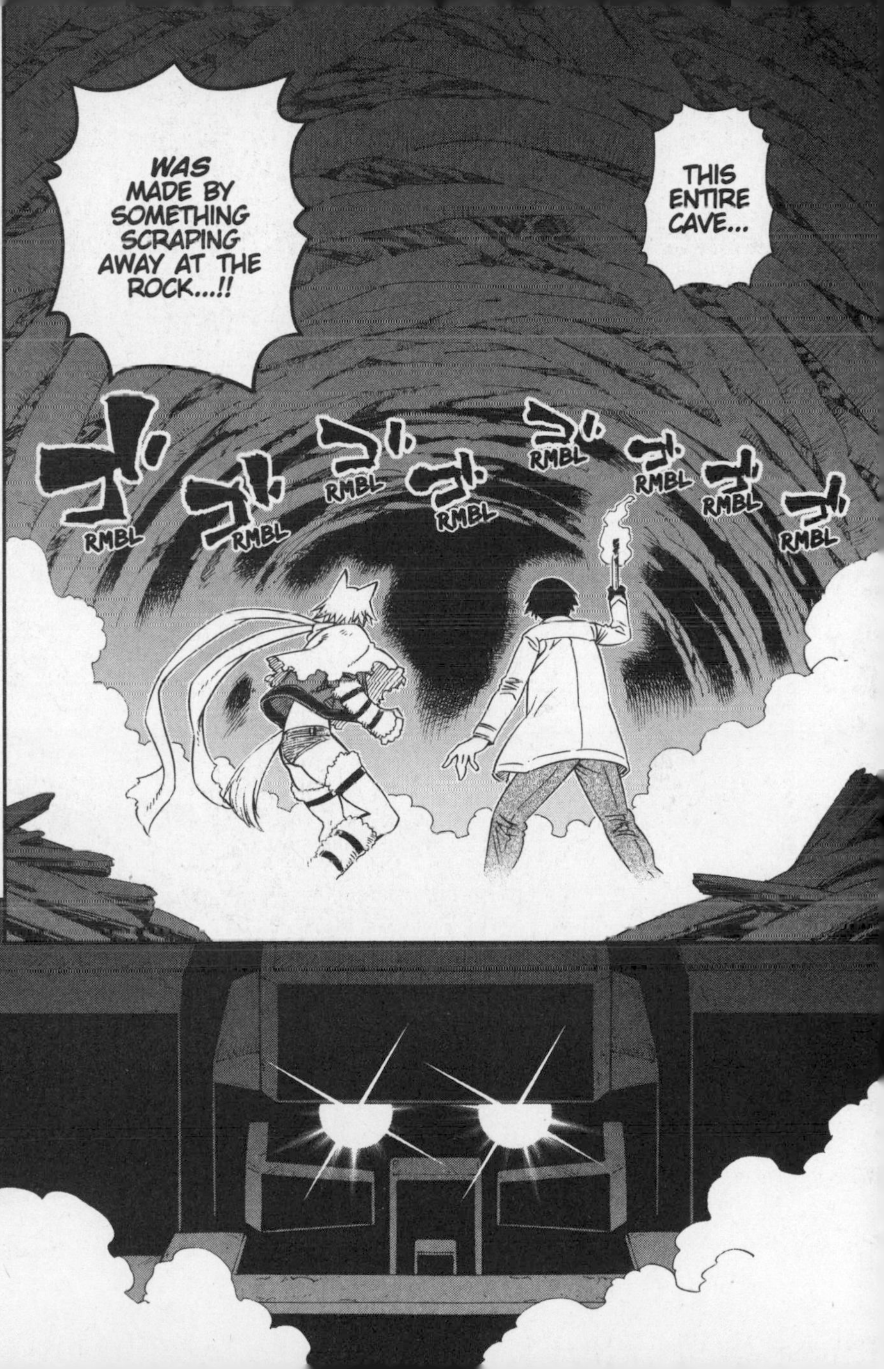
THIS ENTIRE CAVE...
WAS MADE BY SOMETHING SCRAPING AWAY AT THE ROCK...!!
ゴ RMBL
ゴ RMBL
ゴ RMBL
ゴ RMBL
ゴ RMBL
ゴ RMBL
ゴ RMBL
ゴ RMBL

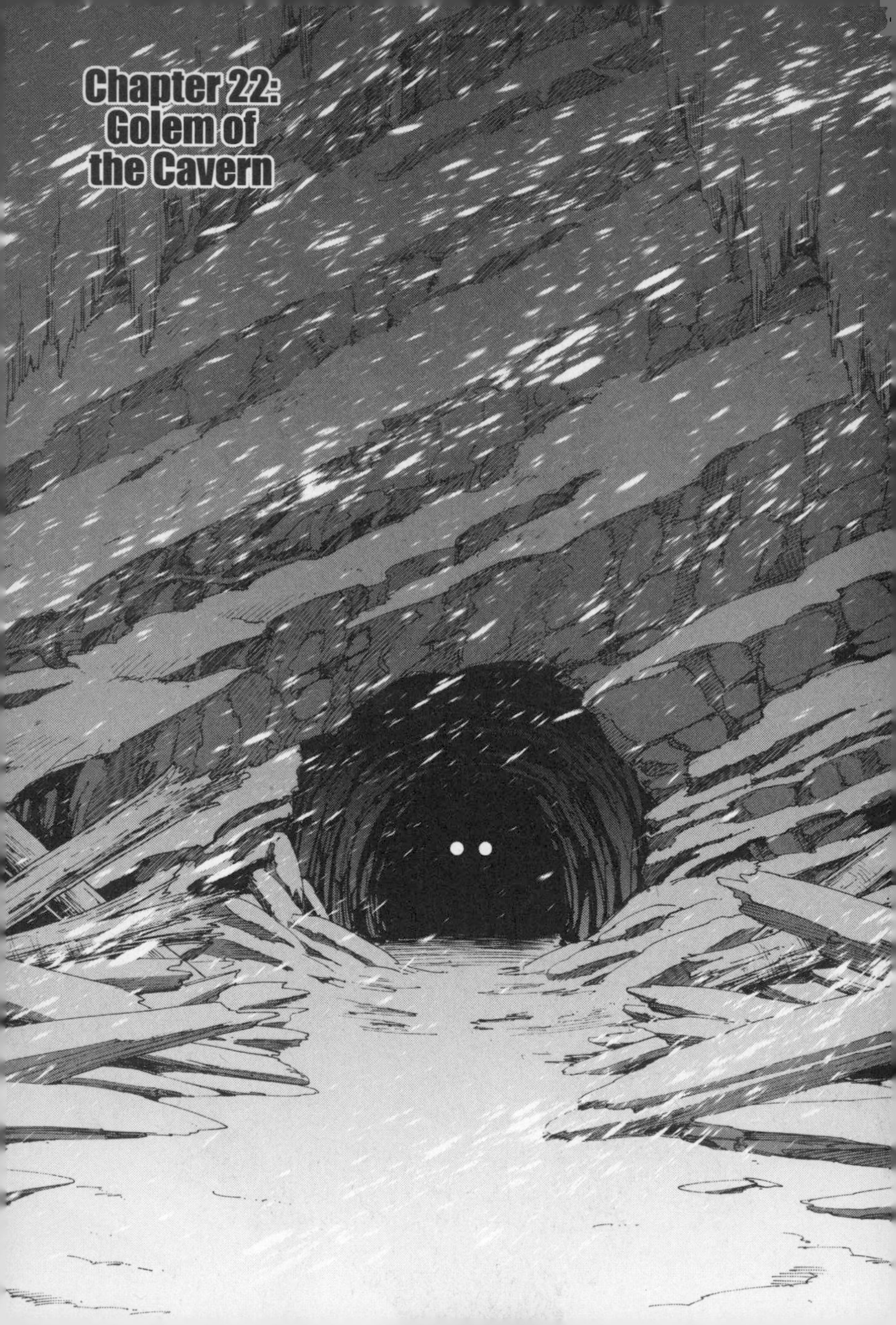
Chapter 22:
Golem of
the Cavern

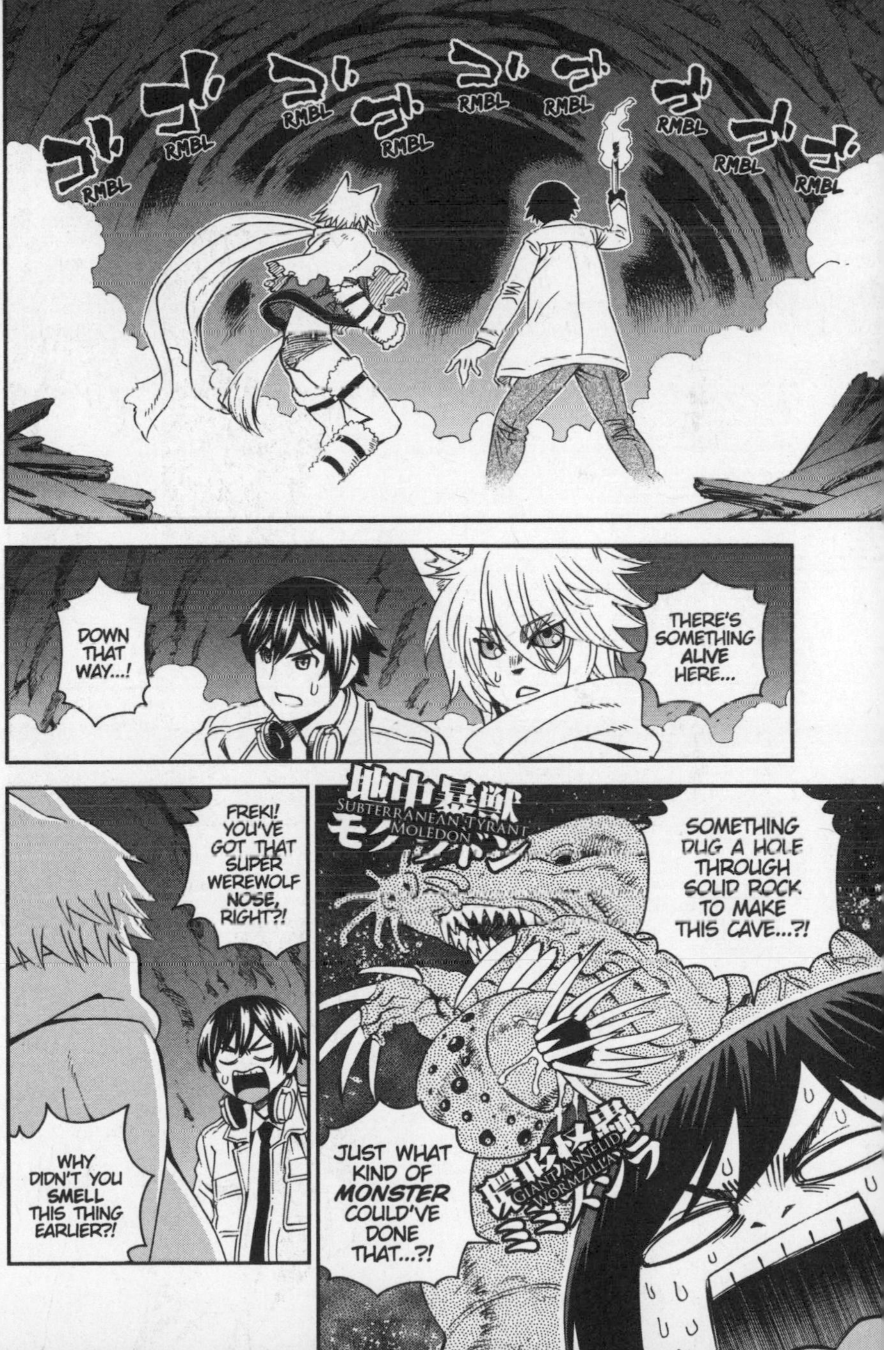
RMBL
RMBL
RMBL
RMBL
RMBL
RMBL
RMBL
RMBL
RMBL
THERE'S SOMETHING ALIVE HERE...
DOWN THAT WAY...!
SOMETHING DUG A HOLE THROUGH SOLID ROCK TO MAKE THIS CAVE...?!
SUBTERRANEAN TYRANT MOLEDON
JUST WHAT KIND OF *MONSTER* COULD'VE DONE THAT...?!
GIANT ANNELID WORMZILLA
FREKI! YOU'VE GOT THAT SUPER WEREWOLF NOSE, RIGHT?!
WHY DIDN'T YOU SMELL THIS THING EARLIER?!

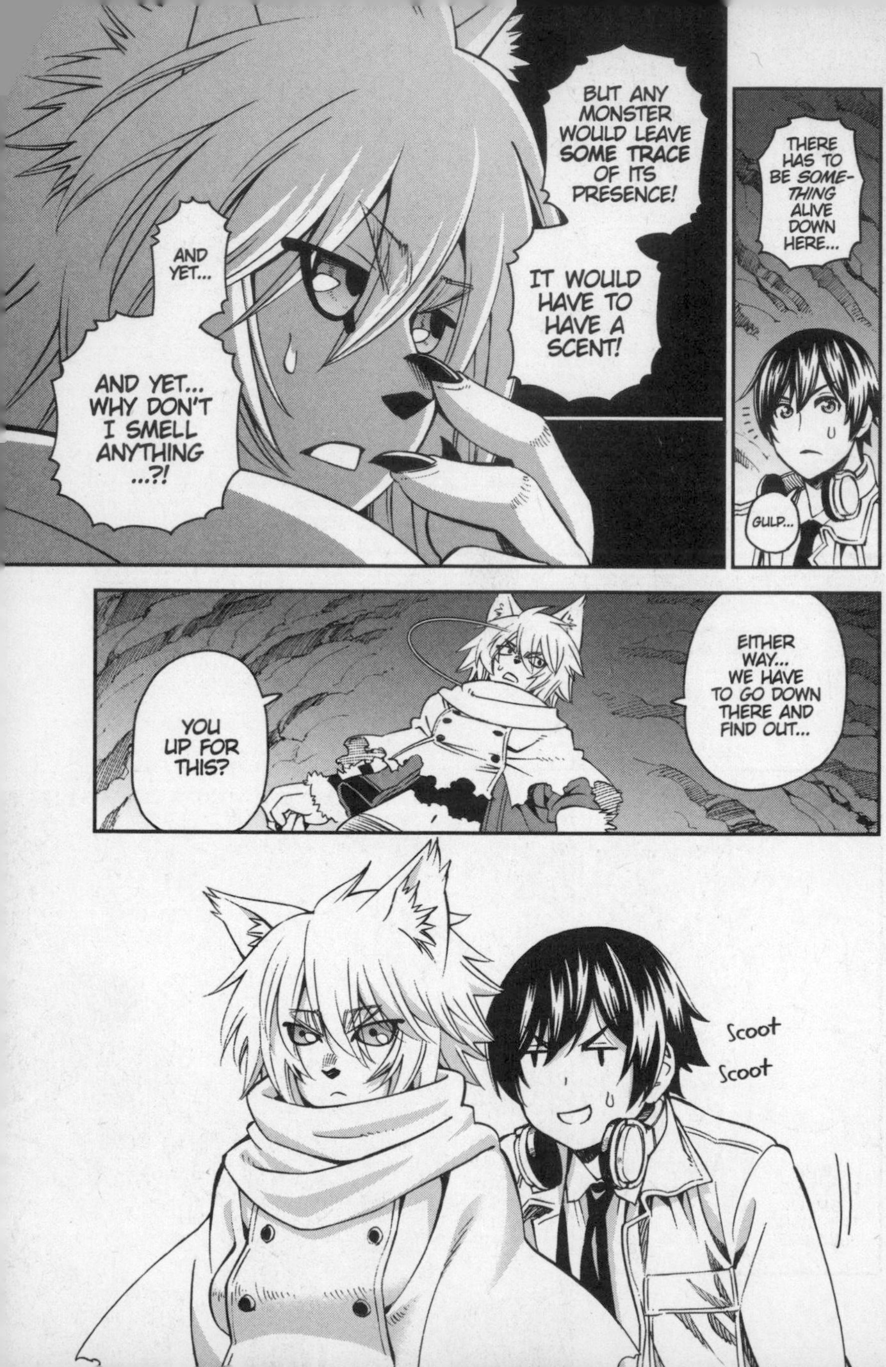
THERE HAS TO BE SOMETHING ALIVE DOWN HERE...
GULP...
BUT ANY MONSTER WOULD LEAVE SOME TRACE OF ITS PRESENCE!
IT WOULD HAVE TO HAVE A SCENT!
AND YET...
AND YET... WHY DON'T I SMELL ANYTHING ...?!
EITHER WAY... WE HAVE TO GO DOWN THERE AND FIND OUT...
YOU UP FOR THIS?
Scoot
Scoot

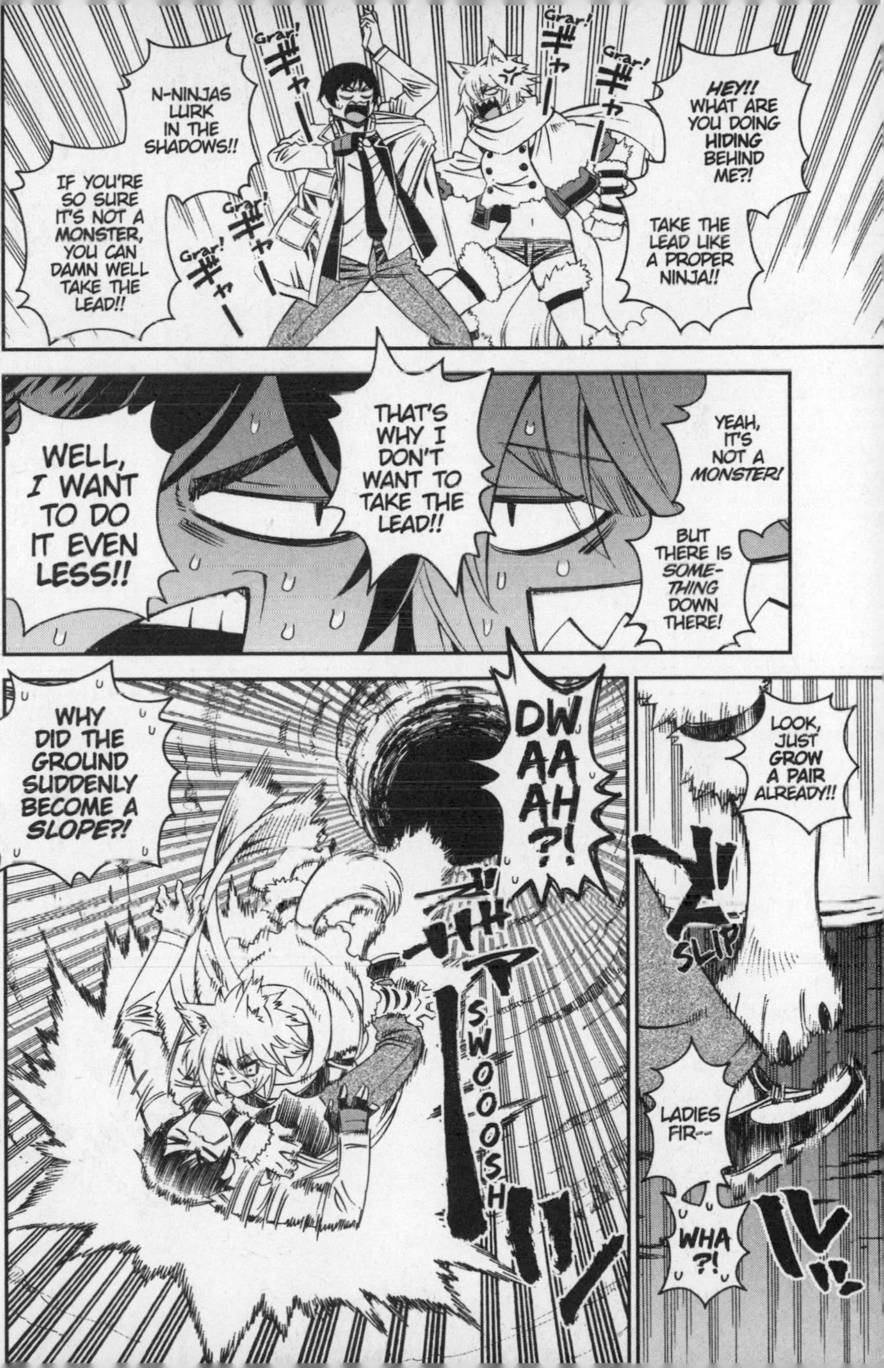
HEY!! WHAT ARE YOU DOING HIDING BEHIND ME?!
TAKE THE LEAD LIKE A PROPER NINJA!!
Grar!
Grar!
N-NINJAS LURK IN THE SHADOWS!!
IF YOU'RE SO SURE IT'S NOT A MONSTER, YOU CAN DAMN WELL TAKE THE LEAD!!
Grar!
Grar!
YEAH, IT'S NOT A *MONSTER!*
BUT THERE IS *SOME-THING* DOWN THERE!
THAT'S WHY I DON'T WANT TO TAKE THE LEAD!!
WELL, *I* WANT TO DO IT EVEN LESS!!
LOOK, JUST GROW A PAIR ALREADY!!
SLIP
LADIES FIR--
WHA?!
DWAAAH?!
WHY DID THE GROUND SUDDENLY BECOME A *SLOPE?!*
SWOOOOSH

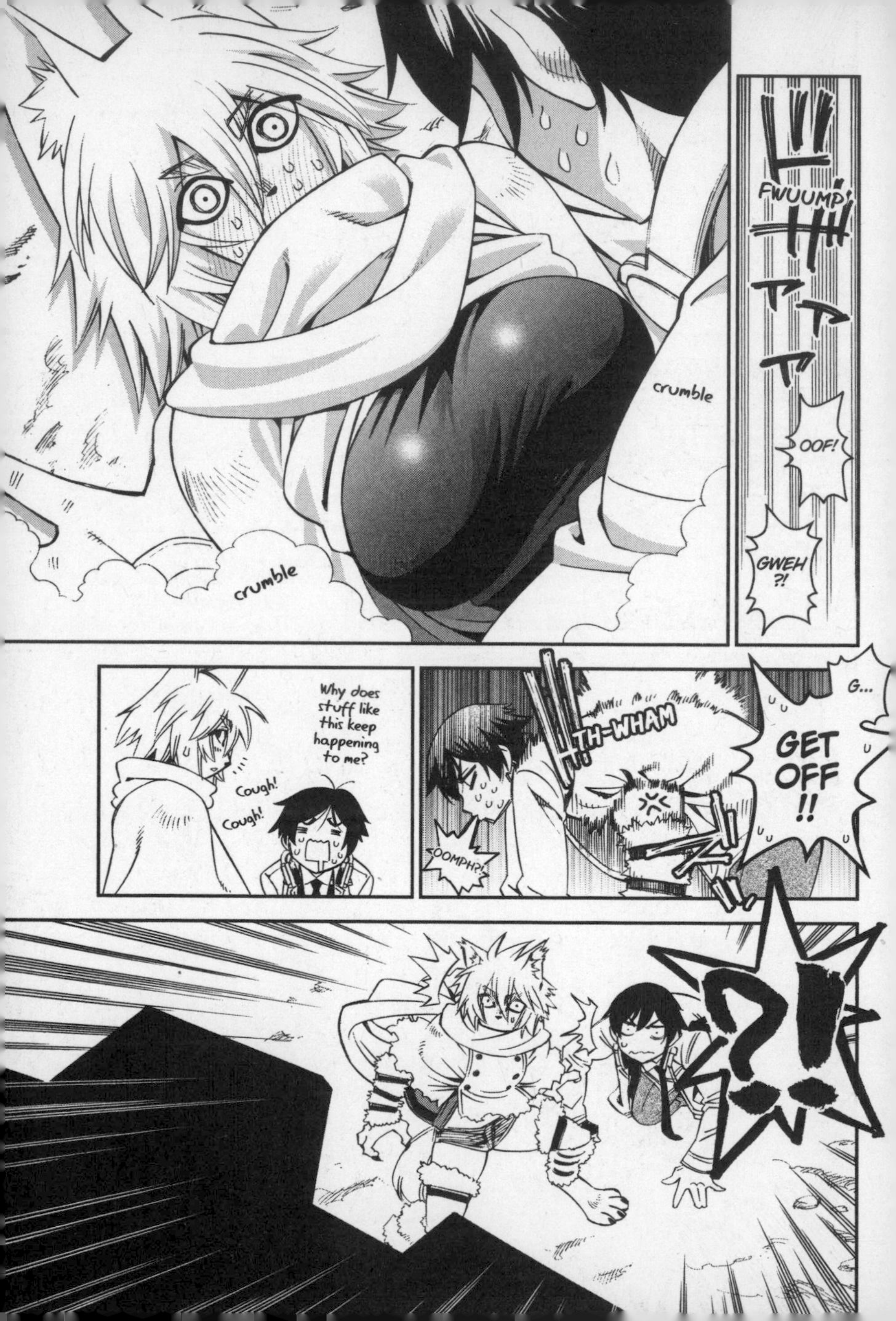
FWUUMP
OOF!
GWEH?!
crumble
crumble
G...
GET OFF!!
TH-WHAM
OOMPH?!
Why does stuff like this keep happening to me?
Cough!
Cough!
?!

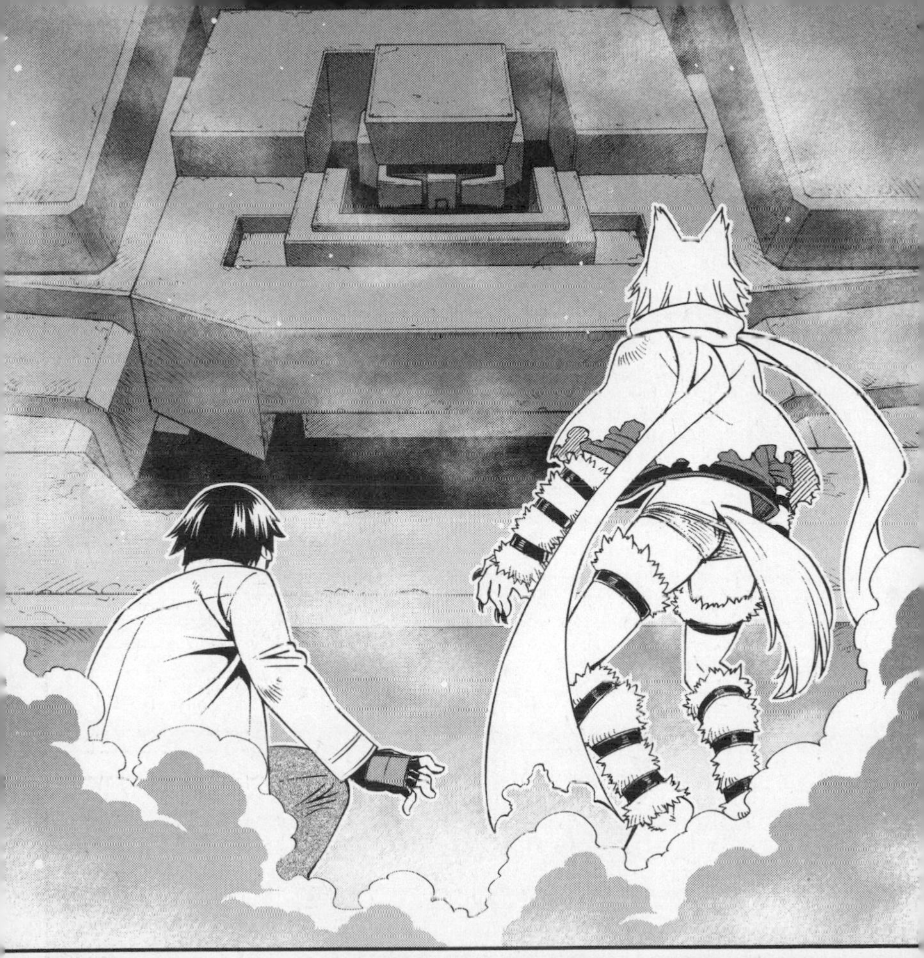
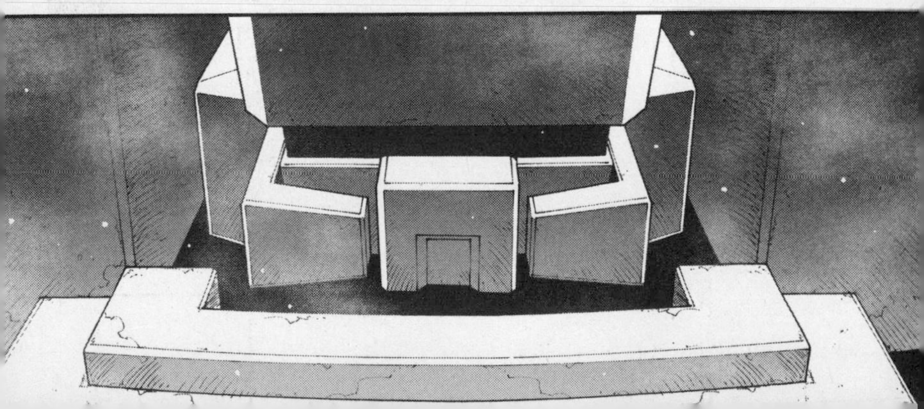

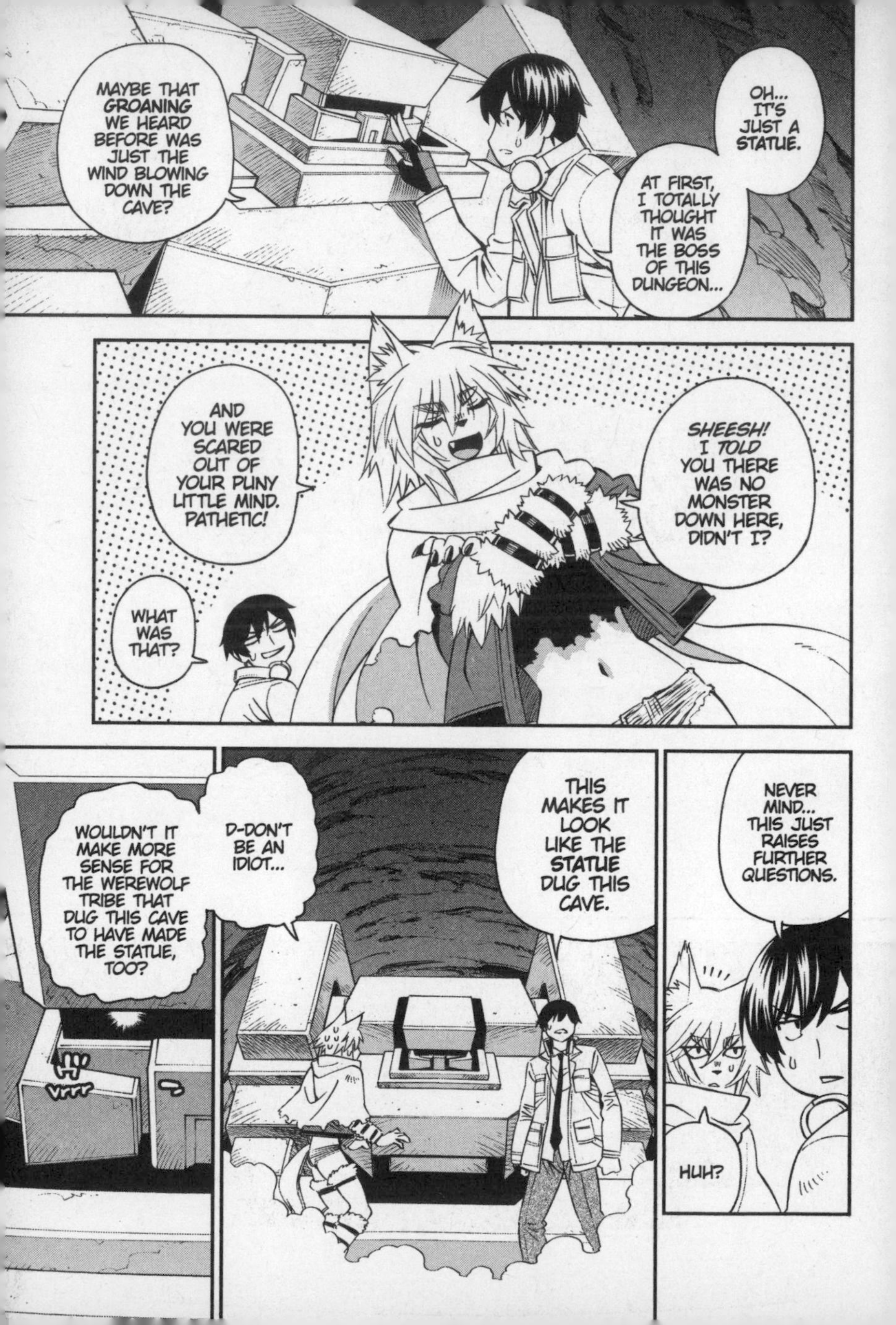
OH... IT'S JUST A STATUE.
AT FIRST, I TOTALLY THOUGHT IT WAS THE BOSS OF THIS DUNGEON...
MAYBE THAT GROANING WE HEARD BEFORE WAS JUST THE WIND BLOWING DOWN THE CAVE?
SHEESH! I *TOLD* YOU THERE WAS NO MONSTER DOWN HERE, DIDN'T I?
AND YOU WERE SCARED OUT OF YOUR PUNY LITTLE MIND. PATHETIC!
WHAT WAS THAT?
NEVER MIND... THIS JUST RAISES FURTHER QUESTIONS.
HUH?
THIS MAKES IT LOOK LIKE THE STATUE DUG THIS CAVE.
D-DON'T BE AN IDIOT...
WOULDN'T IT MAKE MORE SENSE FOR THE WEREWOLF TRIBE THAT DUG THIS CAVE TO HAVE MADE THE STATUE, TOO?
VRRR

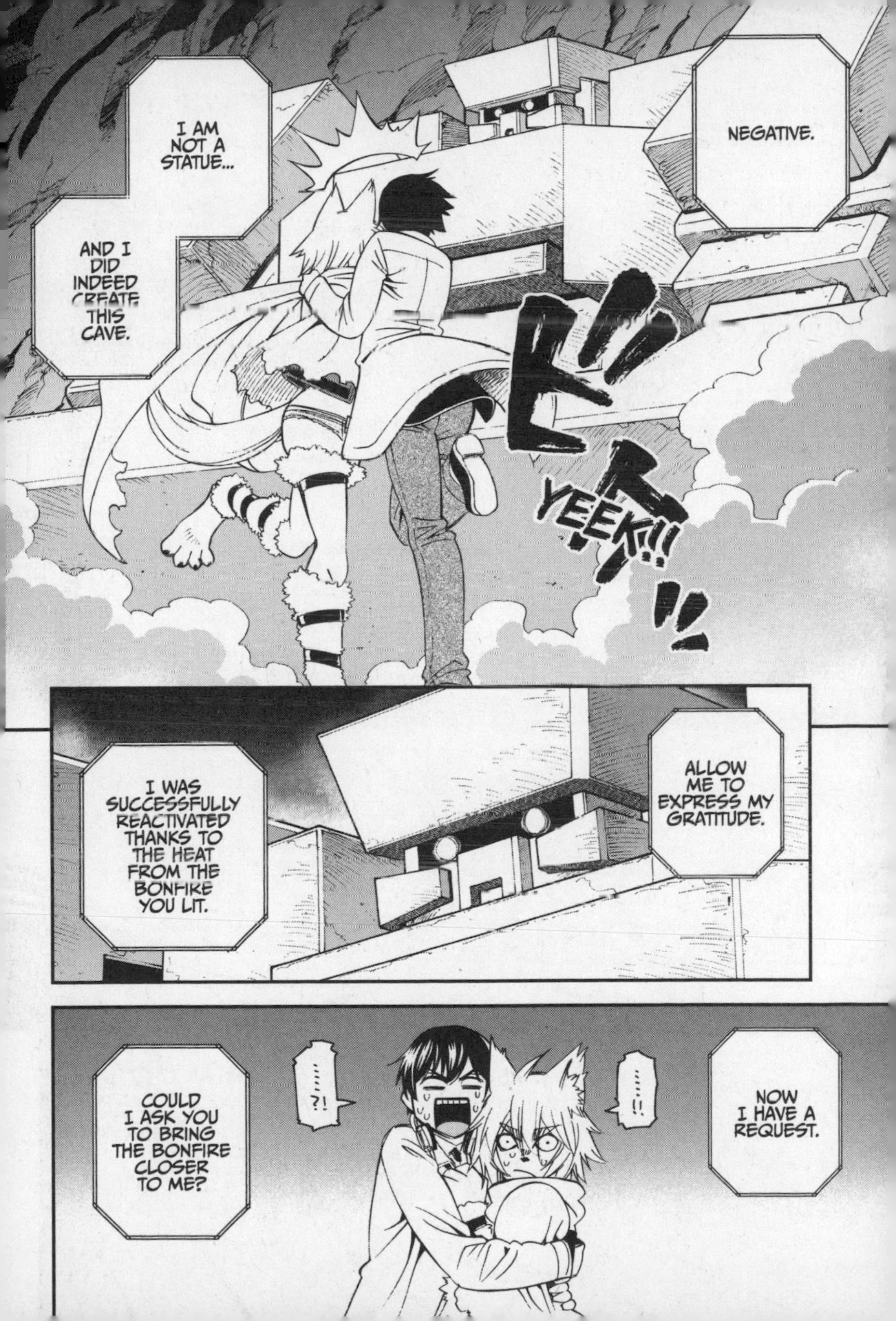
NEGATIVE.
I AM NOT A STATUE...
AND I DID INDEED CREATE THIS CAVE.
YEEK!!
!!
ALLOW ME TO EXPRESS MY GRATITUDE.
I WAS SUCCESSFULLY REACTIVATED THANKS TO THE HEAT FROM THE BONFIRE YOU LIT.
NOW I HAVE A REQUEST.
......!!
......?!
COULD I ASK YOU TO BRING THE BONFIRE CLOSER TO ME?

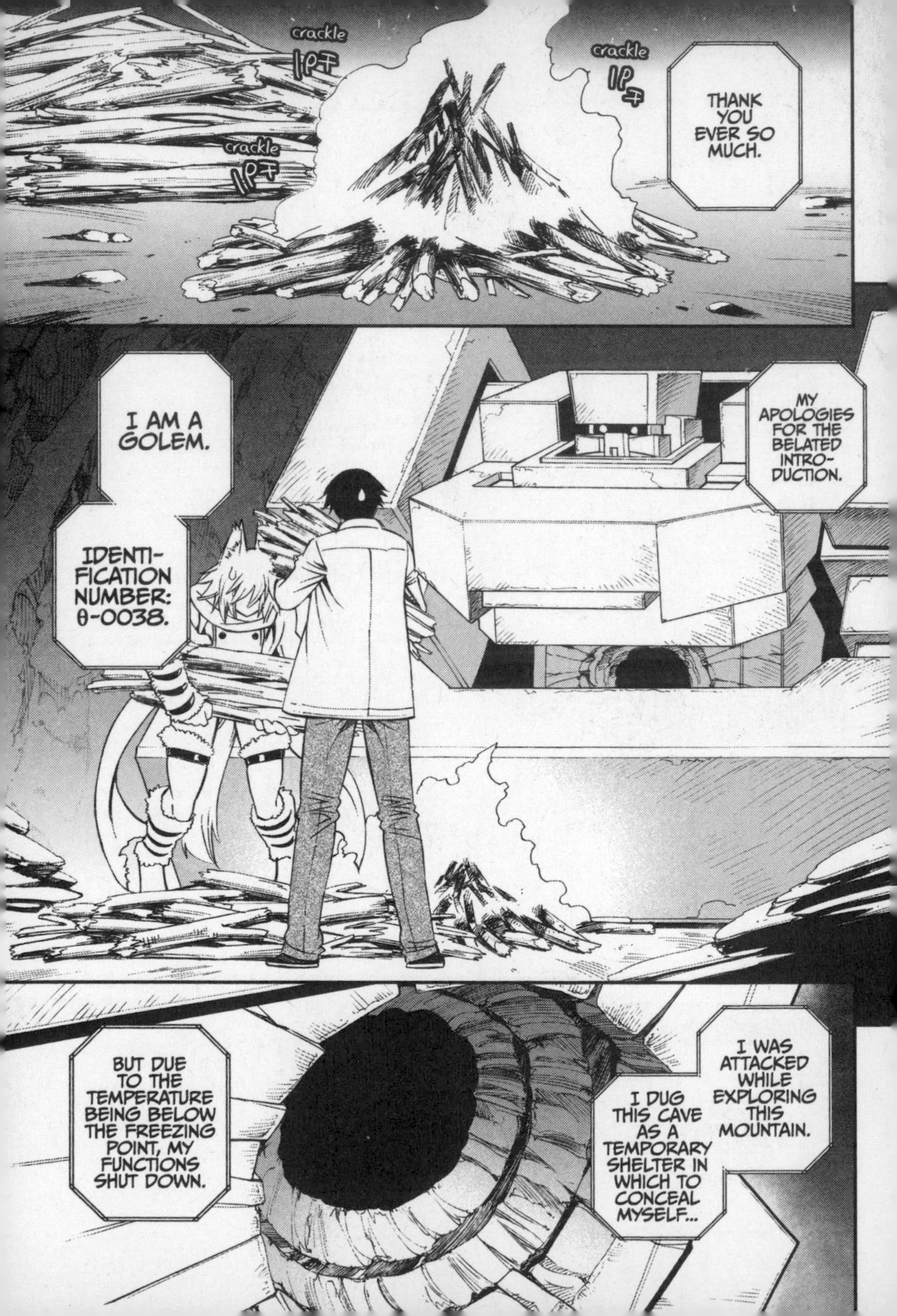
THANK YOU EVER SO MUCH.
crackle
crackle
crackle
MY APOLOGIES FOR THE BELATED INTRO-DUCTION.
I AM A GOLEM.
IDENTI-FICATION NUMBER: θ-0038.
I WAS ATTACKED WHILE EXPLORING THIS MOUNTAIN.
I DUG THIS CAVE AS A TEMPORARY SHELTER IN WHICH TO CONCEAL MYSELF...
BUT DUE TO THE TEMPERATURE BEING BELOW THE FREEZING POINT, MY FUNCTIONS SHUT DOWN.

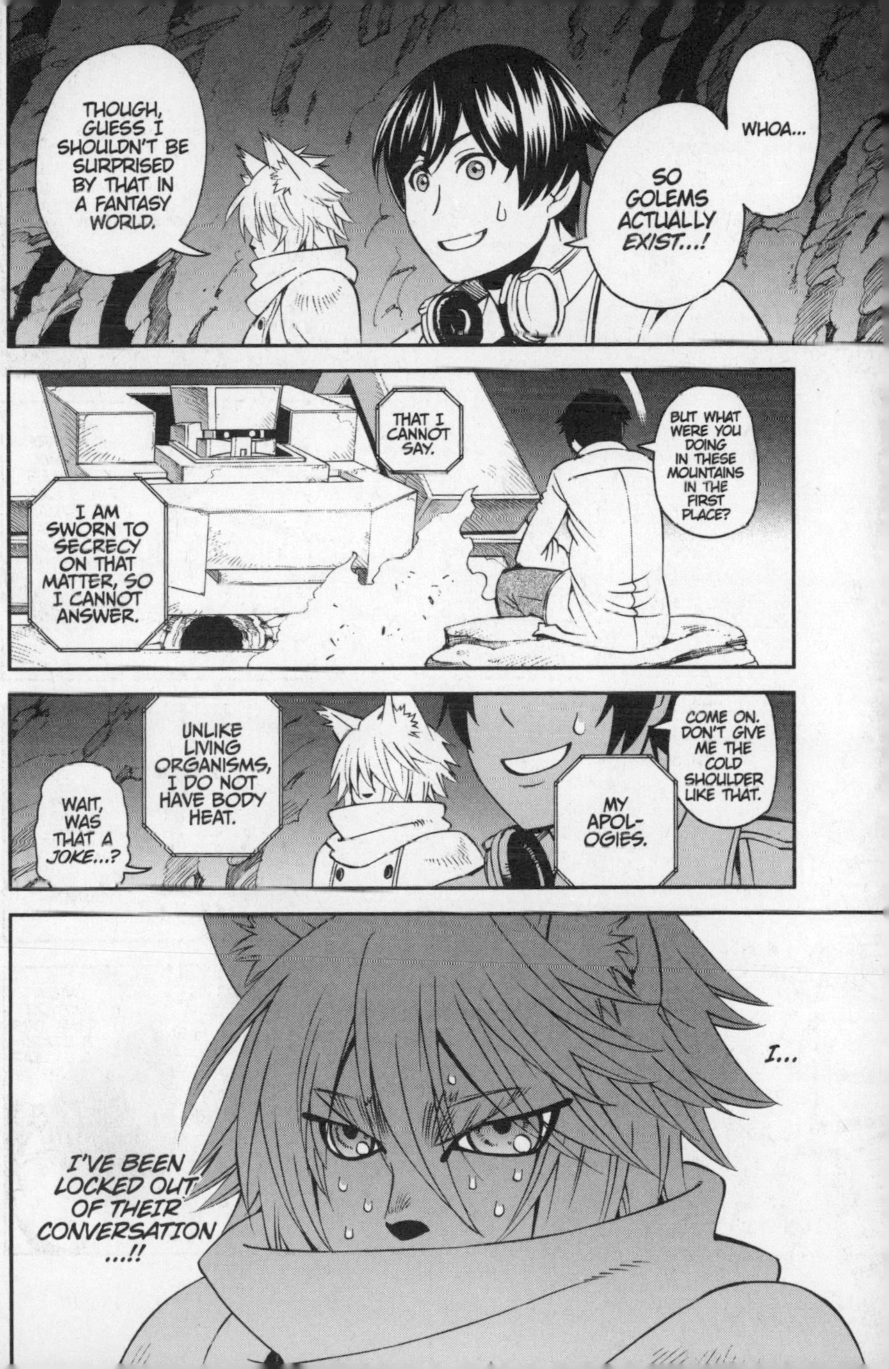
WHOA... SO GOLEMS ACTUALLY *EXIST*...!
THOUGH, GUESS I SHOULDN'T BE SURPRISED BY THAT IN A FANTASY WORLD.
BUT WHAT WERE YOU DOING IN THESE MOUNTAINS IN THE FIRST PLACE?
THAT I CANNOT SAY.
I AM SWORN TO SECRECY ON THAT MATTER, SO I CANNOT ANSWER.
COME ON. DON'T GIVE ME THE COLD SHOULDER LIKE THAT.
MY APOLOGIES.
UNLIKE LIVING ORGANISMS, I DO NOT HAVE BODY HEAT.
WAIT, WAS THAT A *JOKE*...?
I...
I'VE BEEN LOCKED OUT OF THEIR CONVERSATION ...!!

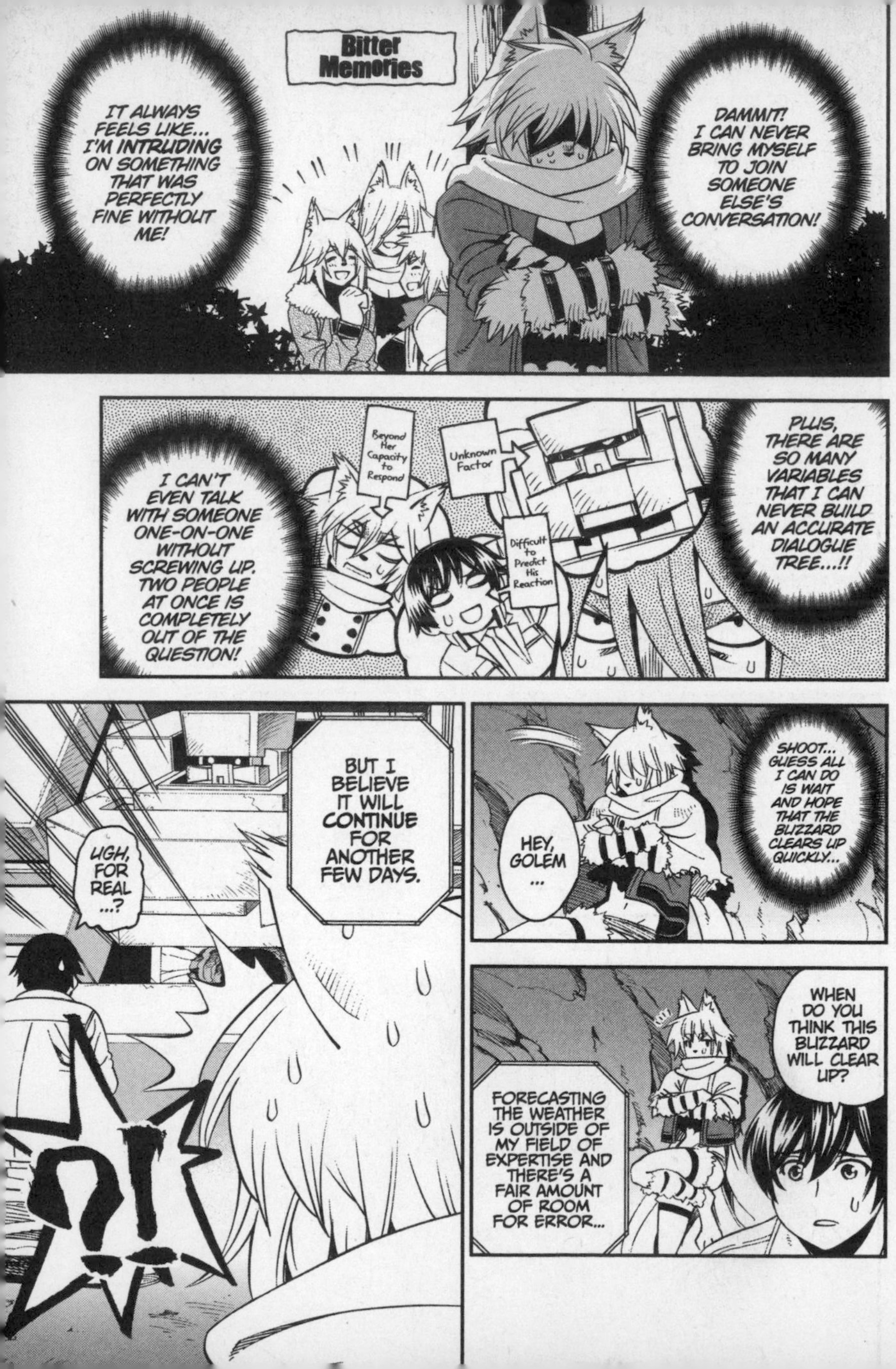
Bitter Memories
DAMMIT! I CAN NEVER BRING MYSELF TO JOIN SOMEONE ELSE'S CONVERSATION!
IT ALWAYS FEELS LIKE... I'M INTRUDING ON SOMETHING THAT WAS PERFECTLY FINE WITHOUT ME!
PLUS, THERE ARE SO MANY VARIABLES THAT I CAN NEVER BUILD AN ACCURATE DIALOGUE TREE...!!
Unknown Factor
Beyond Her Capacity to Respond
Difficult to Predict His Reaction
I CAN'T EVEN TALK WITH SOMEONE ONE-ON-ONE WITHOUT SCREWING UP. TWO PEOPLE AT ONCE IS COMPLETELY OUT OF THE QUESTION!
SHOOT... GUESS ALL I CAN DO IS WAIT AND HOPE THAT THE BLIZZARD CLEARS UP QUICKLY...
HEY, GOLEM ...
WHEN DO YOU THINK THIS BLIZZARD WILL CLEAR UP?
FORECASTING THE WEATHER IS OUTSIDE OF MY FIELD OF EXPERTISE AND THERE'S A FAIR AMOUNT OF ROOM FOR ERROR...
BUT I BELIEVE IT WILL CONTINUE FOR ANOTHER FEW DAYS.
UGH, FOR REAL ...?
?!

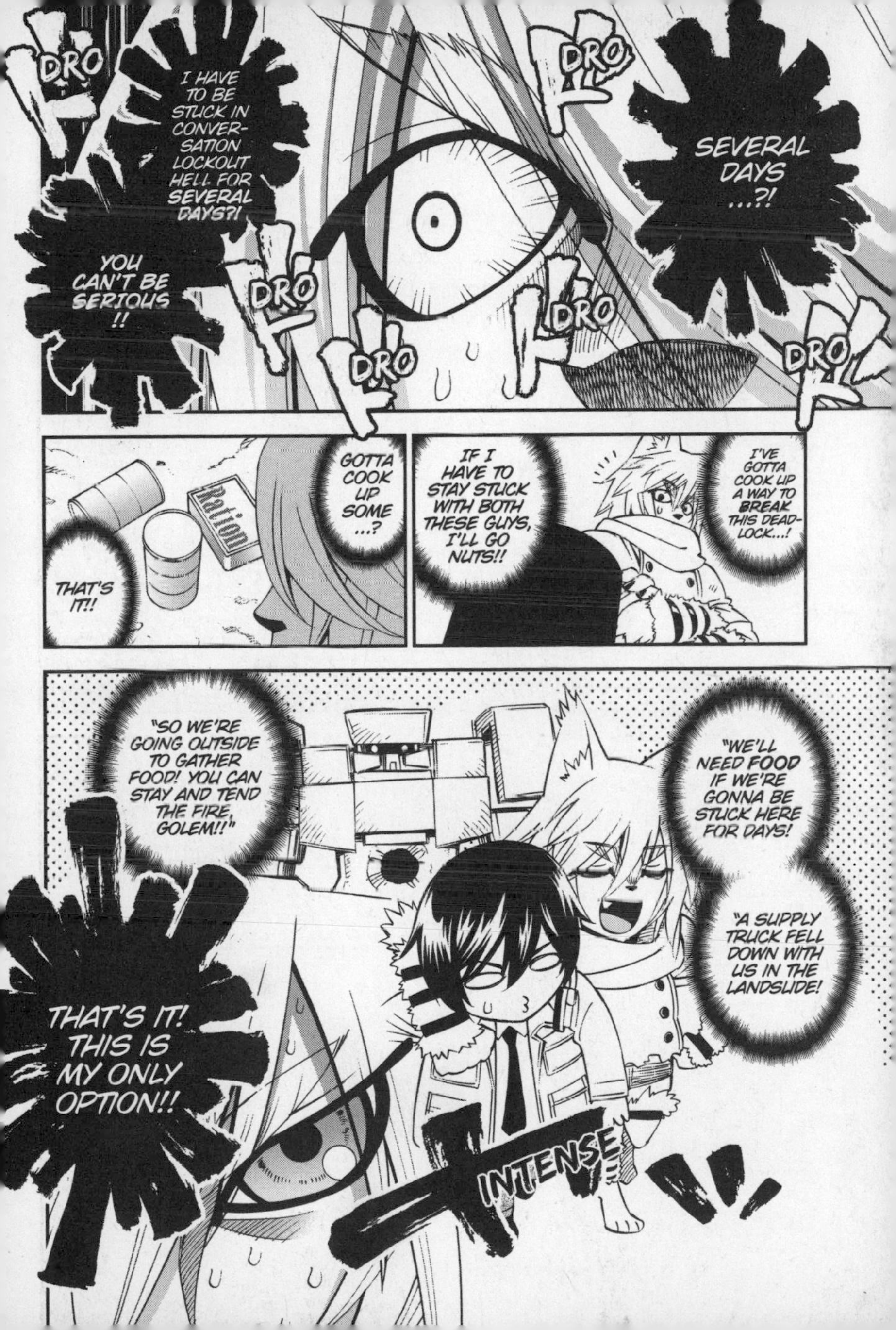
DRO
SEVERAL DAYS ...?!
DRO
I HAVE TO BE STUCK IN CONVER-SATION LOCKOUT HELL FOR SEVERAL DAYS?!
YOU CAN'T BE SERIOUS!!
DRO
DRO
DRO
DRO
I'VE GOTTA COOK UP A WAY TO BREAK THIS DEAD-LOCK...!
IF I HAVE TO STAY STUCK WITH BOTH THESE GUYS, I'LL GO NUTS!!
GOTTA COOK UP SOME ...?
Ration
THAT'S IT!!
"WE'LL NEED FOOD IF WE'RE GONNA BE STUCK HERE FOR DAYS!
"A SUPPLY TRUCK FELL DOWN WITH US IN THE LANDSLIDE!
"SO WE'RE GOING OUTSIDE TO GATHER FOOD! YOU CAN STAY AND TEND THE FIRE, GOLEM!!"
THAT'S IT! THIS IS MY ONLY OPTION!!
INTENSE

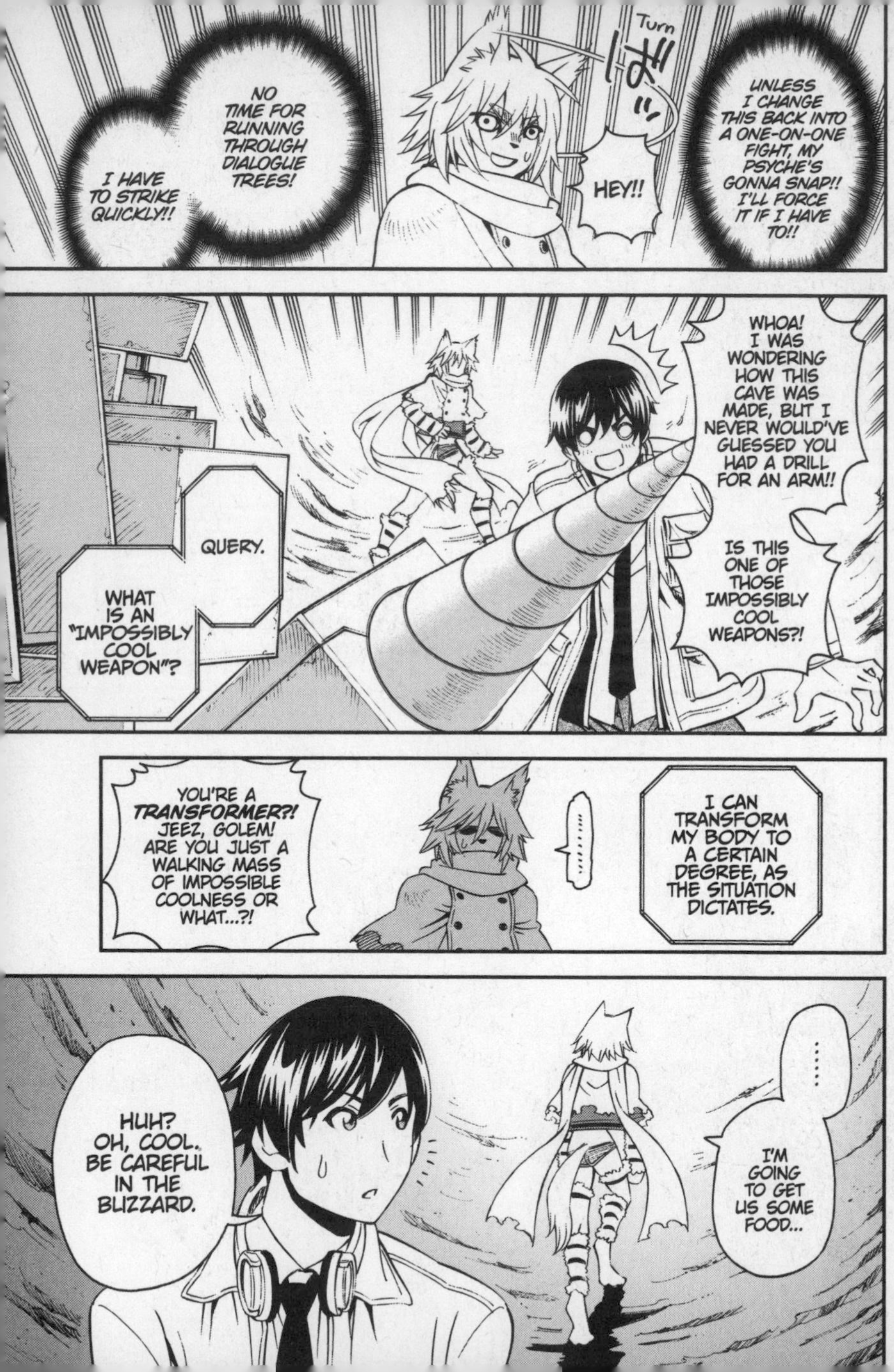
Turn
UNLESS I CHANGE THIS BACK INTO A ONE-ON-ONE FIGHT, MY PSYCHE'S GONNA SNAP!! I'LL FORCE IT IF I HAVE TO!!
HEY!!
NO TIME FOR RUNNING THROUGH DIALOGUE TREES!
I HAVE TO STRIKE QUICKLY!!
WHOA! I WAS WONDERING HOW THIS CAVE WAS MADE, BUT I NEVER WOULD'VE GUESSED YOU HAD A DRILL FOR AN ARM!!
IS THIS ONE OF THOSE IMPOSSIBLY COOL WEAPONS?!
QUERY.
WHAT IS AN "IMPOSSIBLY COOL WEAPON"?
I CAN TRANSFORM MY BODY TO A CERTAIN DEGREE, AS THE SITUATION DICTATES.
....
YOU'RE A *TRANSFORMER?!* JEEZ, GOLEM! ARE YOU JUST A WALKING MASS OF IMPOSSIBLE COOLNESS OR WHAT...?!
......
I'M GOING TO GET US SOME FOOD...
HUH? OH, COOL. BE CAREFUL IN THE BLIZZARD.

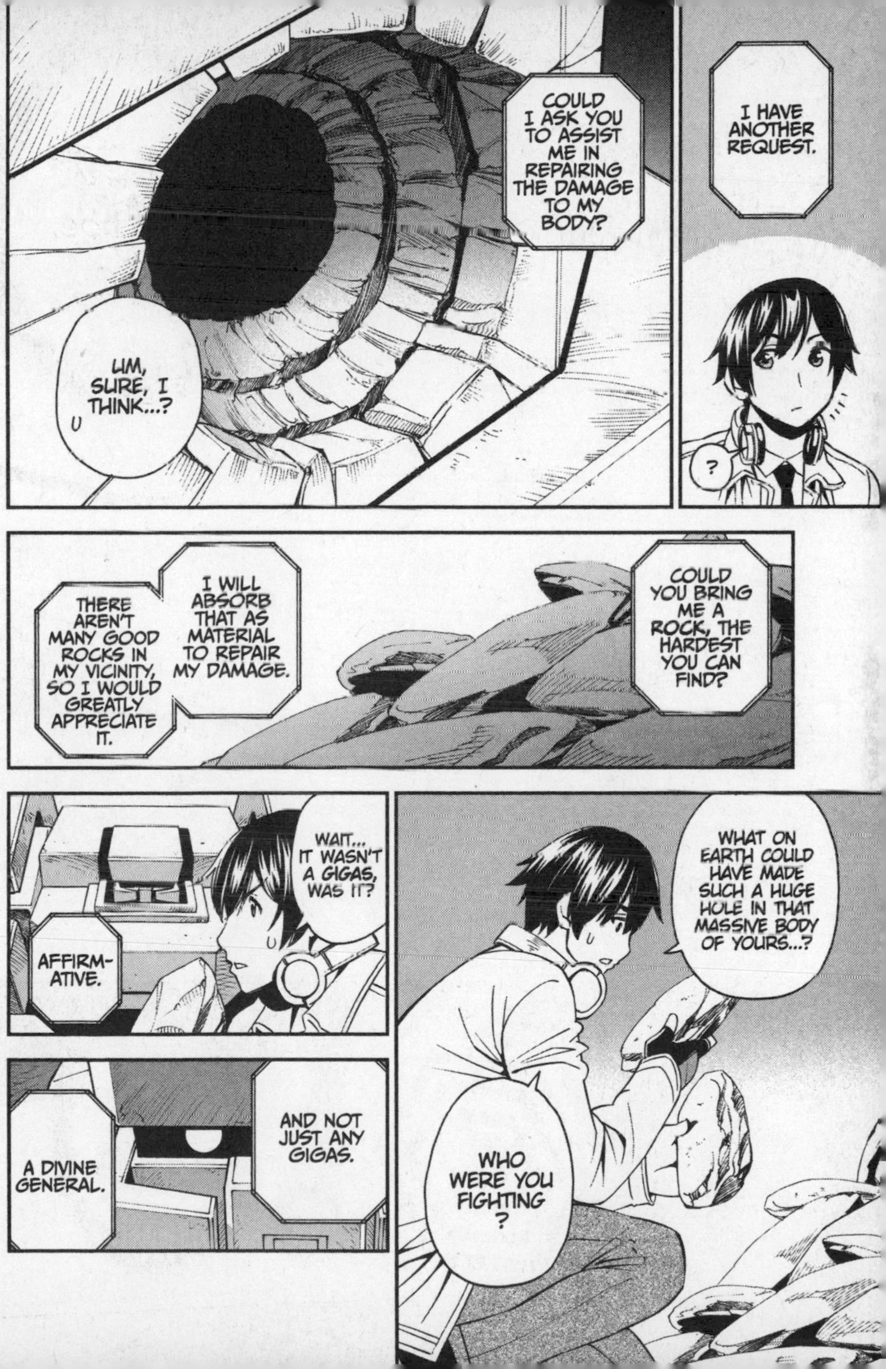
I HAVE ANOTHER REQUEST.
?
COULD I ASK YOU TO ASSIST ME IN REPAIRING THE DAMAGE TO MY BODY?
UM, SURE, I THINK...?
COULD YOU BRING ME A ROCK, THE HARDEST YOU CAN FIND?
I WILL ABSORB THAT AS MATERIAL TO REPAIR MY DAMAGE.
THERE AREN'T MANY GOOD ROCKS IN MY VICINITY, SO I WOULD GREATLY APPRECIATE IT.
WHAT ON EARTH COULD HAVE MADE SUCH A HUGE HOLE IN THAT MASSIVE BODY OF YOURS...?
WHO WERE YOU FIGHTING?
WAIT... IT WASN'T A GIGAS, WAS IT?
AFFIRMATIVE.
AND NOT JUST ANY GIGAS.
A DIVINE GENERAL.

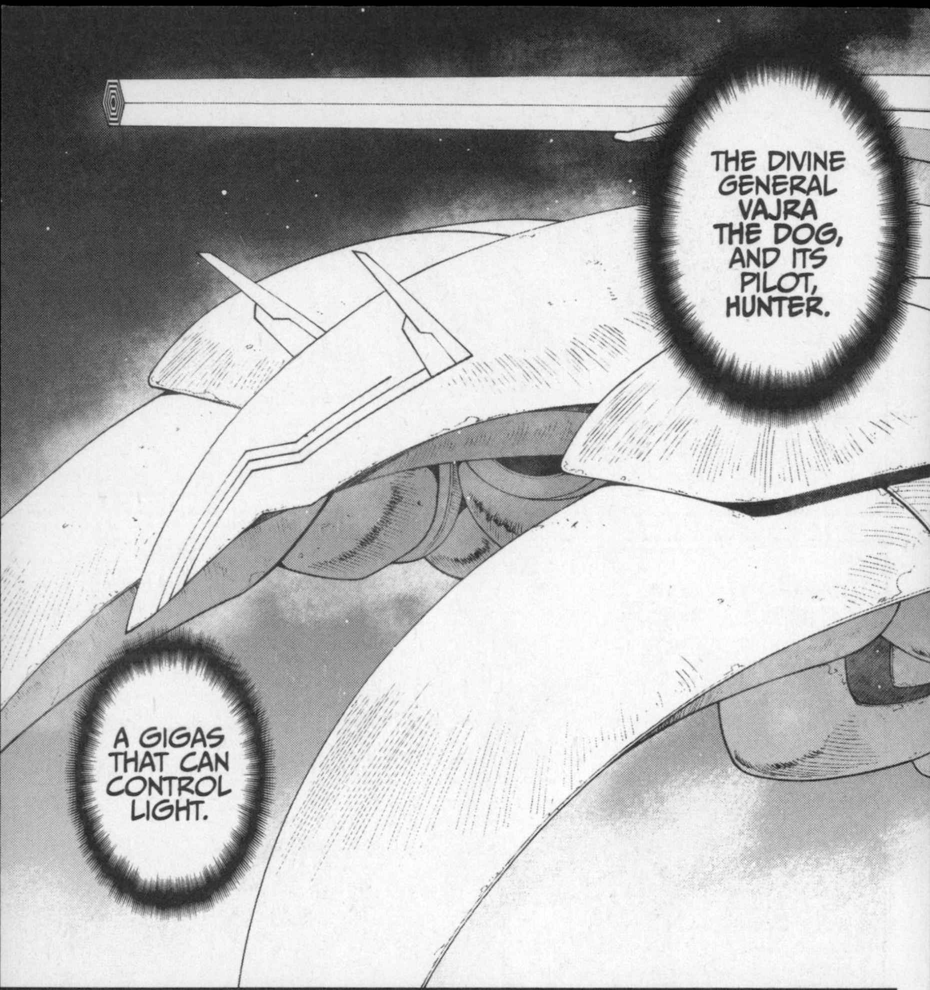
THE DIVINE GENERAL VAJRA THE DOG, AND ITS PILOT, HUNTER.
A GIGAS THAT CAN CONTROL LIGHT.
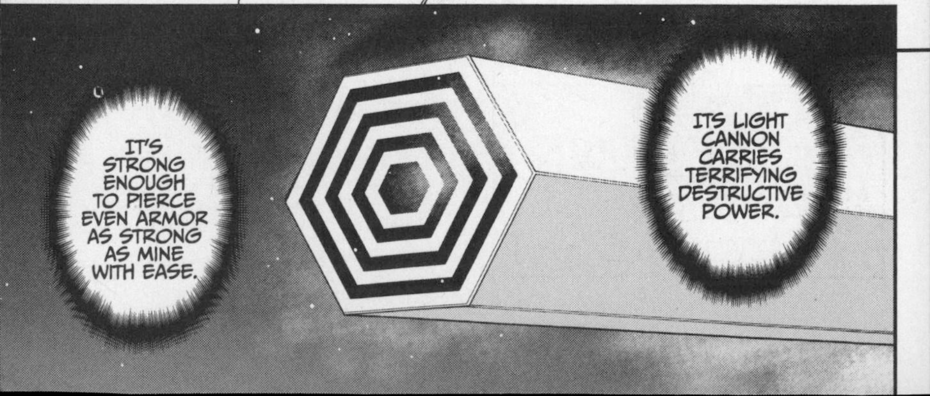
ITS LIGHT CANNON CARRIES TERRIFYING DESTRUCTIVE POWER.
IT'S STRONG ENOUGH TO PIERCE EVEN ARMOR AS STRONG AS MINE WITH EASE.

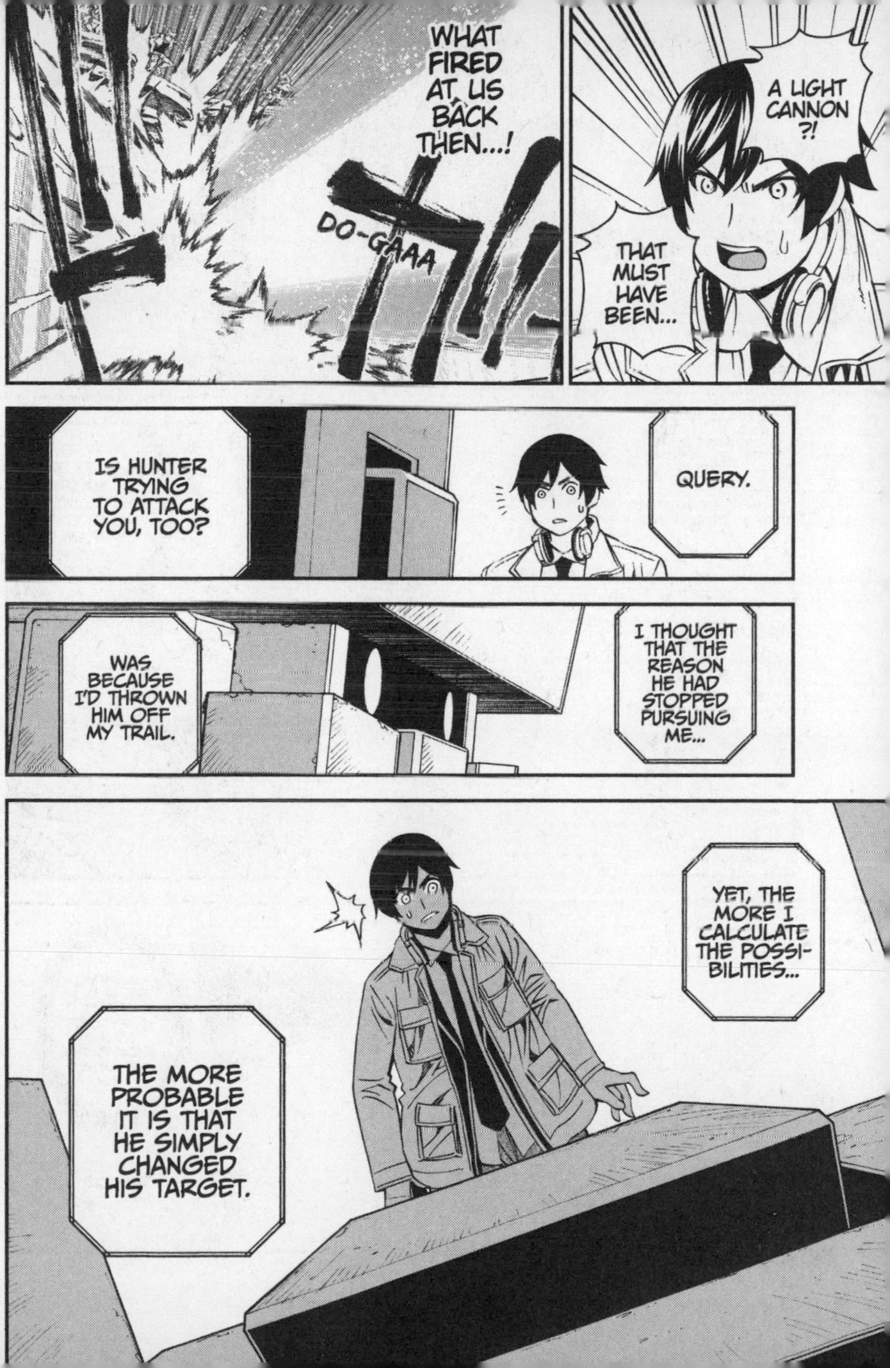

A LIGHT CANNON ?!
THAT MUST HAVE BEEN...
WHAT FIRED AT US BACK THEN...!
DO-GAAA
QUERY.
IS HUNTER TRYING TO ATTACK YOU, TOO?
I THOUGHT THAT THE REASON HE HAD STOPPED PURSUING ME...
WAS BECAUSE I'D THROWN HIM OFF MY TRAIL.
YET, THE MORE I CALCULATE THE POSSI-BILITIES...
THE MORE PROBABLE IT IS THAT HE SIMPLY CHANGED HIS TARGET.

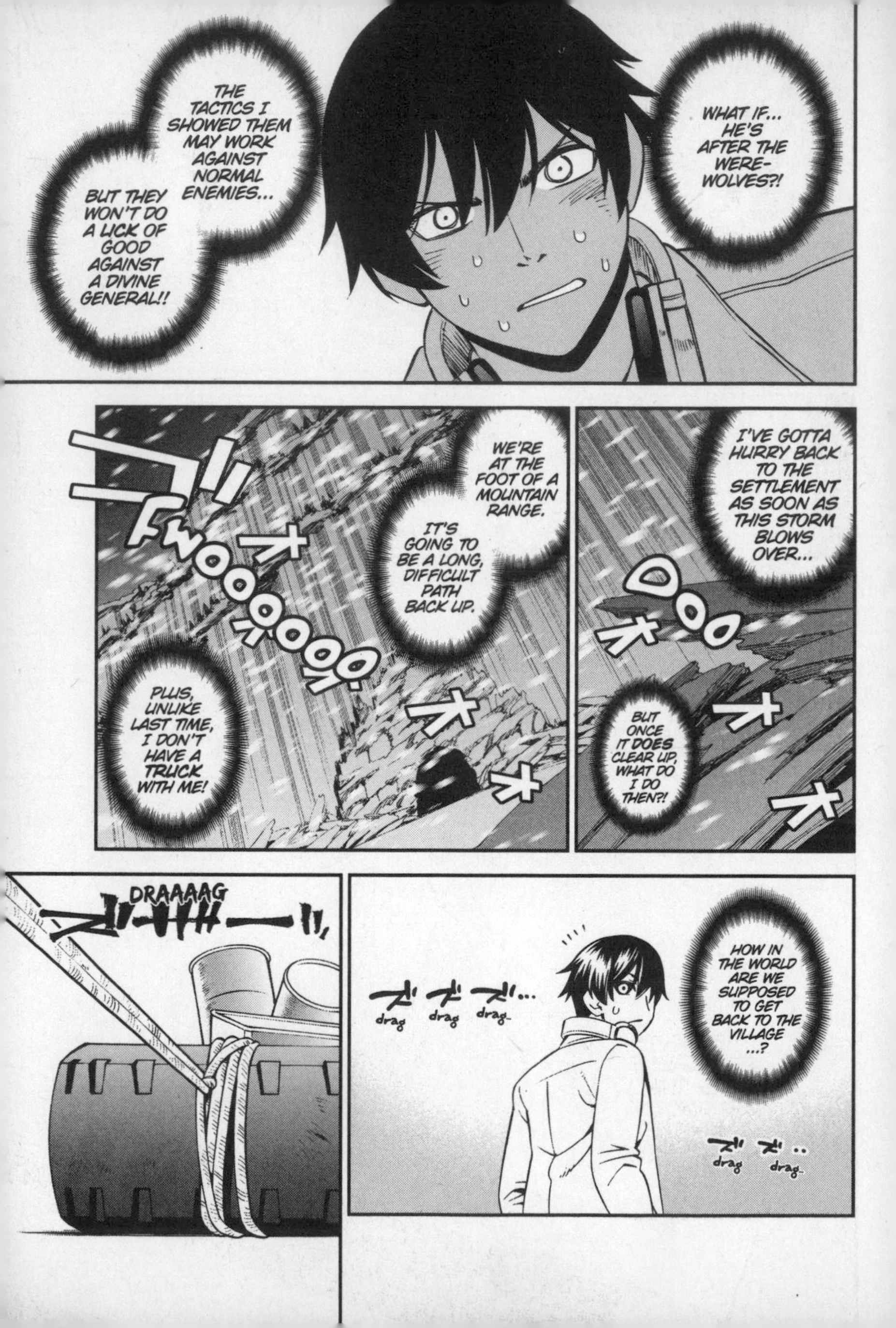
WHAT IF... HE'S AFTER THE WERE-WOLVES?!
THE TACTICS I SHOWED THEM MAY WORK AGAINST NORMAL ENEMIES...
BUT THEY WON'T DO A LICK OF GOOD AGAINST A DIVINE GENERAL!!
I'VE GOTTA HURRY BACK TO THE SETTLEMENT AS SOON AS THIS STORM BLOWS OVER...
DOO
BUT ONCE IT DOES CLEAR UP, WHAT DO I DO THEN?!
FWOOOOOO
WE'RE AT THE FOOT OF A MOUNTAIN RANGE.
IT'S GOING TO BE A LONG, DIFFICULT PATH BACK UP.
PLUS, UNLIKE LAST TIME, I DON'T HAVE A TRUCK WITH ME!
HOW IN THE WORLD ARE WE SUPPOSED TO GET BACK TO THE VILLAGE ...?
drag drag drag
drag drag
DRAAAAG

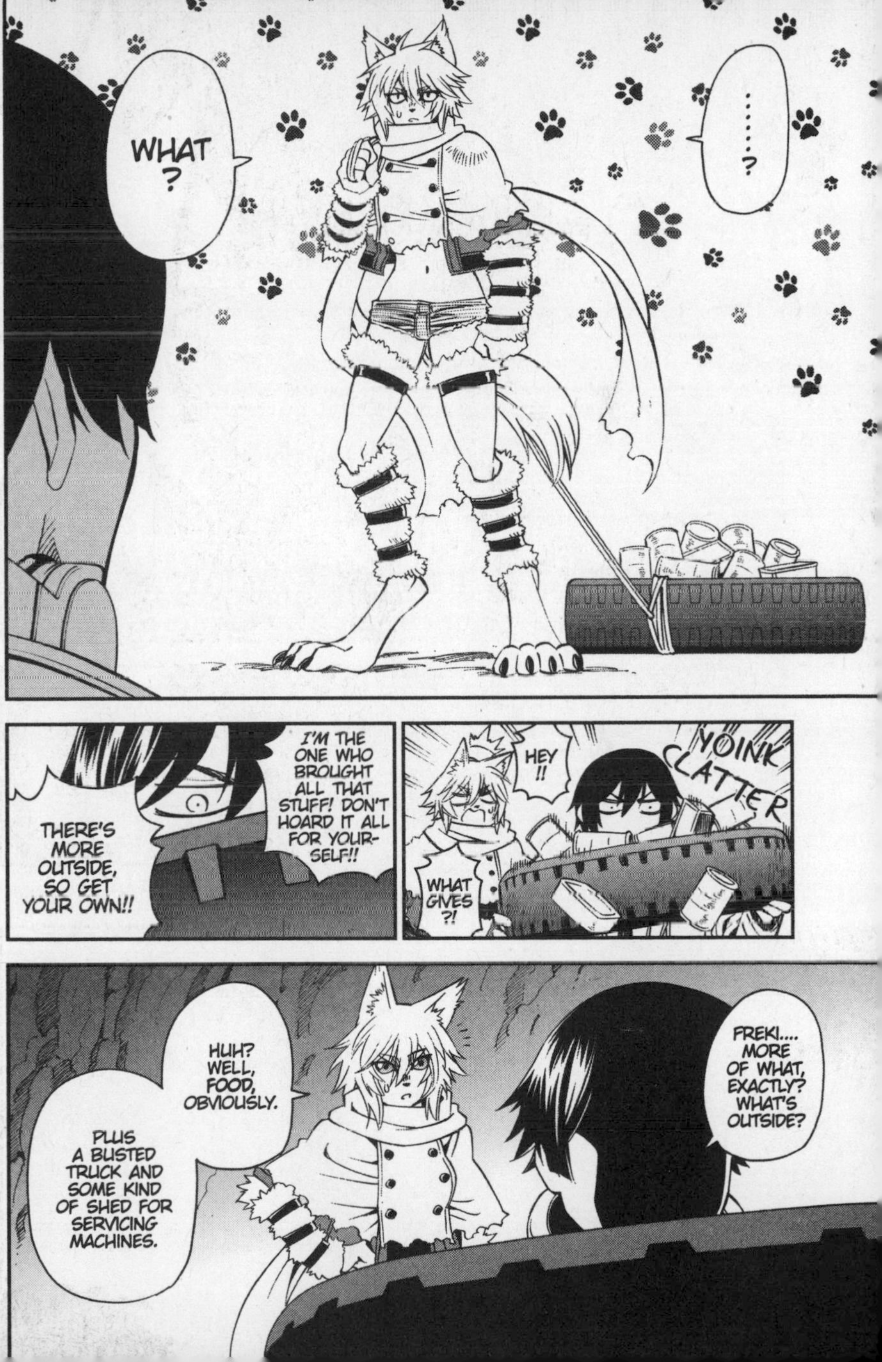
......?
WHAT?
YOINK CLATTER
HEY!!
WHAT GIVES?!
I'M THE ONE WHO BROUGHT ALL THAT STUFF! DON'T HOARD IT ALL FOR YOURSELF!!
THERE'S MORE OUTSIDE, SO GET YOUR OWN!!
FREKI.... MORE OF WHAT, EXACTLY? WHAT'S OUTSIDE?
HUH? WELL, FOOD, OBVIOUSLY.
PLUS A BUSTED TRUCK AND SOME KIND OF SHED FOR SERVICING MACHINES.

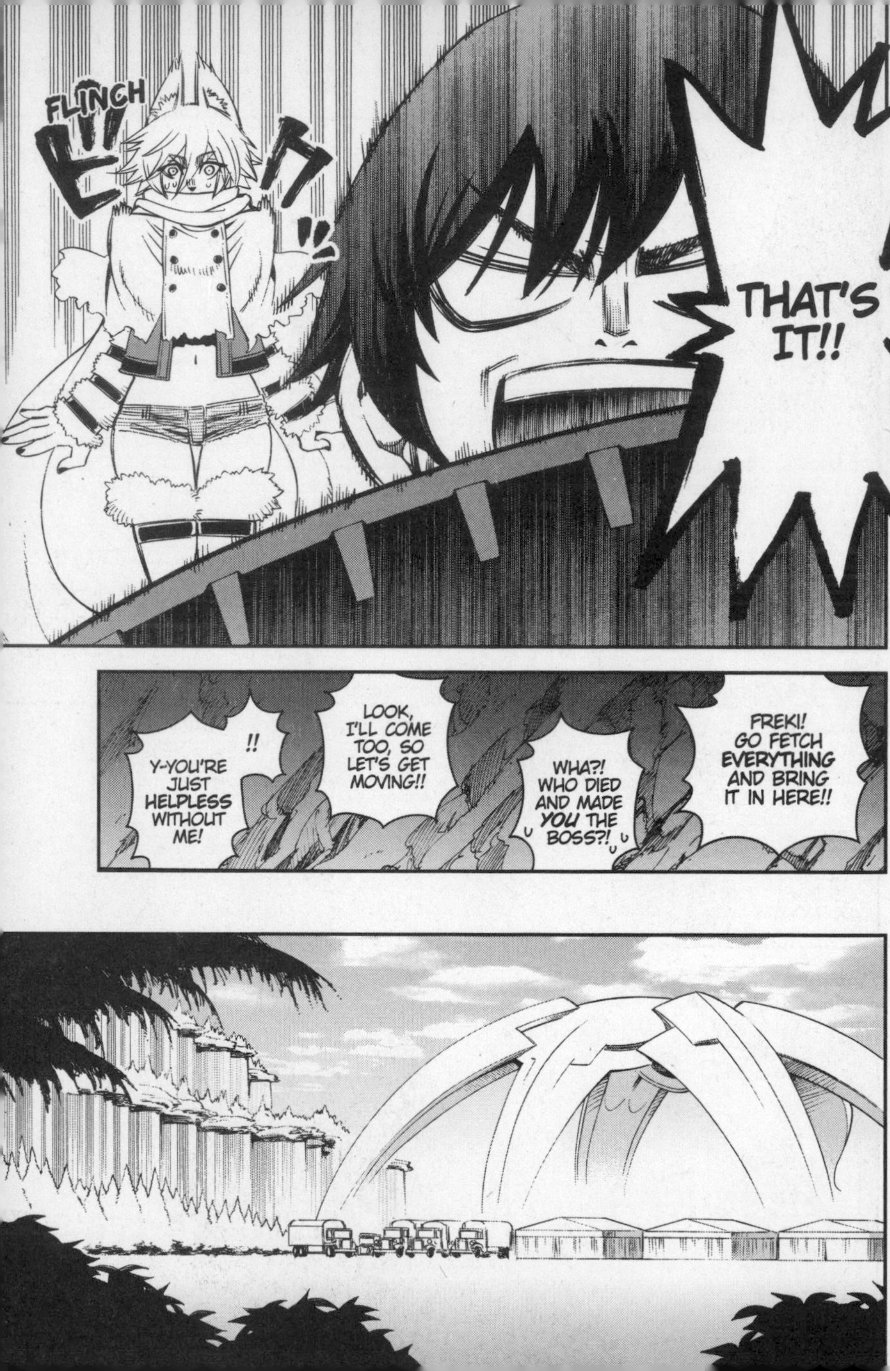
THAT'S IT!!
FLINCH
FREKI! GO FETCH EVERYTHING AND BRING IT IN HERE!!
WHA?! WHO DIED AND MADE YOU THE BOSS?!
LOOK, I'LL COME TOO, SO LET'S GET MOVING!!
!!
Y-YOU'RE JUST HELPLESS WITHOUT ME!

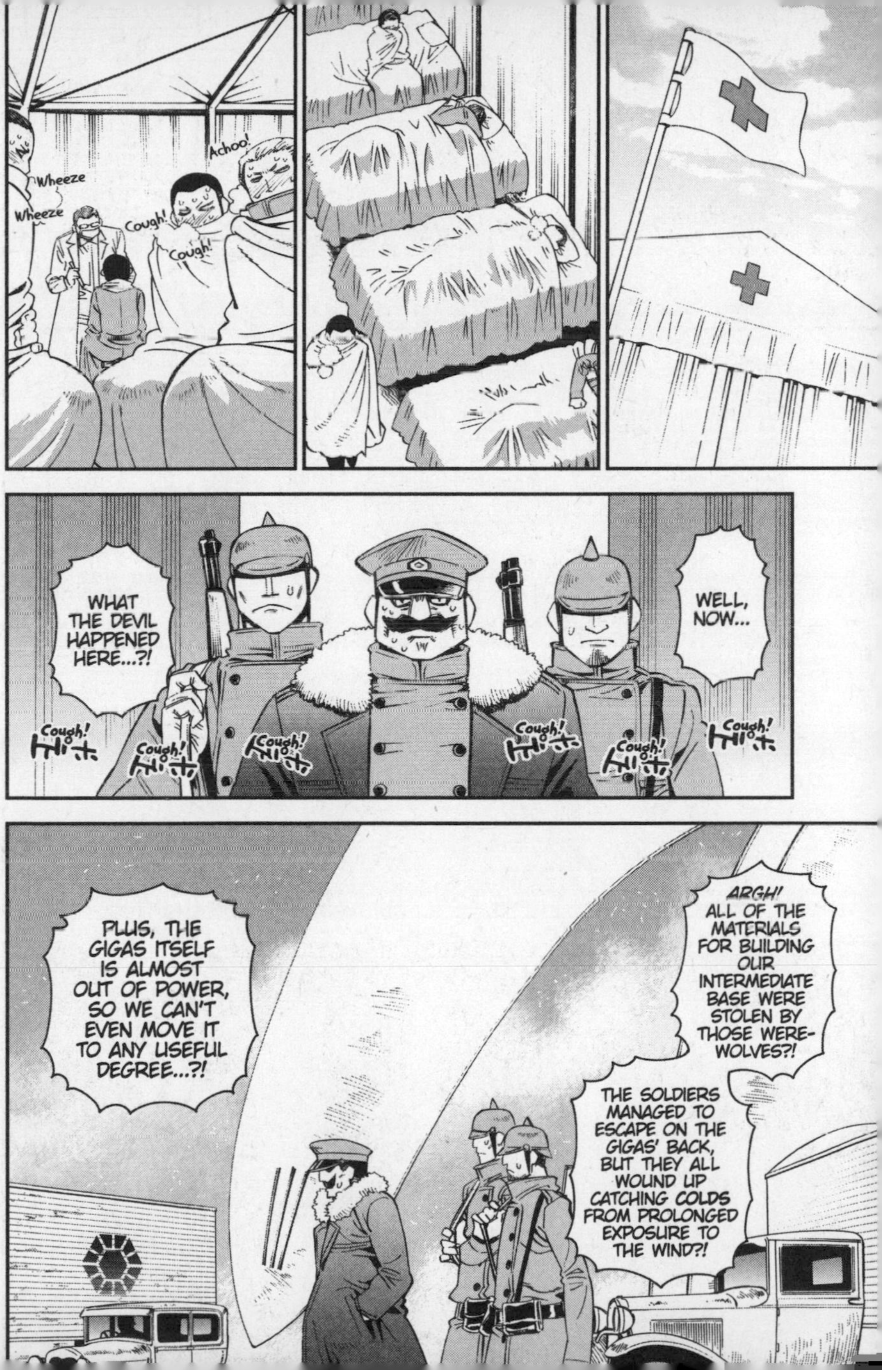
Achoo!
Wheeze
Wheeze
Cough!
Cough!
WELL, NOW...
WHAT THE DEVIL HAPPENED HERE...?!
Cough!
Cough!
Cough!
Cough!
Cough!
ARGH! ALL OF THE MATERIALS FOR BUILDING OUR INTERMEDIATE BASE WERE STOLEN BY THOSE WERE-WOLVES?!
THE SOLDIERS MANAGED TO ESCAPE ON THE GIGAS' BACK, BUT THEY ALL WOUND UP CATCHING COLDS FROM PROLONGED EXPOSURE TO THE WIND?!
PLUS, THE GIGAS ITSELF IS ALMOST OUT OF POWER, SO WE CAN'T EVEN MOVE IT TO ANY USEFUL DEGREE...?!

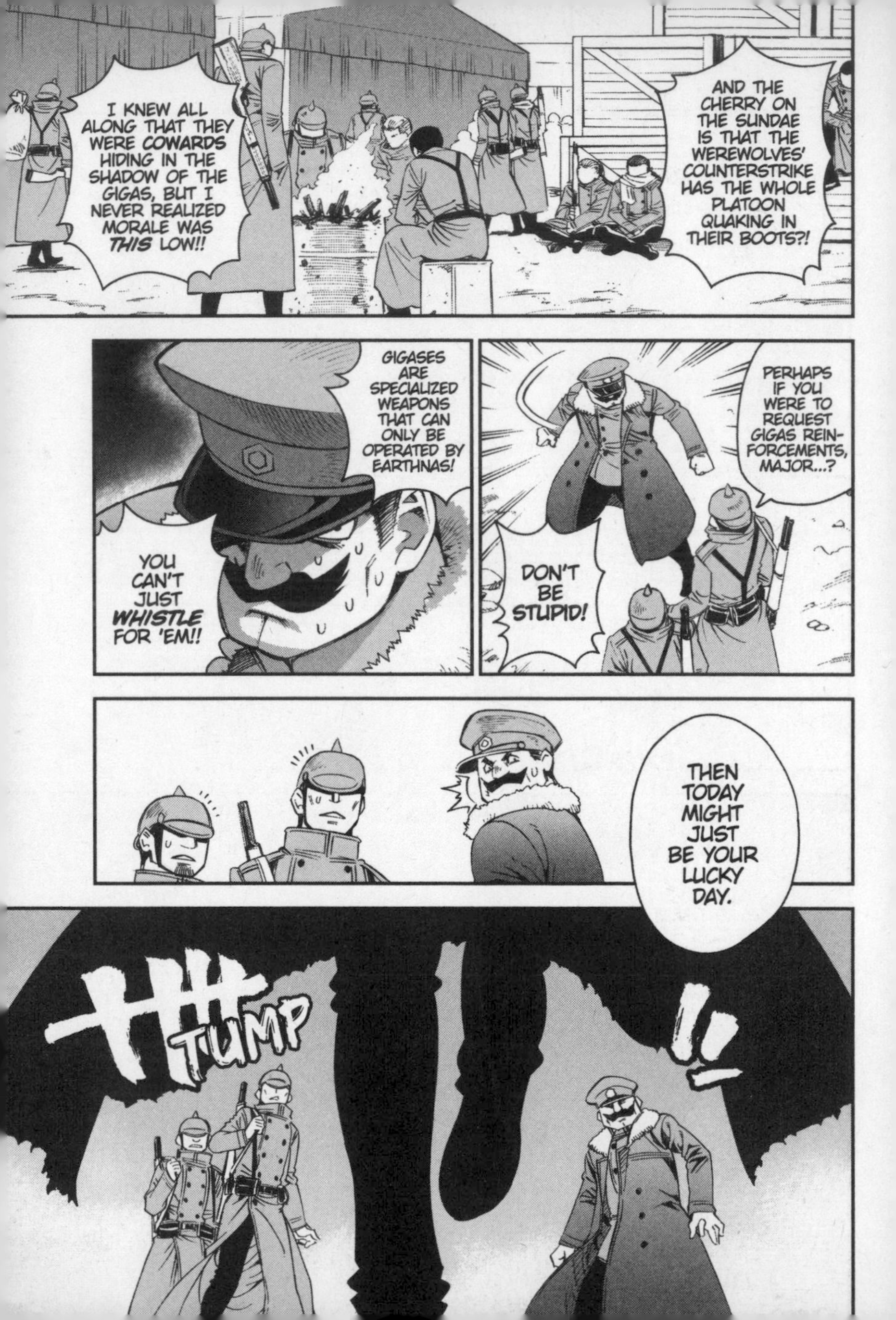
AND THE CHERRY ON THE SUNDAE IS THAT THE WEREWOLVES' COUNTERSTRIKE HAS THE WHOLE PLATOON QUAKING IN THEIR BOOTS?!
I KNEW ALL ALONG THAT THEY WERE COWARDS HIDING IN THE SHADOW OF THE GIGAS, BUT I NEVER REALIZED MORALE WAS THIS LOW!!
PERHAPS IF YOU WERE TO REQUEST GIGAS REIN-FORCEMENTS, MAJOR...?
DON'T BE STUPID!
GIGASES ARE SPECIALIZED WEAPONS THAT CAN ONLY BE OPERATED BY EARTHNAS!
YOU CAN'T JUST WHISTLE FOR 'EM!!
THEN TODAY MIGHT JUST BE YOUR LUCKY DAY.
TUMP
!!

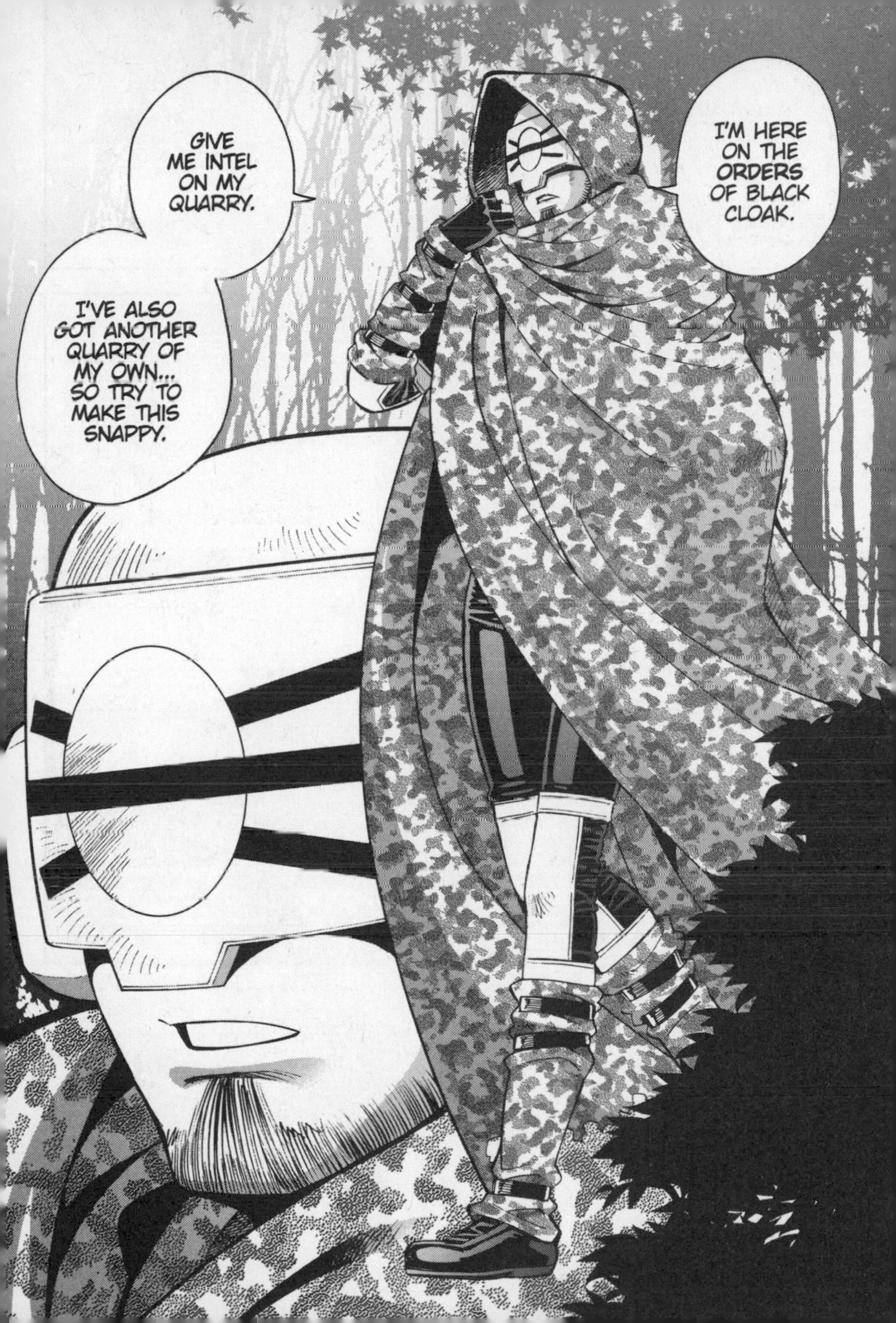
I'M HERE ON THE ORDERS OF BLACK CLOAK.
GIVE ME INTEL ON MY QUARRY.
I'VE ALSO GOT ANOTHER QUARRY OF MY OWN... SO TRY TO MAKE THIS SNAPPY.

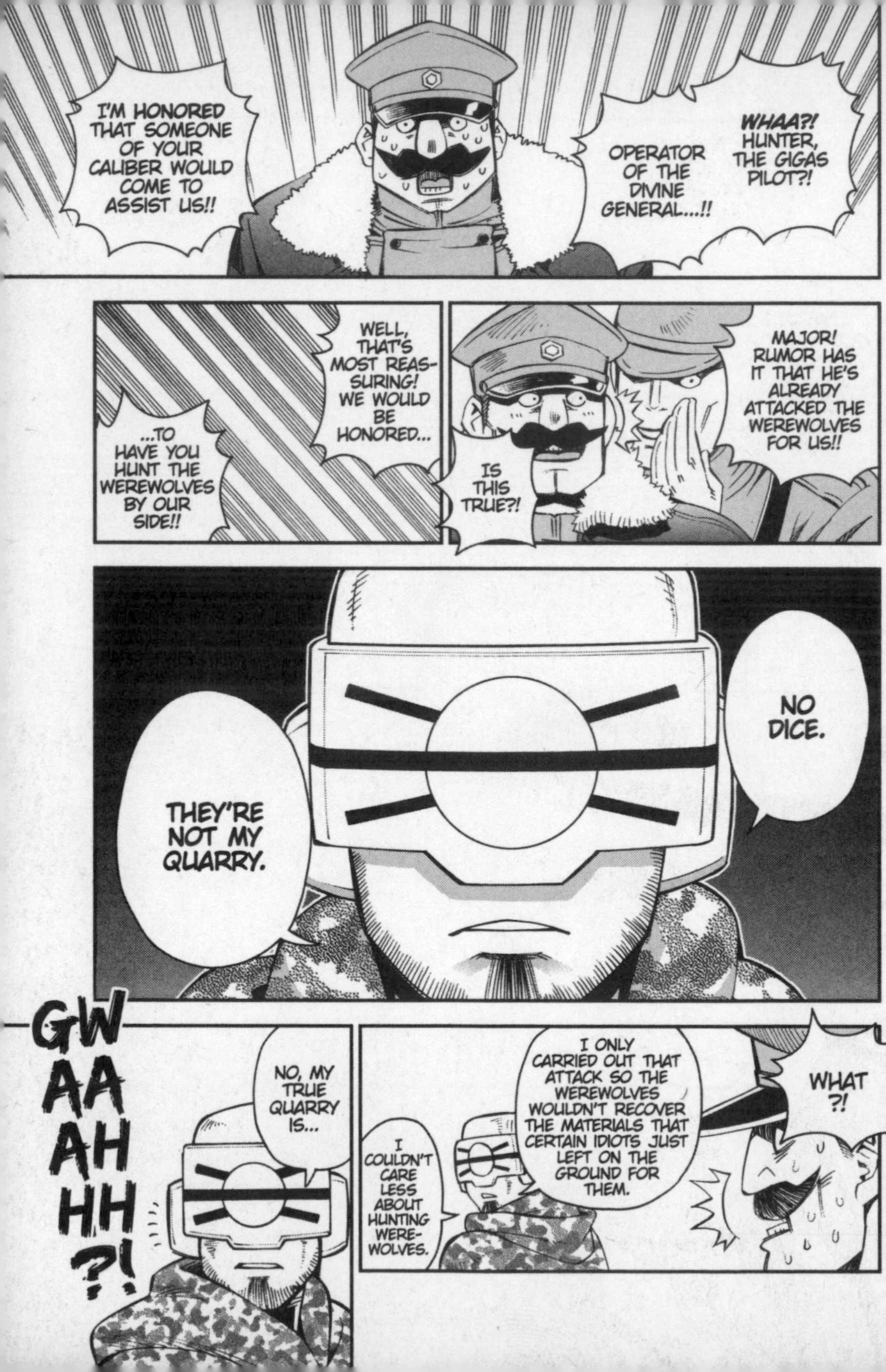
WHAA?! HUNTER, THE GIGAS PILOT?!
OPERATOR OF THE DIVINE GENERAL...!!
I'M HONORED THAT SOMEONE OF YOUR CALIBER WOULD COME TO ASSIST US!!
MAJOR! RUMOR HAS IT THAT HE'S ALREADY ATTACKED THE WEREWOLVES FOR US!!
IS THIS TRUE?!
WELL, THAT'S MOST REAS-SURING! WE WOULD BE HONORED...
...TO HAVE YOU HUNT THE WEREWOLVES BY OUR SIDE!!
NO DICE.
THEY'RE NOT MY QUARRY.
WHAT?!
I ONLY CARRIED OUT THAT ATTACK SO THE WEREWOLVES WOULDN'T RECOVER THE MATERIALS THAT CERTAIN IDIOTS JUST LEFT ON THE GROUND FOR THEM.
I COULDN'T CARE LESS ABOUT HUNTING WERE-WOLVES.
NO, MY TRUE QUARRY IS...
GWAAAHHH?!

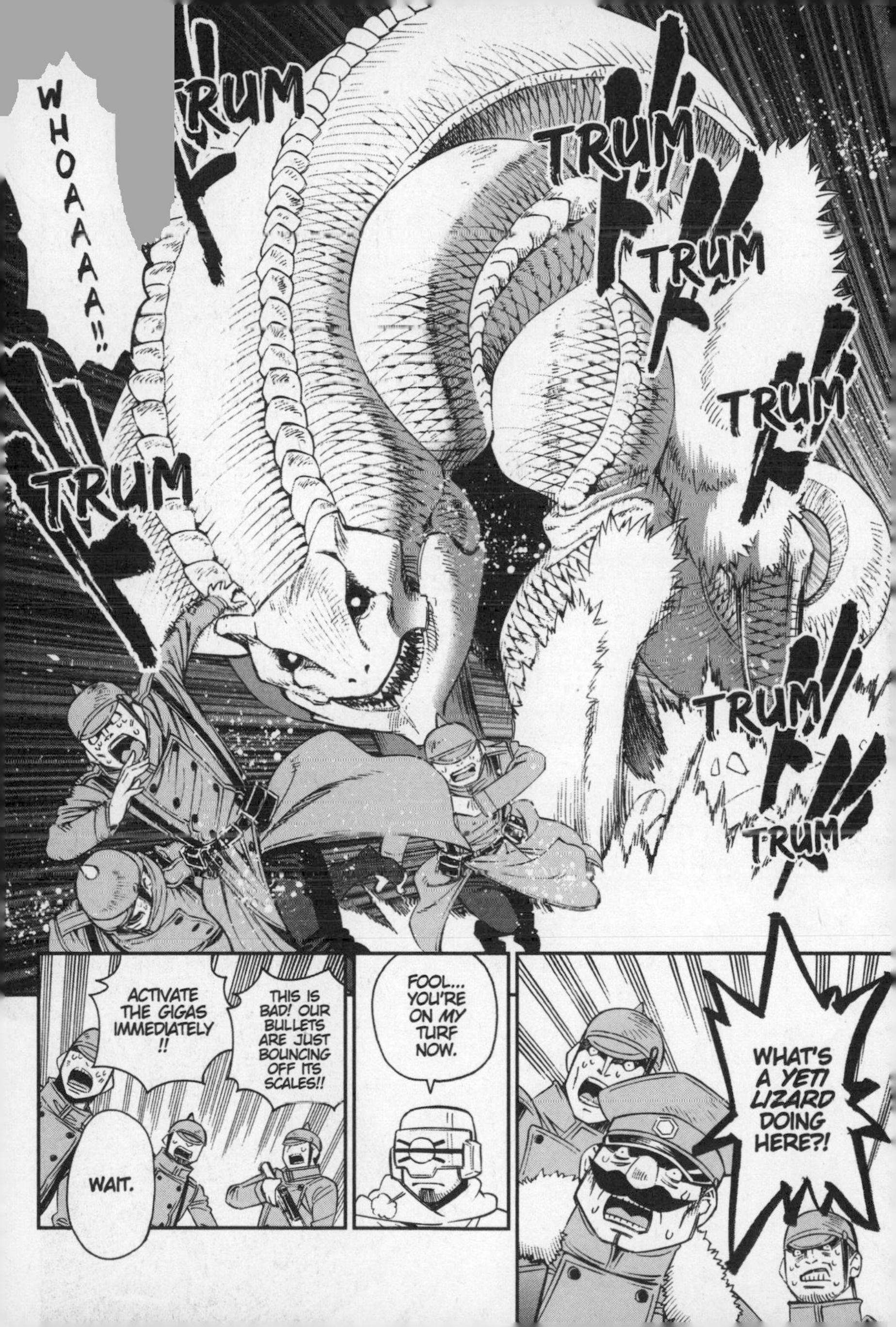
TRUM
TRUM
TRUM
TRUM
TRUM
TRUM
TRUM
WHOAAAAA!!
TRUM
WHAT'S A YETI LIZARD DOING HERE?!
FOOL... YOU'RE ON MY TURF NOW.
THIS IS BAD! OUR BULLETS ARE JUST BOUNCING OFF ITS SCALES!!
ACTIVATE THE GIGAS IMMEDIATELY!!
WAIT.

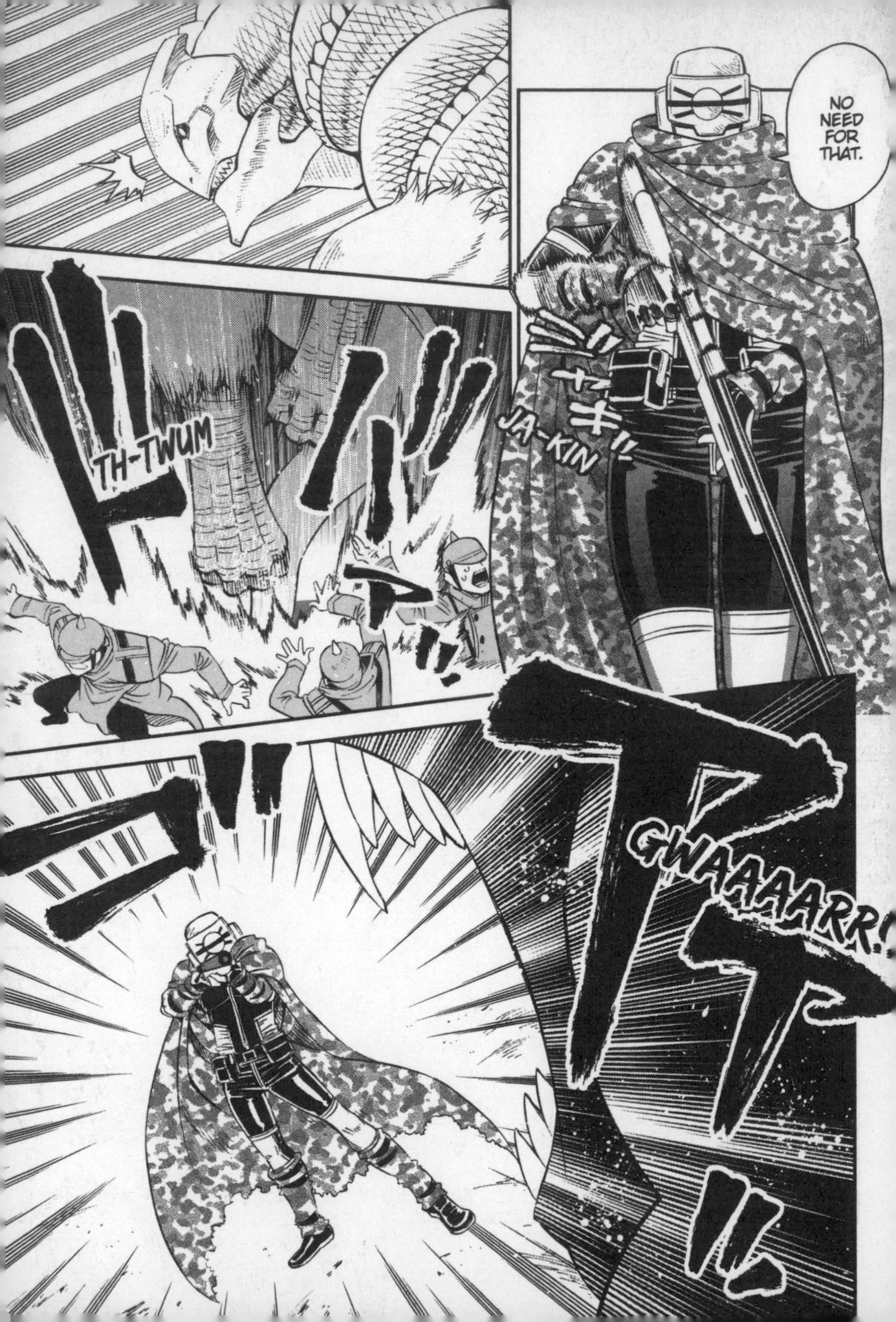
NO NEED FOR THAT.
JA-KIN!!
TH-TWUM
GWAAAAARR!!

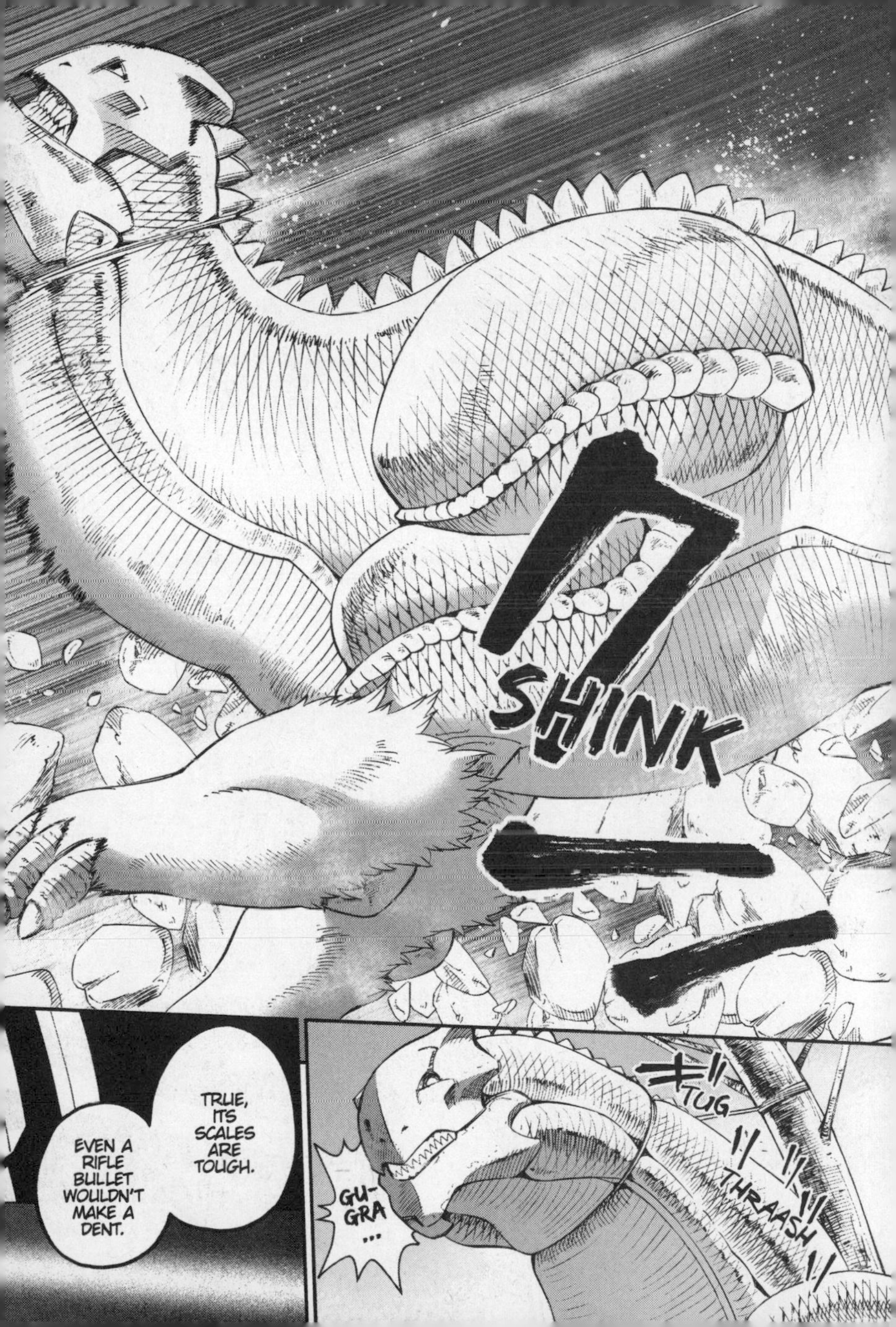
SHINK
TUG
THRAASH
GU-GRA...
TRUE, ITS SCALES ARE TOUGH.
EVEN A RIFLE BULLET WOULDN'T MAKE A DENT.

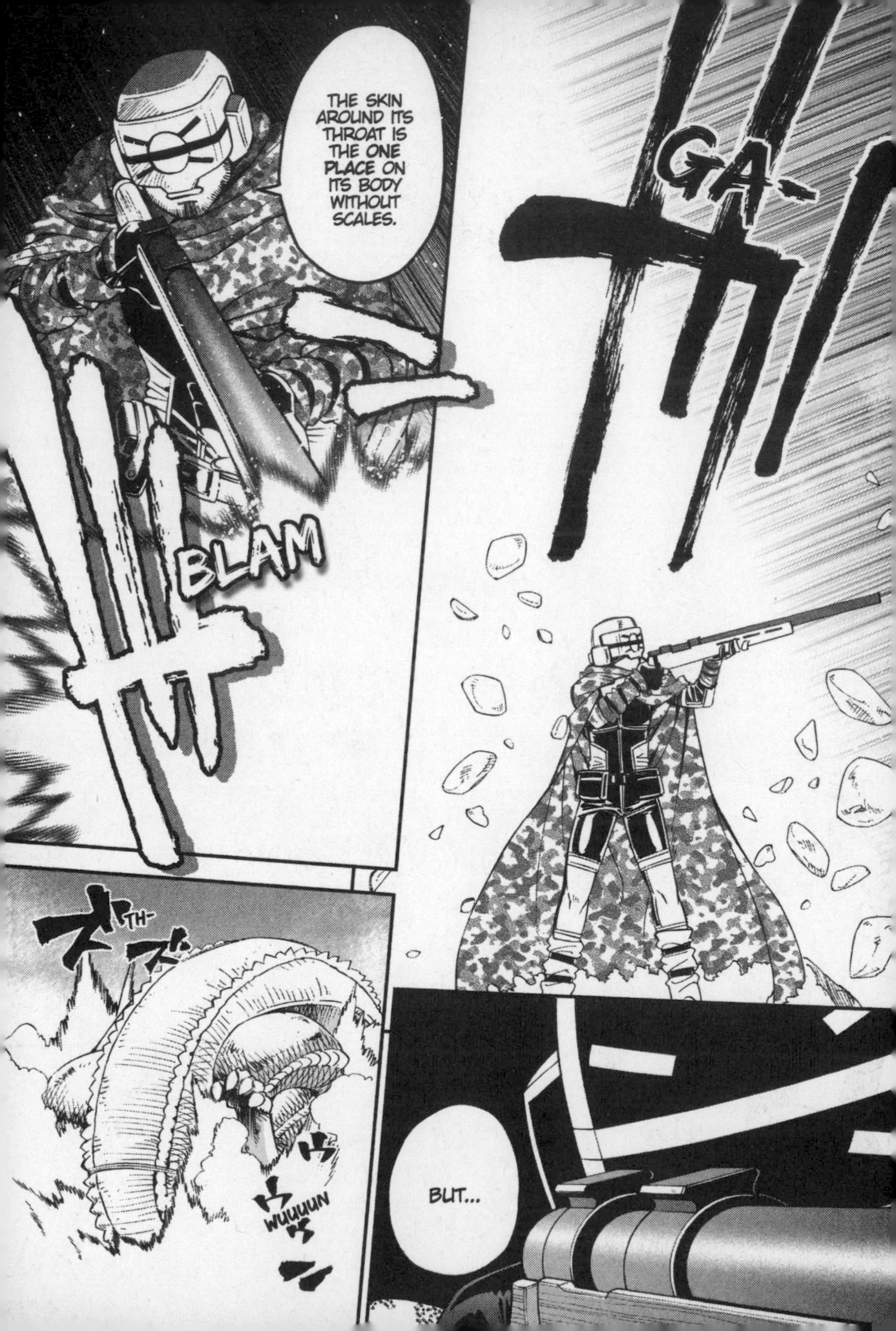
GA-
THE SKIN AROUND ITS THROAT IS THE ONE PLACE ON ITS BODY WITHOUT SCALES.
BLAM
BUT...
TH-
WUUUUN

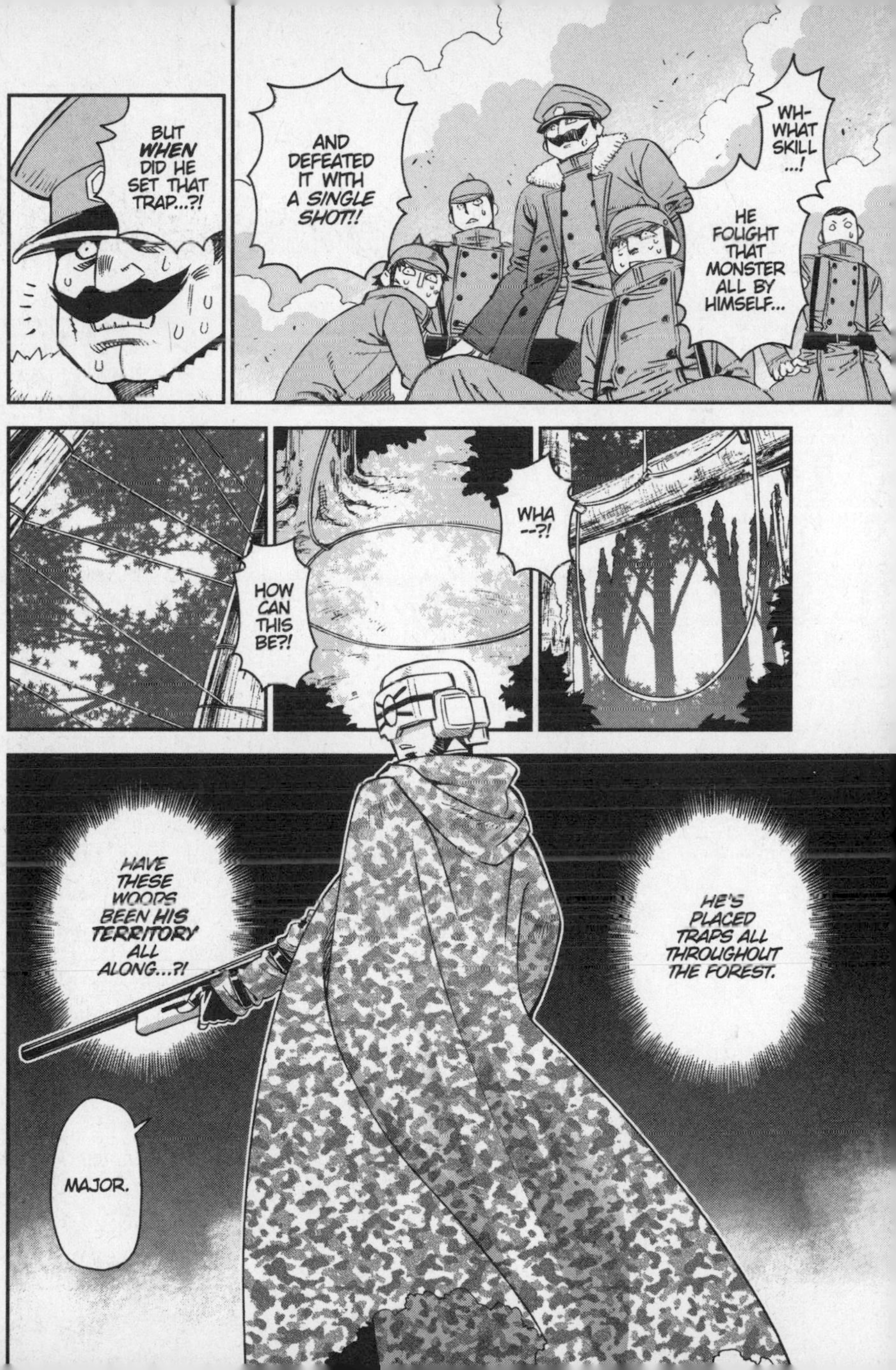
WH-WHAT SKILL...!
HE FOUGHT THAT MONSTER ALL BY HIMSELF...
AND DEFEATED IT WITH A SINGLE SHOT!!
BUT WHEN DID HE SET THAT TRAP...?!
WHA--?!
HOW CAN THIS BE?!
HE'S PLACED TRAPS ALL THROUGHOUT THE FOREST.
HAVE THESE WOODS BEEN HIS TERRITORY ALL ALONG...?!
MAJOR.

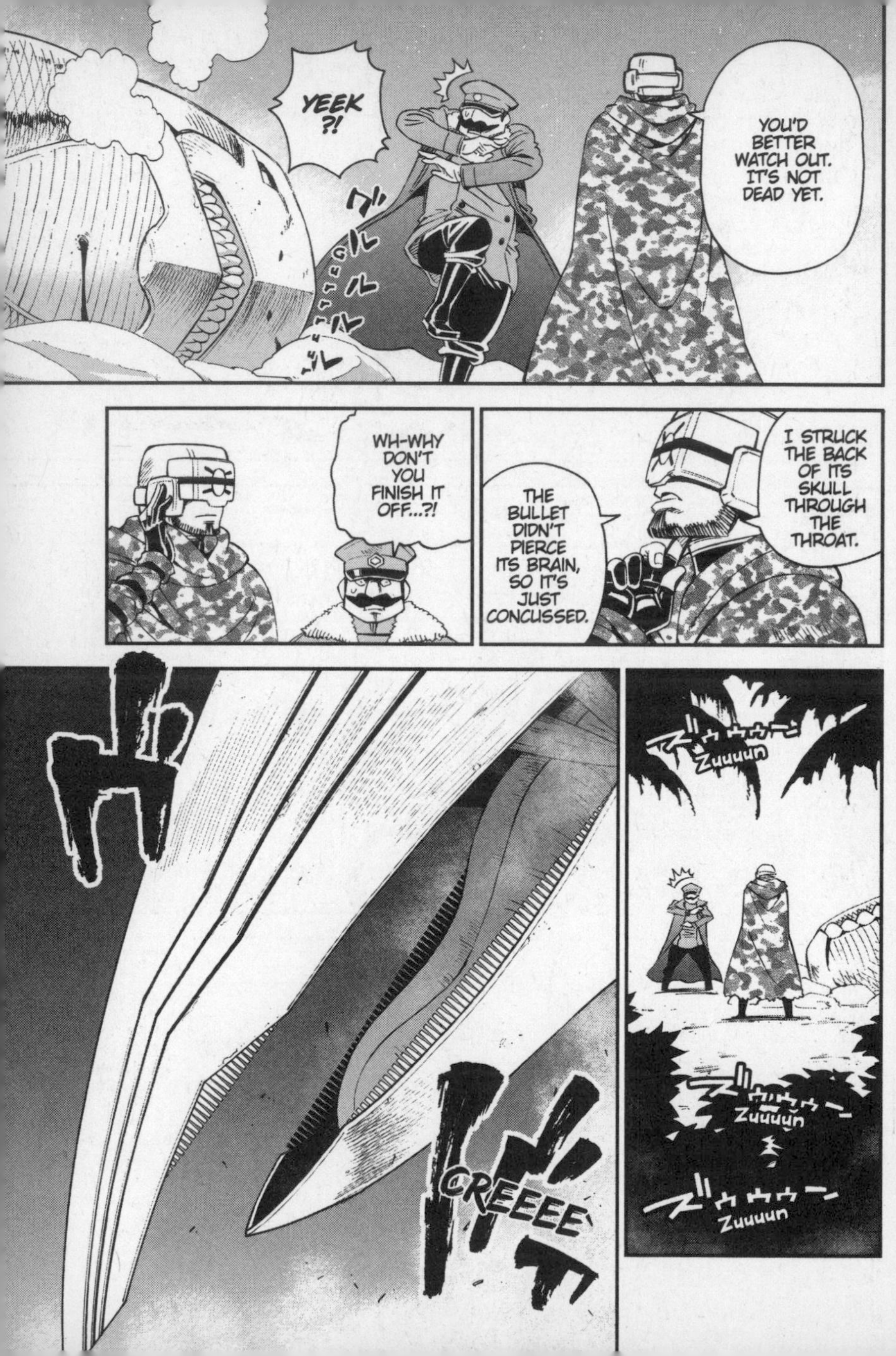
YOU'D BETTER WATCH OUT. IT'S NOT DEAD YET.
YEEK ?!
I STRUCK THE BACK OF ITS SKULL THROUGH THE THROAT.
THE BULLET DIDN'T PIERCE ITS BRAIN, SO IT'S JUST CONCUSSED.
WH-WHY DON'T YOU FINISH IT OFF...?!
Zuuuun
Zuuuun
Zuuuun
CREEEEE

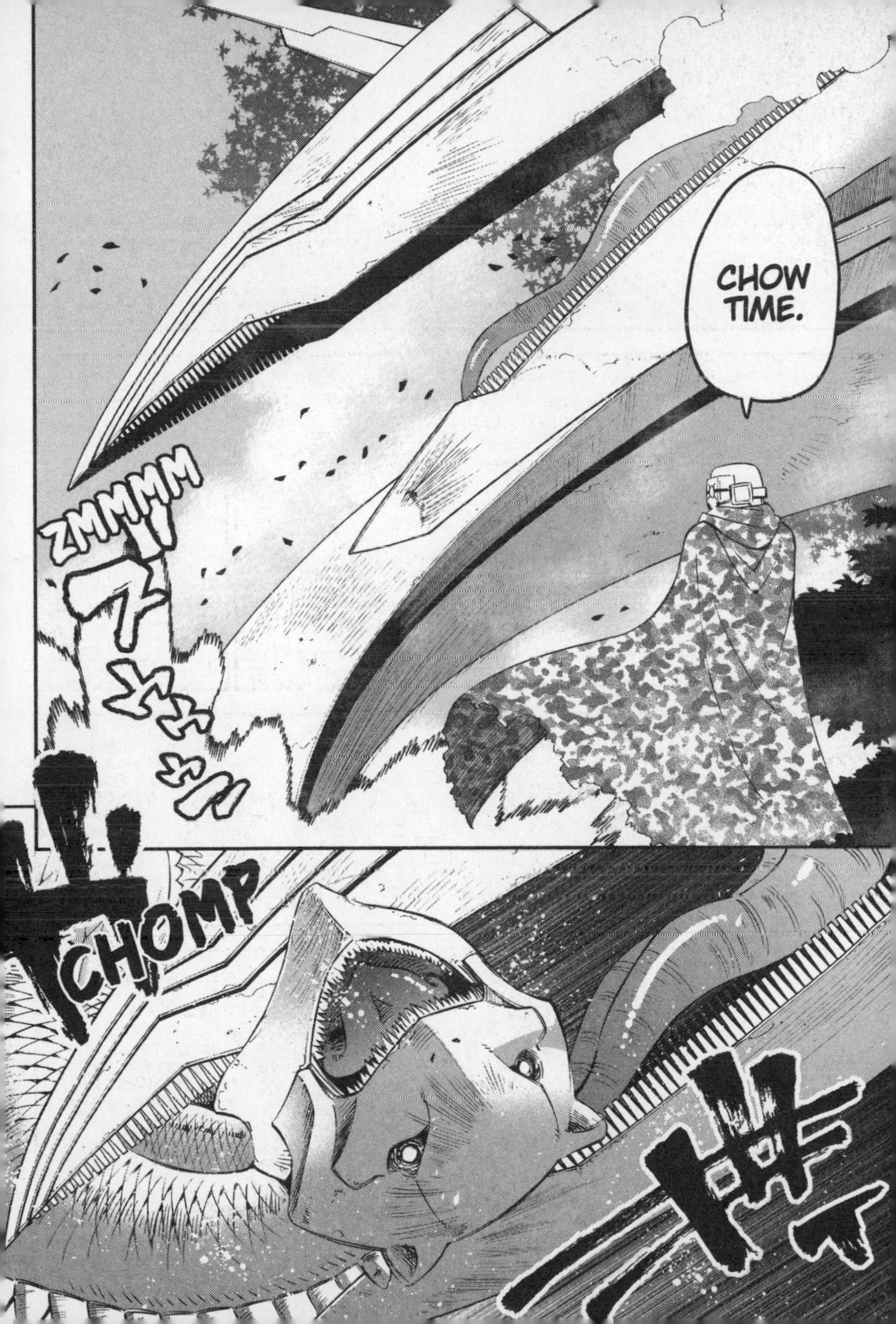
CHOW TIME.
ZMMMM
CHOMP

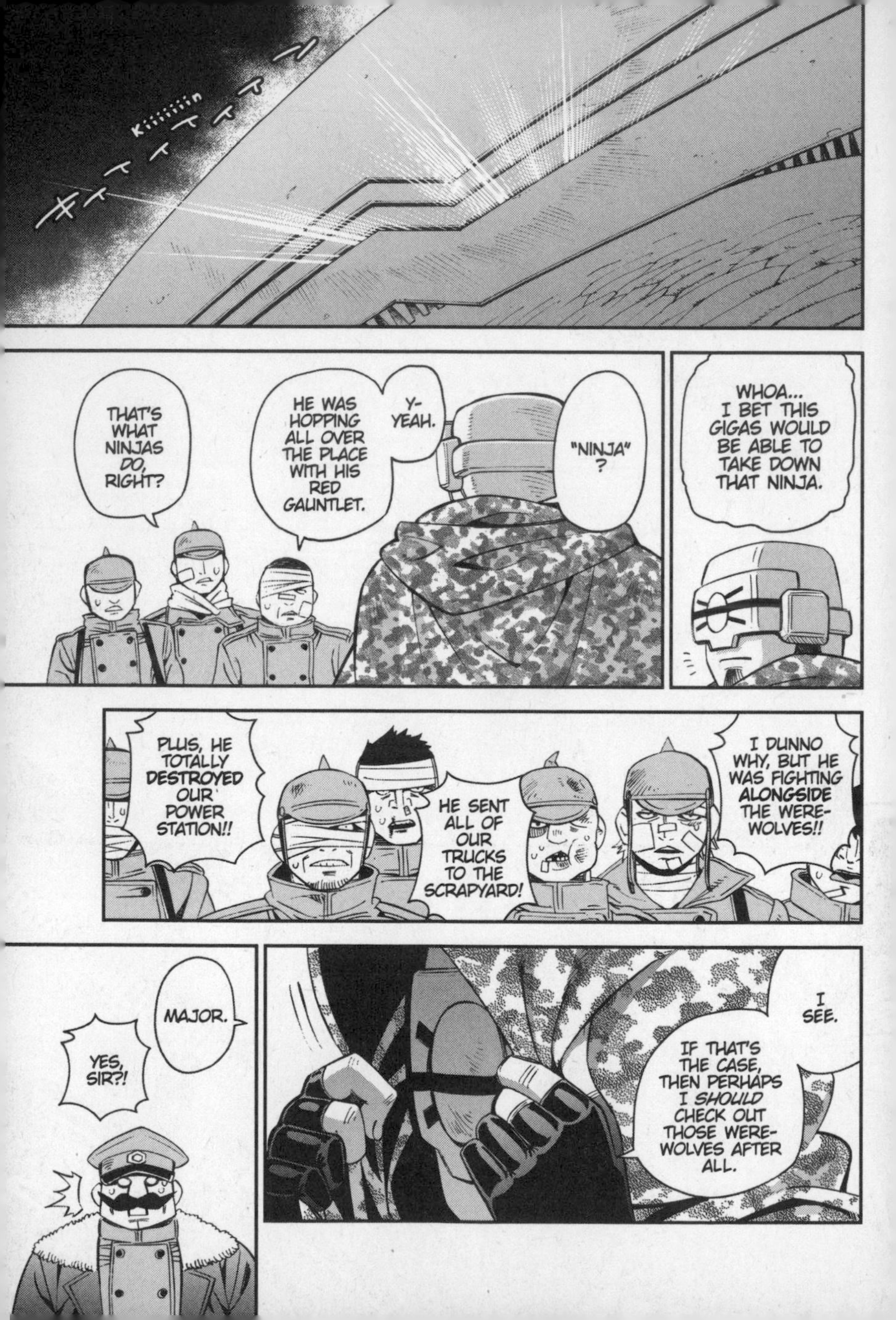
Kiiiiiin
WHOA... I BET THIS GIGAS WOULD BE ABLE TO TAKE DOWN THAT NINJA.
"NINJA" ?
Y- YEAH.
HE WAS HOPPING ALL OVER THE PLACE WITH HIS RED GAUNTLET.
THAT'S WHAT NINJAS *DO*, RIGHT?
I DUNNO WHY, BUT HE WAS FIGHTING **ALONGSIDE** THE WERE-WOLVES!!
HE SENT ALL OF OUR TRUCKS TO THE SCRAPYARD!
PLUS, HE TOTALLY **DESTROYED** OUR POWER STATION!!
I SEE.
IF THAT'S THE CASE, THEN PERHAPS I *SHOULD* CHECK OUT THOSE WERE-WOLVES AFTER ALL.
MAJOR.
YES, SIR?!

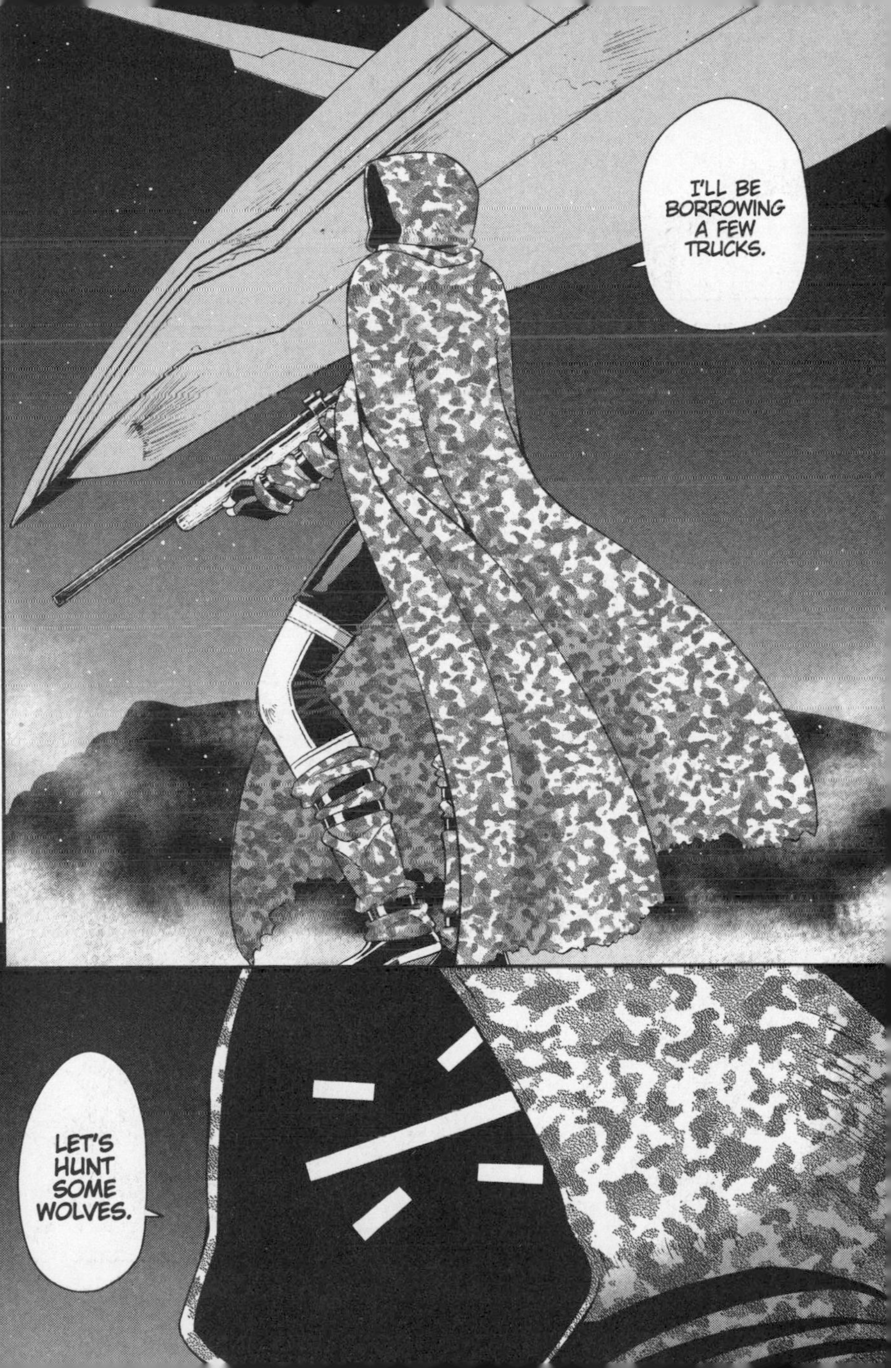
I'LL BE BORROWING A FEW TRUCKS.
LET'S HUNT SOME WOLVES.

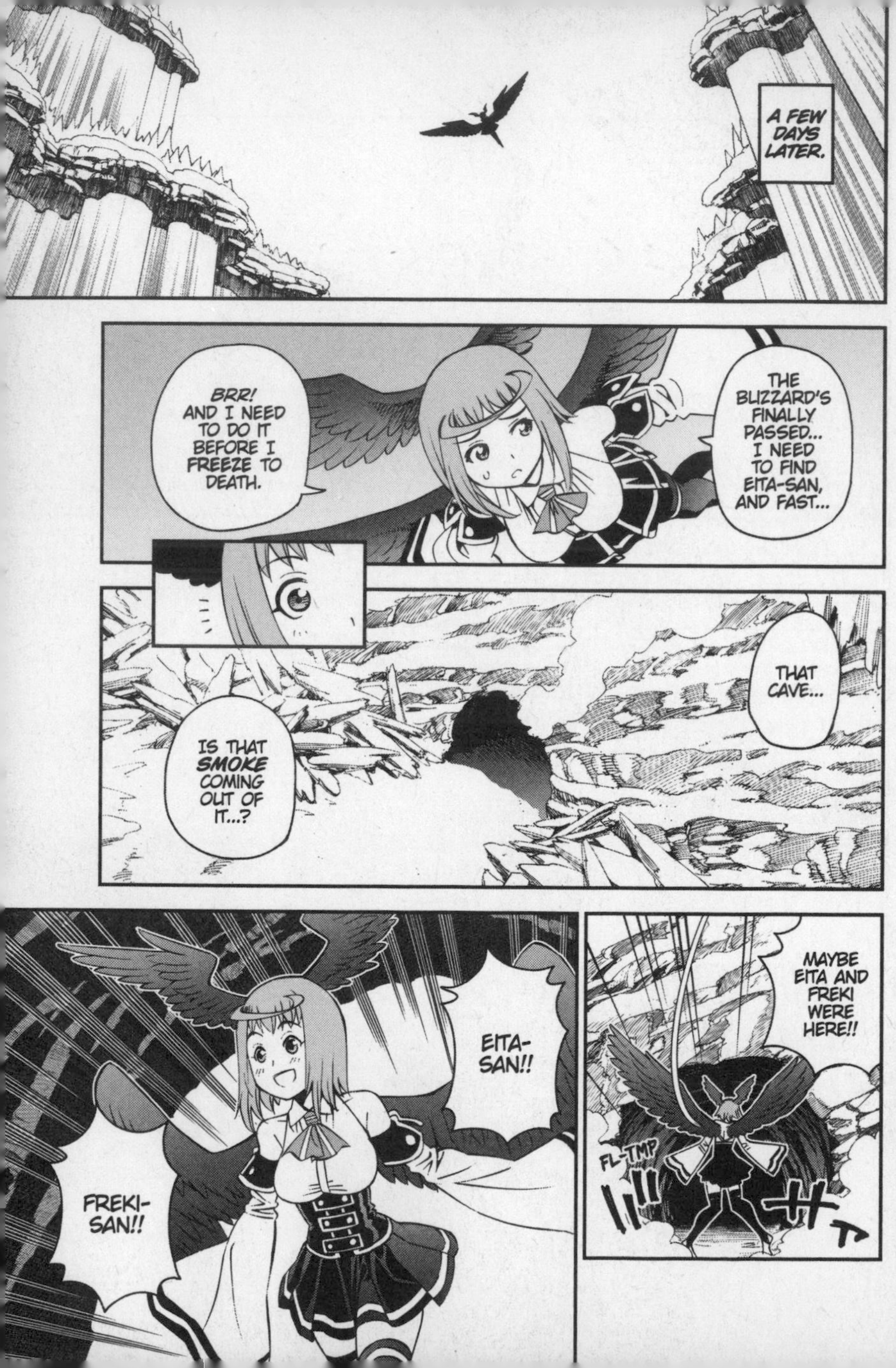
A FEW DAYS LATER.
THE BLIZZARD'S FINALLY PASSED... I NEED TO FIND EITA-SAN, AND FAST...
BRR! AND I NEED TO DO IT BEFORE I FREEZE TO DEATH.
THAT CAVE...
IS THAT **SMOKE** COMING OUT OF IT...?
MAYBE EITA AND FREKI WERE HERE!!
FL-TMP
EITA-SAN!!
FREKI-SAN!!

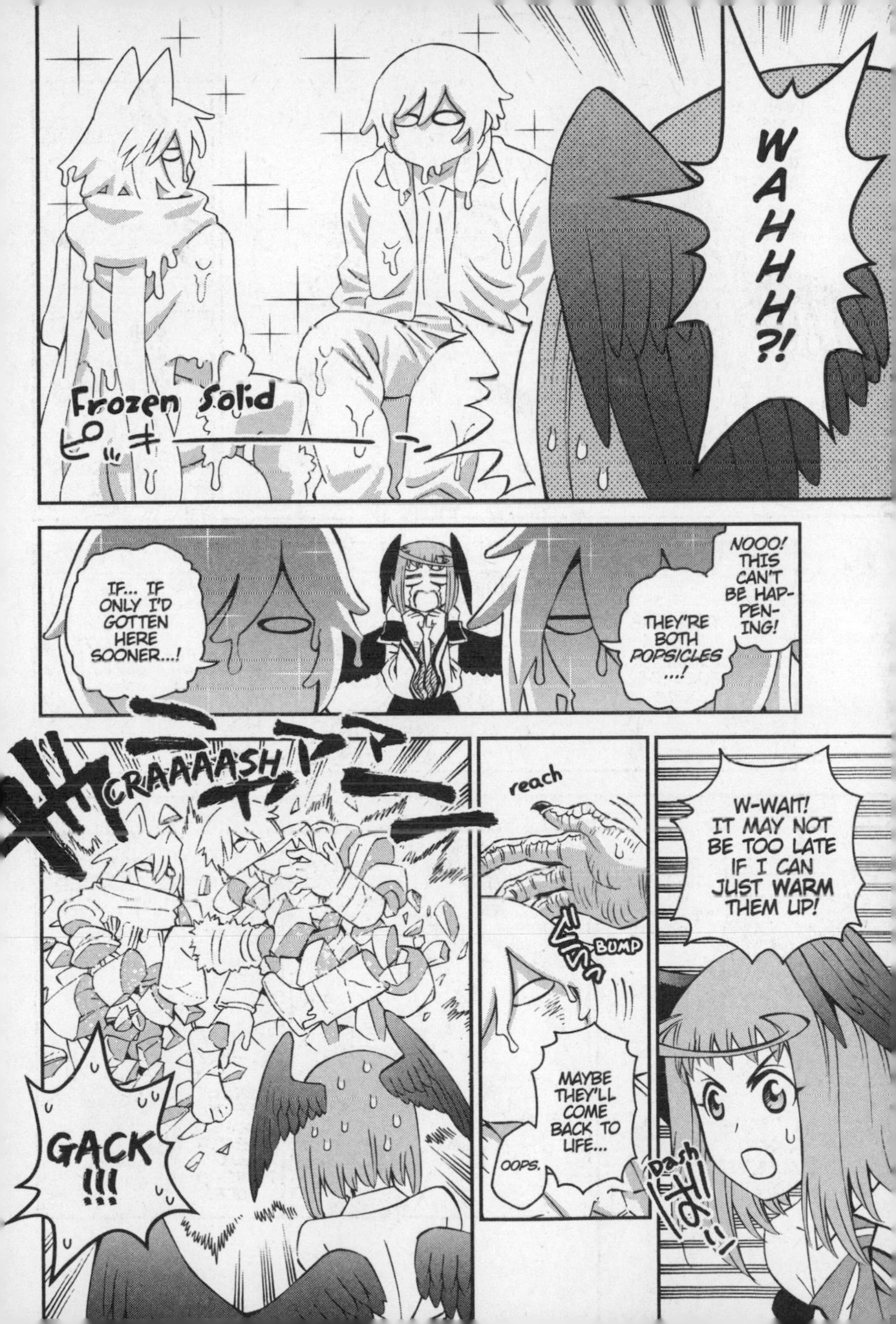
WAHHH?!
Frozen Solid
NOOO! THIS CAN'T BE HAP-PEN-ING!
THEY'RE BOTH *POPSICLES* ...!
IF... IF ONLY I'D GOTTEN HERE SOONER...!
W-WAIT! IT MAY NOT BE TOO LATE IF I CAN JUST WARM THEM UP!
Dash
reach
MAYBE THEY'LL COME BACK TO LIFE...
BUMP
OOPS.
CRAAAASH
GACK !!!

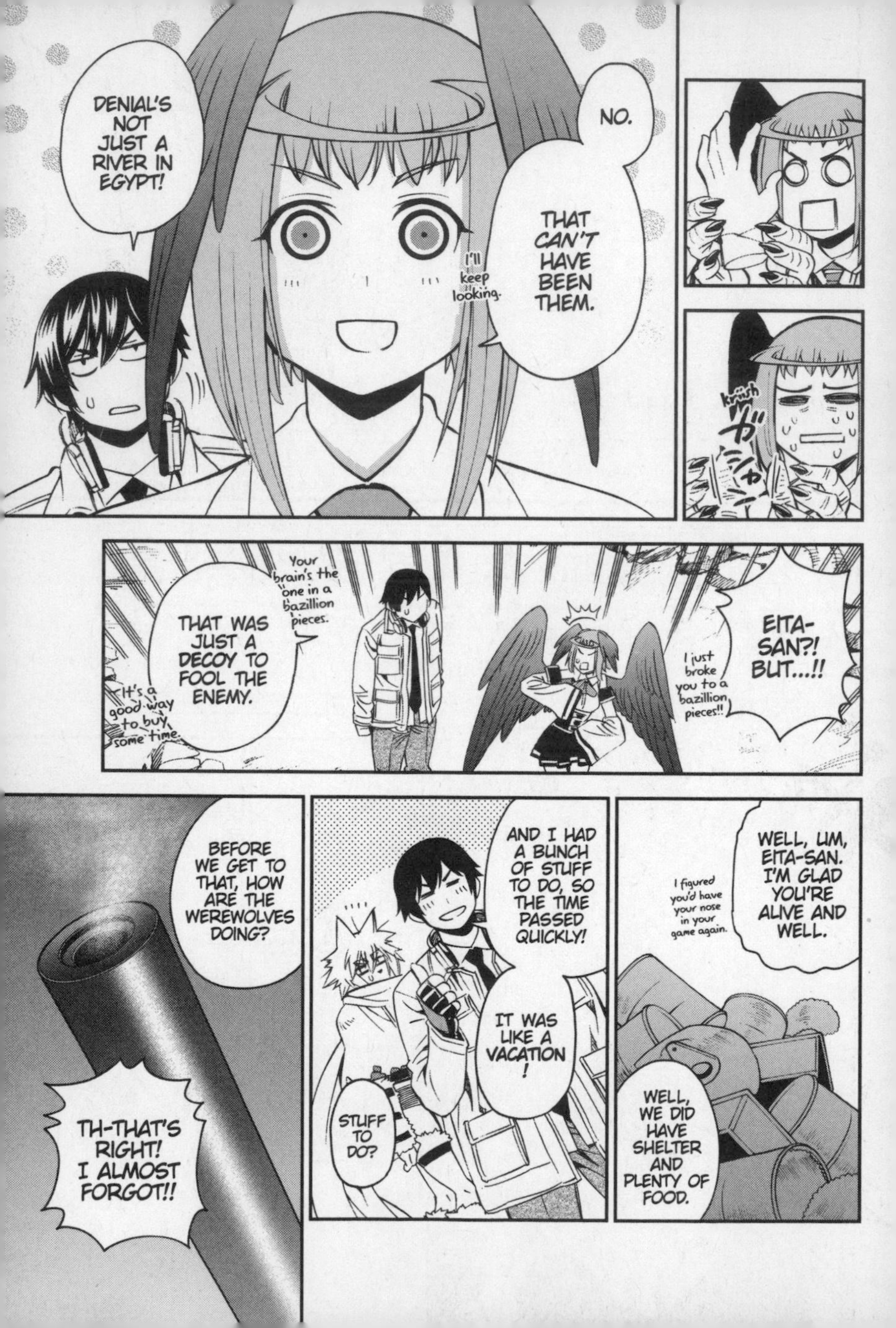
kriish
NO.
THAT CAN'T HAVE BEEN THEM.
I'll keep looking.
DENIAL'S NOT JUST A RIVER IN EGYPT!
EITA-SAN?! BUT...!!
I just broke you to a bazillion pieces!!
THAT WAS JUST A DECOY TO FOOL THE ENEMY.
Your brain's the one in a bazillion pieces.
It's a good way to buy some time.
WELL, UM, EITA-SAN. I'M GLAD YOU'RE ALIVE AND WELL.
I figured you'd have your nose in your game again.
WELL, WE DID HAVE SHELTER AND PLENTY OF FOOD.
AND I HAD A BUNCH OF STUFF TO DO, SO THE TIME PASSED QUICKLY!
IT WAS LIKE A VACATION!
STUFF TO DO?
BEFORE WE GET TO THAT, HOW ARE THE WEREWOLVES DOING?
TH-THAT'S RIGHT! I ALMOST FORGOT!!

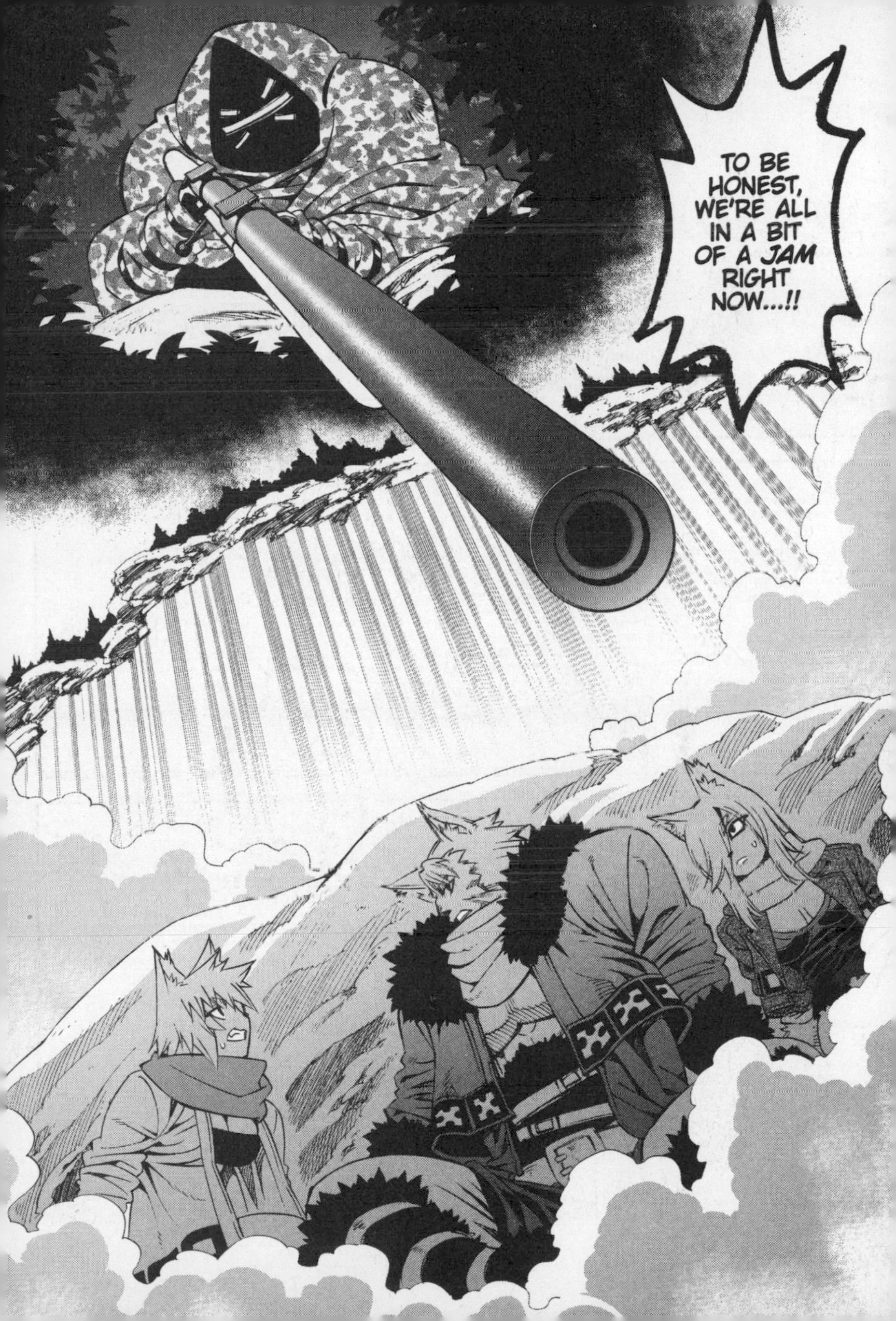
TO BE HONEST, WE'RE ALL IN A BIT OF A JAM RIGHT NOW...!!

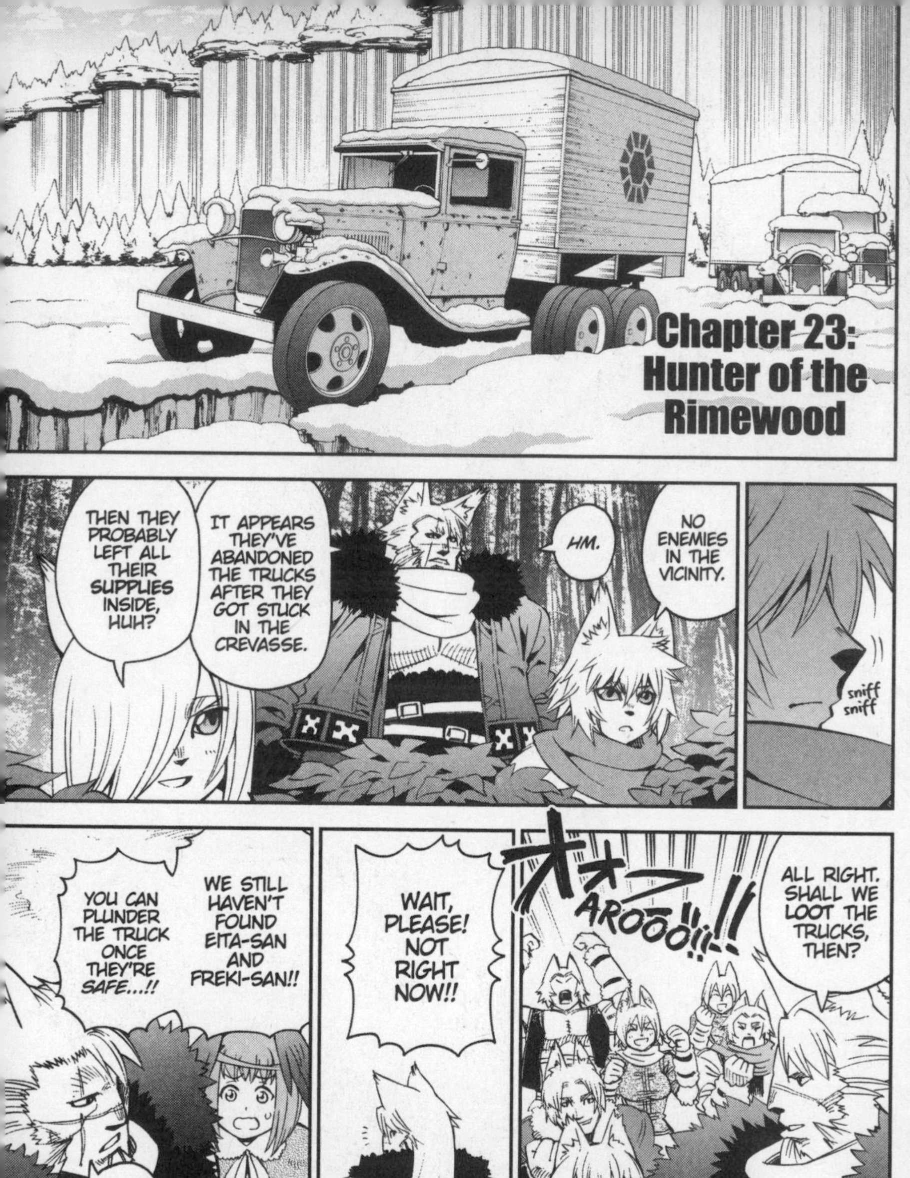
Chapter 23: Hunter of the Rimewood
sniff sniff
NO ENEMIES IN THE VICINITY.
HM.
IT APPEARS THEY'VE ABANDONED THE TRUCKS AFTER THEY GOT STUCK IN THE CREVASSE.
THEN THEY PROBABLY LEFT ALL THEIR SUPPLIES INSIDE, HUH?
ALL RIGHT. SHALL WE LOOT THE TRUCKS, THEN?
AROOOO!!!
WAIT, PLEASE! NOT RIGHT NOW!!
WE STILL HAVEN'T FOUND EITA-SAN AND FREKI-SAN!!
YOU CAN PLUNDER THE TRUCK ONCE THEY'RE SAFE...!!
TRUE. HOW-EVER...

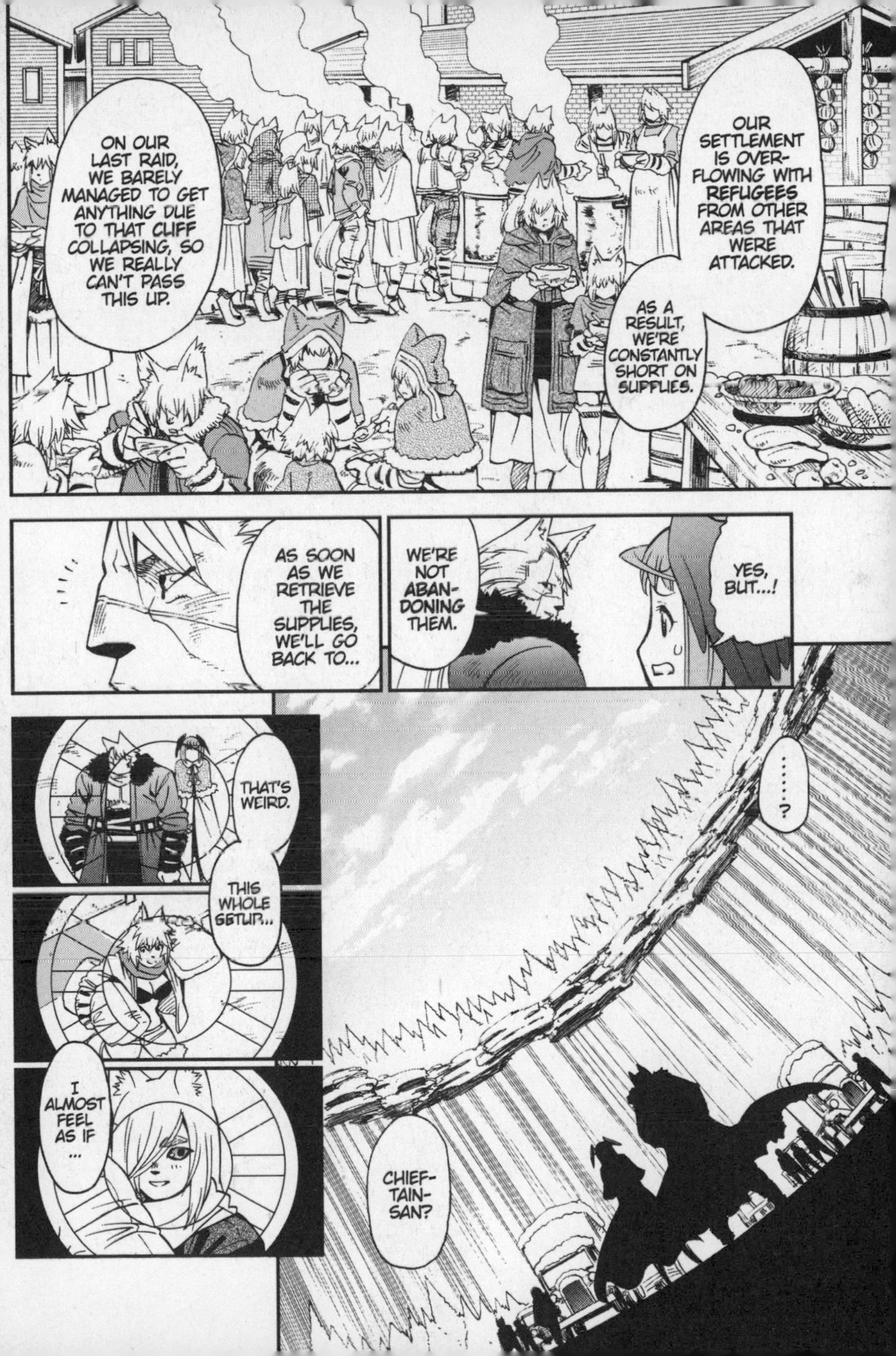
OUR SETTLEMENT IS OVER-FLOWING WITH REFUGEES FROM OTHER AREAS THAT WERE ATTACKED.
AS A RESULT, WE'RE CONSTANTLY SHORT ON SUPPLIES.
ON OUR LAST RAID, WE BARELY MANAGED TO GET ANYTHING DUE TO THAT CLIFF COLLAPSING, SO WE REALLY CAN'T PASS THIS UP.
YES, BUT...!
WE'RE NOT ABAN-DONING THEM.
AS SOON AS WE RETRIEVE THE SUPPLIES, WE'LL GO BACK TO...
......?
THAT'S WEIRD.
THIS WHOLE SETUP...
I ALMOST FEEL AS IF ...
CHIEF-TAIN-SAN?

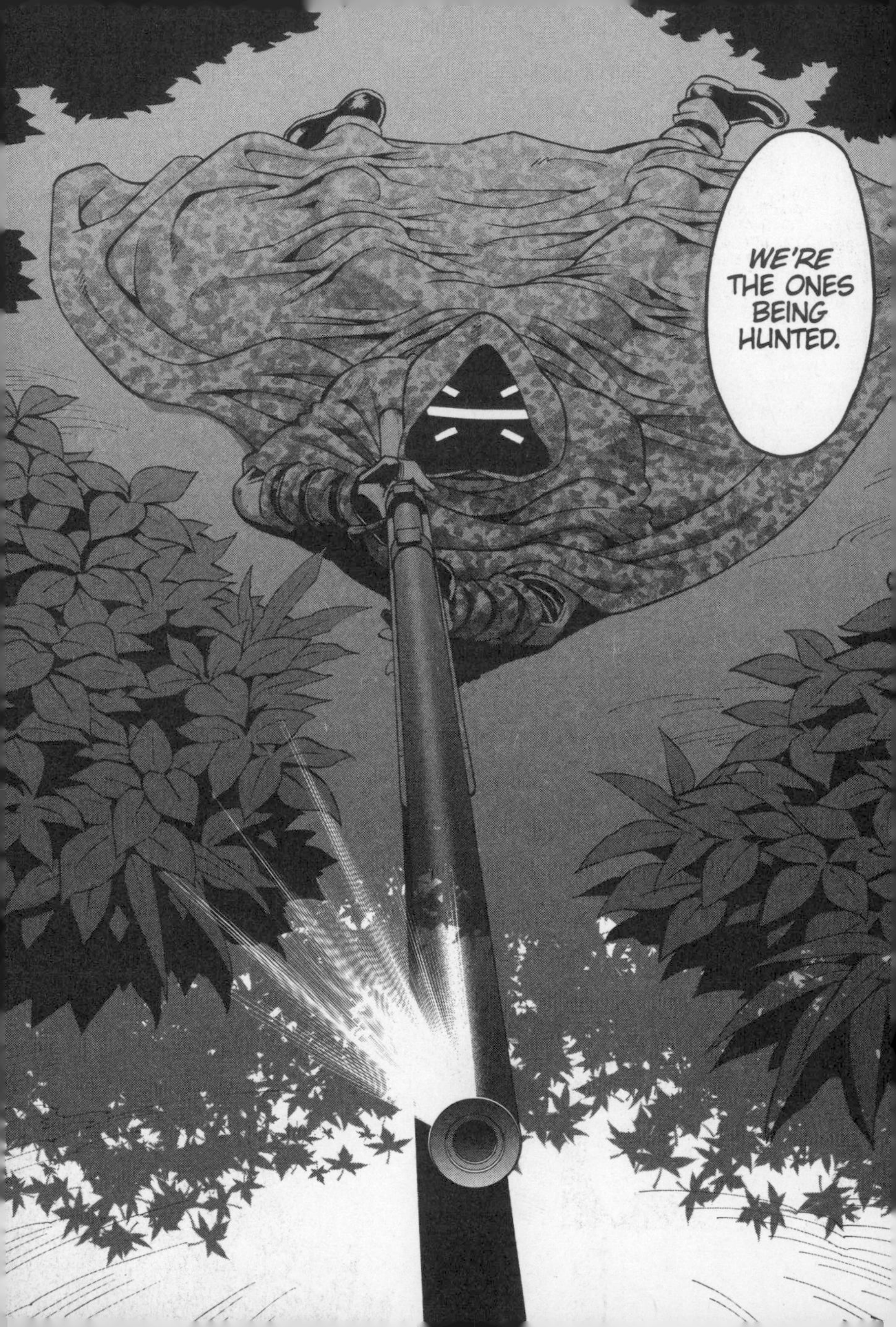
WE'RE THE ONES BEING HUNTED.

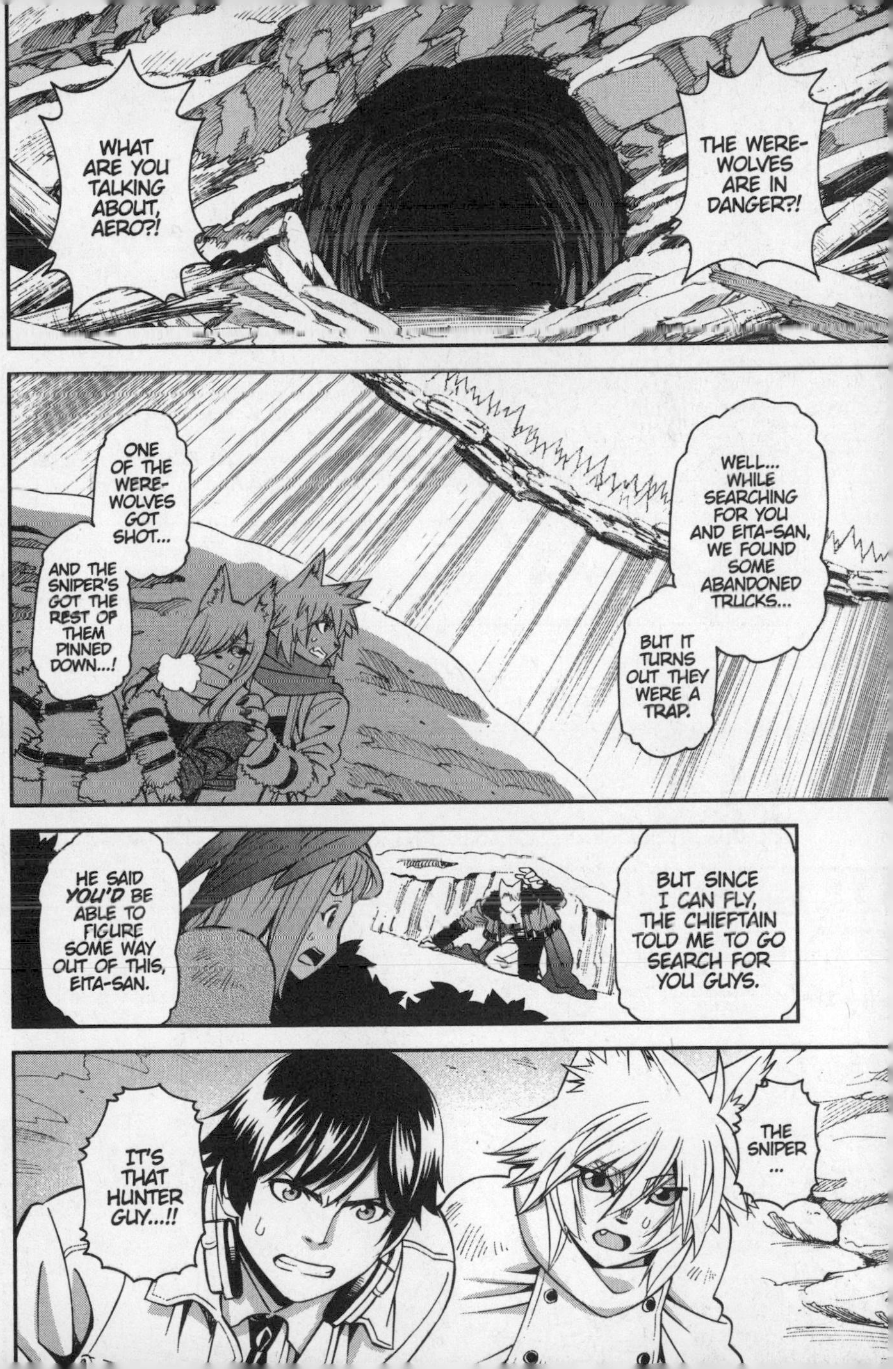
THE WERE-WOLVES ARE IN DANGER?!
WHAT ARE YOU TALKING ABOUT, AERO?!
WELL... WHILE SEARCHING FOR YOU AND EITA-SAN, WE FOUND SOME ABANDONED TRUCKS...
BUT IT TURNS OUT THEY WERE A TRAP.
ONE OF THE WERE-WOLVES GOT SHOT...
AND THE SNIPER'S GOT THE REST OF THEM PINNED DOWN...!
BUT SINCE I CAN FLY, THE CHIEFTAIN TOLD ME TO GO SEARCH FOR YOU GUYS.
HE SAID *YOU'D* BE ABLE TO FIGURE SOME WAY OUT OF THIS, EITA-SAN.
THE SNIPER ...
IT'S THAT HUNTER GUY...!!

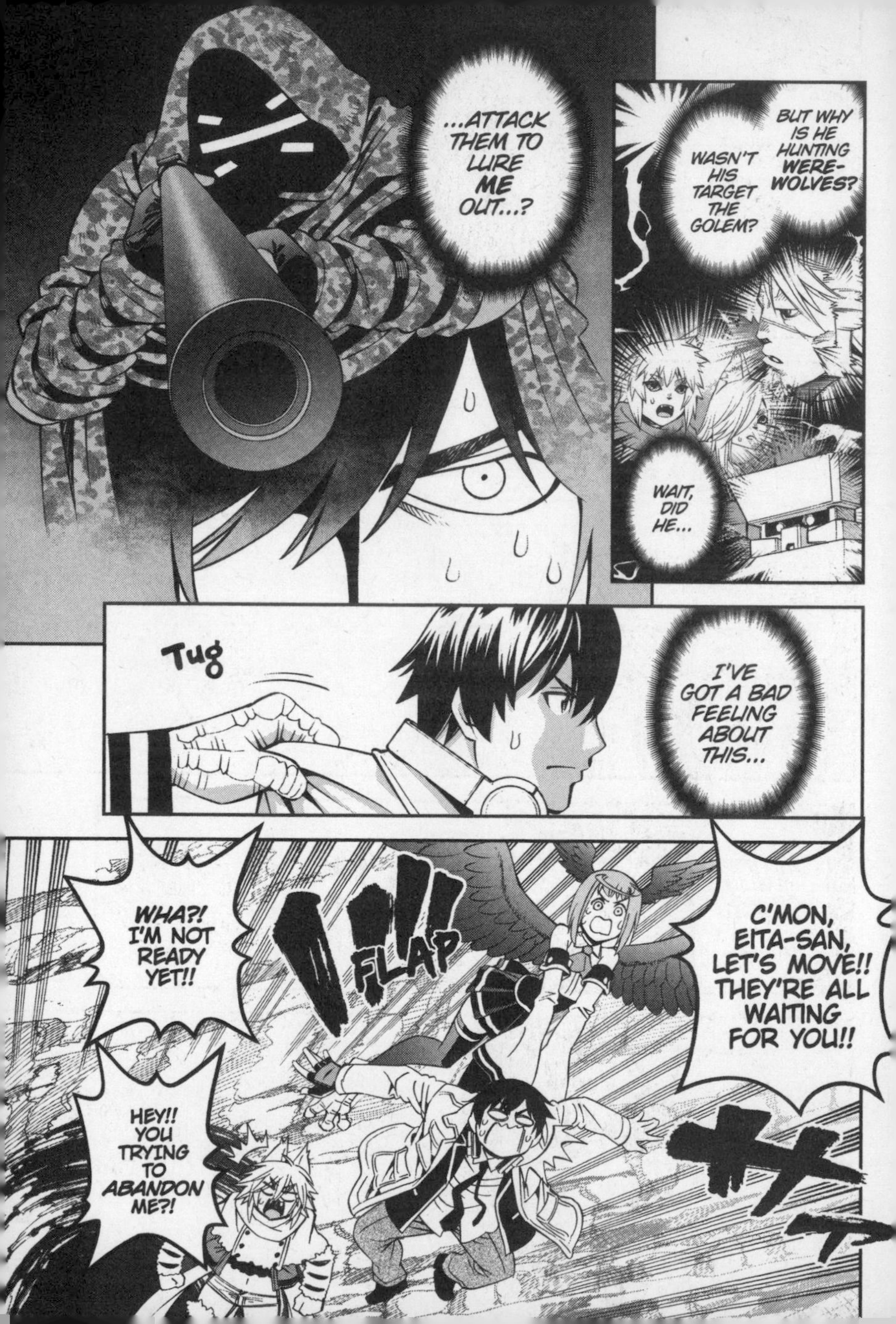
BUT WHY IS HE HUNTING WERE-WOLVES?
WASN'T HIS TARGET THE GOLEM?
WAIT, DID HE...
...ATTACK THEM TO LURE ME OUT...?
I'VE GOT A BAD FEELING ABOUT THIS...
Tug
C'MON, EITA-SAN, LET'S MOVE!! THEY'RE ALL WAITING FOR YOU!!
FLAP
WHA?! I'M NOT READY YET!!
HEY!! YOU TRYING TO ABANDON ME?!

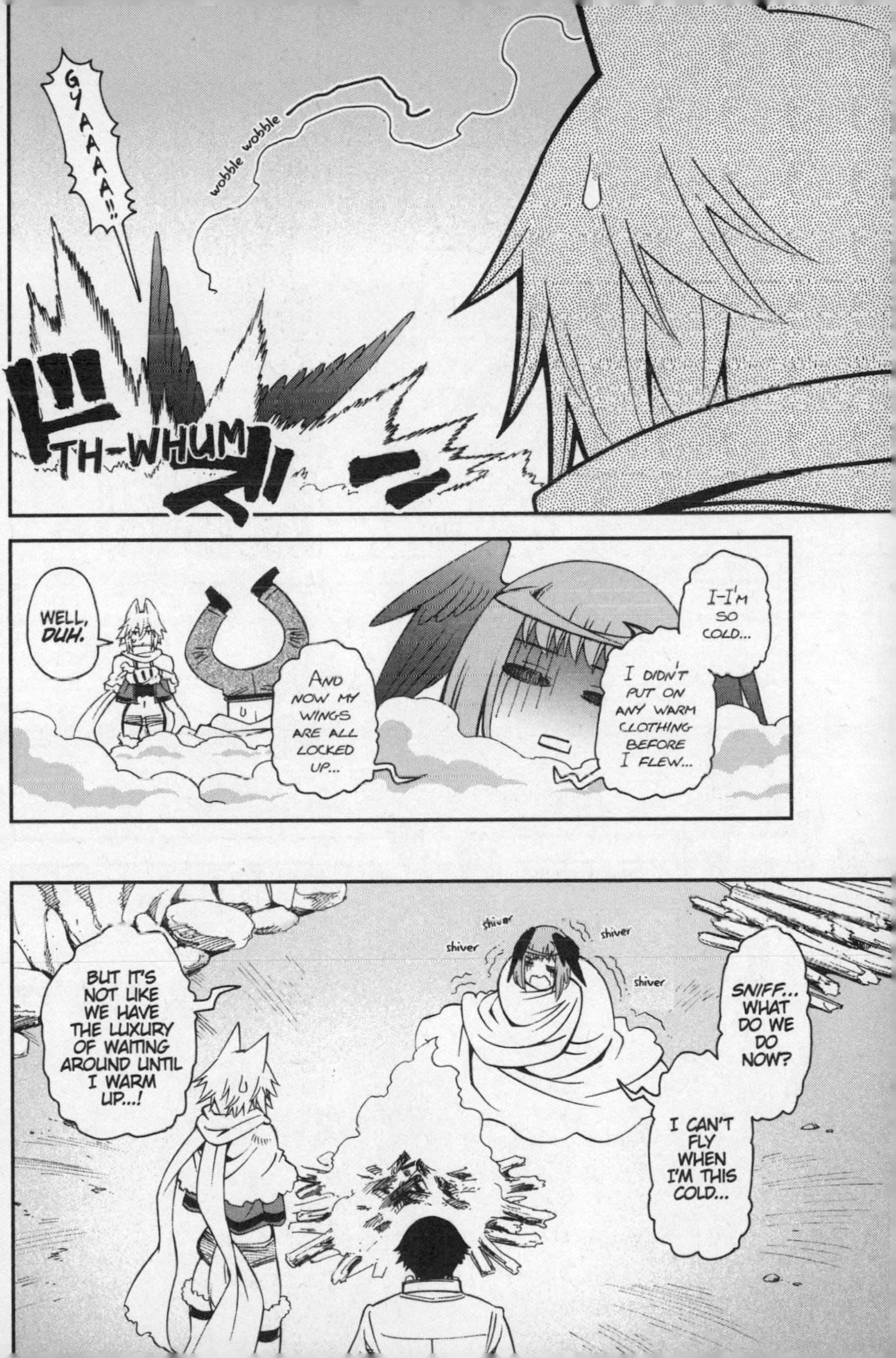
wobble wobble
GYAAAA!!
TH-WHUM
I-I'M SO COLD...
I DIDN'T PUT ON ANY WARM CLOTHING BEFORE I FLEW...
AND NOW MY WINGS ARE ALL LOCKED UP...
WELL, DUH.
shiver shiver shiver shiver
SNIFF... WHAT DO WE DO NOW?
I CAN'T FLY WHEN I'M THIS COLD...
BUT IT'S NOT LIKE WE HAVE THE LUXURY OF WAITING AROUND UNTIL I WARM UP...!

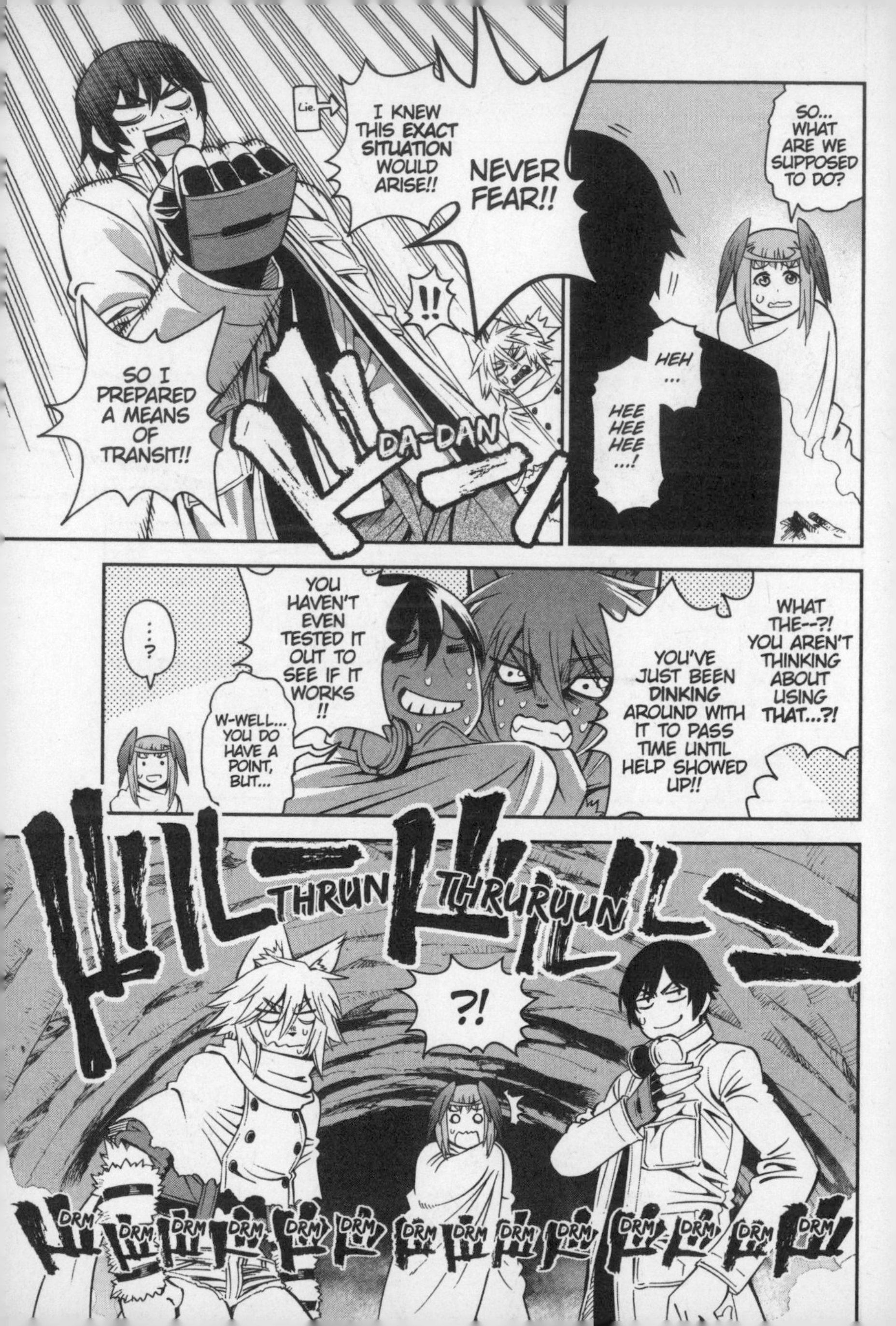
SO... WHAT ARE WE SUPPOSED TO DO?
HEH... HEE HEE HEE...!
NEVER FEAR!!
Lie.
I KNEW THIS EXACT SITUATION WOULD ARISE!!
!!
SO I PREPARED A MEANS OF TRANSIT!!
DA-DAN
WHAT THE--?! YOU AREN'T THINKING ABOUT USING THAT...?!
YOU'VE JUST BEEN DINKING AROUND WITH IT TO PASS TIME UNTIL HELP SHOWED UP!!
YOU HAVEN'T EVEN TESTED IT OUT TO SEE IF IT WORKS!!
...?
W-WELL... YOU DO HAVE A POINT, BUT...
THRUN
THRURUUN
?!
DRM DRM DRM DRM DRM DRM DRM DRM DRM DRM DRM DRM DRM

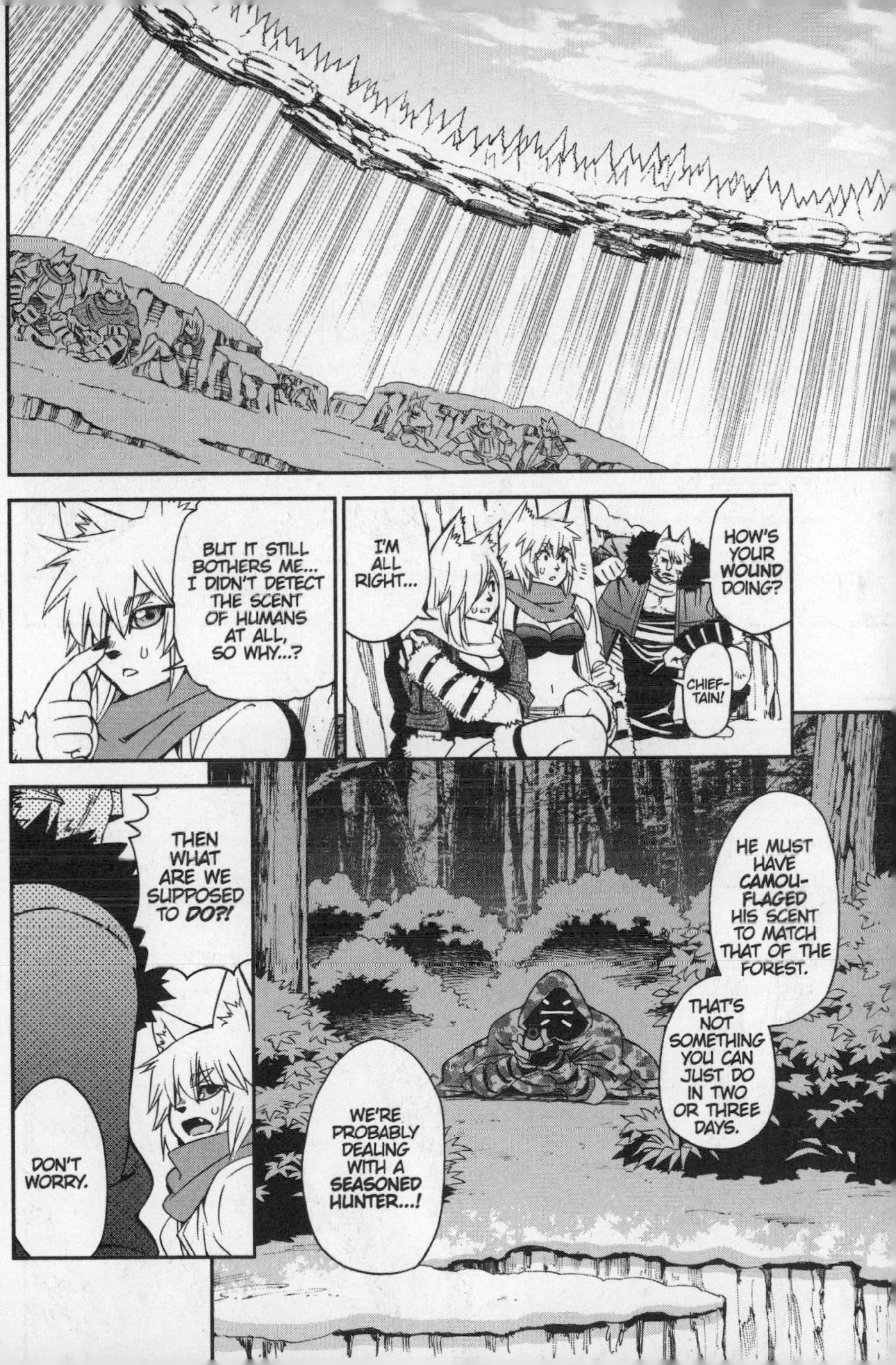
HOW'S YOUR WOUND DOING?
CHIEF-TAIN!
I'M ALL RIGHT...
BUT IT STILL BOTHERS ME... I DIDN'T DETECT THE SCENT OF HUMANS AT ALL, SO WHY...?
HE MUST HAVE CAMOU-FLAGED HIS SCENT TO MATCH THAT OF THE FOREST.
THAT'S NOT SOMETHING YOU CAN JUST DO IN TWO OR THREE DAYS.
WE'RE PROBABLY DEALING WITH A SEASONED HUNTER...!
THEN WHAT ARE WE SUPPOSED TO DO?!
DON'T WORRY.

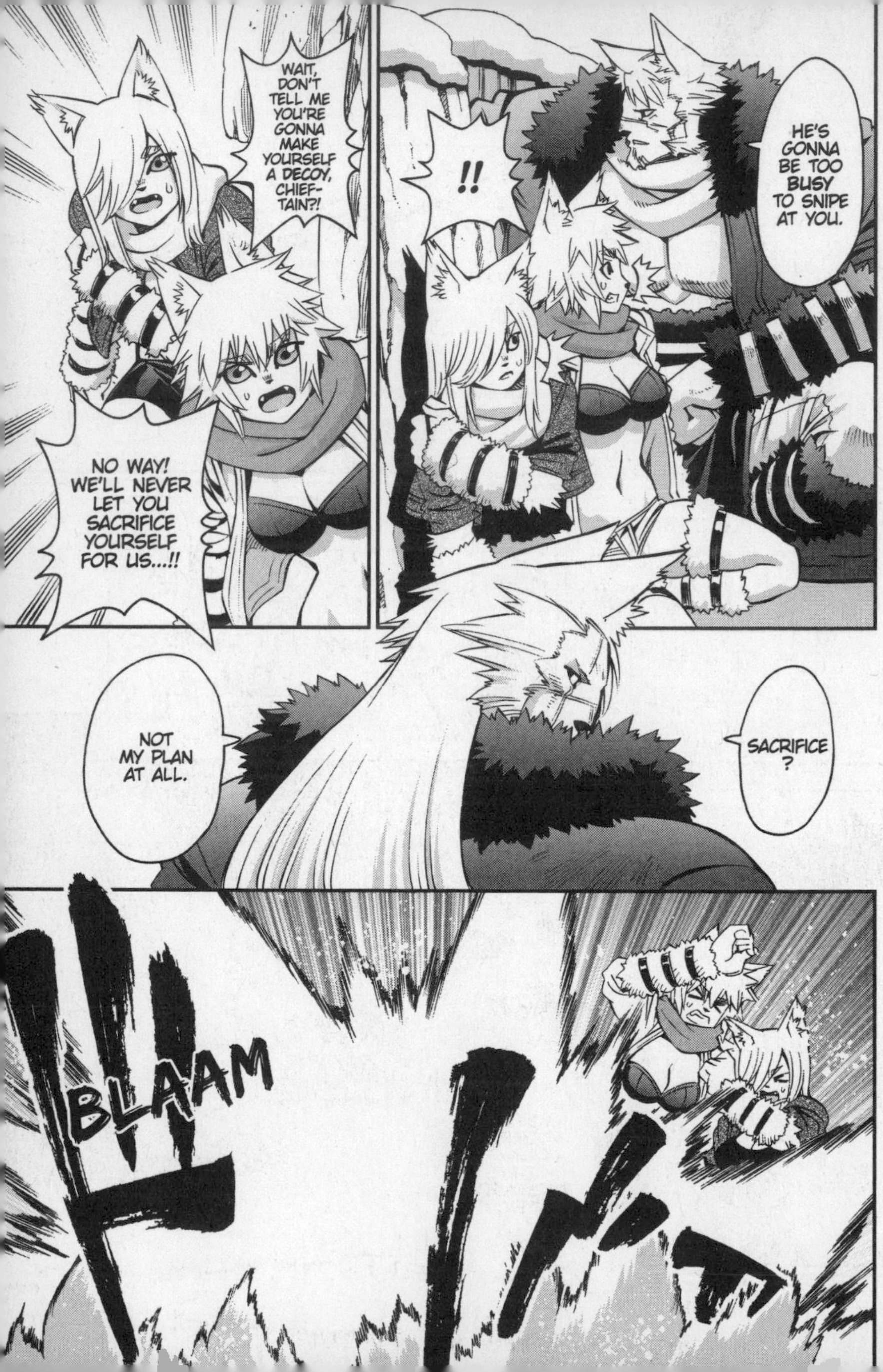
HE'S GONNA BE TOO BUSY TO SNIPE AT YOU.
!!
WAIT, DON'T TELL ME YOU'RE GONNA MAKE YOURSELF A DECOY, CHIEF-TAIN?!
NO WAY! WE'LL NEVER LET YOU SACRIFICE YOURSELF FOR US...!!
SACRIFICE?
NOT MY PLAN AT ALL.
BLAAM

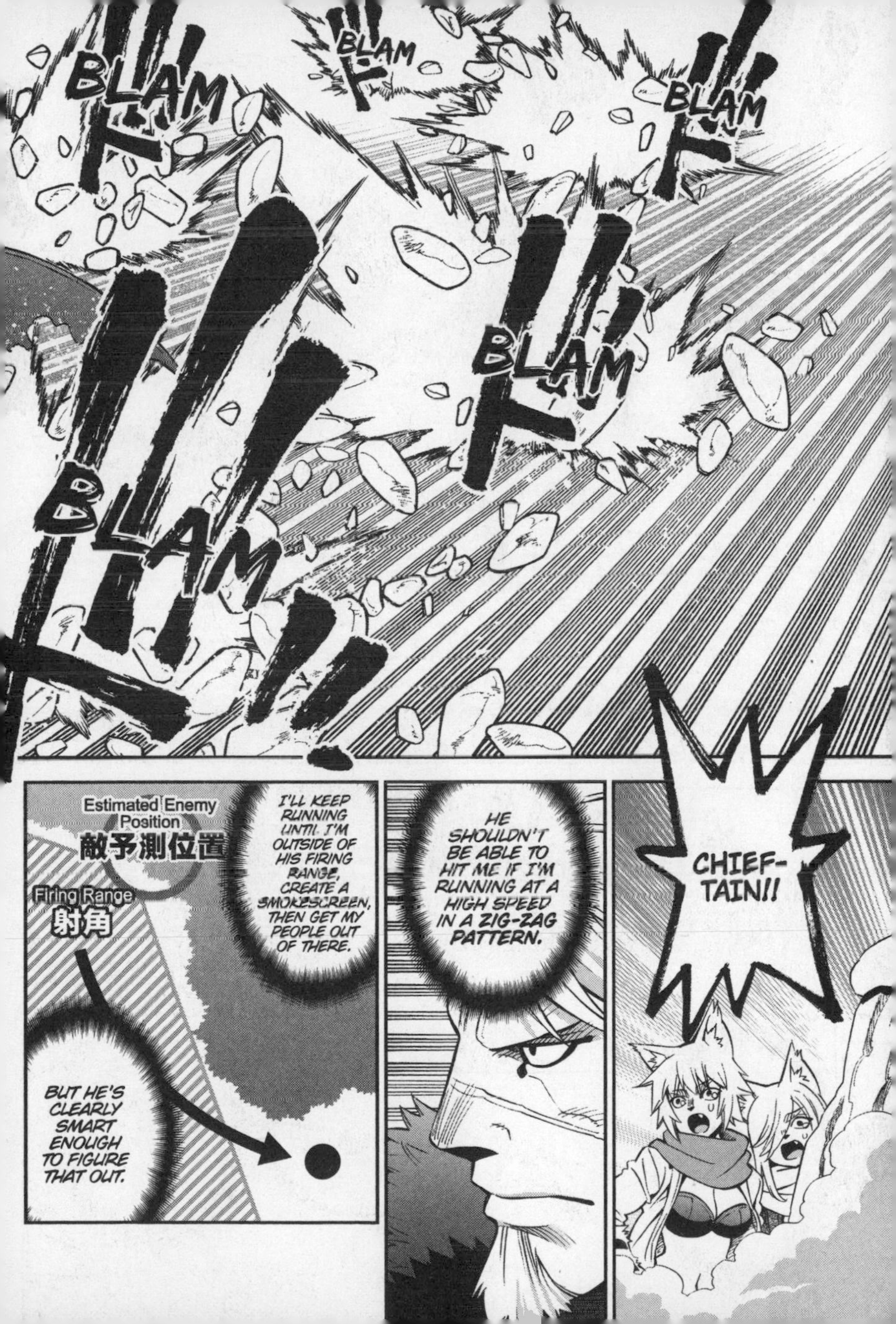
BLAM
BLAM
BLAM
BLAM
BLAM
CHIEF-TAIN!!
HE SHOULDN'T BE ABLE TO HIT ME IF I'M RUNNING AT A HIGH SPEED IN A ZIG-ZAG PATTERN.
I'LL KEEP RUNNING UNTIL I'M OUTSIDE OF HIS FIRING RANGE, CREATE A SMOKESCREEN, THEN GET MY PEOPLE OUT OF THERE.
Estimated Enemy Position
敵予測位置
Firing Range
射角
BUT HE'S CLEARLY SMART ENOUGH TO FIGURE THAT OUT.

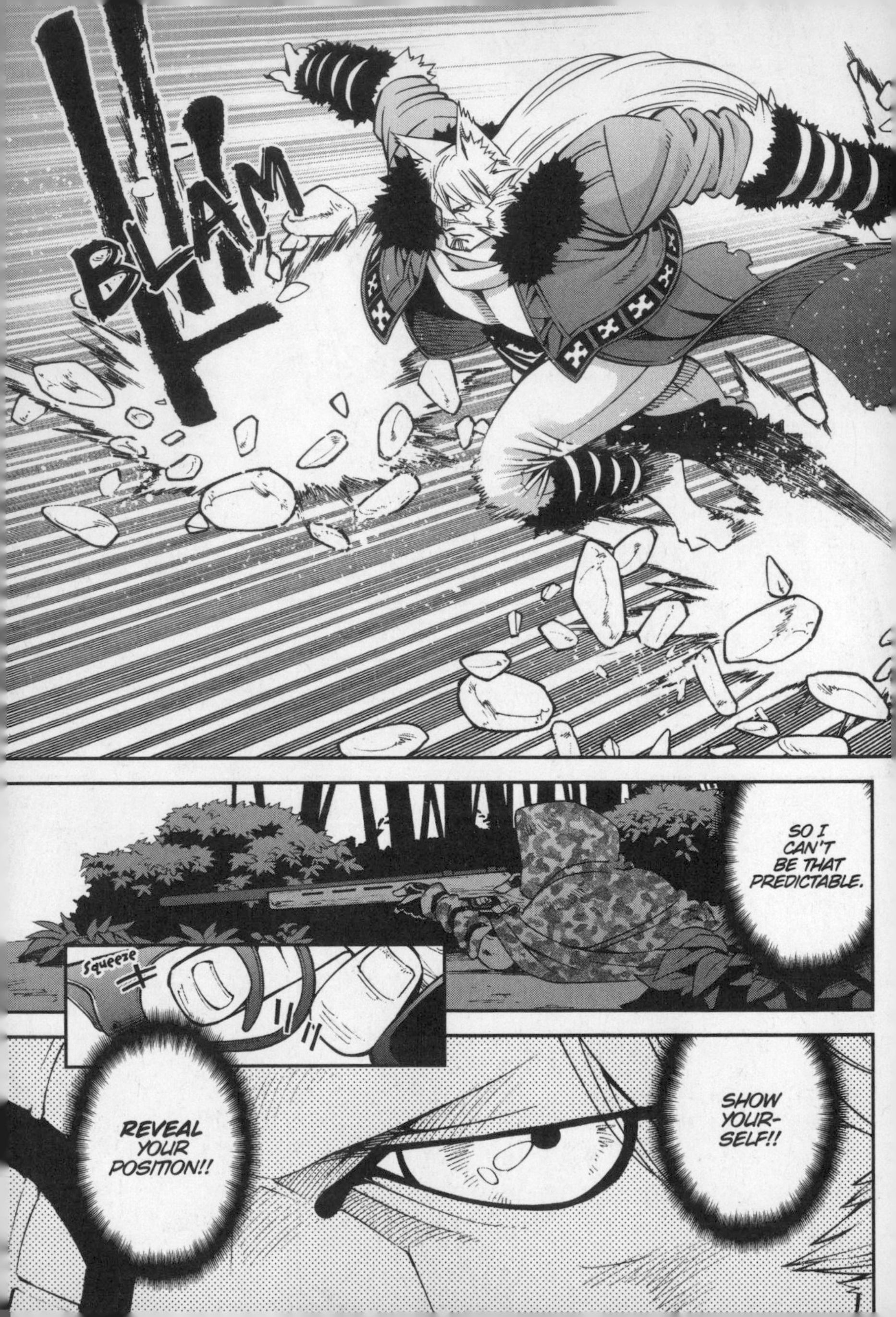
BLAM
SO I CAN'T BE THAT PREDICTABLE.
Squeeze
SHOW YOUR-SELF!!
REVEAL YOUR POSITION!!

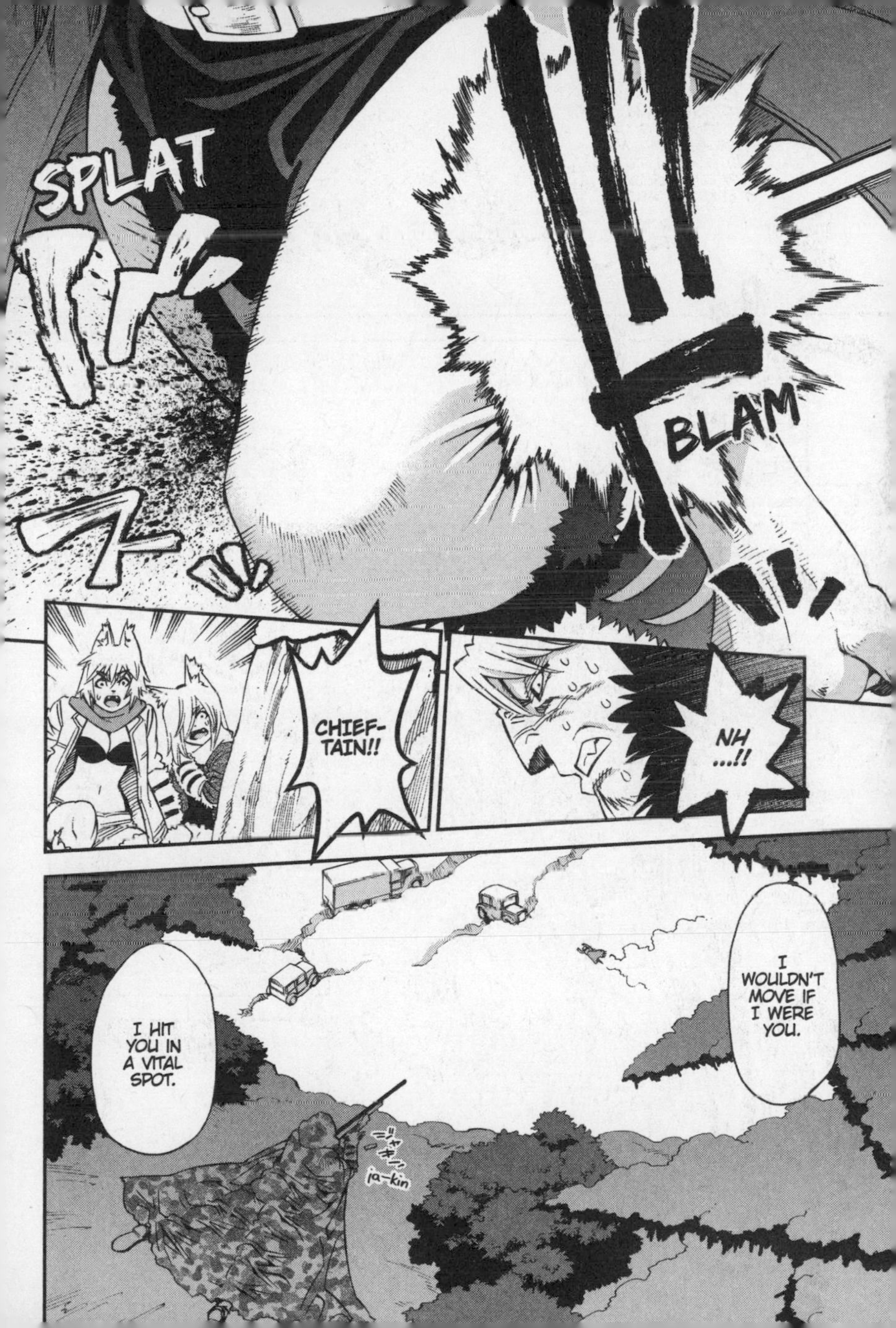
BLAM
SPLAT
NH ...!!
CHIEF-TAIN!!
I WOULDN'T MOVE IF I WERE YOU.
I HIT YOU IN A VITAL SPOT.
ja-kin

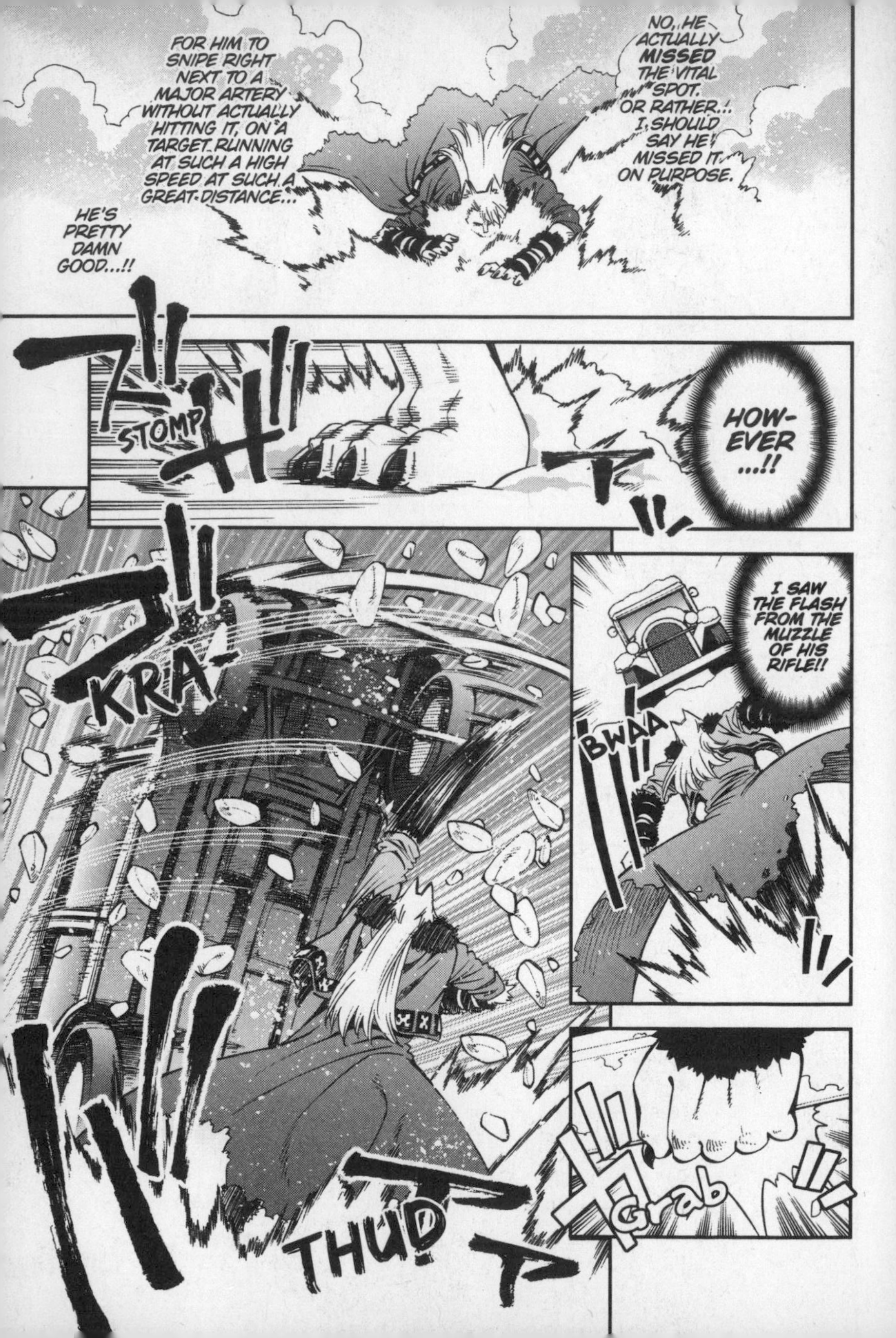
NO, HE ACTUALLY MISSED THE VITAL SPOT. OR RATHER... I SHOULD SAY HE MISSED IT ON PURPOSE.
FOR HIM TO SNIPE RIGHT NEXT TO A MAJOR ARTERY WITHOUT ACTUALLY HITTING IT, ON A TARGET RUNNING AT SUCH A HIGH SPEED AT SUCH A GREAT DISTANCE...
HE'S PRETTY DAMN GOOD...!!
HOW-EVER...!!
STOMP
I SAW THE FLASH FROM THE MUZZLE OF HIS RIFLE!!
BWAA
KRA
Grab
THUD

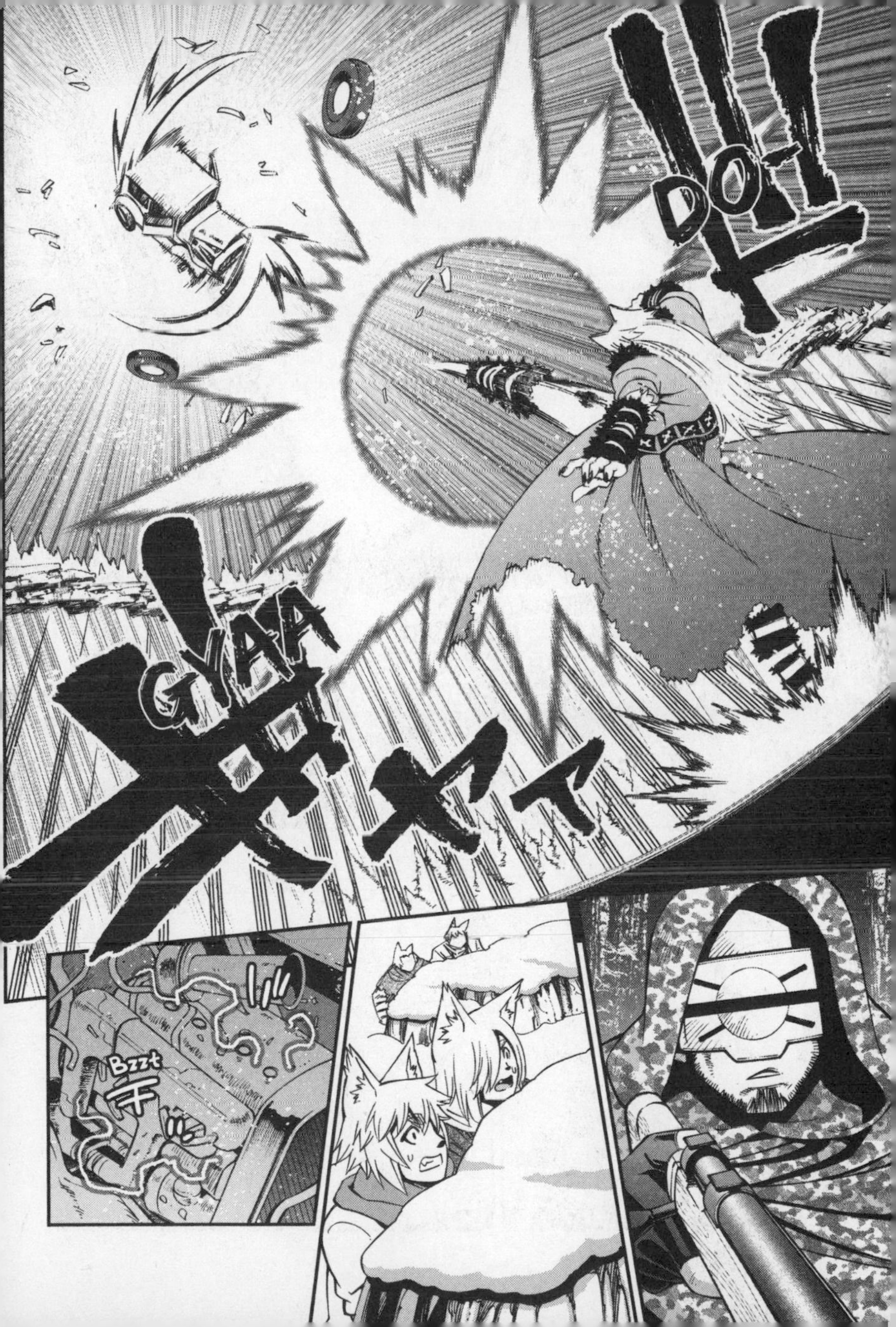
DOH!!
GYAA
Bzzt

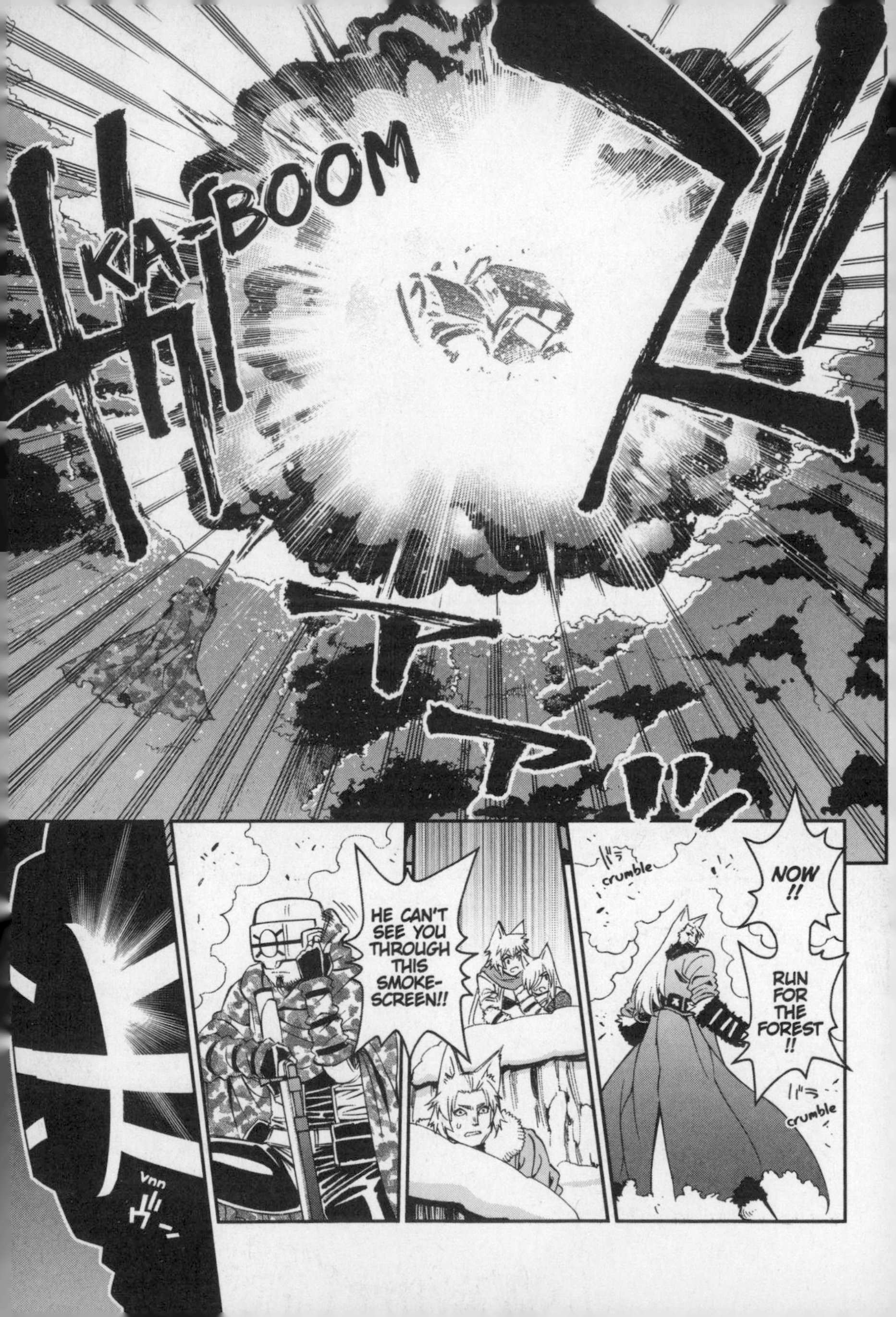
KA-BOOM
crumble
NOW!!
RUN FOR THE FOREST!!
crumble
HE CAN'T SEE YOU THROUGH THIS SMOKE-SCREEN!!
vnn

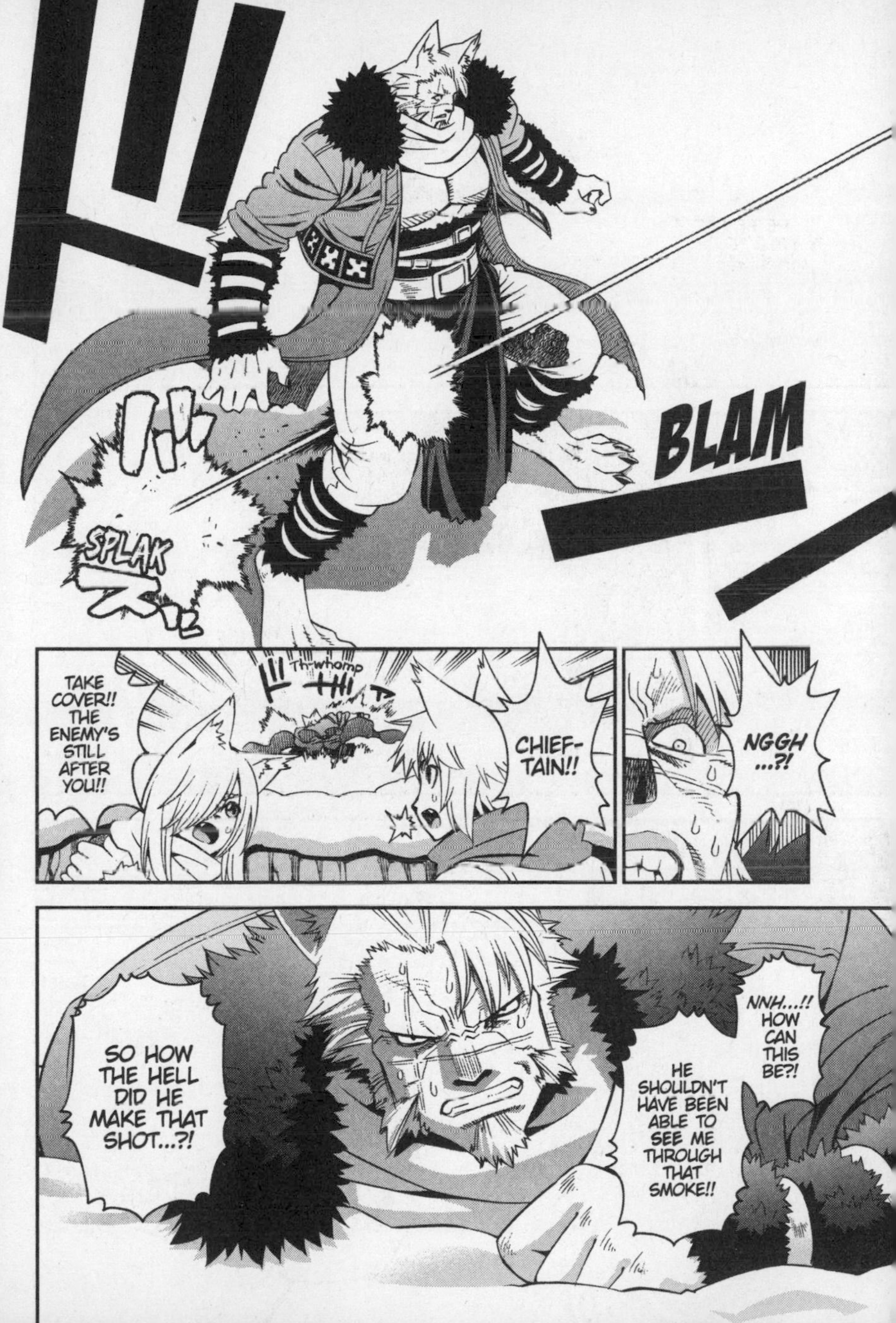
BLAM
SPLAK
NGGH ...?!
Th-whomp
CHIEF-TAIN!!
TAKE COVER!! THE ENEMY'S STILL AFTER YOU!!
NNH...!! HOW CAN THIS BE?!
HE SHOULDN'T HAVE BEEN ABLE TO SEE ME THROUGH THAT SMOKE!!
SO HOW THE HELL DID HE MAKE THAT SHOT...?!

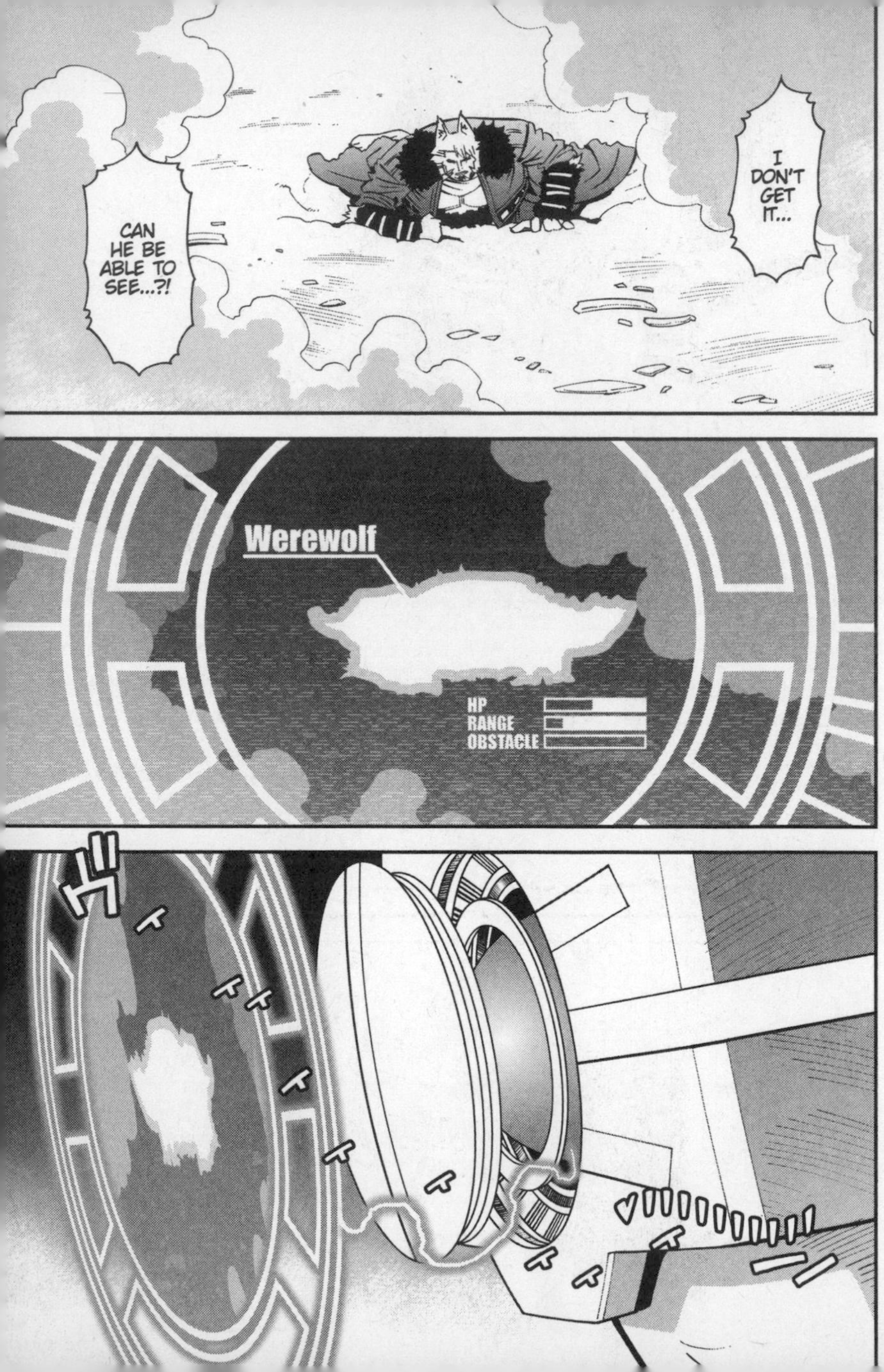
I DON'T GET IT...
CAN HE BE ABLE TO SEE...?!
Werewolf
HP
RANGE
OBSTACLE

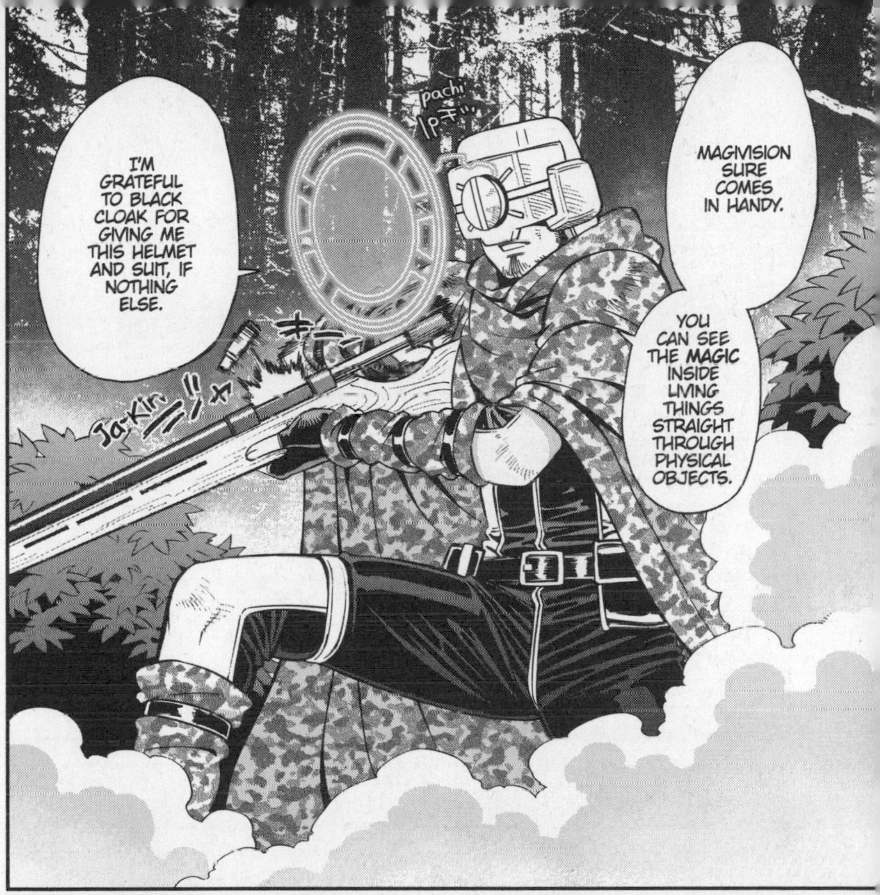
pachi
MAGIVISION SURE COMES IN HANDY.
YOU CAN SEE THE MAGIC INSIDE LIVING THINGS STRAIGHT THROUGH PHYSICAL OBJECTS.
I'M GRATEFUL TO BLACK CLOAK FOR GIVING ME THIS HELMET AND SUIT, IF NOTHING ELSE.
Ja-kin
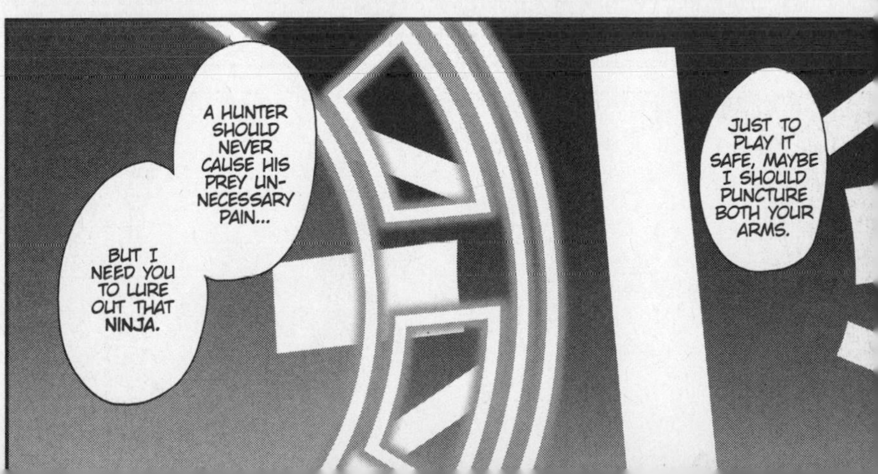
JUST TO PLAY IT SAFE, MAYBE I SHOULD PUNCTURE BOTH YOUR ARMS.
A HUNTER SHOULD NEVER CAUSE HIS PREY UN-NECESSARY PAIN...
BUT I NEED YOU TO LURE OUT THAT NINJA.

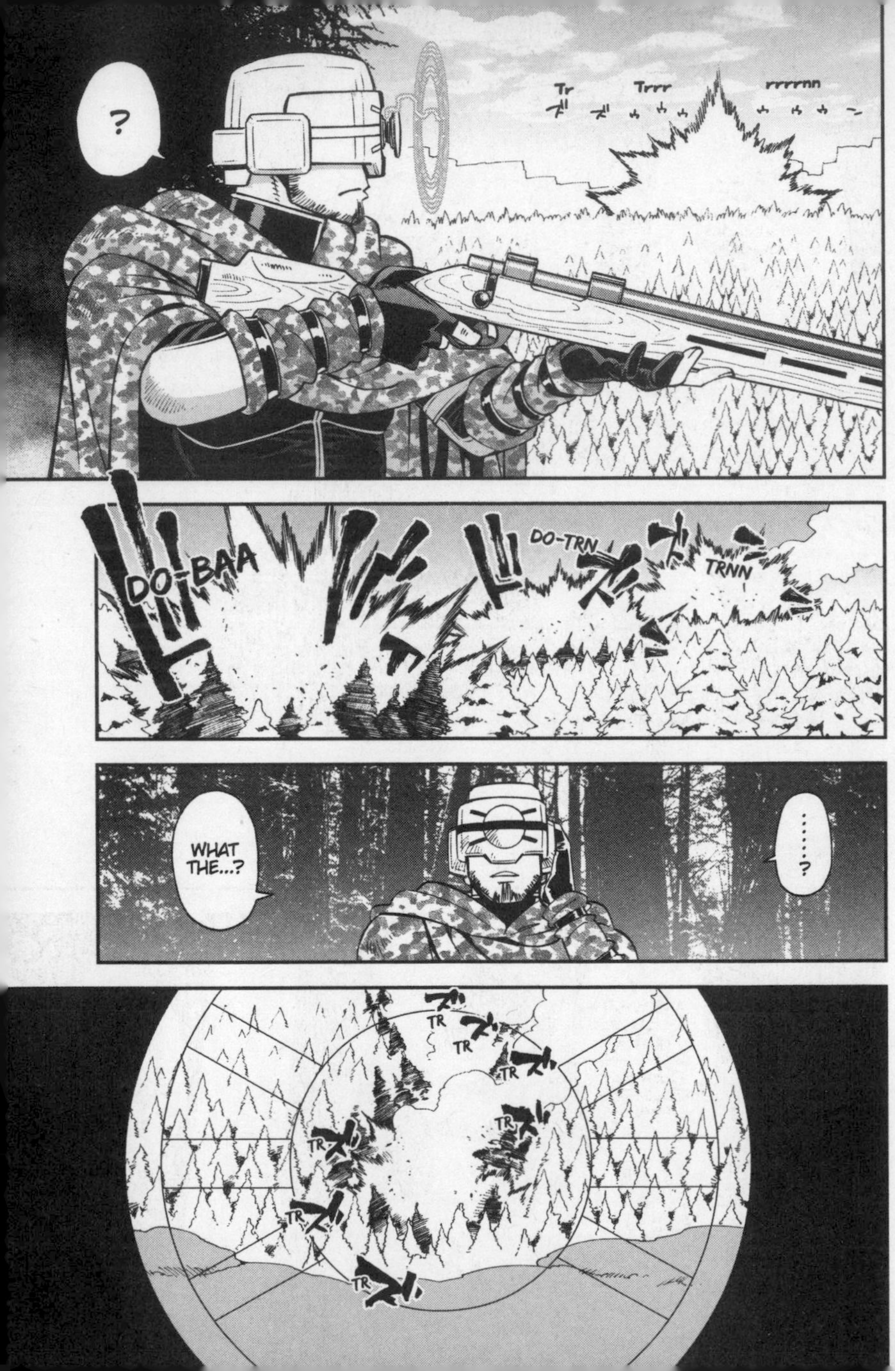
Tr Trrr rrrrnn
?
DO-TRN
TRNN
DO-BAA
......?
WHAT THE...?
TR
TR
TR
TR
TR
TR
TR

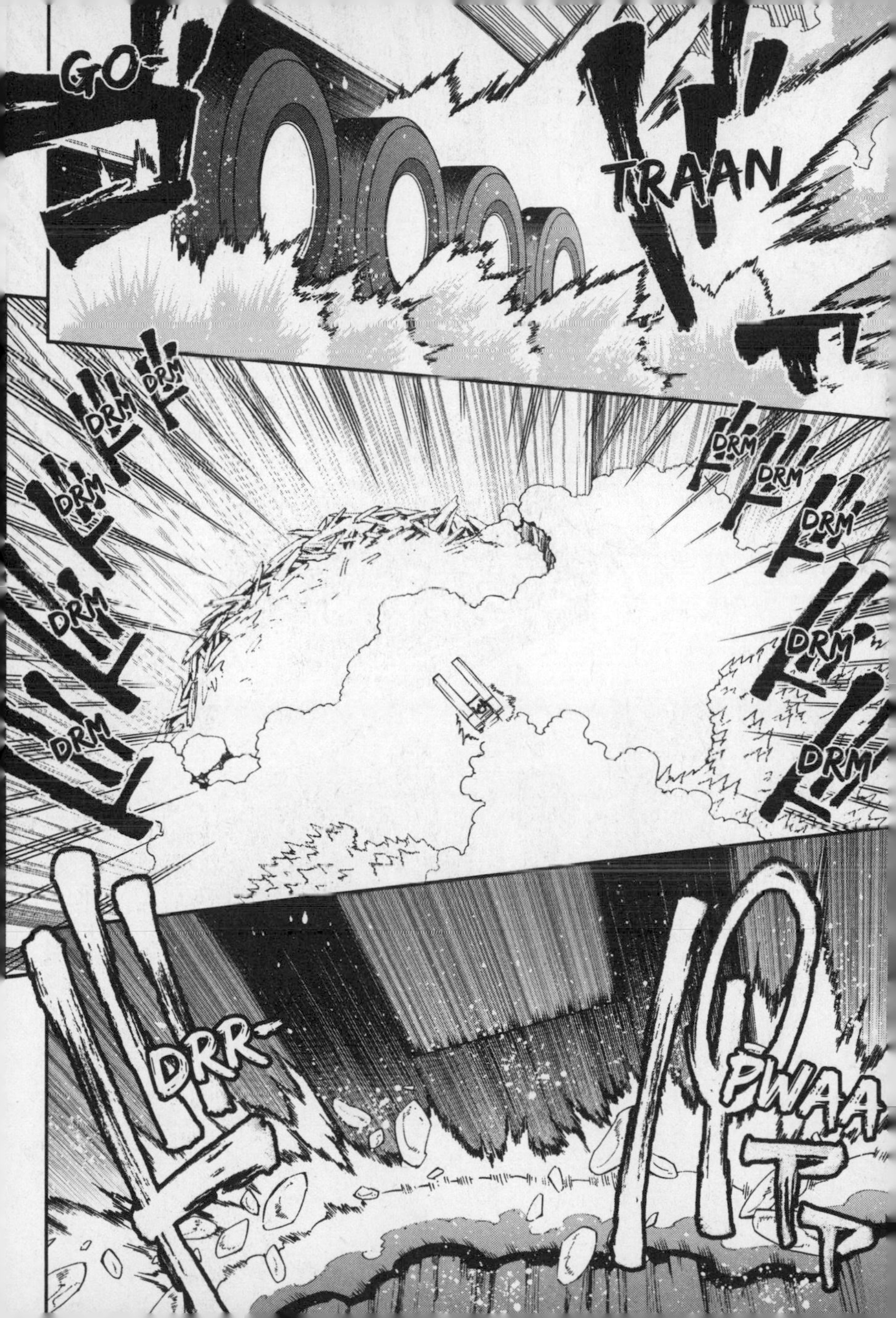
GO-
TRAAN
DRM
DRM
DRM
DRM
DRM
DRM
DRM
DRM
DRM
DRM
PWAAT
DRR-

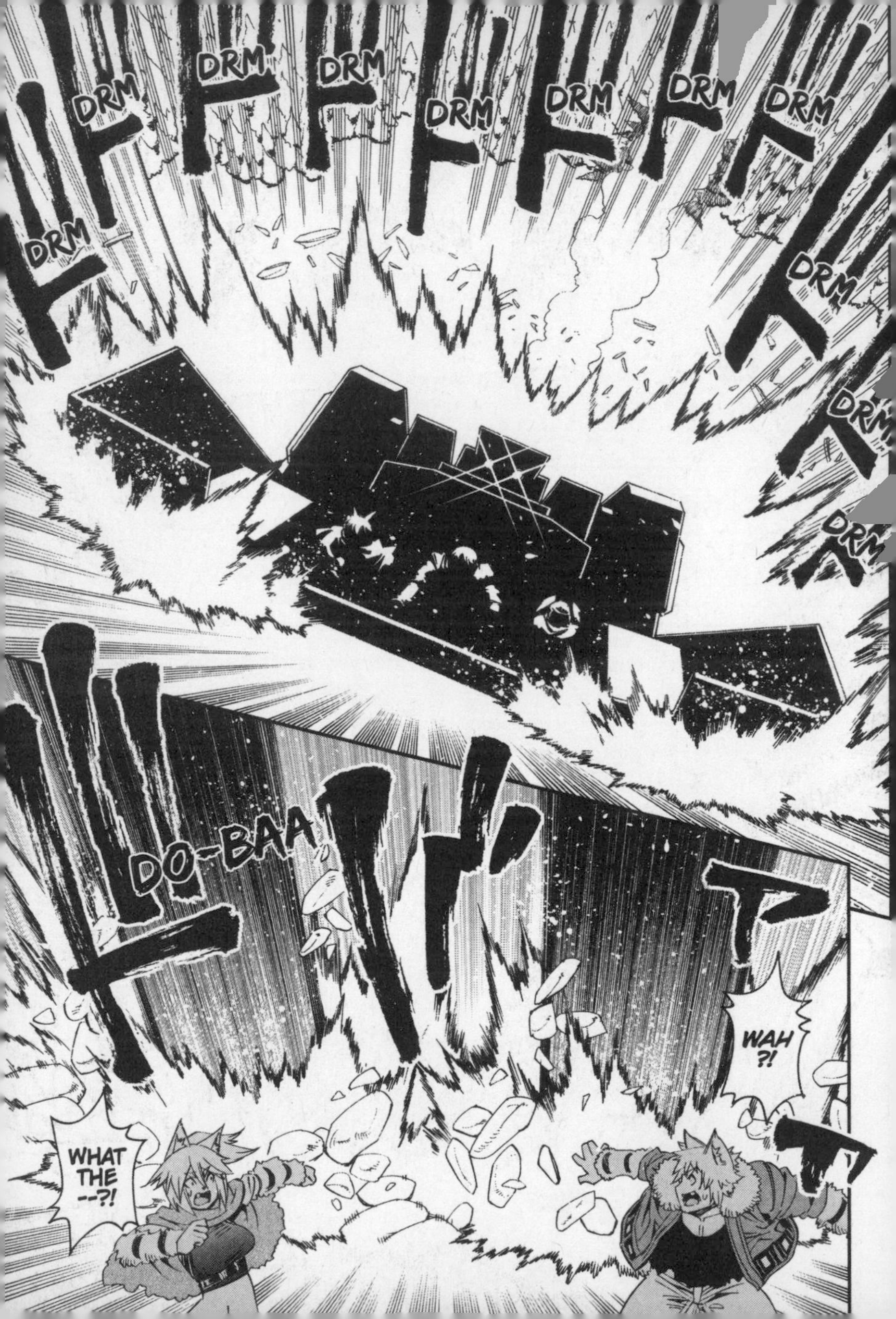
DRM
DRM
DRM
DRM
DRM
DRM
DRM
DRM
DRM
DRM
DRM
DO-BAA
WAH ?!
WHAT THE --?!

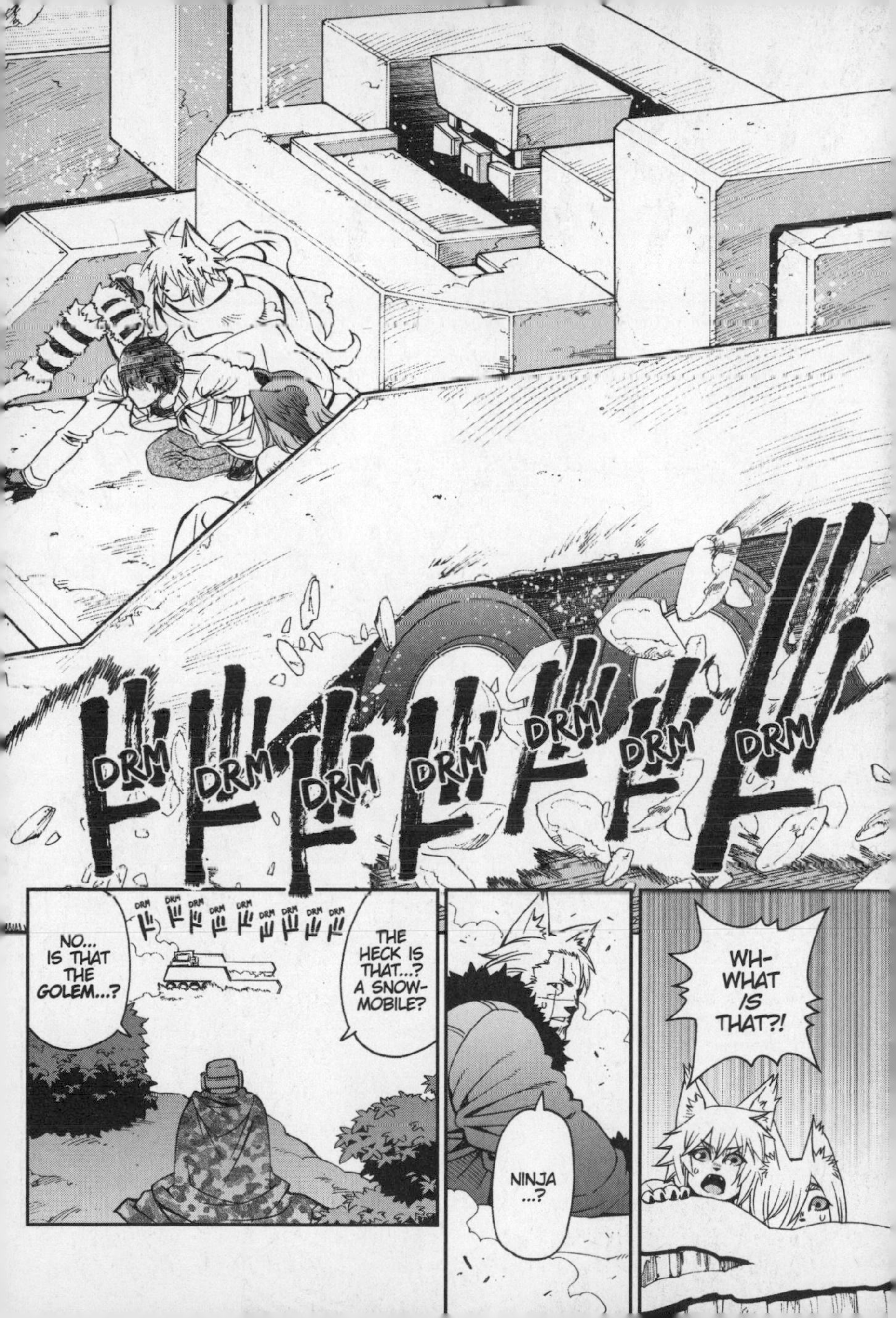
DRM DRM DRM DRM DRM DRM DRM
WH- WHAT IS THAT?!
NINJA ...?
THE HECK IS THAT...? A SNOW-MOBILE?
NO... IS THAT THE GOLEM...?
DRM DRM DRM DRM DRM DRM DRM DRM DRM

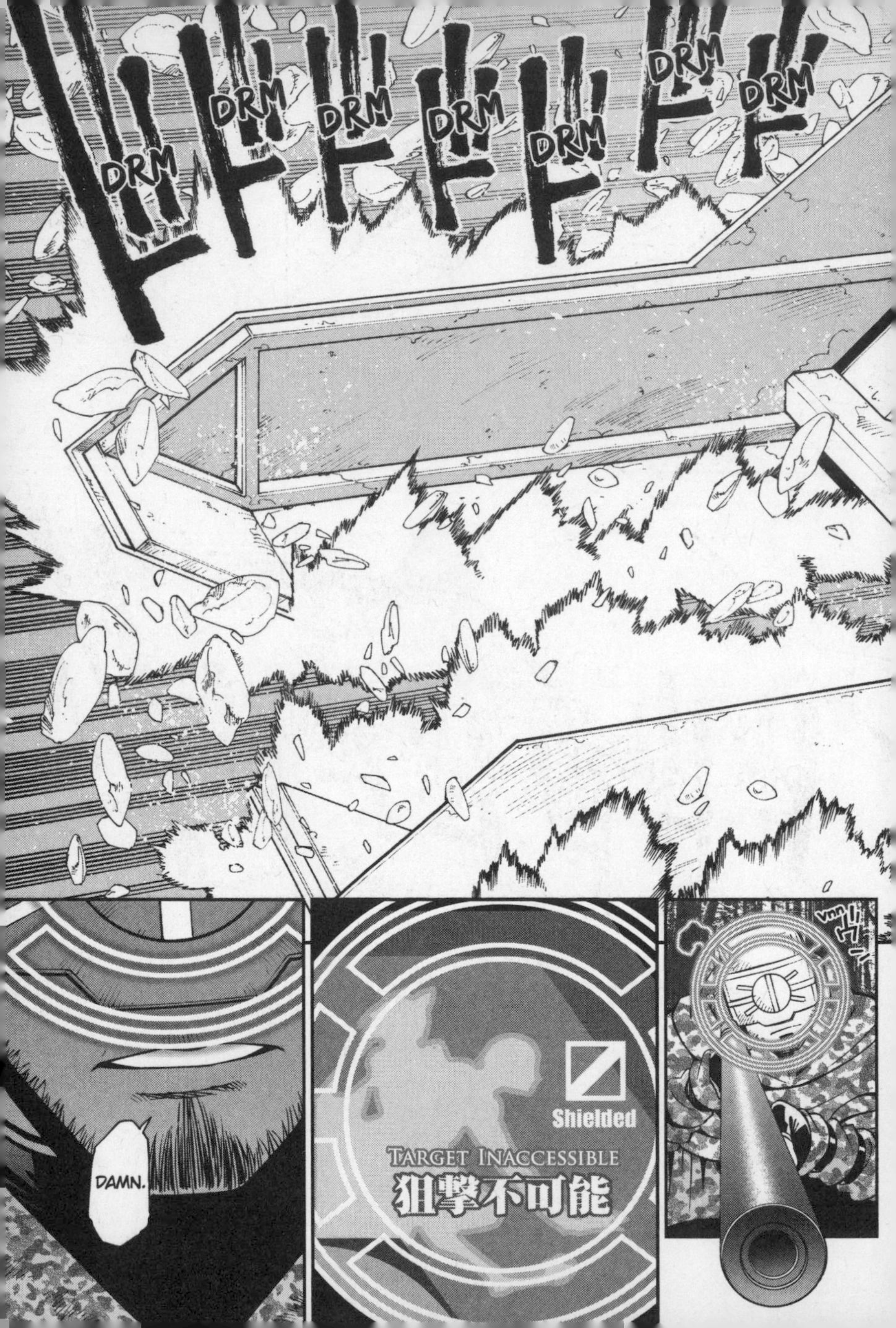
DRM
DRM
DRM
DRM
DRM
DRM
DRM
vnn
Shielded
TARGET INACCESSIBLE
狙撃不可能
DAMN.

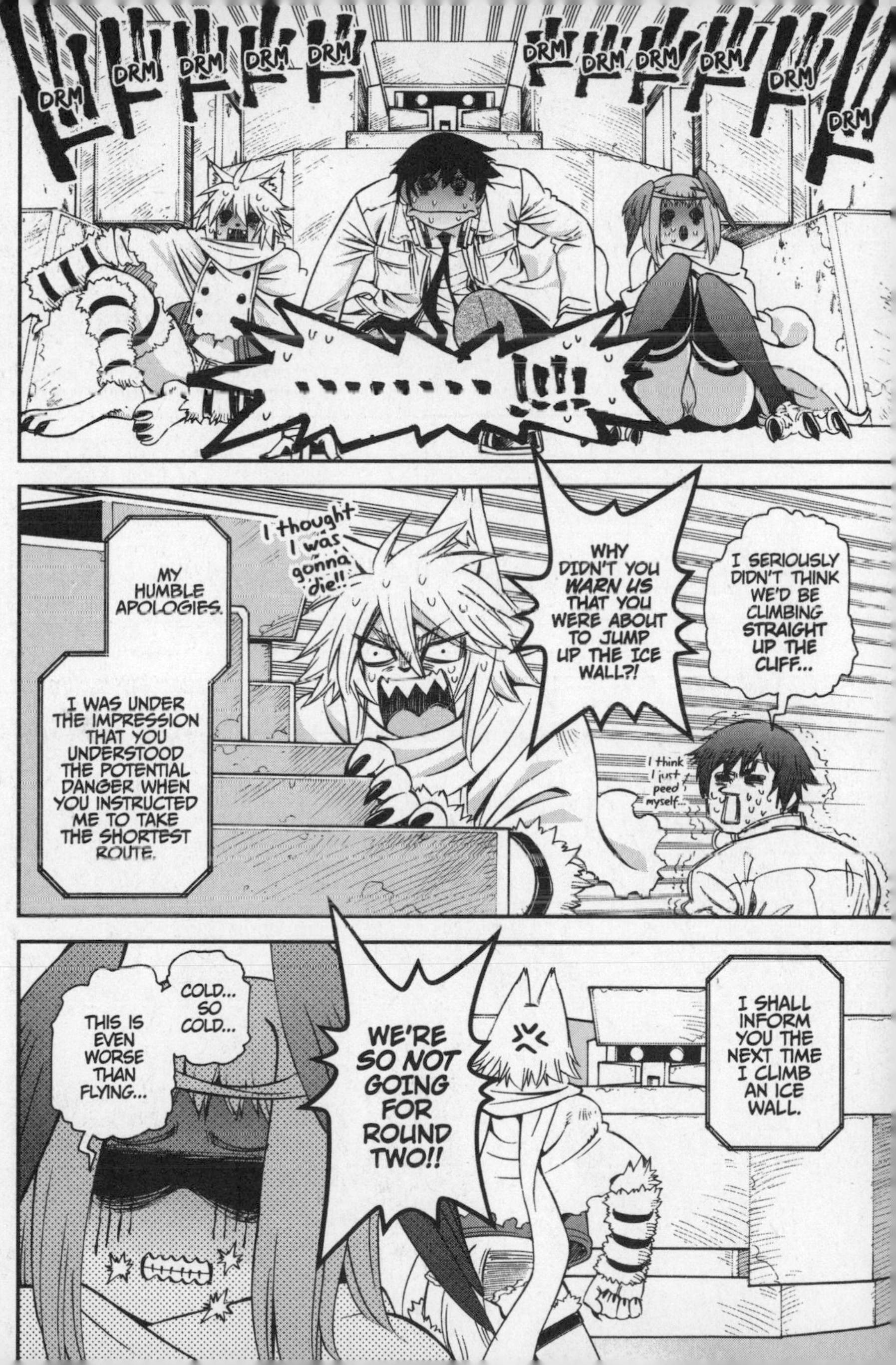
DRM DRM DRM DRM DRM DRM
DRM DRM DRM DRM DRM
..........!!!
I SERIOUSLY DIDN'T THINK WE'D BE CLIMBING STRAIGHT UP THE CLIFF...
I think I just peed myself...
WHY DIDN'T YOU *WARN US* THAT YOU WERE ABOUT TO JUMP UP THE ICE WALL?!
I thought I was gonna die!!
MY HUMBLE APOLOGIES.
I WAS UNDER THE IMPRESSION THAT YOU UNDERSTOOD THE POTENTIAL DANGER WHEN YOU INSTRUCTED ME TO TAKE THE SHORTEST ROUTE.
I SHALL INFORM YOU THE NEXT TIME I CLIMB AN ICE WALL.
WE'RE SO *NOT* GOING FOR ROUND TWO!!
COLD... SO COLD...
THIS IS EVEN WORSE THAN FLYING...

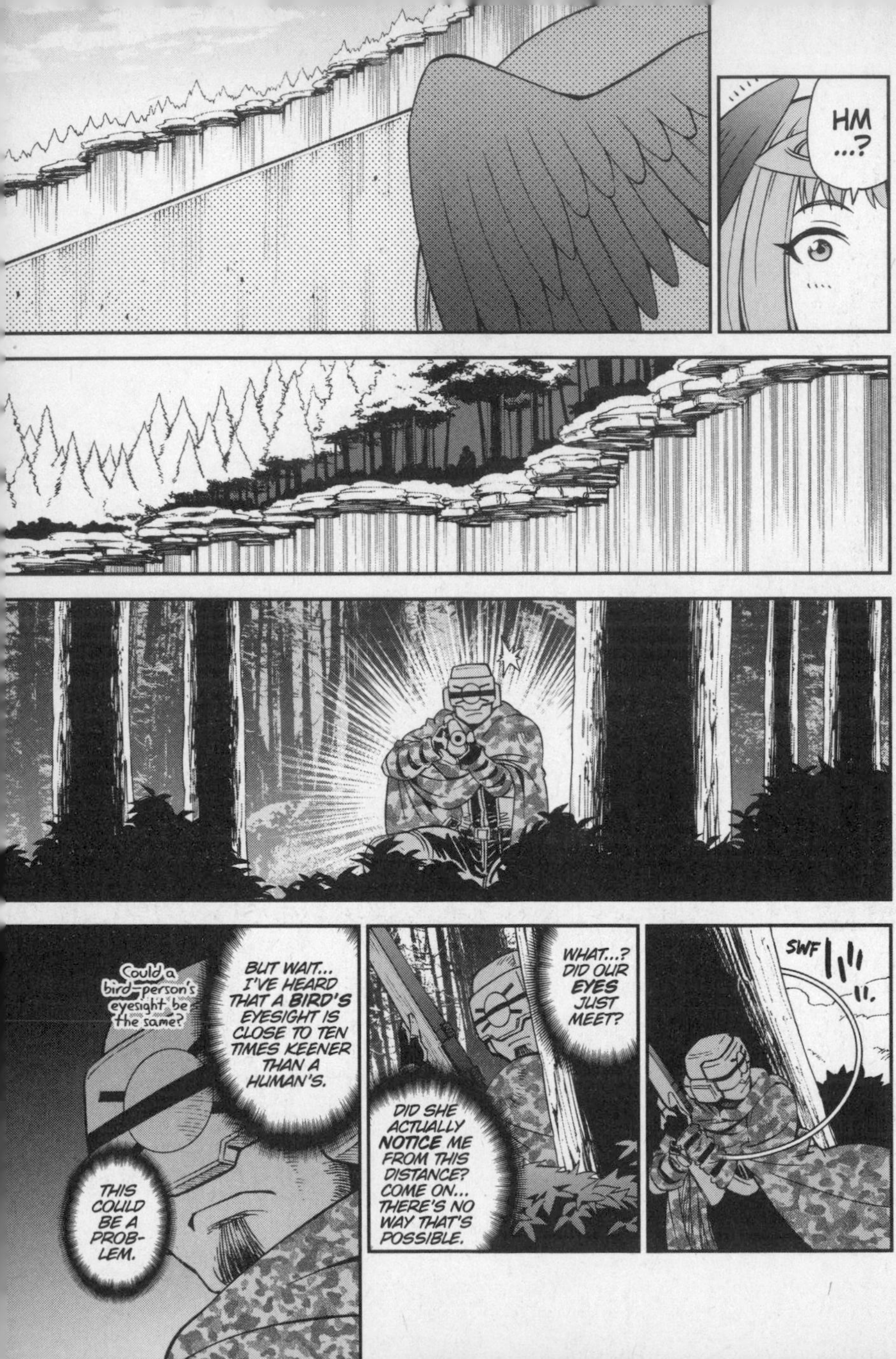
HM ...?
...
SWF
WHAT...? DID OUR EYES JUST MEET?
DID SHE ACTUALLY NOTICE ME FROM THIS DISTANCE? COME ON... THERE'S NO WAY THAT'S POSSIBLE.
BUT WAIT... I'VE HEARD THAT A BIRD'S EYESIGHT IS CLOSE TO TEN TIMES KEENER THAN A HUMAN'S.
Could a bird-person's eyesight be the same?
THIS COULD BE A PROB-LEM.

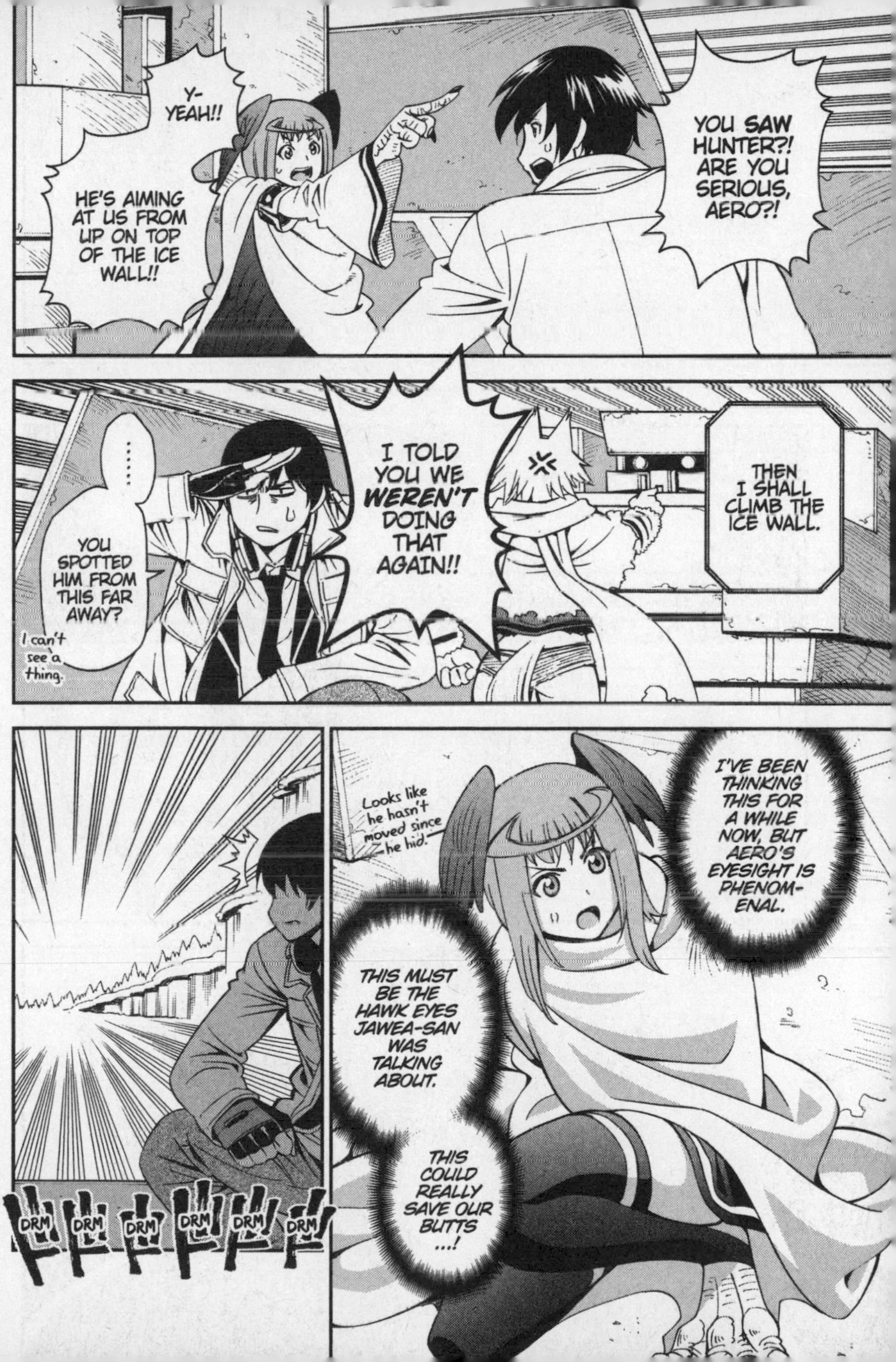
YOU SAW HUNTER?! ARE YOU SERIOUS, AERO?!
Y-YEAH!!
HE'S AIMING AT US FROM UP ON TOP OF THE ICE WALL!!
THEN I SHALL CLIMB THE ICE WALL.
I TOLD YOU WE WEREN'T DOING THAT AGAIN!!
......
YOU SPOTTED HIM FROM THIS FAR AWAY?
I can't see a thing.
I'VE BEEN THINKING THIS FOR A WHILE NOW, BUT AERO'S EYESIGHT IS PHENOMENAL.
Looks like he hasn't moved since he hid.
THIS MUST BE THE HAWK EYES JAWEA-SAN WAS TALKING ABOUT.
THIS COULD REALLY SAVE OUR BUTTS ...!
DRM DRM DRM DRM DRM DRM

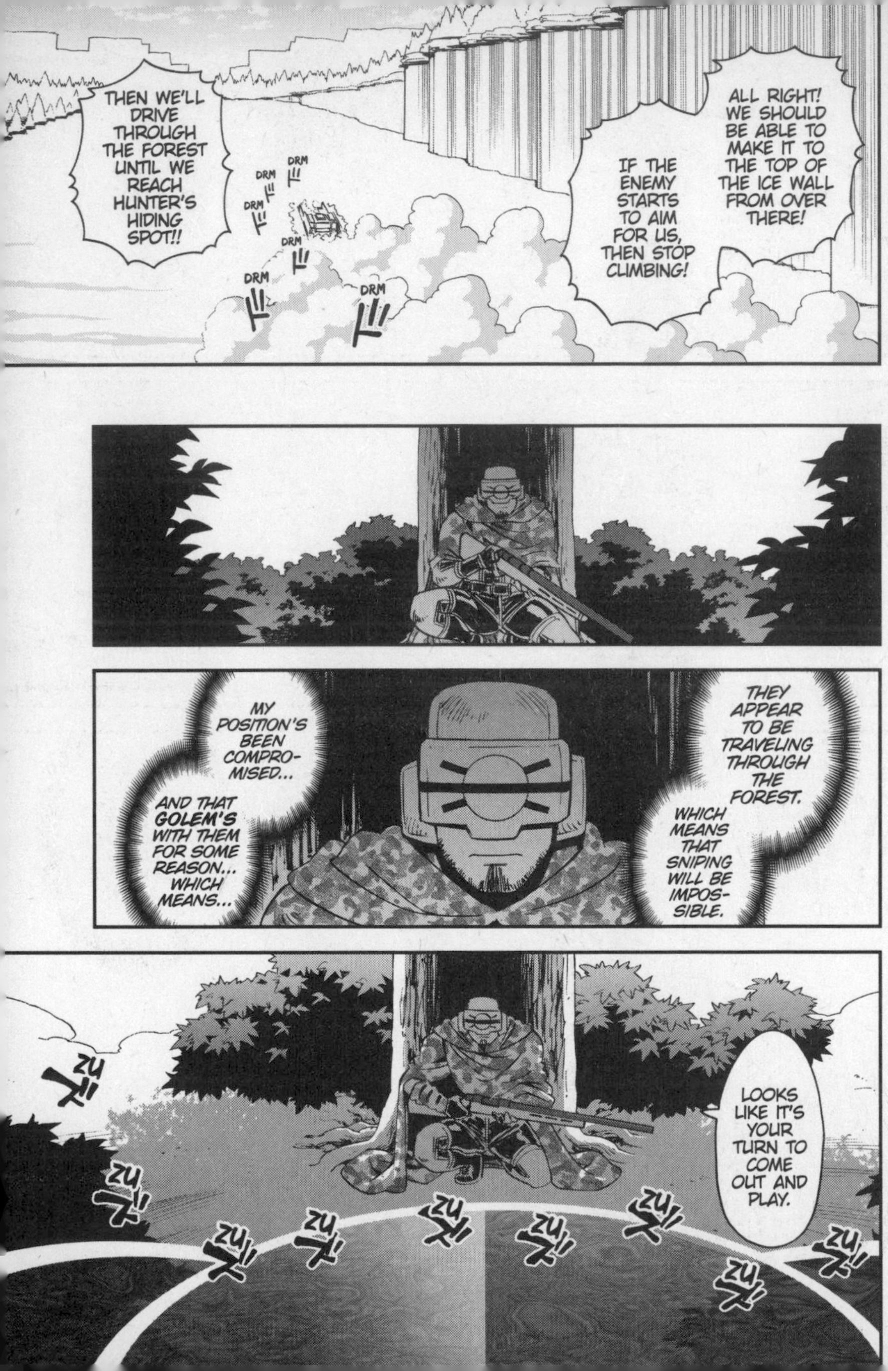
ALL RIGHT! WE SHOULD BE ABLE TO MAKE IT TO THE TOP OF THE ICE WALL FROM OVER THERE!
IF THE ENEMY STARTS TO AIM FOR US, THEN STOP CLIMBING!
THEN WE'LL DRIVE THROUGH THE FOREST UNTIL WE REACH HUNTER'S HIDING SPOT!!
DRM DRM DRM DRM DRM DRM
THEY APPEAR TO BE TRAVELING THROUGH THE FOREST.
WHICH MEANS THAT SNIPING WILL BE IMPOSSIBLE.
MY POSITION'S BEEN COMPROMISED...
AND THAT **GOLEM'S** WITH THEM FOR SOME REASON... WHICH MEANS...
LOOKS LIKE IT'S YOUR TURN TO COME OUT AND PLAY.
ZU ZU ZU ZU ZU ZU ZU ZU ZU

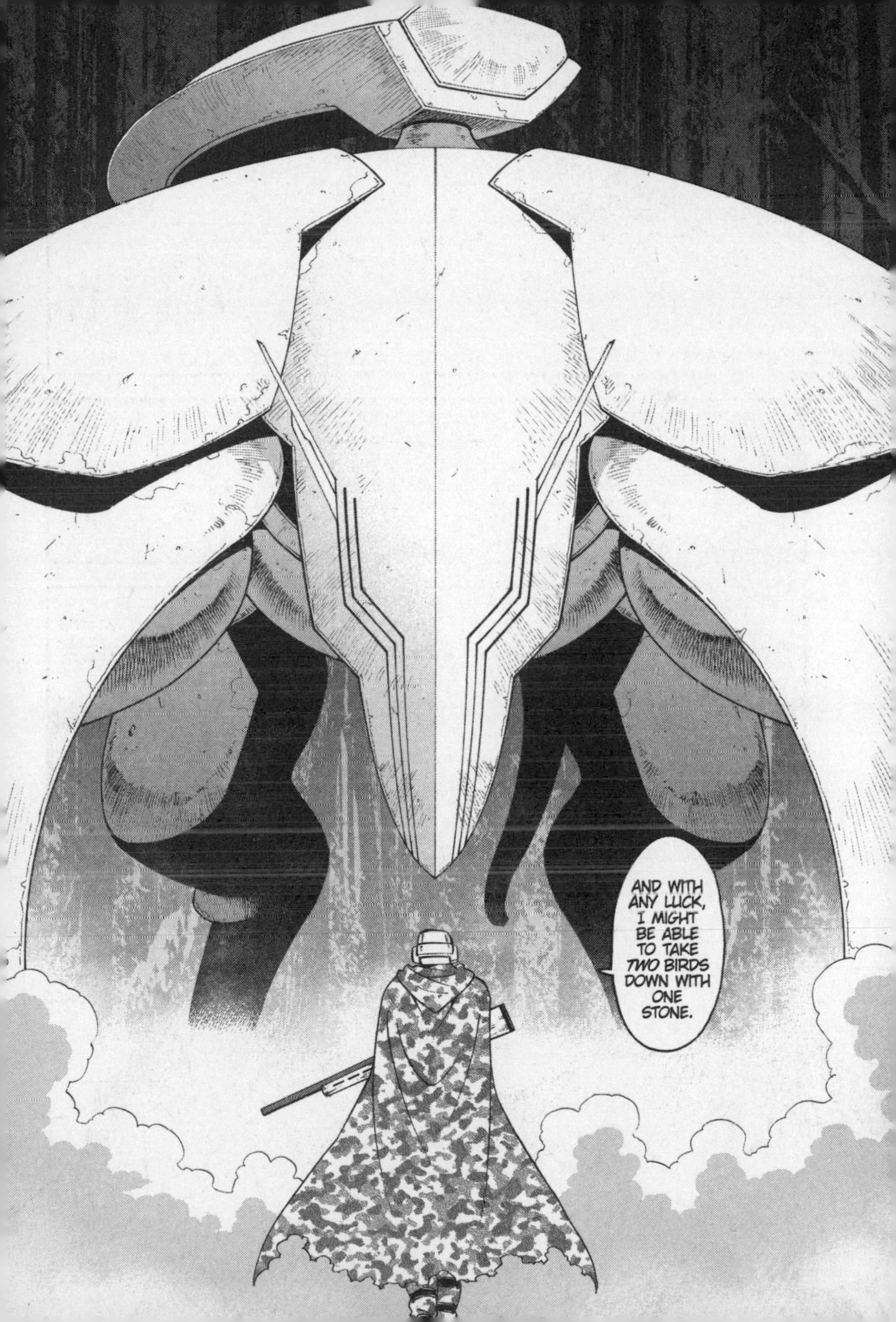
AND WITH ANY LUCK, I MIGHT BE ABLE TO TAKE *TWO* BIRDS DOWN WITH ONE STONE.

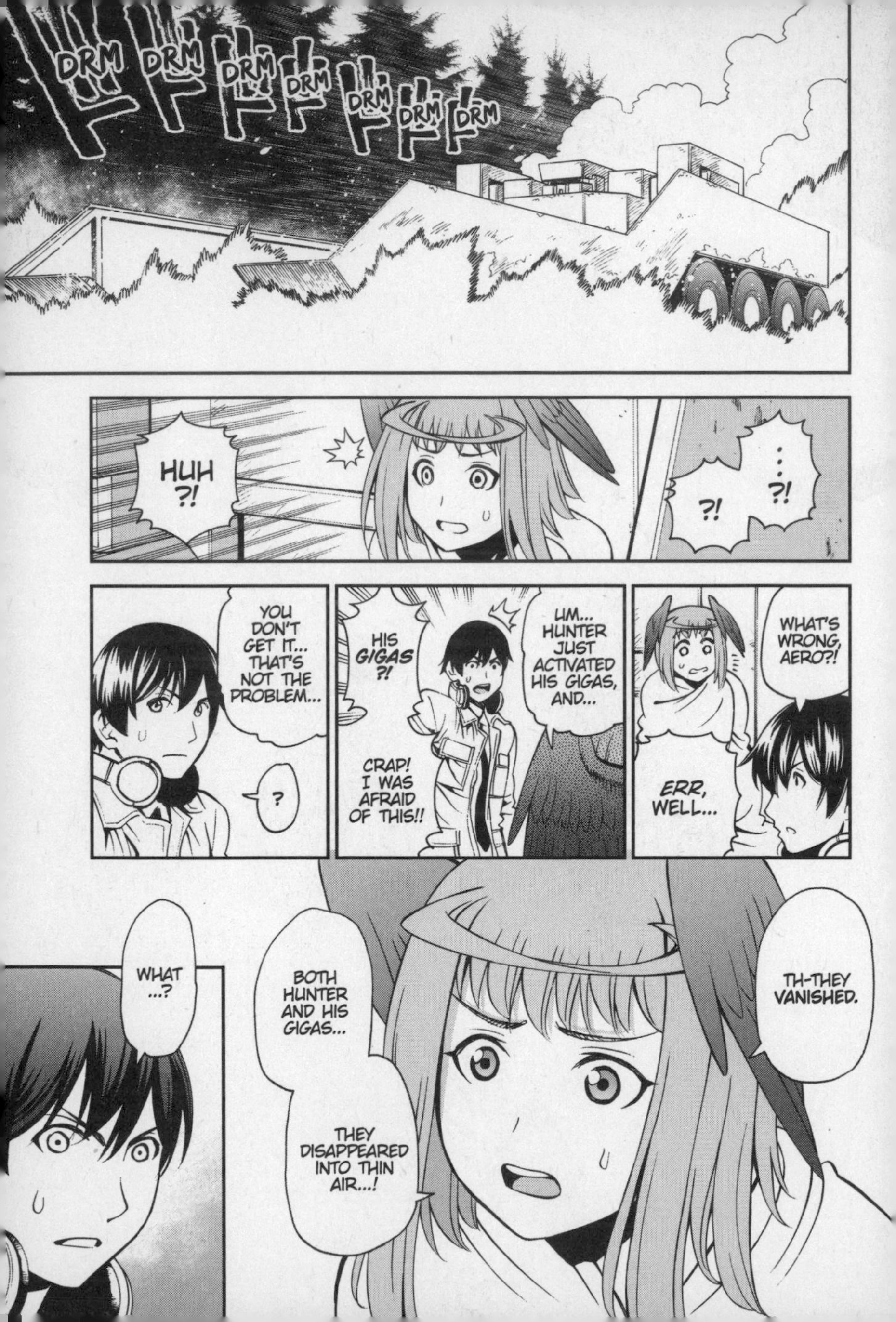
DRM DRM DRM DRM DRM DRM DRM
...?!
?!
HUH?!
WHAT'S WRONG, AERO?!
ERR, WELL...
UM... HUNTER JUST ACTIVATED HIS GIGAS, AND...
HIS GIGAS?!
CRAP! I WAS AFRAID OF THIS!!
YOU DON'T GET IT... THAT'S NOT THE PROBLEM...
?
TH-THEY VANISHED.
BOTH HUNTER AND HIS GIGAS...
WHAT...?
THEY DISAPPEARED INTO THIN AIR...!

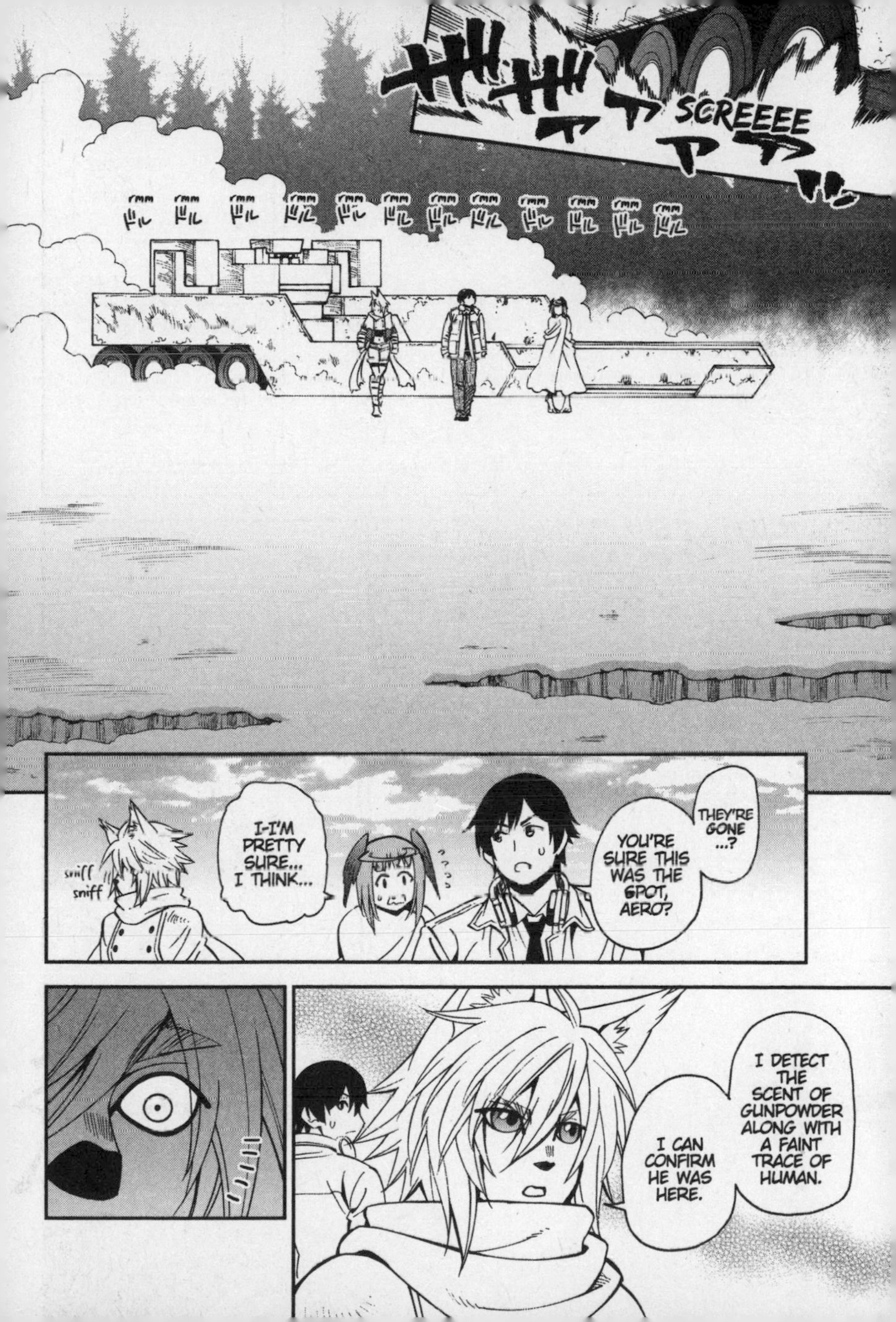
SCREEEEE
rmm rmm rmm rmm rmm rmm rmm rmm rmm rmm rmm rmm
ドル ドル ドル ドル ドル ドル ドル ドル ドル ドル ドル ドル
THEY'RE GONE ...?
YOU'RE SURE THIS WAS THE SPOT, AERO?
I-I'M PRETTY SURE... I THINK...
sniff sniff
I DETECT THE SCENT OF GUNPOWDER ALONG WITH A FAINT TRACE OF HUMAN.
I CAN CONFIRM HE WAS HERE.

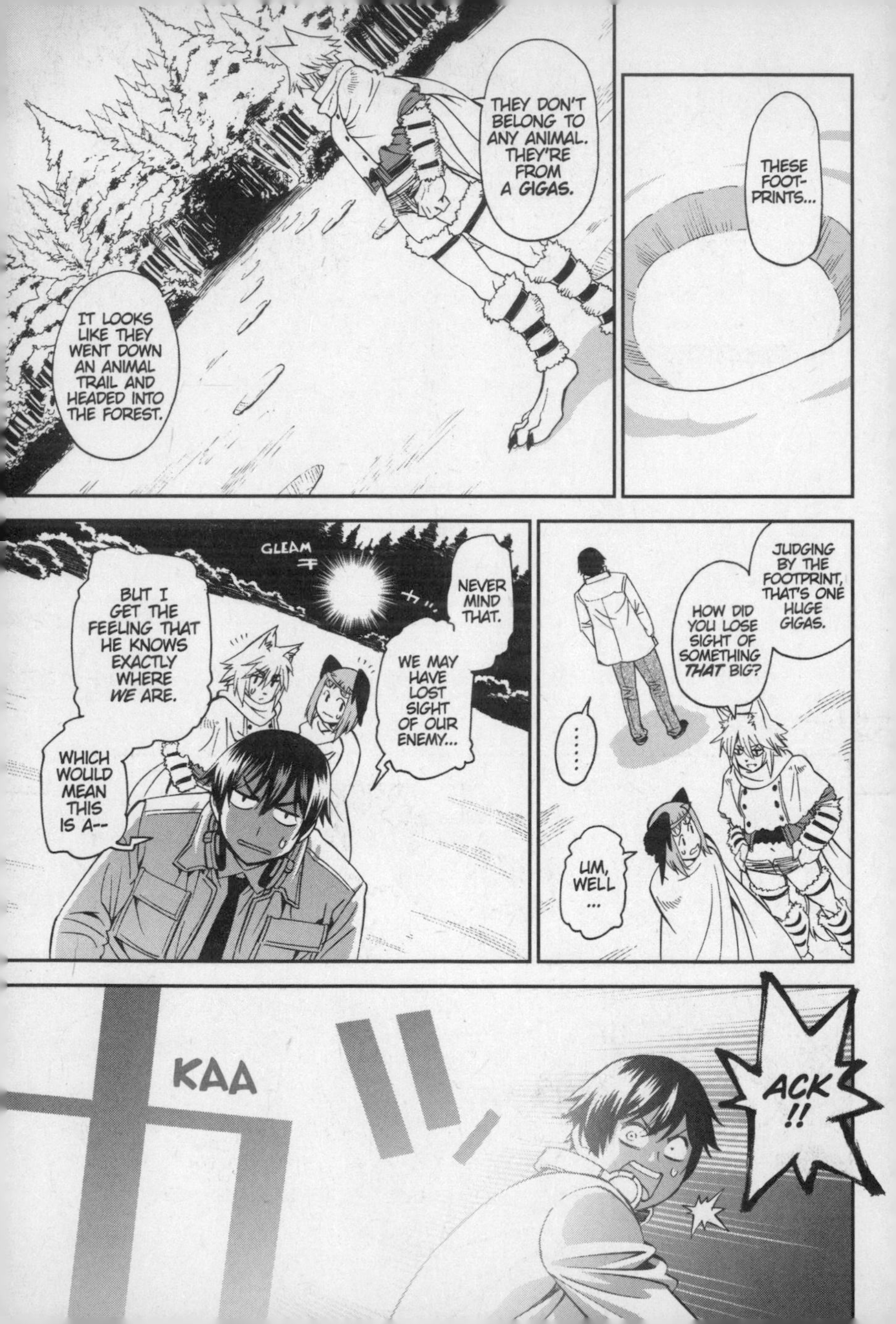
THESE FOOT-PRINTS...
THEY DON'T BELONG TO ANY ANIMAL. THEY'RE FROM A GIGAS.
IT LOOKS LIKE THEY WENT DOWN AN ANIMAL TRAIL AND HEADED INTO THE FOREST.
JUDGING BY THE FOOTPRINT, THAT'S ONE HUGE GIGAS.
HOW DID YOU LOSE SIGHT OF SOMETHING THAT BIG?
......
UM, WELL ...
GLEAM
NEVER MIND THAT.
WE MAY HAVE LOST SIGHT OF OUR ENEMY...
BUT I GET THE FEELING THAT HE KNOWS EXACTLY WHERE WE ARE.
WHICH WOULD MEAN THIS IS A--
ACK !!
KAA

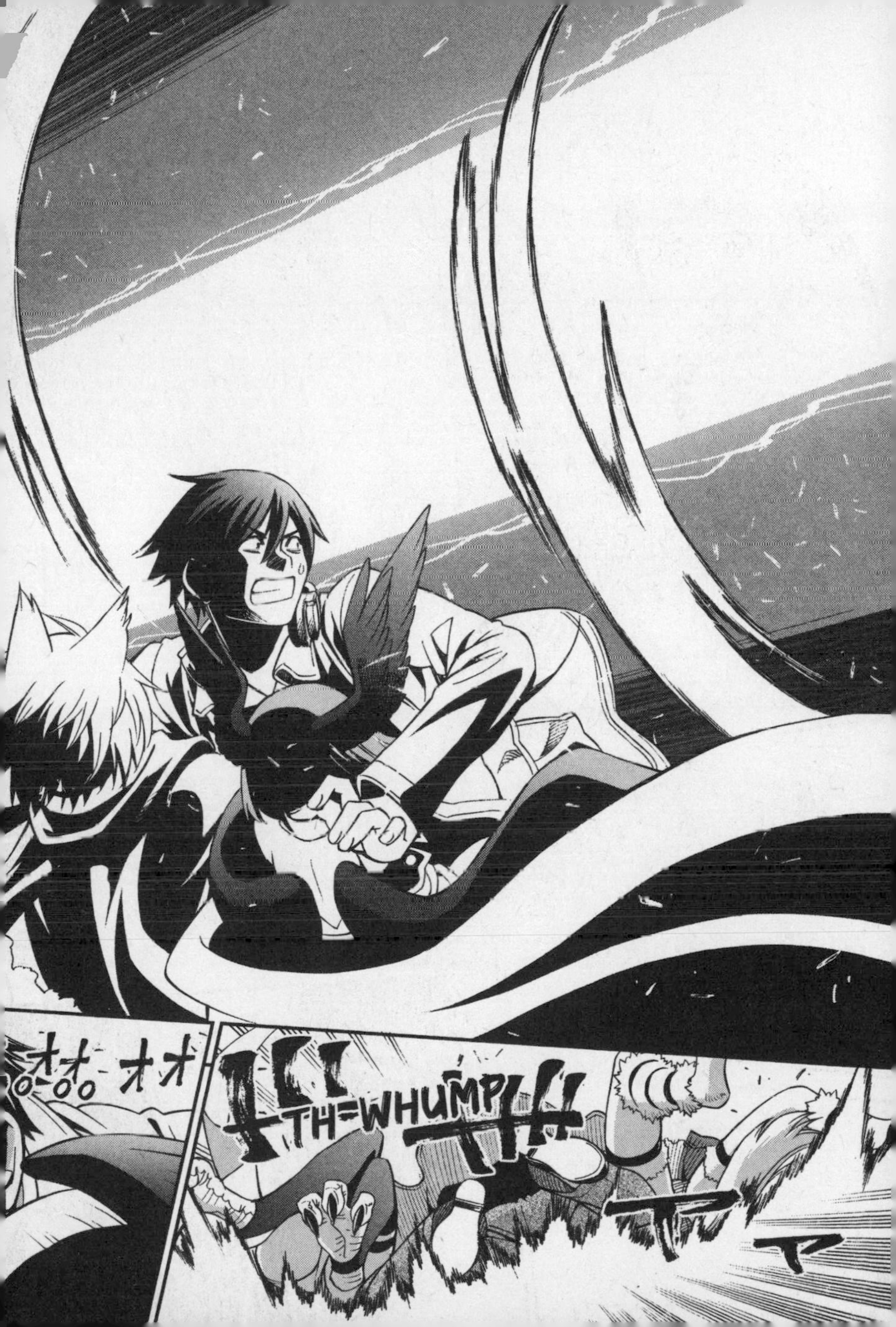
TH-WHUMP
オオ オオ

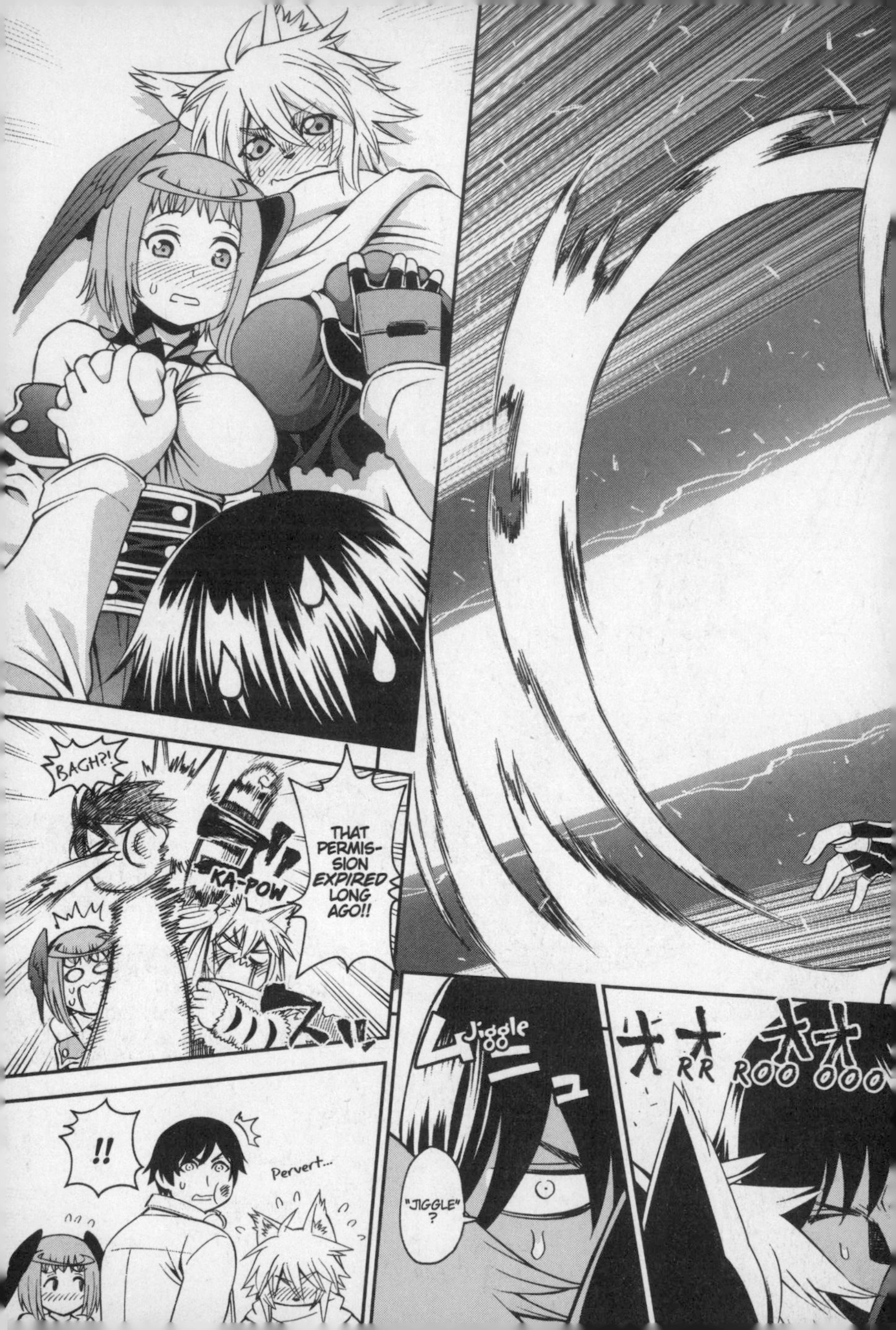
BAGH?!
KA-POW
THAT PERMISSION EXPIRED LONG AGO!!
RR ROO OOO
Jiggle
"JIGGLE"?
!!
Pervert...

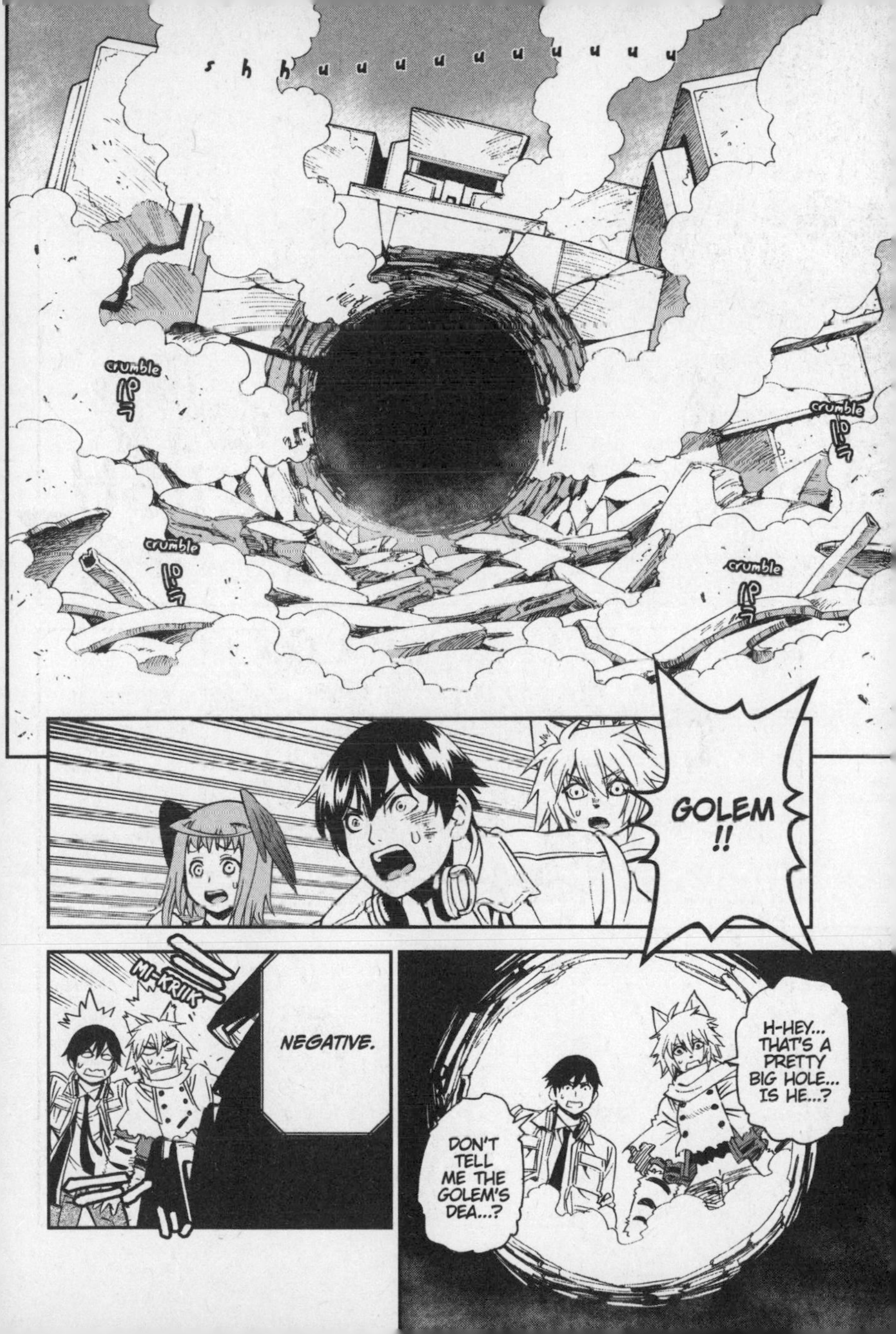
shhuuuuuuuuuuu
crumble
crumble
crumble
crumble
GOLEM!!
H-HEY... THAT'S A PRETTY BIG HOLE... IS HE...?
DON'T TELL ME THE GOLEM'S DEA...?
NEGATIVE.
MI-KRIIK

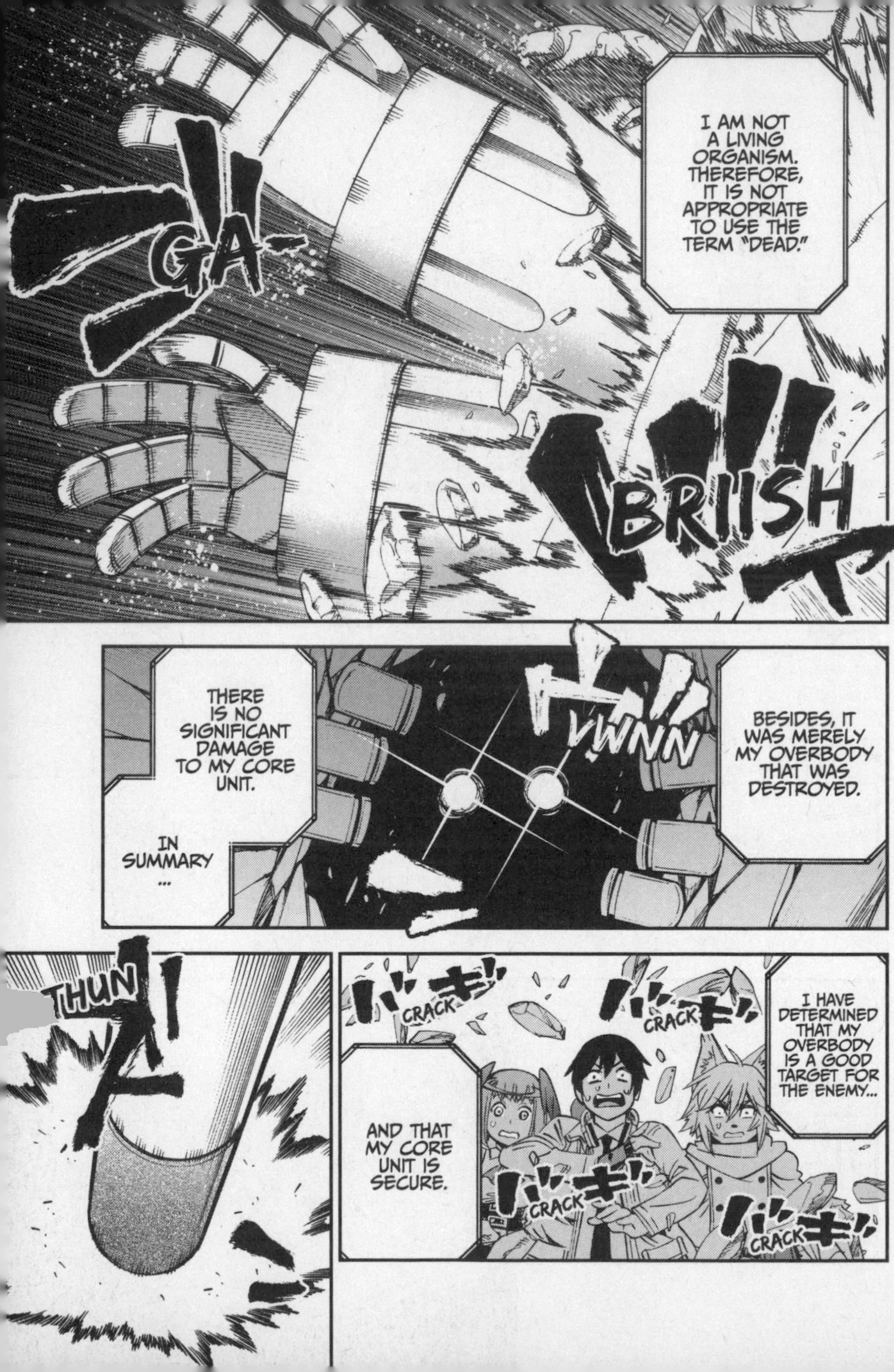
I AM NOT A LIVING ORGANISM. THEREFORE, IT IS NOT APPROPRIATE TO USE THE TERM "DEAD."
BRIISH
GA
BESIDES, IT WAS MERELY MY OVERBODY THAT WAS DESTROYED.
VWNNN
THERE IS NO SIGNIFICANT DAMAGE TO MY CORE UNIT.
IN SUMMARY ...
I HAVE DETERMINED THAT MY OVERBODY IS A GOOD TARGET FOR THE ENEMY...
CRACK
CRACK
AND THAT MY CORE UNIT IS SECURE.
CRACK
CRACK
THUN

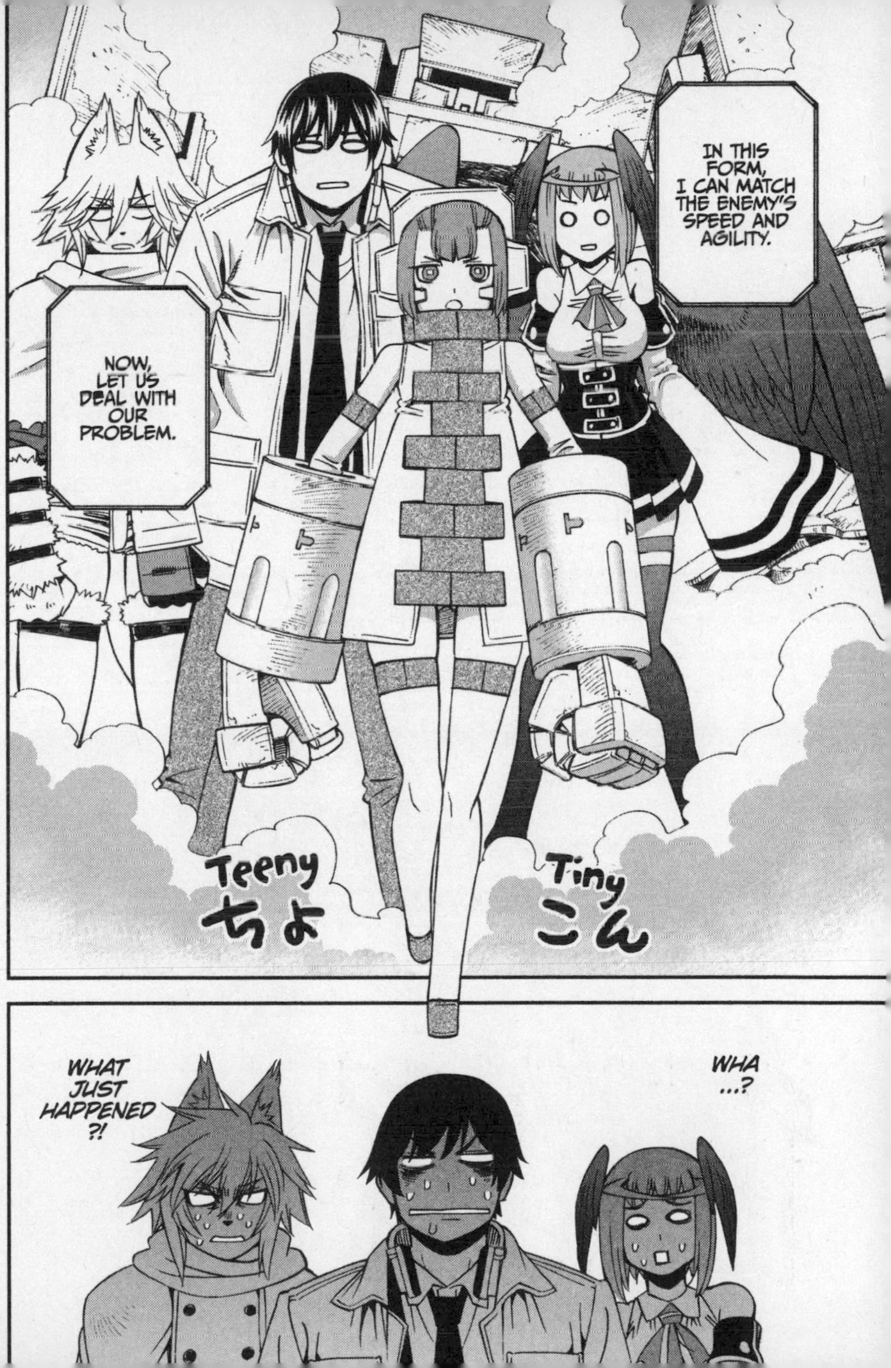
IN THIS FORM, I CAN MATCH THE ENEMY'S SPEED AND AGILITY.
NOW, LET US DEAL WITH OUR PROBLEM.
Teeny ちょ
Tiny こん
WHA ...?
WHAT JUST HAPPENED ?!

12BEAST

トゥエルヴビースト

~OMAKE~

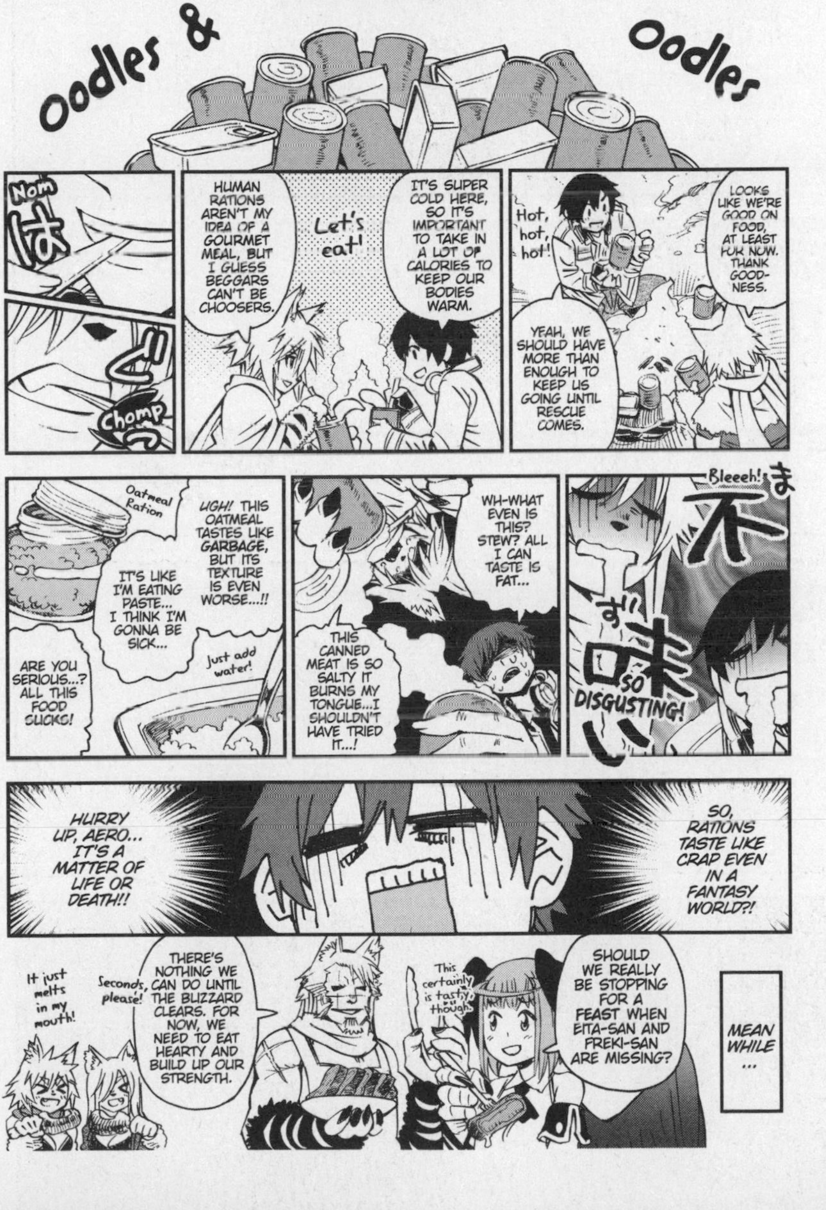
Oodles & Oodles
LOOKS LIKE WE'RE GOOD ON FOOD, AT LEAST FOR NOW. THANK GOODNESS.
Hot, hot, hot!
YEAH, WE SHOULD HAVE MORE THAN ENOUGH TO KEEP US GOING UNTIL RESCUE COMES.
IT'S SUPER COLD HERE, SO IT'S IMPORTANT TO TAKE IN A LOT OF CALORIES TO KEEP OUR BODIES WARM.
Let's eat!
HUMAN RATIONS AREN'T MY IDEA OF A GOURMET MEAL, BUT I GUESS BEGGARS CAN'T BE CHOOSERS.
Nom
Chomp
Bleeeh!
SO DISGUSTING!
WH-WHAT EVEN IS THIS? STEW? ALL I CAN TASTE IS FAT...
THIS CANNED MEAT IS SO SALTY IT BURNS MY TONGUE...I SHOULDN'T HAVE TRIED IT...!
UGH! THIS OATMEAL TASTES LIKE GARBAGE, BUT ITS TEXTURE IS EVEN WORSE...!!
Oatmeal Ration
IT'S LIKE I'M EATING PASTE... I THINK I'M GONNA BE SICK...
just add water!
ARE YOU SERIOUS...? ALL THIS FOOD SUCKS!
SO, RATIONS TASTE LIKE CRAP EVEN IN A FANTASY WORLD?!
HURRY UP, AERO... IT'S A MATTER OF LIFE OR DEATH!!
MEANWHILE...
SHOULD WE REALLY BE STOPPING FOR A FEAST WHEN EITA-SAN AND FREKI-SAN ARE MISSING?
This certainly is tasty, though.
THERE'S NOTHING WE CAN DO UNTIL THE BLIZZARD CLEARS. FOR NOW, WE NEED TO EAT HEARTY AND BUILD UP OUR STRENGTH.
Seconds, please!
It just melts in my mouth!

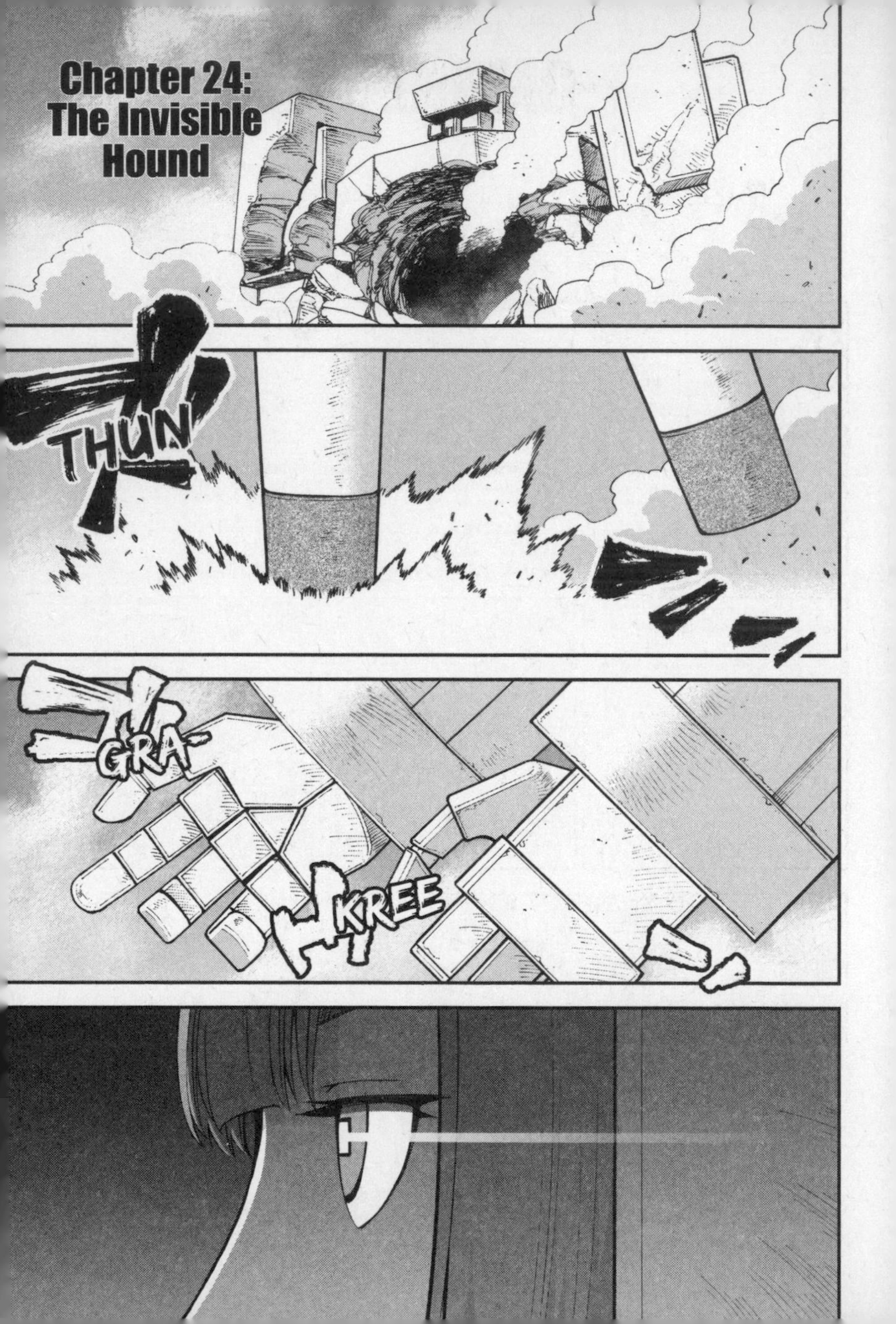
Chapter 24: The Invisible Hound
THUN
GRA-
KREE

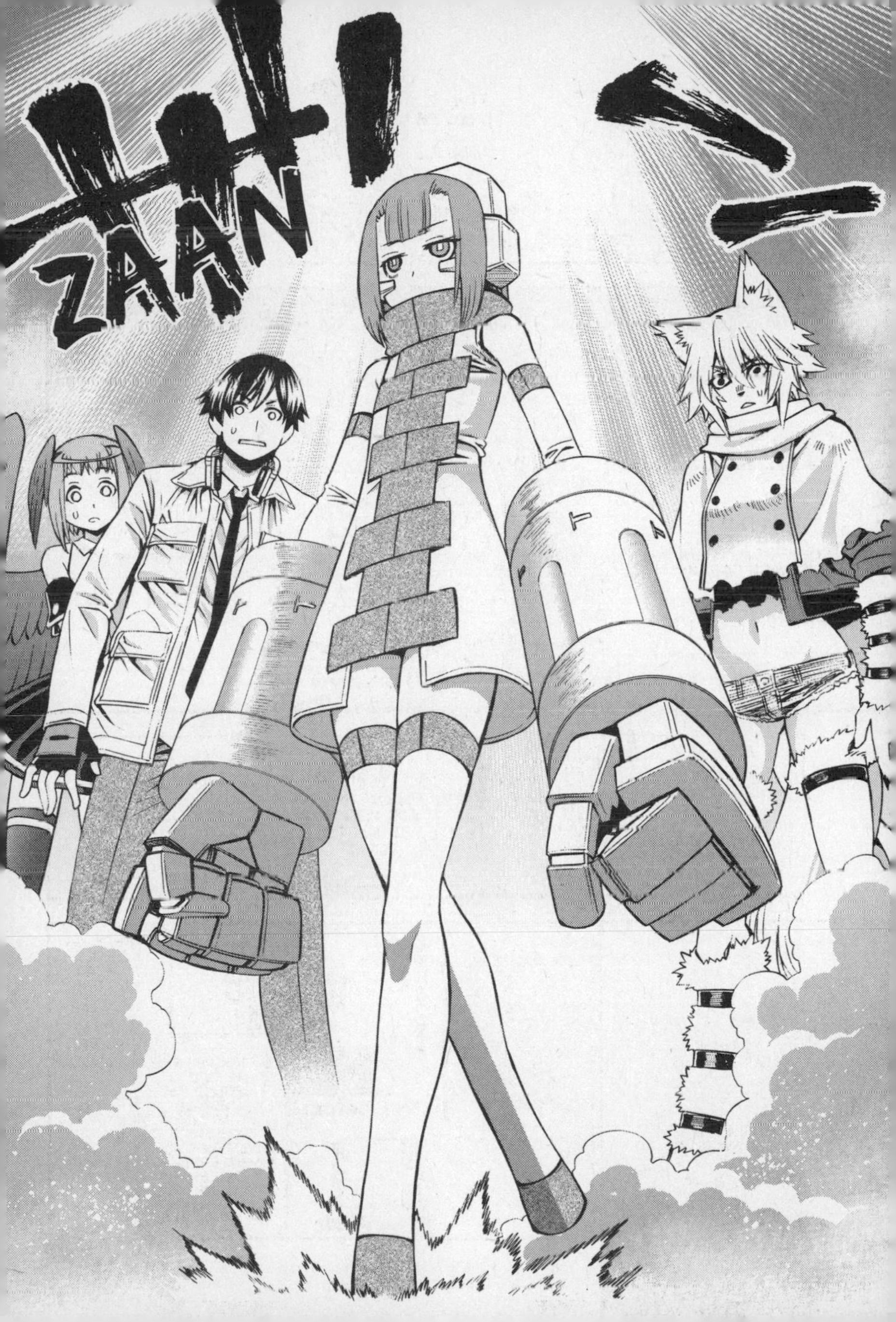
ZAAN

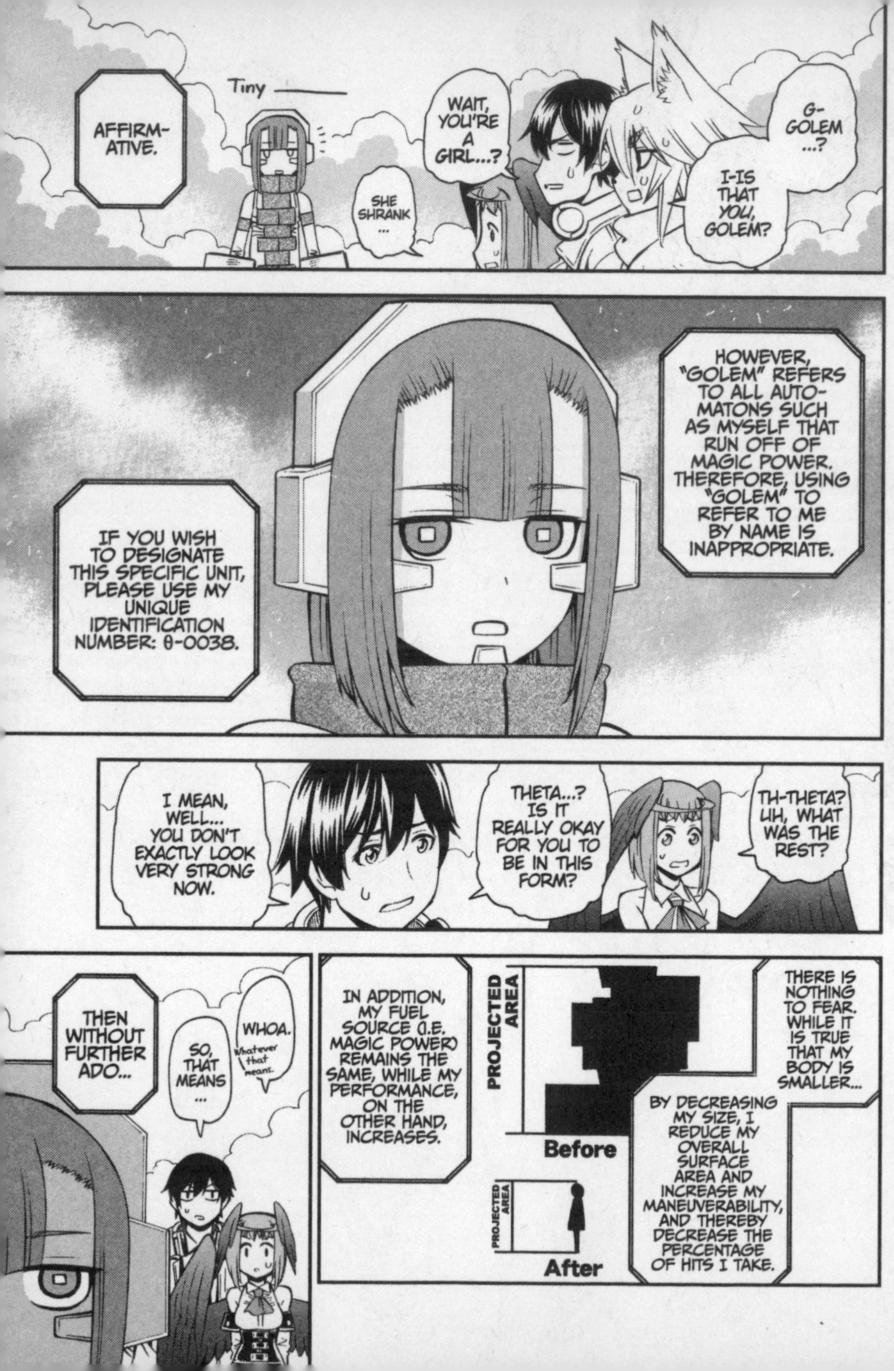
G-GOLEM...?
I-IS THAT YOU, GOLEM?
WAIT, YOU'RE A GIRL...?
SHE SHRANK...
Tiny
AFFIRMATIVE.
HOWEVER, "GOLEM" REFERS TO ALL AUTOMATONS SUCH AS MYSELF THAT RUN OFF OF MAGIC POWER. THEREFORE, USING "GOLEM" TO REFER TO ME BY NAME IS INAPPROPRIATE.
IF YOU WISH TO DESIGNATE THIS SPECIFIC UNIT, PLEASE USE MY UNIQUE IDENTIFICATION NUMBER: θ-0038.
TH-THETA? UH, WHAT WAS THE REST?
THETA...? IS IT REALLY OKAY FOR YOU TO BE IN THIS FORM?
I MEAN, WELL... YOU DON'T EXACTLY LOOK VERY STRONG NOW.
THERE IS NOTHING TO FEAR. WHILE IT IS TRUE THAT MY BODY IS SMALLER...
PROJECTED AREA
Before
BY DECREASING MY SIZE, I REDUCE MY OVERALL SURFACE AREA AND INCREASE MY MANEUVERABILITY, AND THEREBY DECREASE THE PERCENTAGE OF HITS I TAKE.
PROJECTED AREA
After
IN ADDITION, MY FUEL SOURCE (I.E. MAGIC POWER) REMAINS THE SAME, WHILE MY PERFORMANCE, ON THE OTHER HAND, INCREASES.
WHOA.
Whatever that means.
SO, THAT MEANS...
THEN WITHOUT FURTHER ADO...

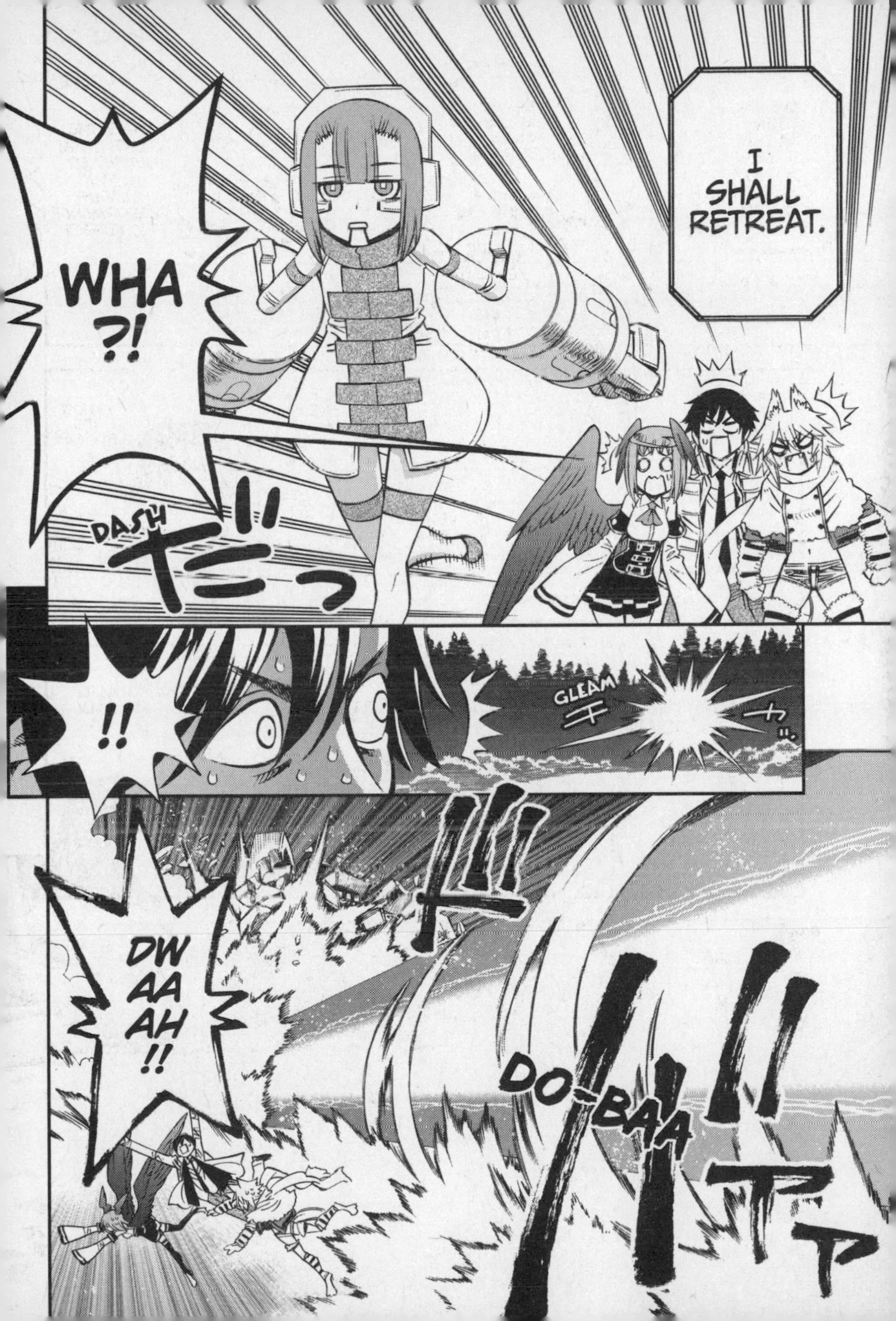

I SHALL RETREAT.
WHA ?!
DASH
GLEAM
!!
DO-BAAA
DWAAAH!!

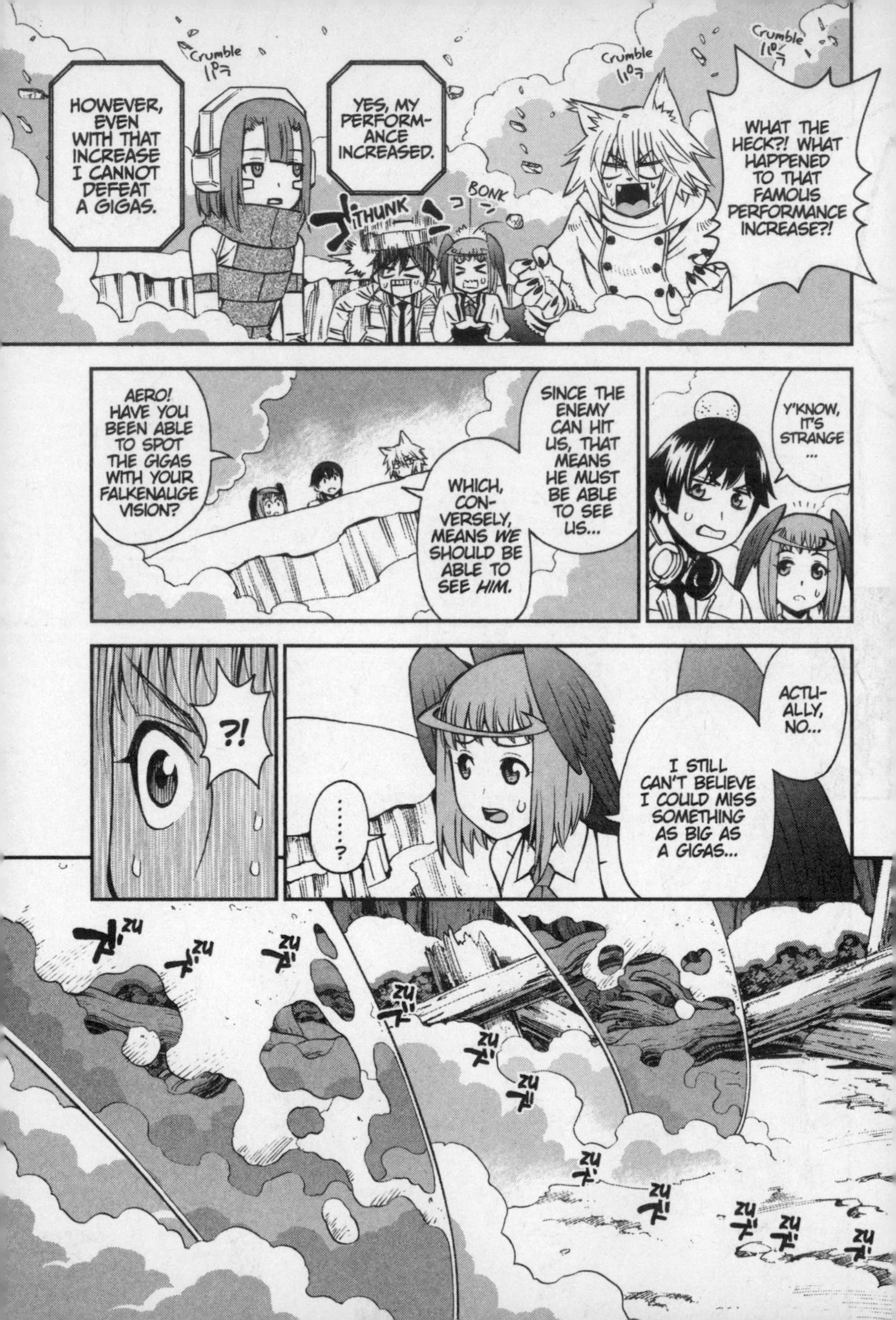
Crumble パラ
WHAT THE HECK?! WHAT HAPPENED TO THAT FAMOUS PERFORMANCE INCREASE?!
Crumble パラ
YES, MY PERFORM-ANCE INCREASED.
BONK
THUNK
HOWEVER, EVEN WITH THAT INCREASE I CANNOT DEFEAT A GIGAS.
Crumble パラ
Y'KNOW, IT'S STRANGE ...
SINCE THE ENEMY CAN HIT US, THAT MEANS HE MUST BE ABLE TO SEE US...
WHICH, CON-VERSELY, MEANS WE SHOULD BE ABLE TO SEE HIM.
AERO! HAVE YOU BEEN ABLE TO SPOT THE GIGAS WITH YOUR FALKENAUGE VISION?
ACTU-ALLY, NO...
I STILL CAN'T BELIEVE I COULD MISS SOMETHING AS BIG AS A GIGAS...
......?
?!
zu
zu
zu
zu
zu
zu
zu
zu
zu
zu
zu

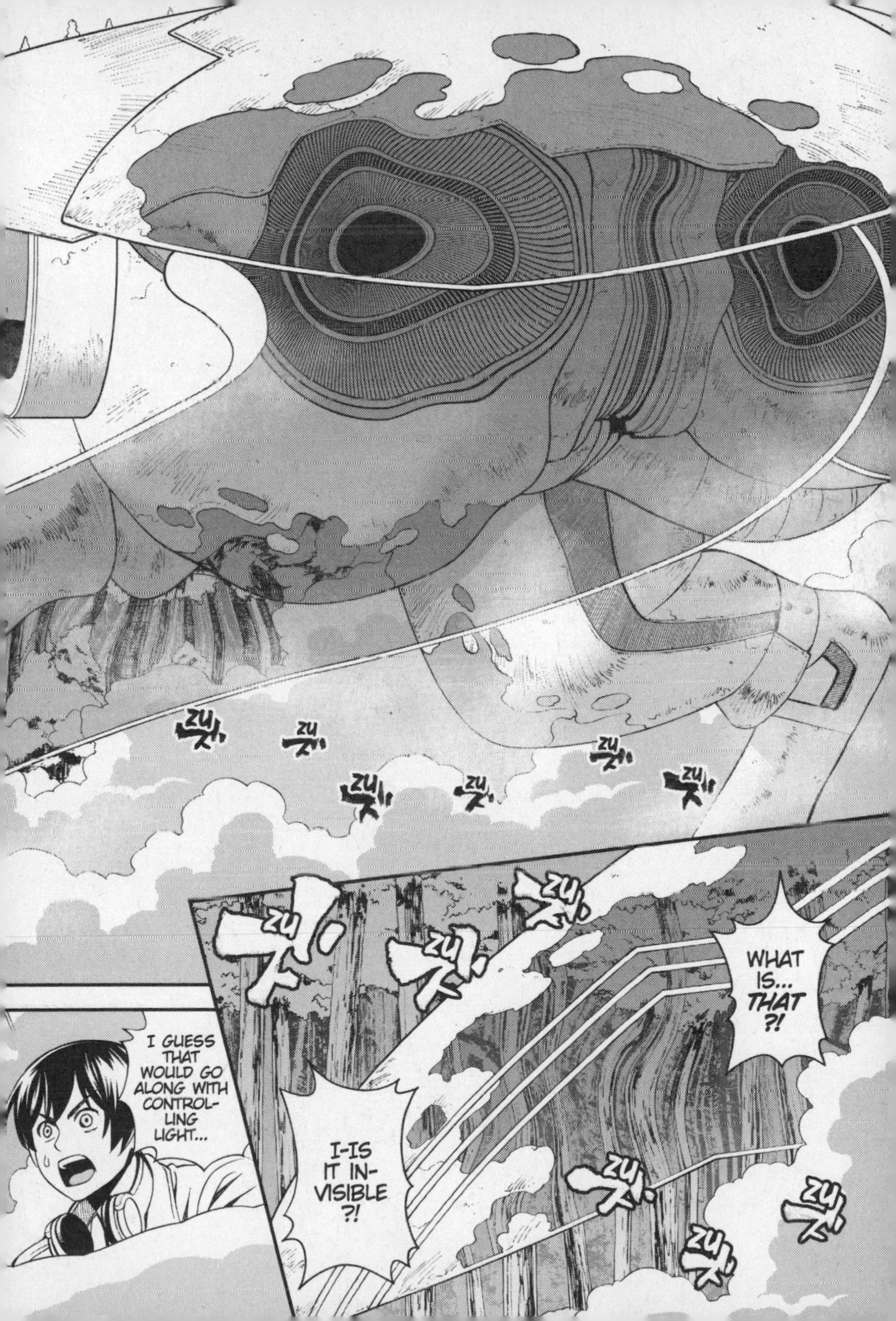
ZU
ZU
ZU
ZU
ZU
ZU
ZU
ZU
ZU
WHAT IS... THAT?!
I-IS IT IN-VISIBLE?!
ZU
ZU
ZU
I GUESS THAT WOULD GO ALONG WITH CONTROL-LING LIGHT...

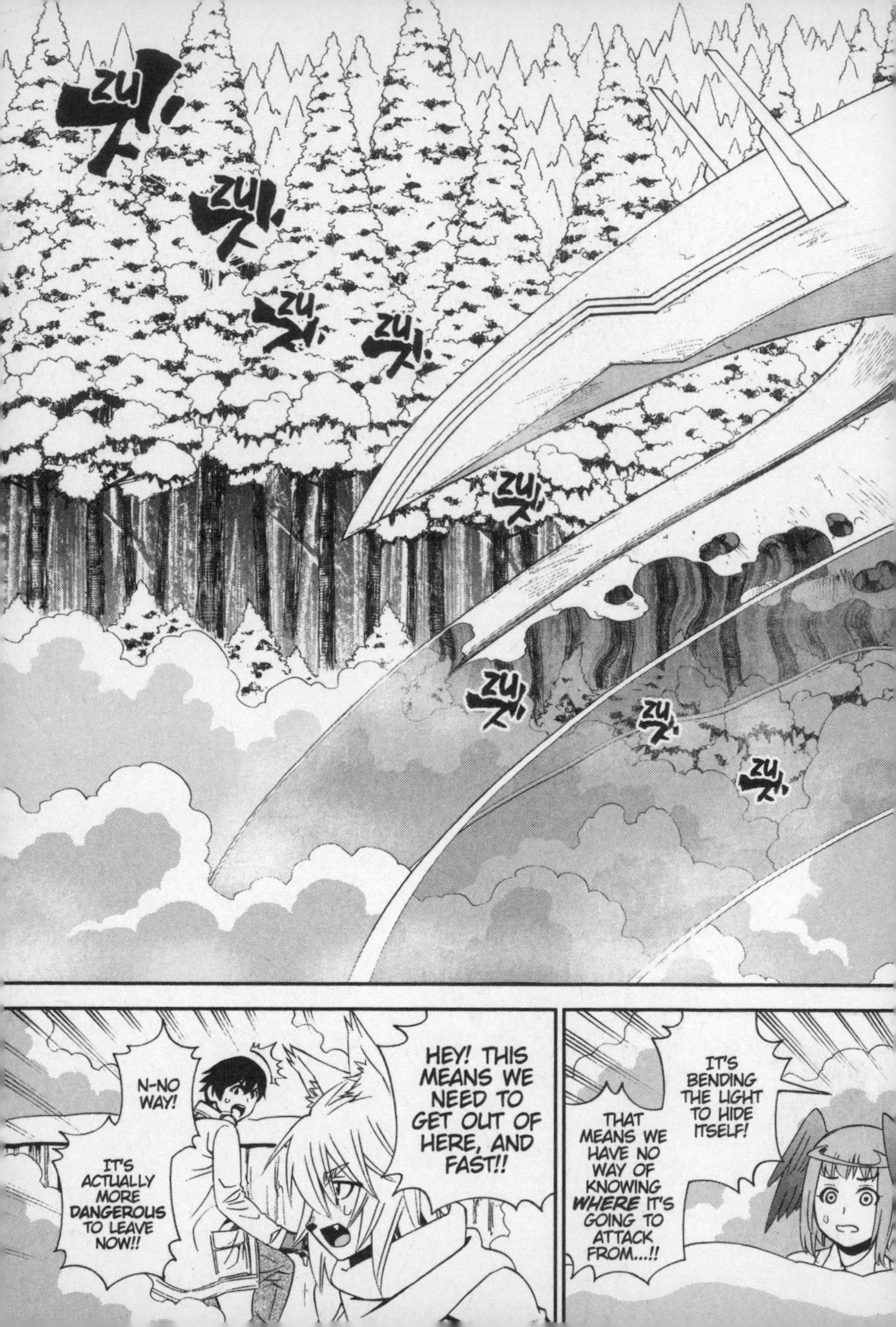
ZU
ZU
ZU
ZU
ZU
ZU
ZU
ZU
IT'S BENDING THE LIGHT TO HIDE ITSELF!
THAT MEANS WE HAVE NO WAY OF KNOWING *WHERE* IT'S GOING TO ATTACK FROM...!!
HEY! THIS MEANS WE NEED TO GET OUT OF HERE, AND FAST!!
N-NO WAY!
IT'S ACTUALLY MORE DANGEROUS TO LEAVE NOW!!

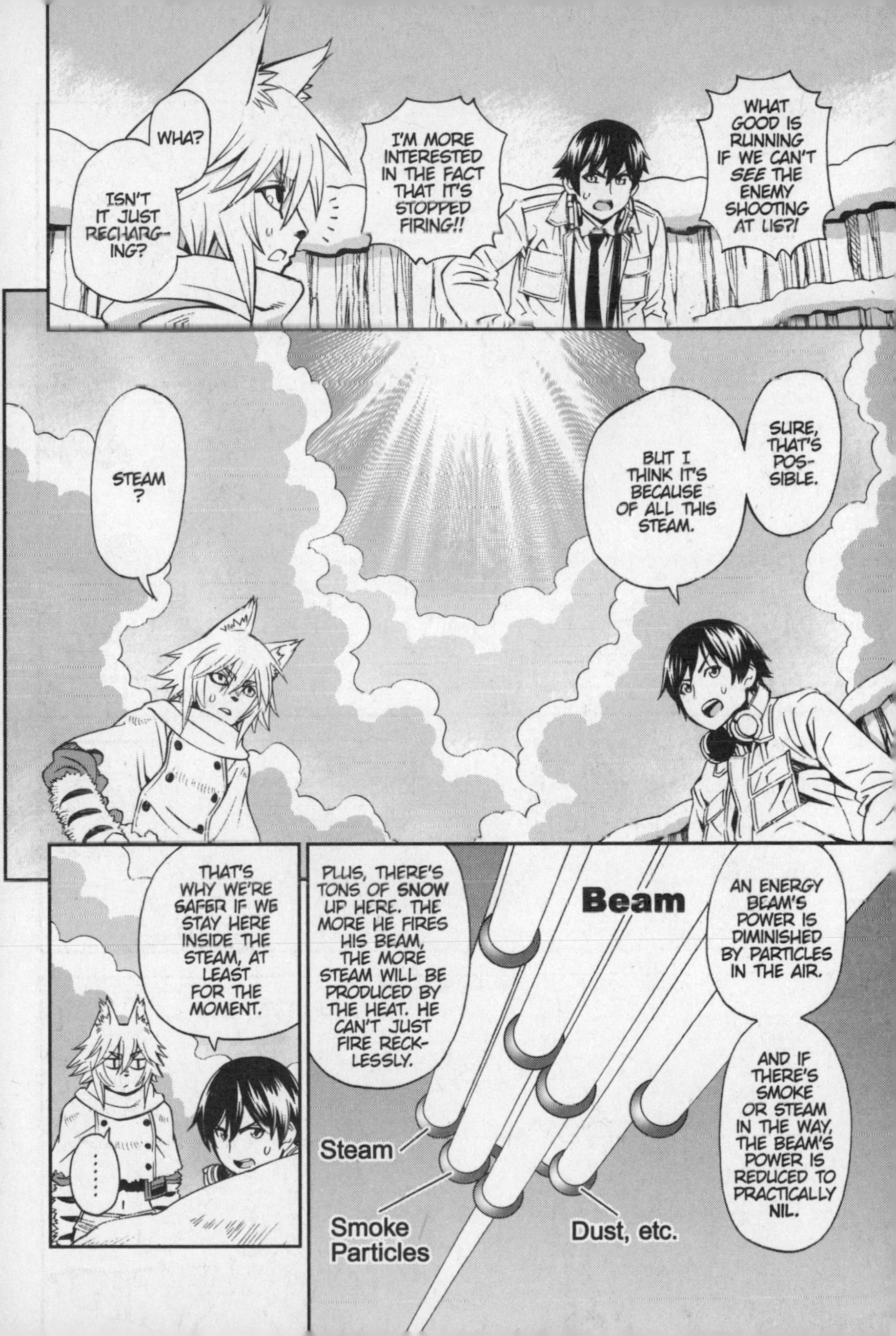
WHAT GOOD IS RUNNING IF WE CAN'T *SEE* THE ENEMY SHOOTING AT US?!
I'M MORE INTERESTED IN THE FACT THAT IT'S STOPPED FIRING!!
WHA?
ISN'T IT JUST RECHARGING?
SURE, THAT'S POSSIBLE.
BUT I THINK IT'S BECAUSE OF ALL THIS STEAM.
STEAM?
AN ENERGY BEAM'S POWER IS DIMINISHED BY PARTICLES IN THE AIR.
Beam
AND IF THERE'S SMOKE OR STEAM IN THE WAY, THE BEAM'S POWER IS REDUCED TO PRACTICALLY NIL.
Dust, etc.
Steam
Smoke Particles
PLUS, THERE'S TONS OF SNOW UP HERE. THE MORE HE FIRES HIS BEAM, THE MORE STEAM WILL BE PRODUCED BY THE HEAT. HE CAN'T JUST FIRE RECKLESSLY.
THAT'S WHY WE'RE SAFER IF WE STAY HERE INSIDE THE STEAM, AT LEAST FOR THE MOMENT.
......

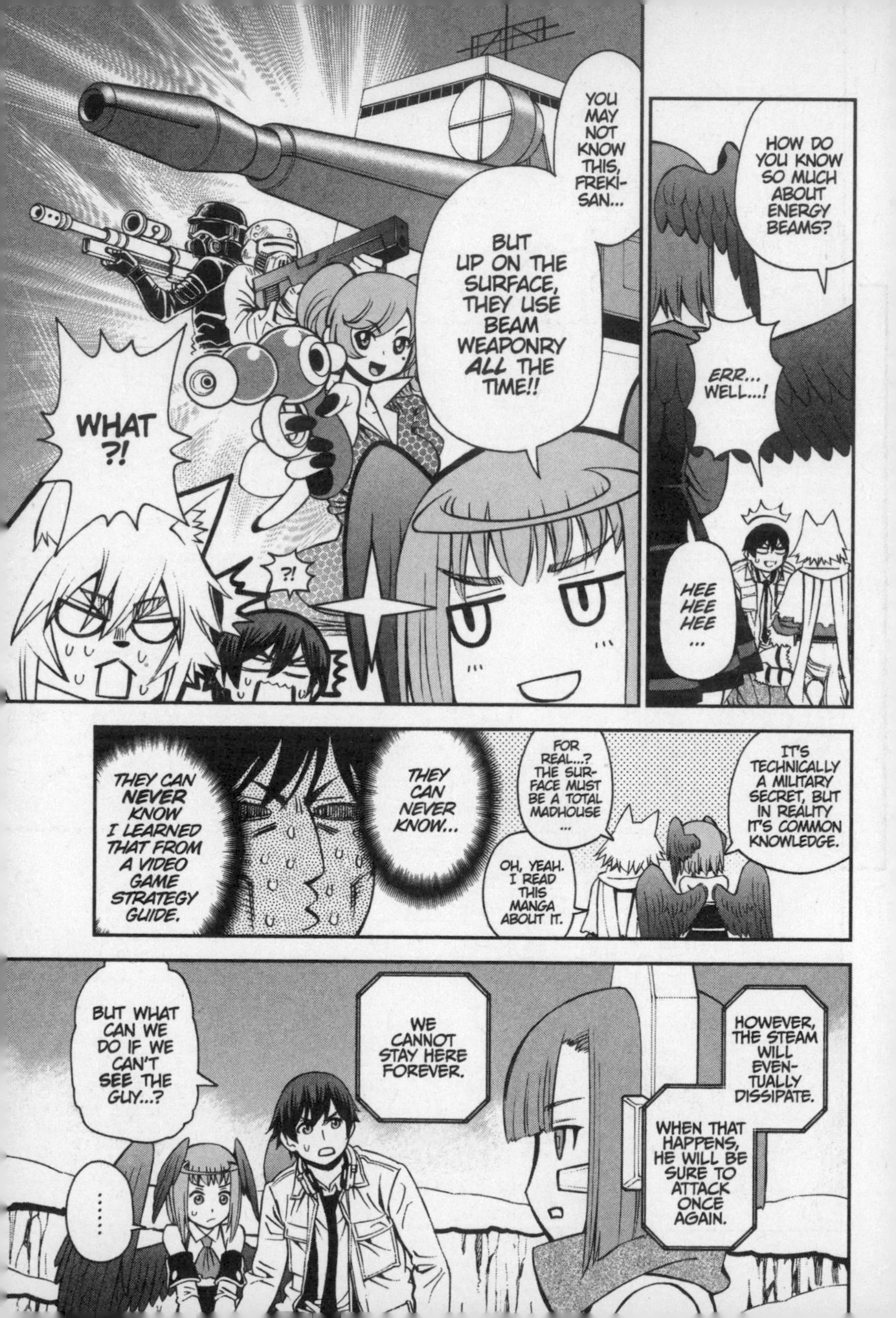
HOW DO YOU KNOW SO MUCH ABOUT ENERGY BEAMS?
ERR... WELL...!
HEE HEE HEE ...
YOU MAY NOT KNOW THIS, FREKI-SAN...
BUT UP ON THE SURFACE, THEY USE BEAM WEAPONRY *ALL* THE TIME!!
WHAT ?!
?!
IT'S TECHNICALLY A MILITARY SECRET, BUT IN REALITY IT'S COMMON KNOWLEDGE.
FOR REAL...? THE SURFACE MUST BE A TOTAL MADHOUSE ...
OH, YEAH. I READ THIS MANGA ABOUT IT.
THEY CAN NEVER KNOW...
THEY CAN NEVER KNOW I LEARNED THAT FROM A VIDEO GAME STRATEGY GUIDE.
HOWEVER, THE STEAM WILL EVENTUALLY DISSIPATE.
WHEN THAT HAPPENS, HE WILL BE SURE TO ATTACK ONCE AGAIN.
WE CANNOT STAY HERE FOREVER.
BUT WHAT CAN WE DO IF WE CAN'T SEE THE GUY...?
......

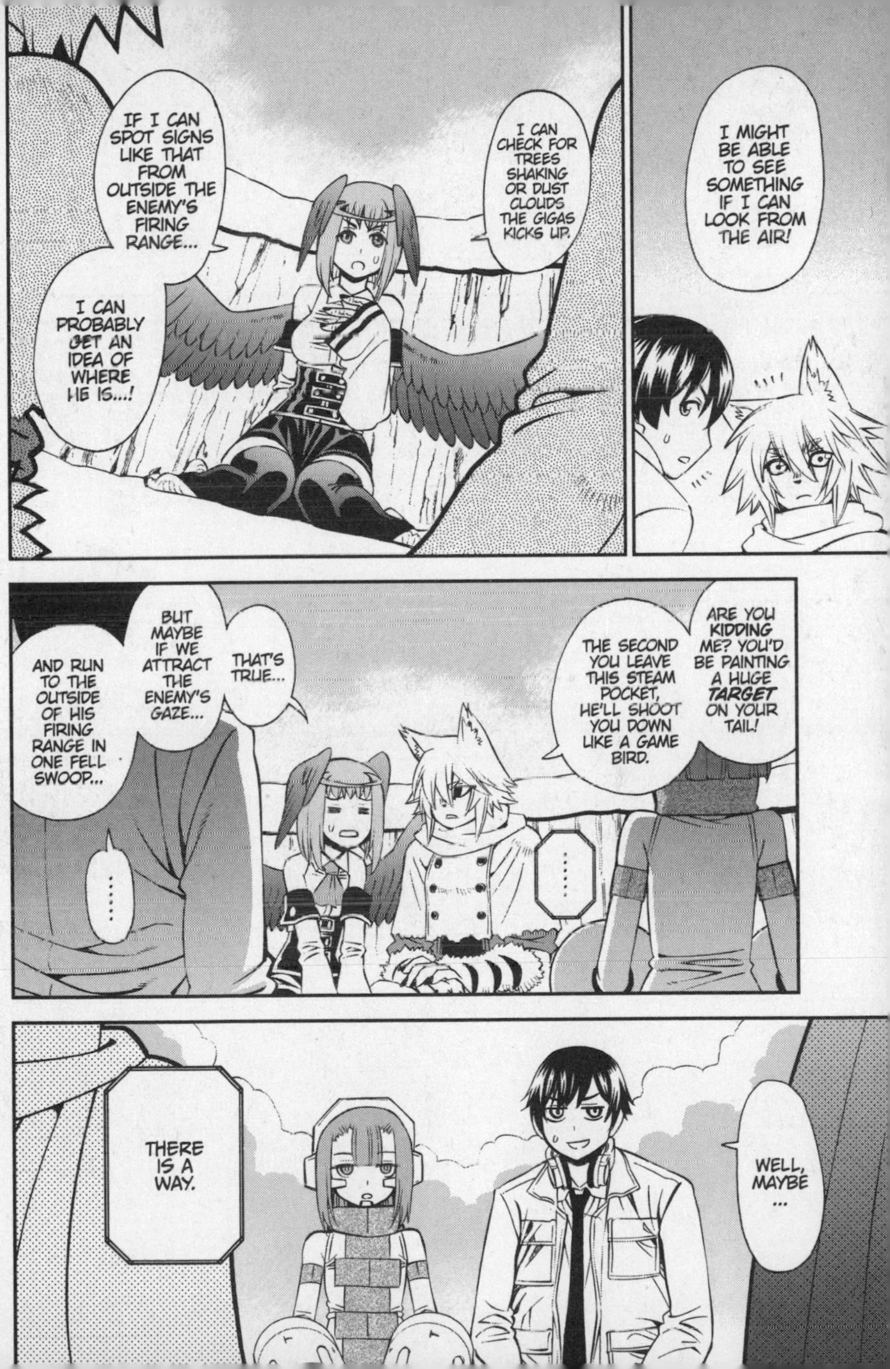
I MIGHT BE ABLE TO SEE SOMETHING IF I CAN LOOK FROM THE AIR!
I CAN CHECK FOR TREES SHAKING OR DUST CLOUDS THE GIGAS KICKS UP.
IF I CAN SPOT SIGNS LIKE THAT FROM OUTSIDE THE ENEMY'S FIRING RANGE...
I CAN PROBABLY GET AN IDEA OF WHERE HE IS...!
ARE YOU KIDDING ME? YOU'D BE PAINTING A HUGE *TARGET* ON YOUR TAIL!
THE SECOND YOU LEAVE THIS STEAM POCKET, HE'LL SHOOT YOU DOWN LIKE A GAME BIRD.
......
THAT'S TRUE...
BUT MAYBE IF WE ATTRACT THE ENEMY'S GAZE...
AND RUN TO THE OUTSIDE OF HIS FIRING RANGE IN ONE FELL SWOOP...
......
WELL, MAYBE ...
THERE IS A WAY.

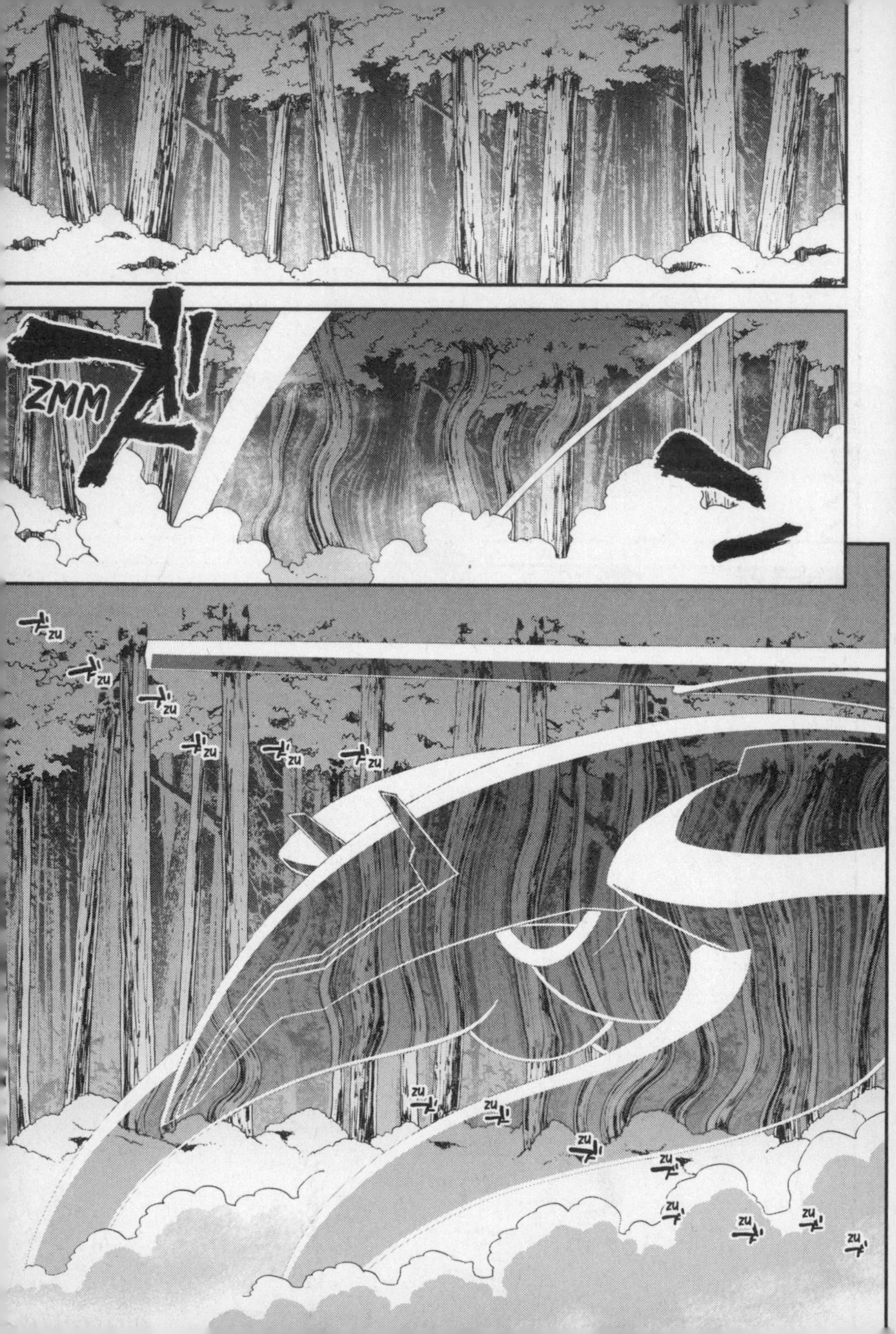
ズ
ZMM
ず zu
ず zu
ず zu
ず zu
ず zu
ず zu
zu ず
zu ず
zu ず
zu ず
zu ず
zu ず
zu ず
zu ず

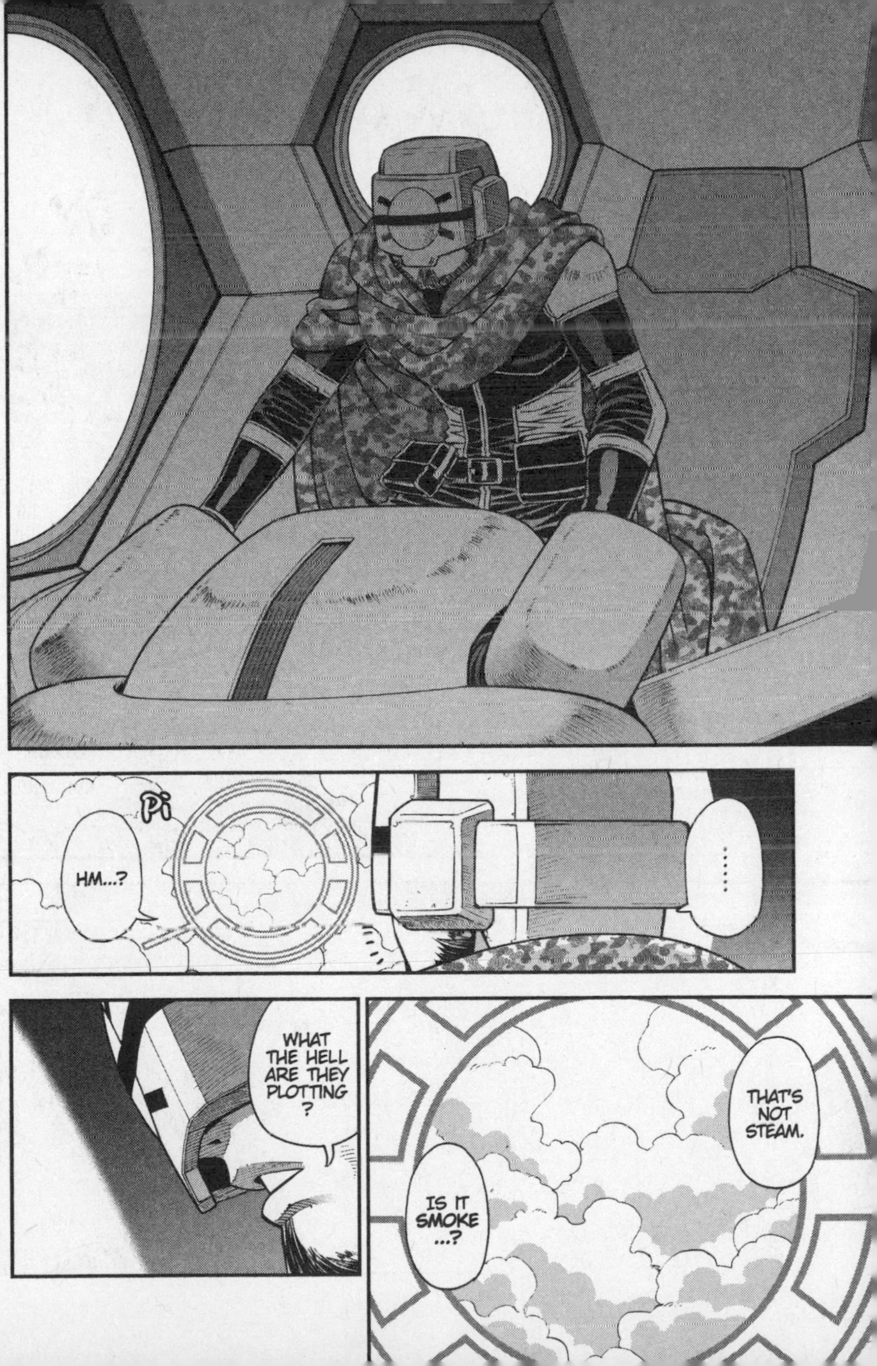
......
Pi
HM...?
THAT'S NOT STEAM.
IS IT SMOKE ...?
WHAT THE HELL ARE THEY PLOTTING ?

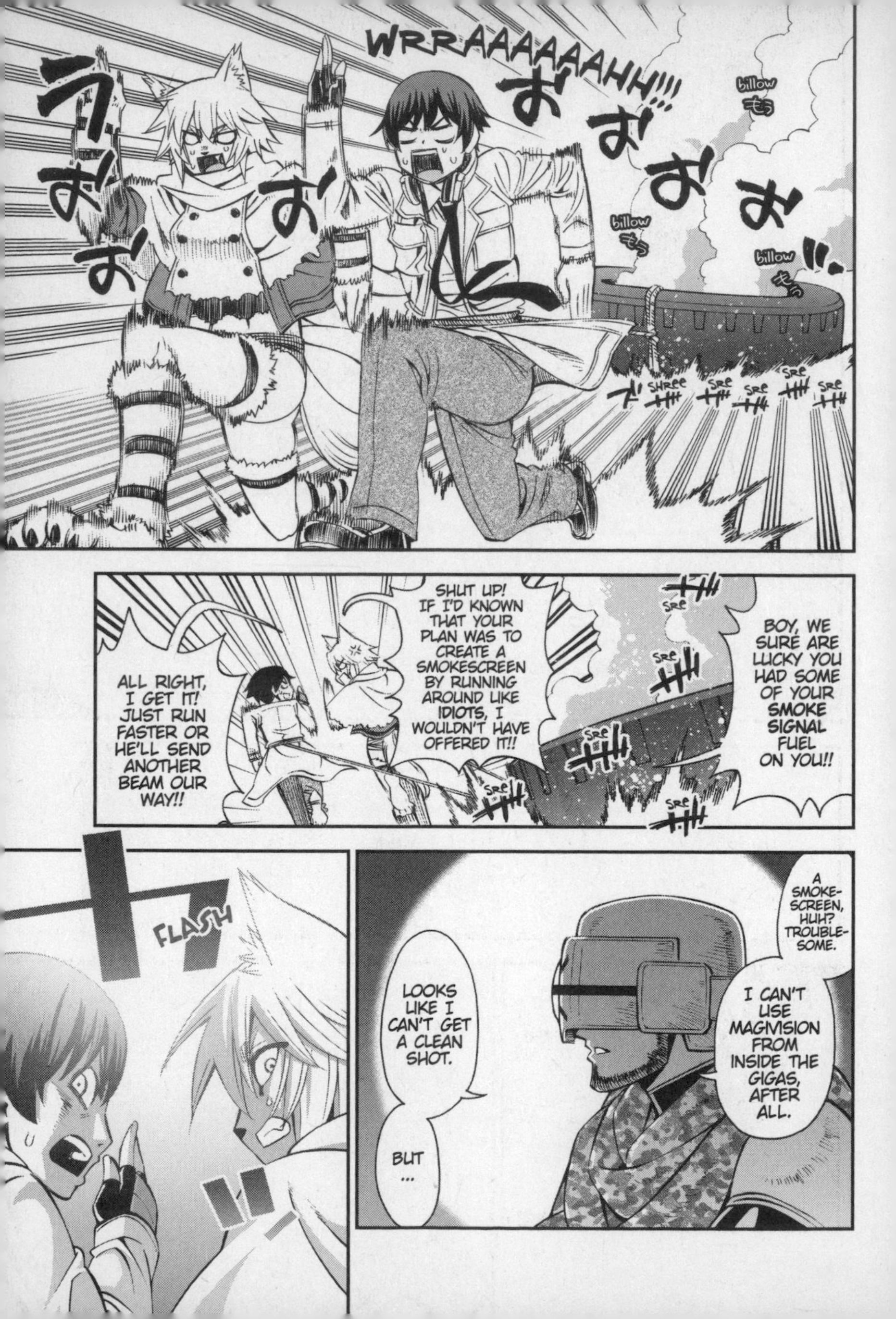
WRRAAAAAAAHH!!!!
billow
billow
billow
SHREE
SRE
SRE
SRE
SRE
BOY, WE SURE ARE LUCKY YOU HAD SOME OF YOUR SMOKE SIGNAL FUEL ON YOU!!
SHUT UP! IF I'D KNOWN THAT YOUR PLAN WAS TO CREATE A SMOKESCREEN BY RUNNING AROUND LIKE IDIOTS, I WOULDN'T HAVE OFFERED IT!!
ALL RIGHT, I GET IT! JUST RUN FASTER OR HE'LL SEND ANOTHER BEAM OUR WAY!!
SRE
SRE
SRE
SRE
SRE
A SMOKE-SCREEN, HUH? TROUBLE-SOME.
I CAN'T USE MAGIVISION FROM INSIDE THE GIGAS, AFTER ALL.
LOOKS LIKE I CAN'T GET A CLEAN SHOT.
BUT ...
FLASH

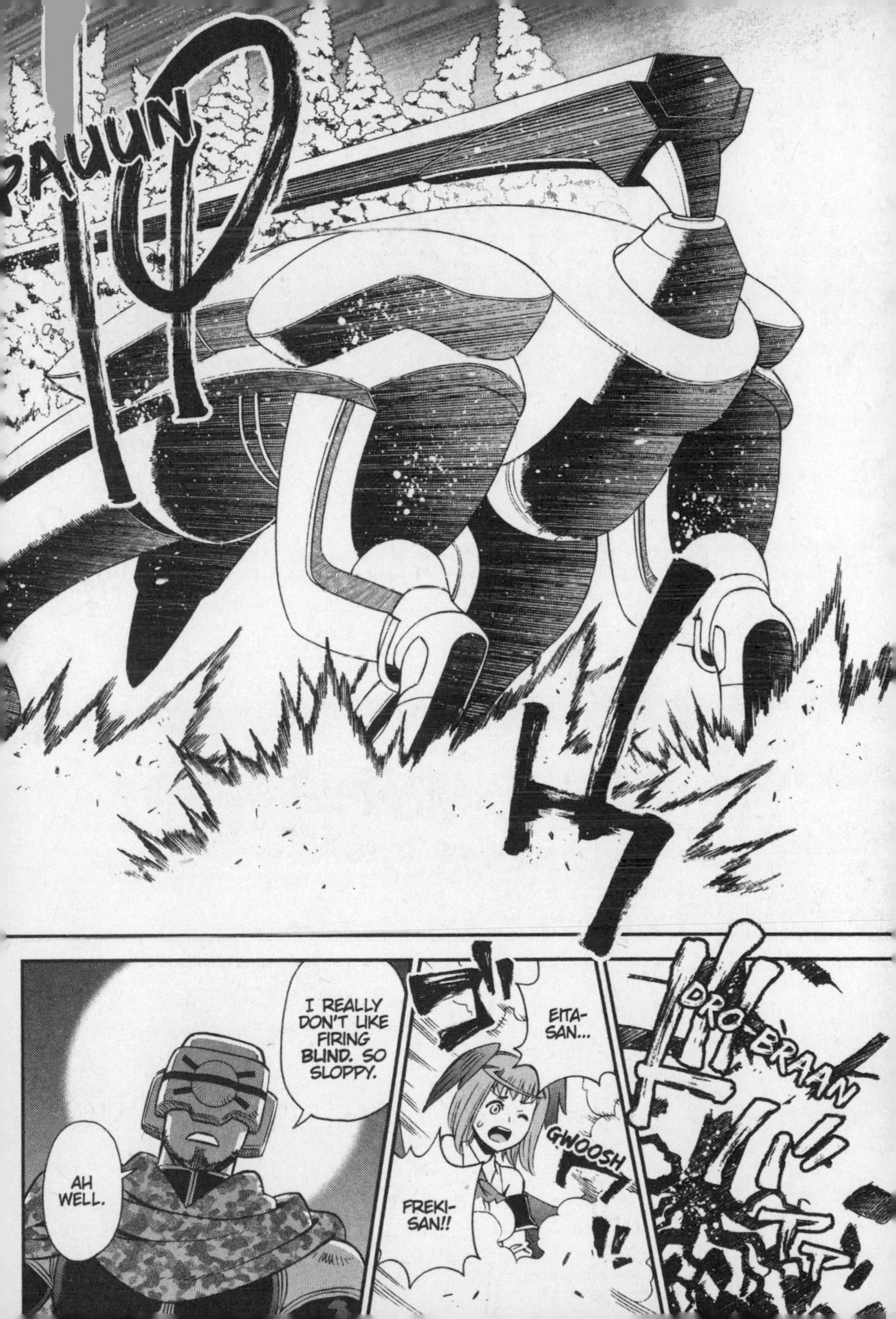
PAUUN
DRO-BRAAN
EITA-SAN...
GWOOSH
FREKI-SAN!!
I REALLY DON'T LIKE FIRING BLIND. SO SLOPPY.
AH WELL.

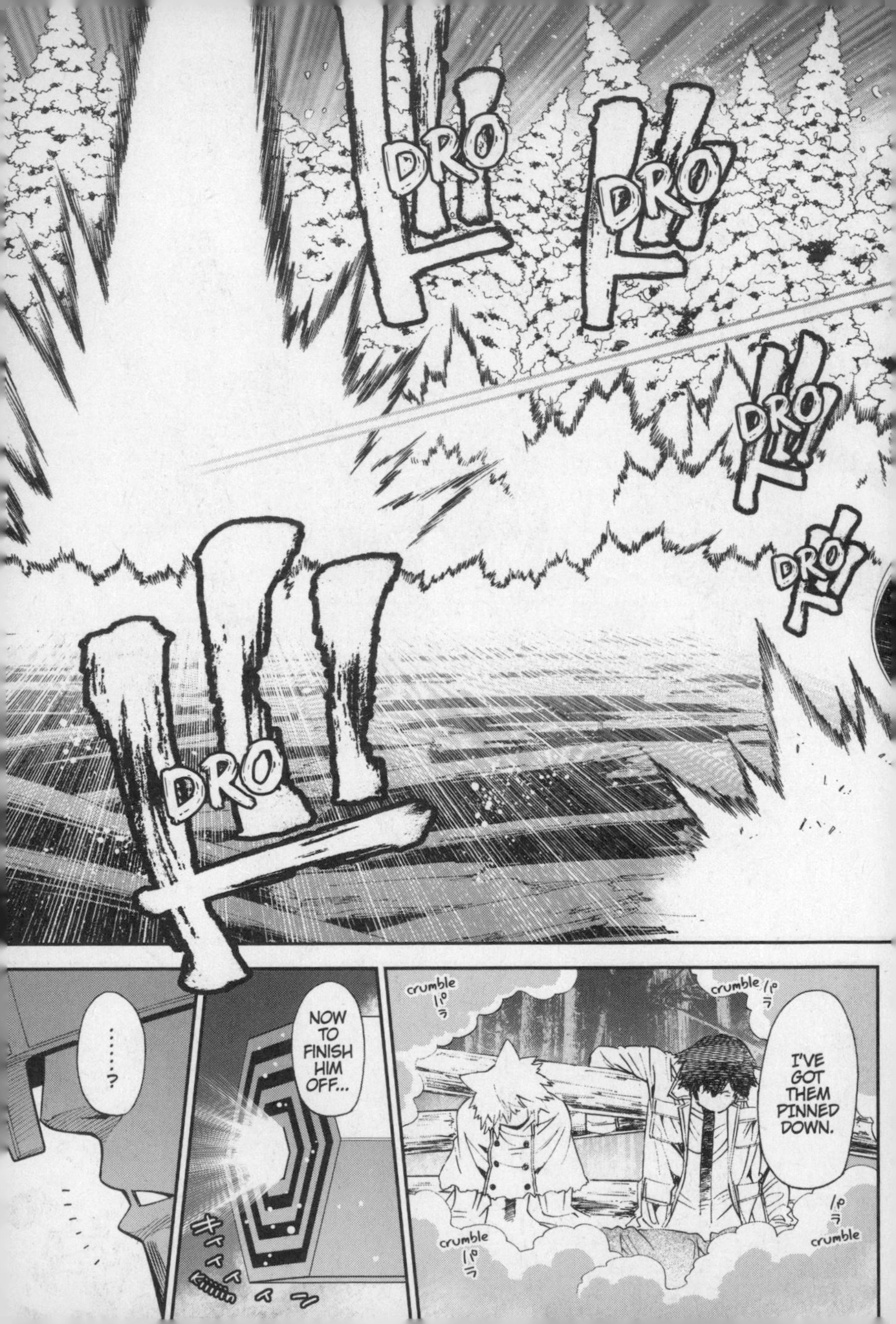
DRO
DRO
DRO
DRO
DRO
crumble パラ
crumble パラ
I'VE GOT THEM PINNED DOWN.
crumble パラ
crumble パラ
NOW TO FINISH HIM OFF...
キィィィン Kiiiiin
......?

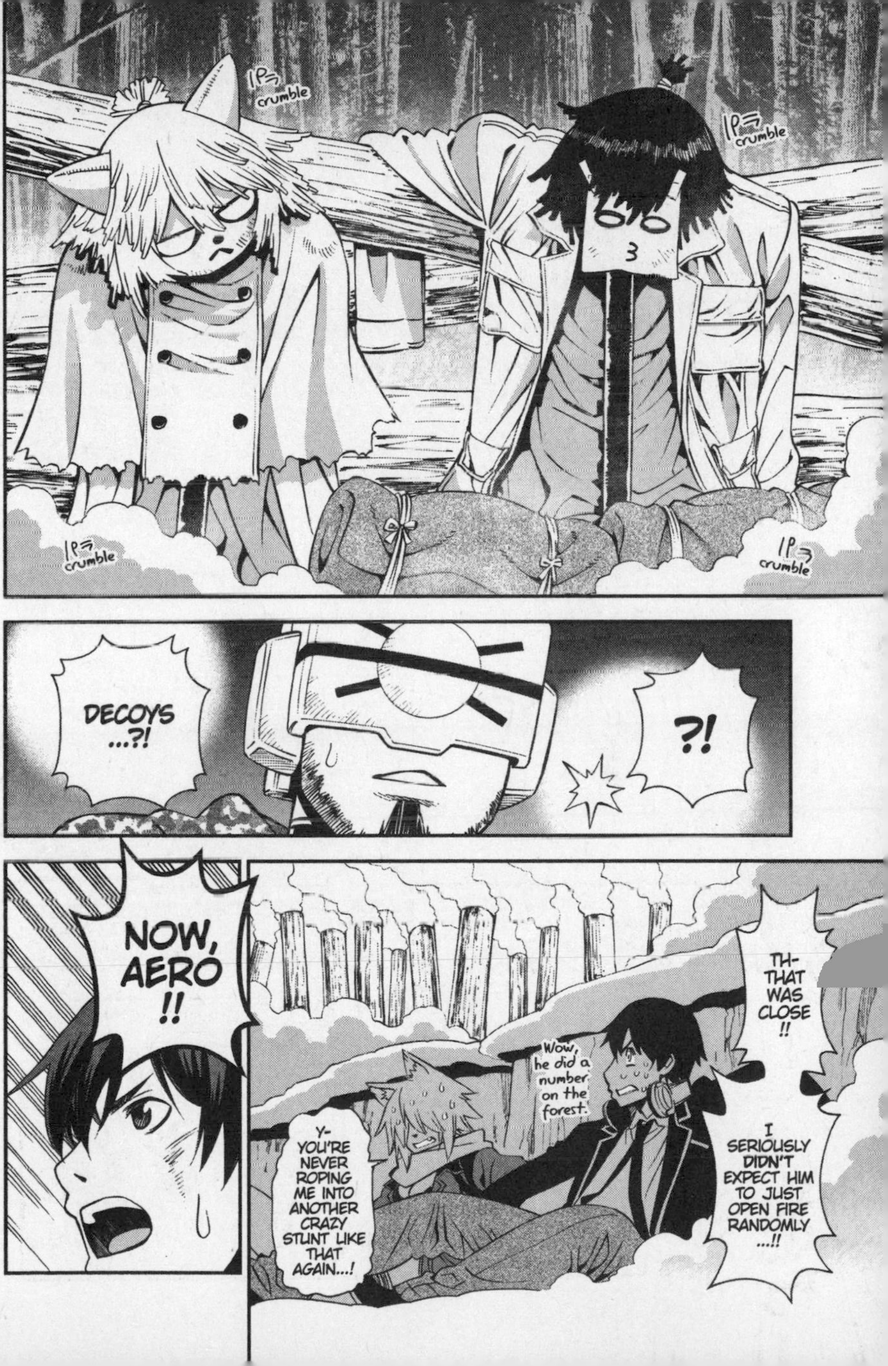
crumble
crumble
crumble
crumble
?!
DECOYS ...?!
TH- THAT WAS CLOSE !!
Wow, he did a number on the forest.
I SERIOUSLY DIDN'T EXPECT HIM TO JUST OPEN FIRE RANDOMLY ...!!
Y- YOU'RE NEVER ROPING ME INTO ANOTHER CRAZY STUNT LIKE THAT AGAIN...!
NOW, AERO !!

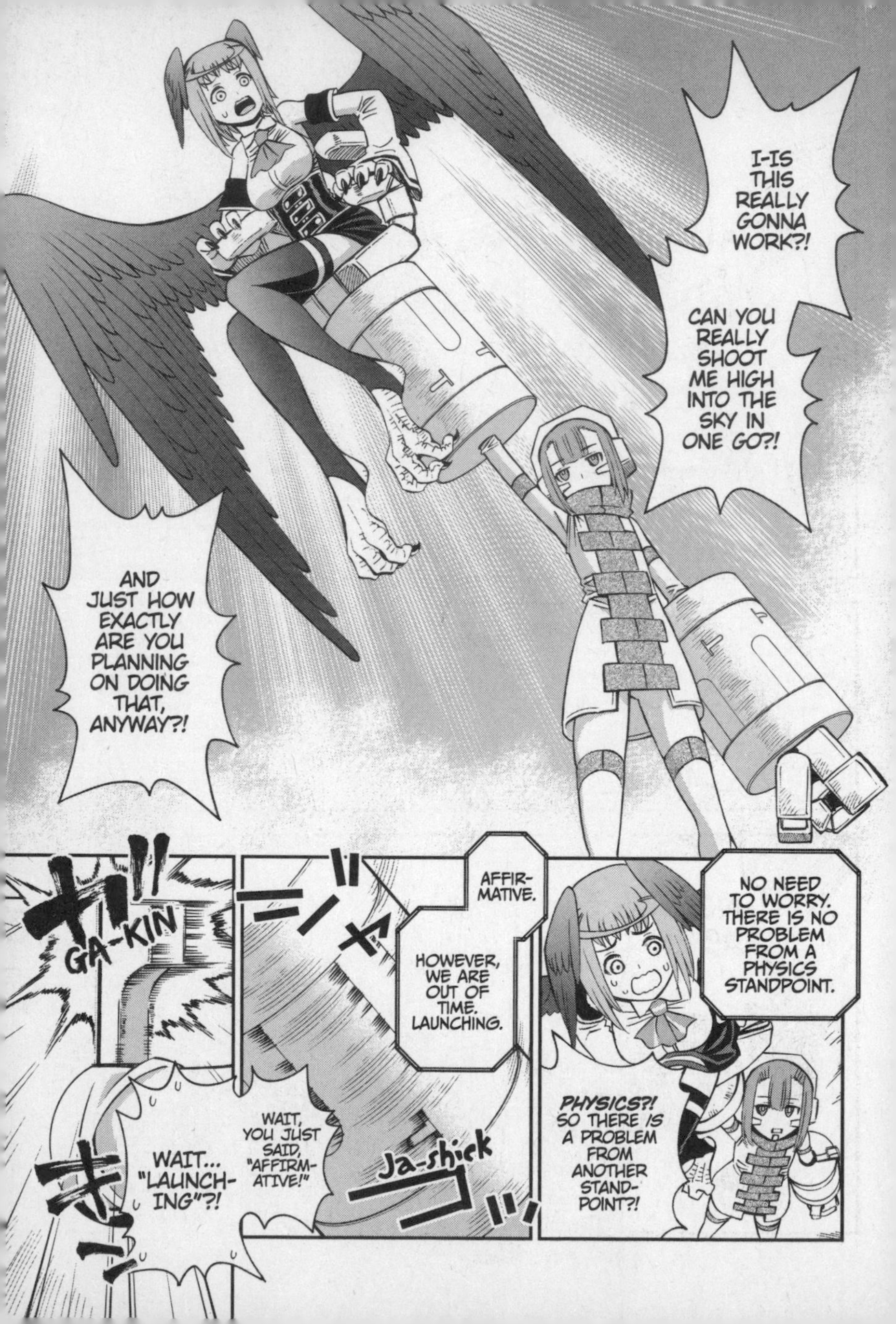
I-IS THIS REALLY GONNA WORK?!
CAN YOU REALLY SHOOT ME HIGH INTO THE SKY IN ONE GO?!
AND JUST HOW EXACTLY ARE YOU PLANNING ON DOING THAT, ANYWAY?!
NO NEED TO WORRY. THERE IS NO PROBLEM FROM A PHYSICS STANDPOINT.
PHYSICS?! SO THERE *IS* A PROBLEM FROM ANOTHER STAND-POINT?!
AFFIRM-ATIVE.
HOWEVER, WE ARE OUT OF TIME. LAUNCHING.
Ja-shick
WAIT, YOU JUST SAID, "AFFIRM-ATIVE!"
GA-KIN
WAIT... "LAUNCH-ING"?!

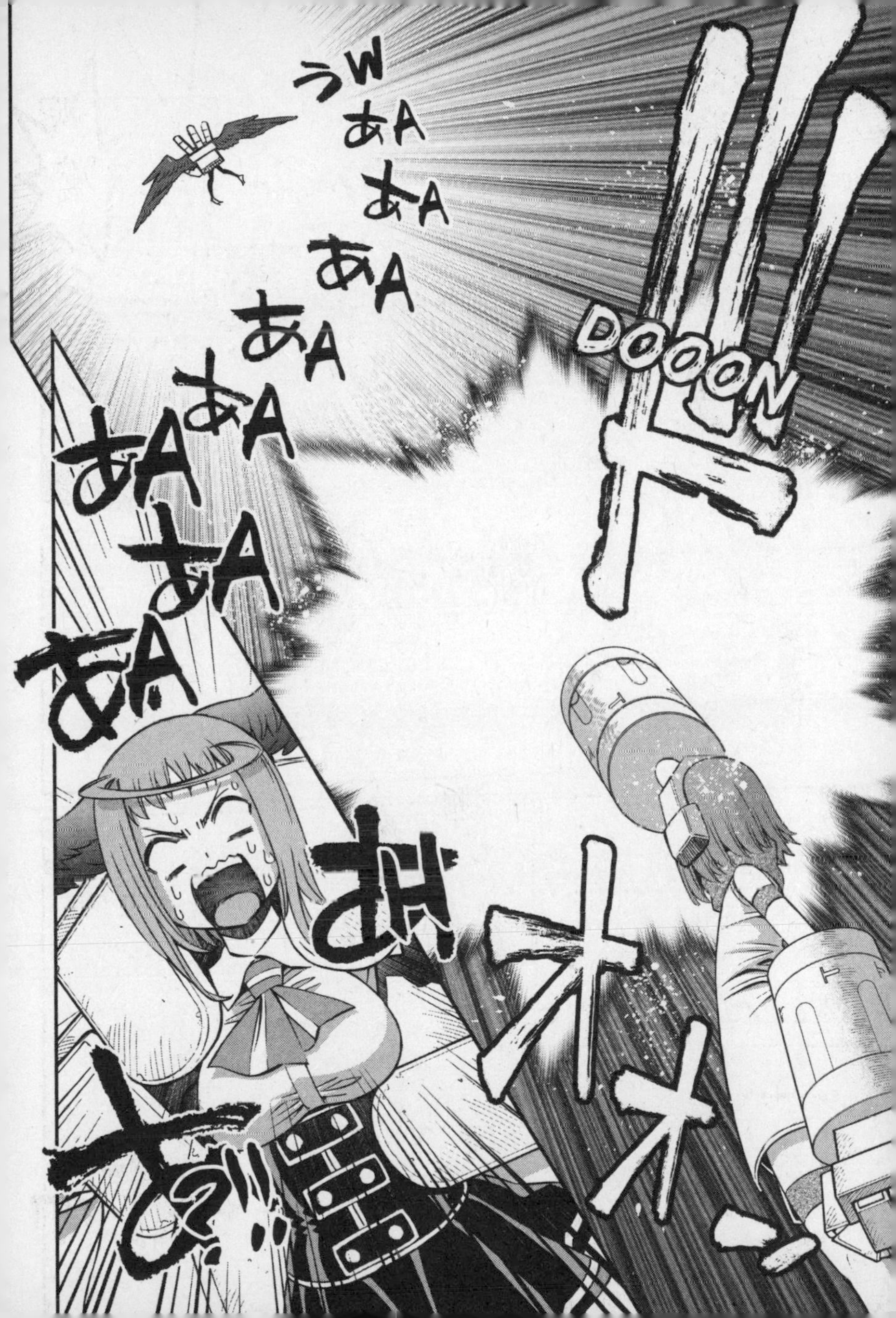

うWあAあAあAあAあAあAあAあAあH
DOOON

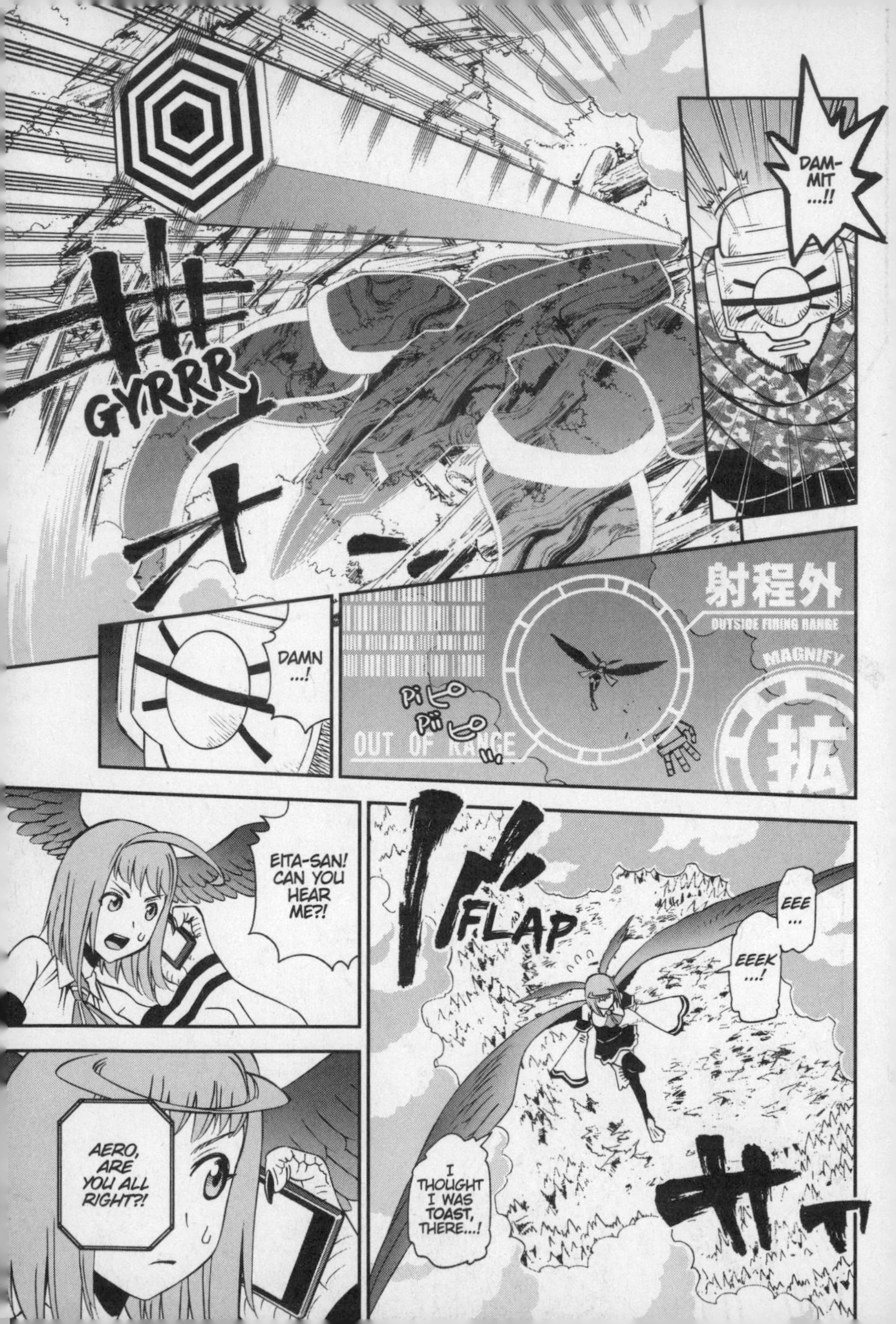
DAM-MIT ...!!
GYRRR
射程外
OUTSIDE FIRING RANGE
MAGNIFY
拡
Pi ピ Pii ピ
OUT OF RANGE
DAMN ...!
EEE ...
EEEK ...!
FLAP
I THOUGHT I WAS TOAST, THERE...!
EITA-SAN! CAN YOU HEAR ME?!
AERO, ARE YOU ALL RIGHT?!

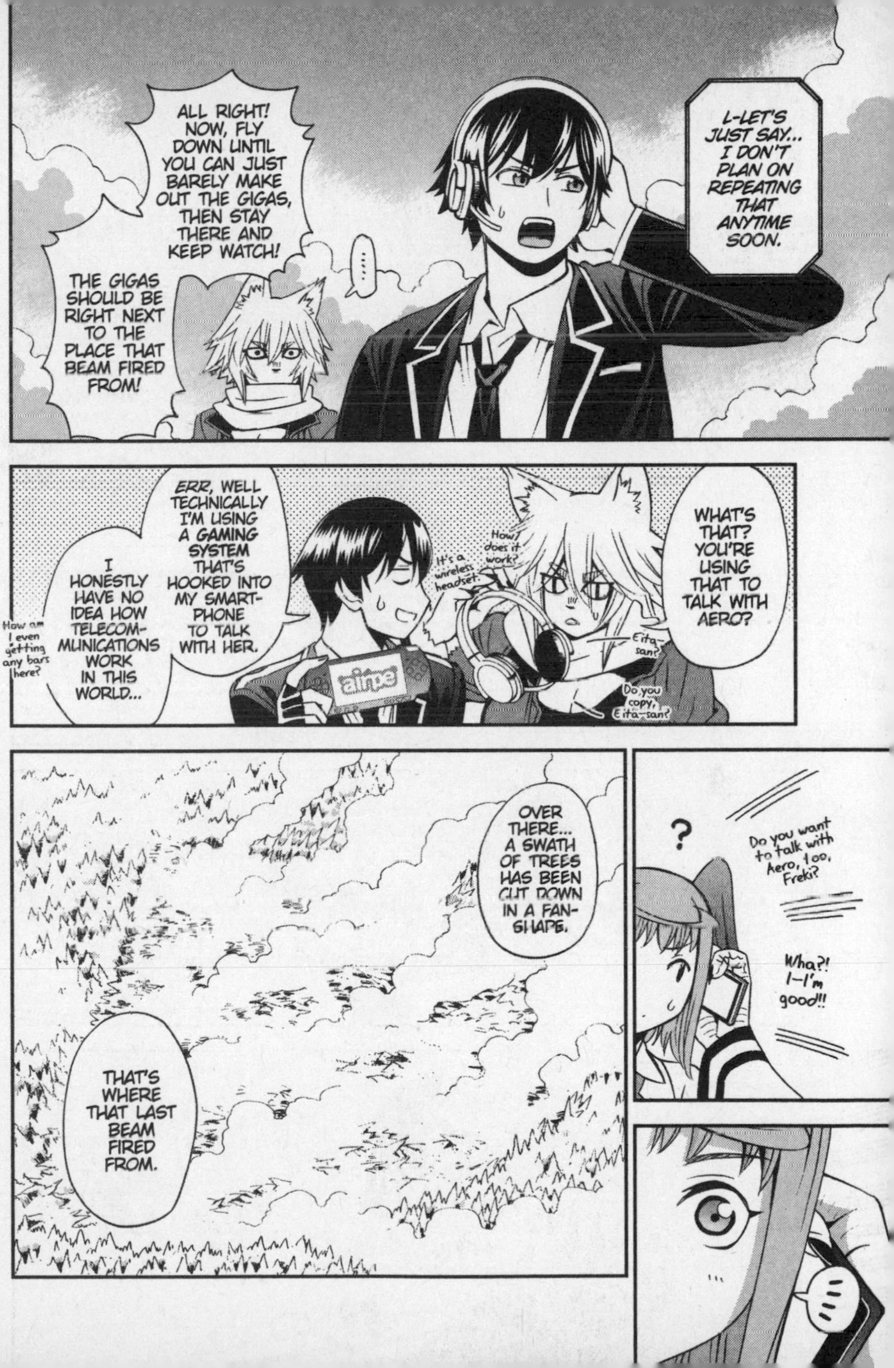
L-LET'S JUST SAY... I DON'T PLAN ON REPEATING THAT ANYTIME SOON.
...
ALL RIGHT! NOW, FLY DOWN UNTIL YOU CAN JUST BARELY MAKE OUT THE GIGAS, THEN STAY THERE AND KEEP WATCH!
THE GIGAS SHOULD BE RIGHT NEXT TO THE PLACE THAT BEAM FIRED FROM!
WHAT'S THAT? YOU'RE USING THAT TO TALK WITH AERO?
Eita-san?
Do you copy, Eita-san?
How does it work?
It's a wireless headset.
ERR, WELL TECHNICALLY I'M USING A GAMING SYSTEM THAT'S HOOKED INTO MY SMART-PHONE TO TALK WITH HER.
airpe
I HONESTLY HAVE NO IDEA HOW TELECOM-MUNICATIONS WORK IN THIS WORLD...
How am I even getting any bars here?
?
Do you want to talk with Aero, too, Freki?
Wha?! I-I'm good!!
...
OVER THERE... A SWATH OF TREES HAS BEEN CUT DOWN IN A FAN-SHAPE.
THAT'S WHERE THAT LAST BEAM FIRED FROM.

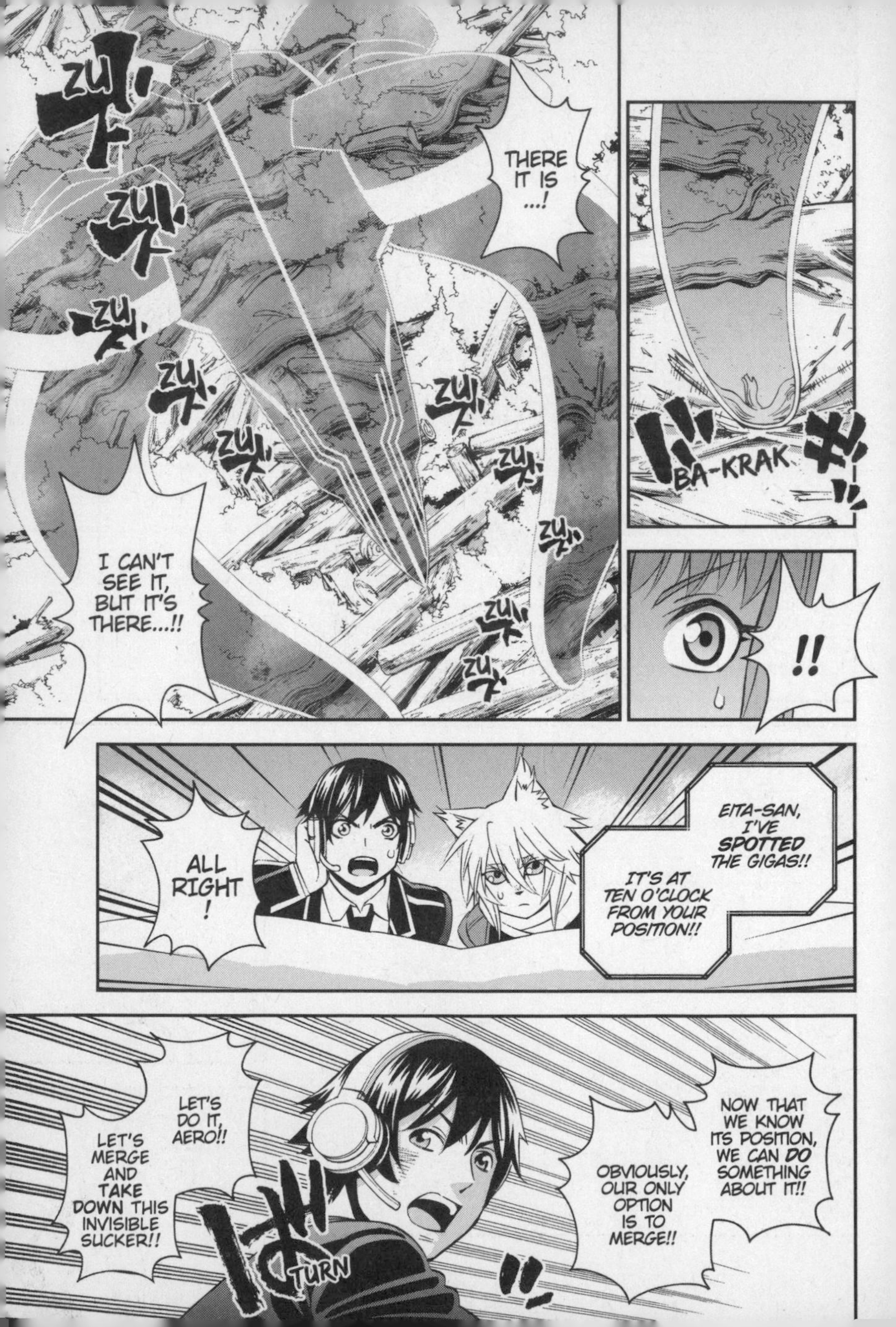
BA-KRAK
!!
THERE IT IS ...!
ZU
ZU
ZU
ZU
ZU
ZU
ZU
ZU
ZU
ZU
ZU
I CAN'T SEE IT, BUT IT'S THERE...!!
EITA-SAN, I'VE SPOTTED THE GIGAS!!
IT'S AT TEN O'CLOCK FROM YOUR POSITION!!
ALL RIGHT!
NOW THAT WE KNOW ITS POSITION, WE CAN DO SOMETHING ABOUT IT!!
OBVIOUSLY, OUR ONLY OPTION IS TO MERGE!!
LET'S DO IT, AERO!!
LET'S MERGE AND TAKE DOWN THIS INVISIBLE SUCKER!!
TURN

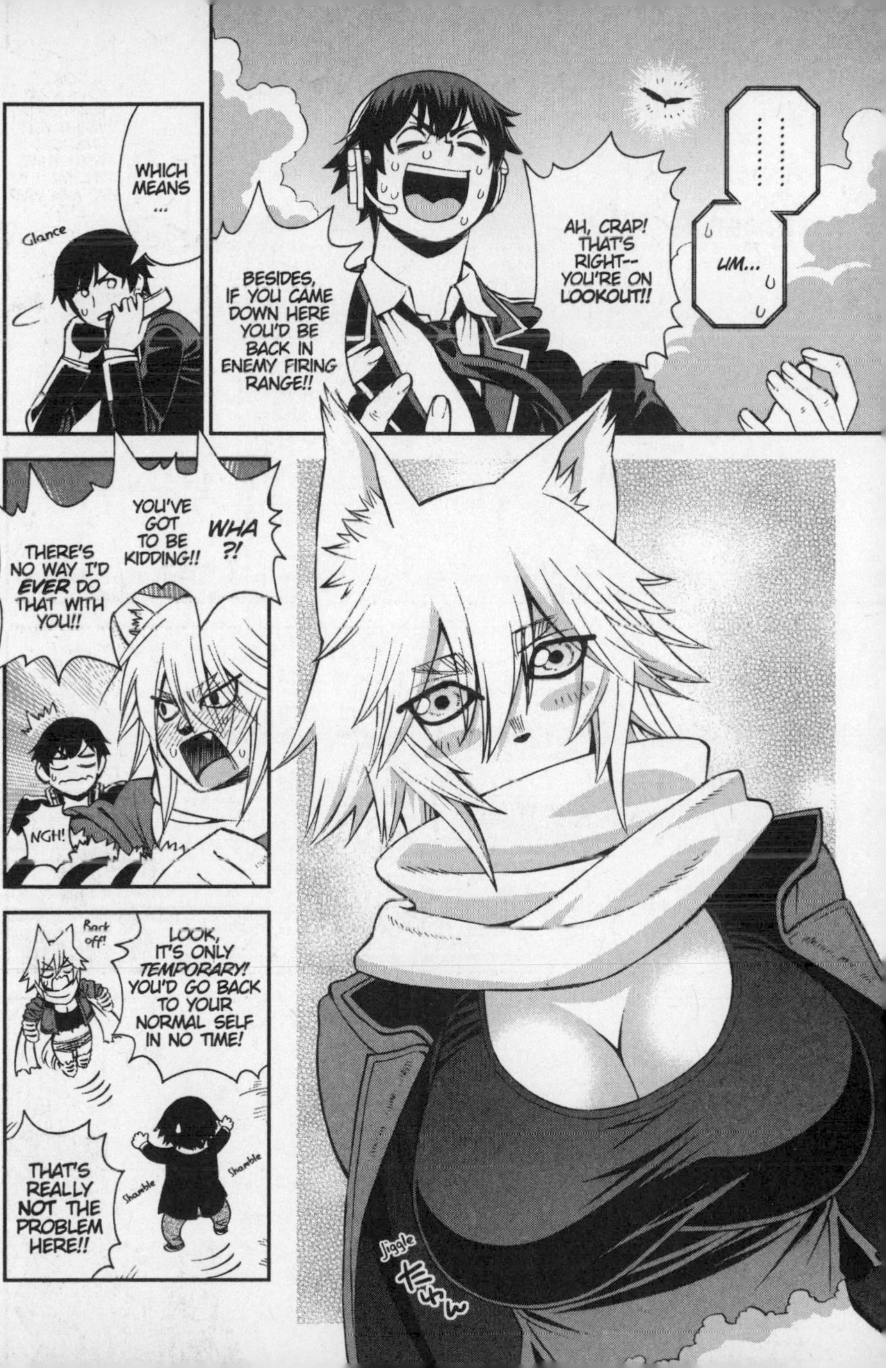
......
UM...
AH, CRAP! THAT'S RIGHT-- YOU'RE ON LOOKOUT!!
BESIDES, IF YOU CAME DOWN HERE YOU'D BE BACK IN ENEMY FIRING RANGE!!
WHICH MEANS ...
Glance
WHA ?!
YOU'VE GOT TO BE KIDDING!!
THERE'S NO WAY I'D *EVER* DO THAT WITH YOU!!
NGH!
LOOK, IT'S ONLY *TEMPORARY!* YOU'D GO BACK TO YOUR NORMAL SELF IN NO TIME!
Back off!
Shamble
Shamble
THAT'S REALLY NOT THE PROBLEM HERE!!
Jiggle

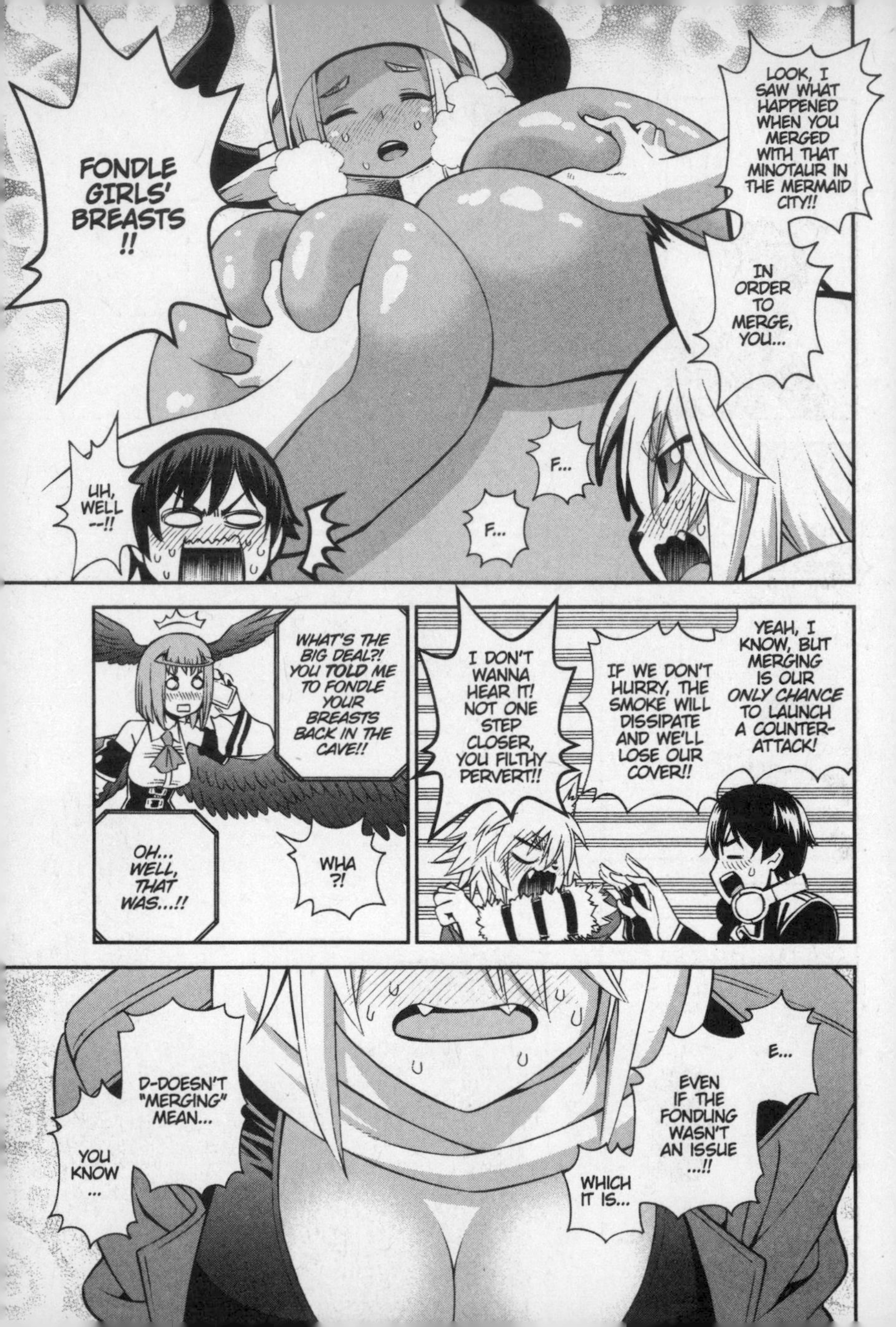
LOOK, I SAW WHAT HAPPENED WHEN YOU MERGED WITH THAT MINOTAUR IN THE MERMAID CITY!!
IN ORDER TO MERGE, YOU...
FONDLE GIRLS' BREASTS!!
F...
F...
UH, WELL--!!
YEAH, I KNOW, BUT MERGING IS OUR *ONLY CHANCE* TO LAUNCH A COUNTER-ATTACK!
IF WE DON'T HURRY, THE SMOKE WILL DISSIPATE AND WE'LL LOSE OUR COVER!!
I DON'T WANNA HEAR IT! NOT ONE STEP CLOSER, YOU FILTHY PERVERT!!
*WHAT'S THE BIG DEAL?! YOU **TOLD** ME TO FONDLE YOUR BREASTS BACK IN THE CAVE!!*
WHA?!
OH... WELL, THAT WAS...!!
E...
EVEN IF THE FONDLING WASN'T AN ISSUE...!!
WHICH IT IS...
D-DOESN'T "MERGING" MEAN...
YOU KNOW...

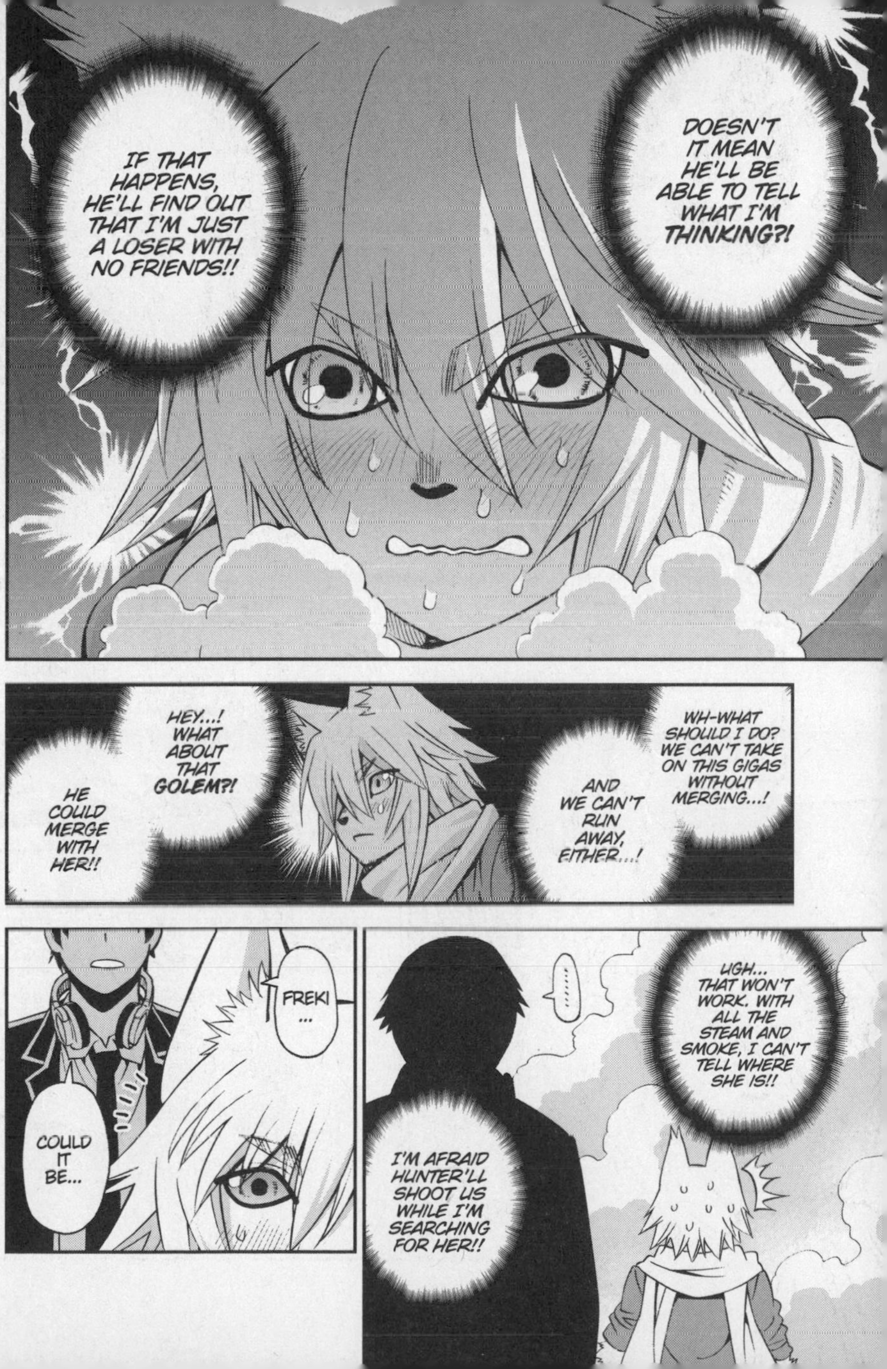
DOESN'T IT MEAN HE'LL BE ABLE TO TELL WHAT I'M THINKING?!
IF THAT HAPPENS, HE'LL FIND OUT THAT I'M JUST A LOSER WITH NO FRIENDS!!
WH-WHAT SHOULD I DO? WE CAN'T TAKE ON THIS GIGAS WITHOUT MERGING...!
AND WE CAN'T RUN AWAY, EITHER...!
HEY...! WHAT ABOUT THAT GOLEM?!
HE COULD MERGE WITH HER!!
UGH... THAT WON'T WORK. WITH ALL THE STEAM AND SMOKE, I CAN'T TELL WHERE SHE IS!!
......
I'M AFRAID HUNTER'LL SHOOT US WHILE I'M SEARCHING FOR HER!!
FREKI...
COULD IT BE...

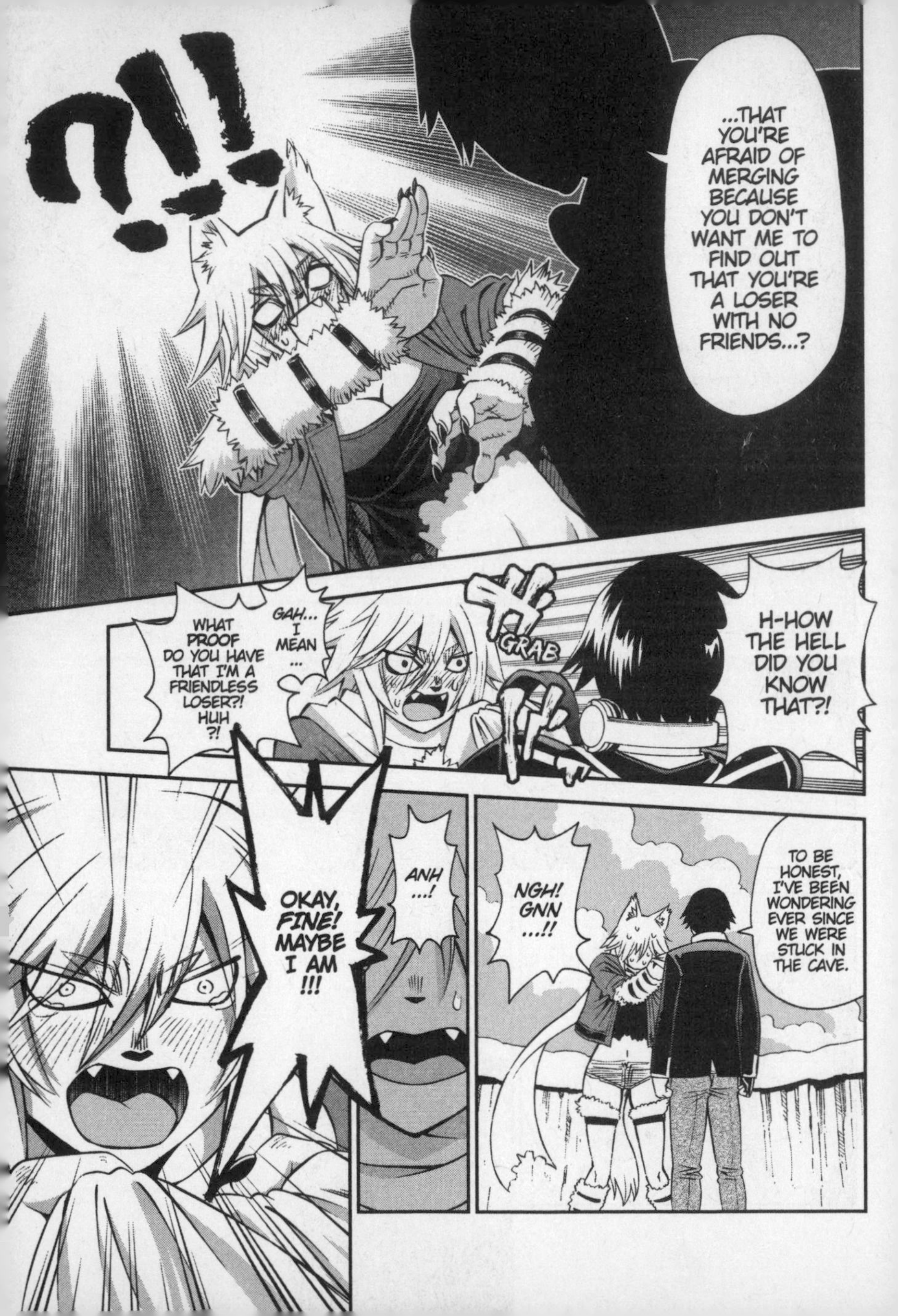
...THAT YOU'RE AFRAID OF MERGING BECAUSE YOU DON'T WANT ME TO FIND OUT THAT YOU'RE A LOSER WITH NO FRIENDS...?
?!!
H-HOW THE HELL DID YOU KNOW THAT?!
GRAB
GAH... I MEAN ...
WHAT PROOF DO YOU HAVE THAT I'M A FRIENDLESS LOSER?! HUH ?!
TO BE HONEST, I'VE BEEN WONDERING EVER SINCE WE WERE STUCK IN THE CAVE.
NGH! GNN ...!!
ANH ...!
OKAY, FINE! MAYBE I AM !!!

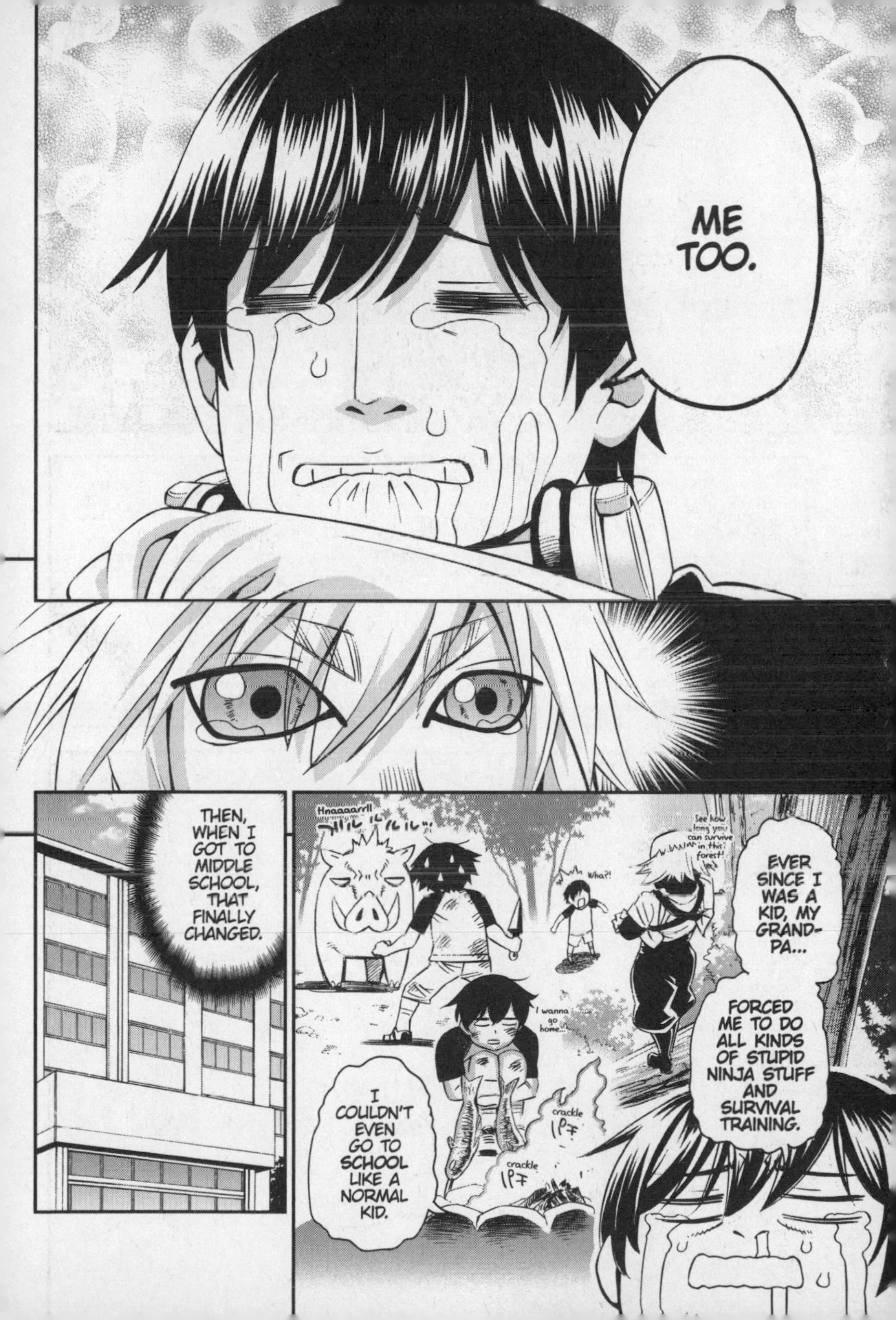
ME TOO.
EVER SINCE I WAS A KID, MY GRAND-PA...
See how long you can survive in this forest!
FORCED ME TO DO ALL KINDS OF STUPID NINJA STUFF AND SURVIVAL TRAINING.
Wha?!
Hnaaaarrll
I wanna go home...
crackle
crackle
I COULDN'T EVEN GO TO SCHOOL LIKE A NORMAL KID.
THEN, WHEN I GOT TO MIDDLE SCHOOL, THAT FINALLY CHANGED.

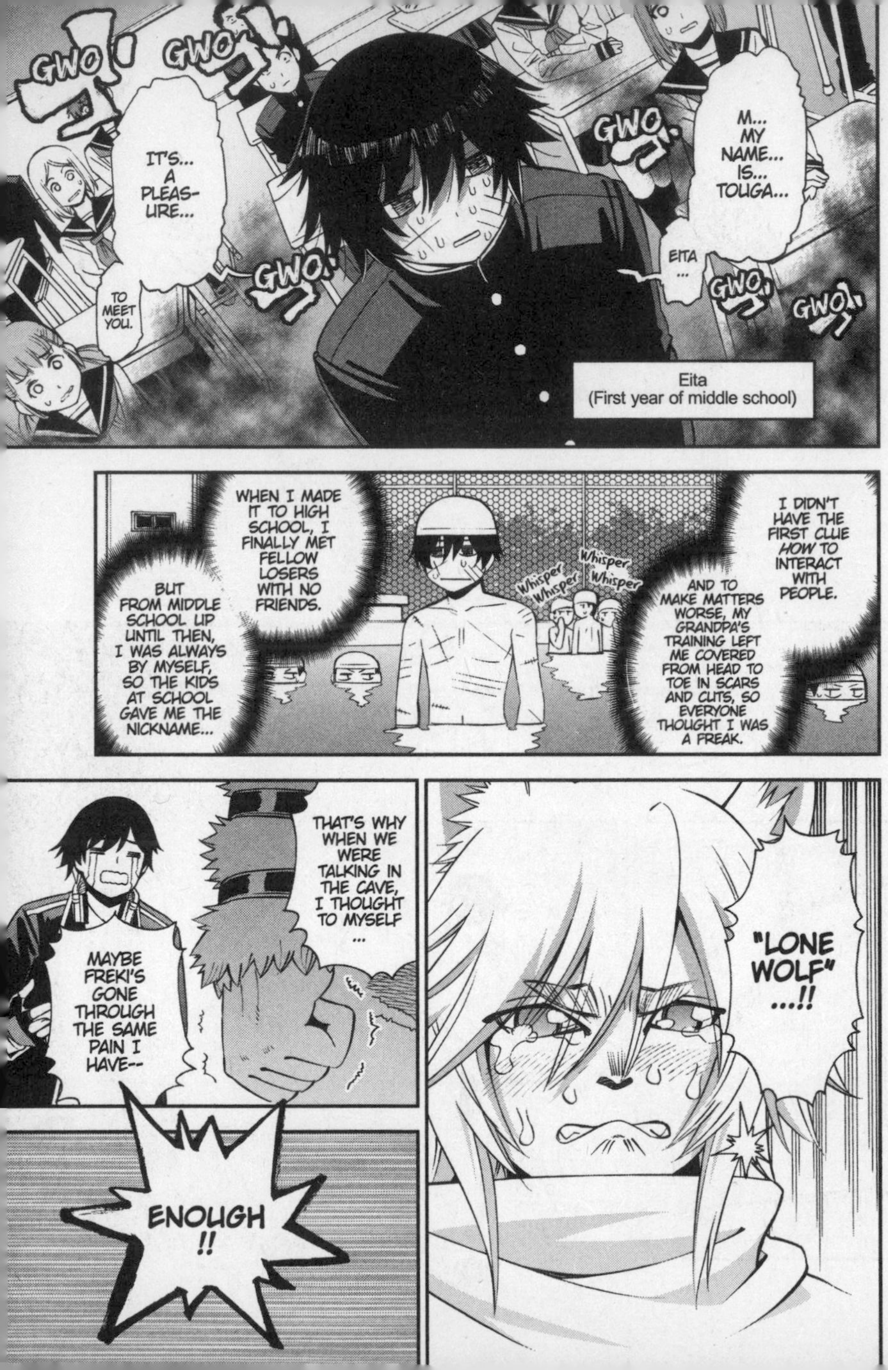
GWO
GWO
M... MY NAME... IS... TOUGA...
GWO
EITA ...
GWO
GWO
GWO
IT'S... A PLEASURE...
TO MEET YOU.
Eita (First year of middle school)
I DIDN'T HAVE THE FIRST CLUE HOW TO INTERACT WITH PEOPLE.
AND TO MAKE MATTERS WORSE, MY GRANDPA'S TRAINING LEFT ME COVERED FROM HEAD TO TOE IN SCARS AND CUTS, SO EVERYONE THOUGHT I WAS A FREAK.
Whisper Whisper
Whisper Whisper
WHEN I MADE IT TO HIGH SCHOOL, I FINALLY MET FELLOW LOSERS WITH NO FRIENDS.
BUT FROM MIDDLE SCHOOL UP UNTIL THEN, I WAS ALWAYS BY MYSELF, SO THE KIDS AT SCHOOL GAVE ME THE NICKNAME...
"LONE WOLF" ...!!
THAT'S WHY WHEN WE WERE TALKING IN THE CAVE, I THOUGHT TO MYSELF ...
MAYBE FREKI'S GONE THROUGH THE SAME PAIN I HAVE--
ENOUGH !!

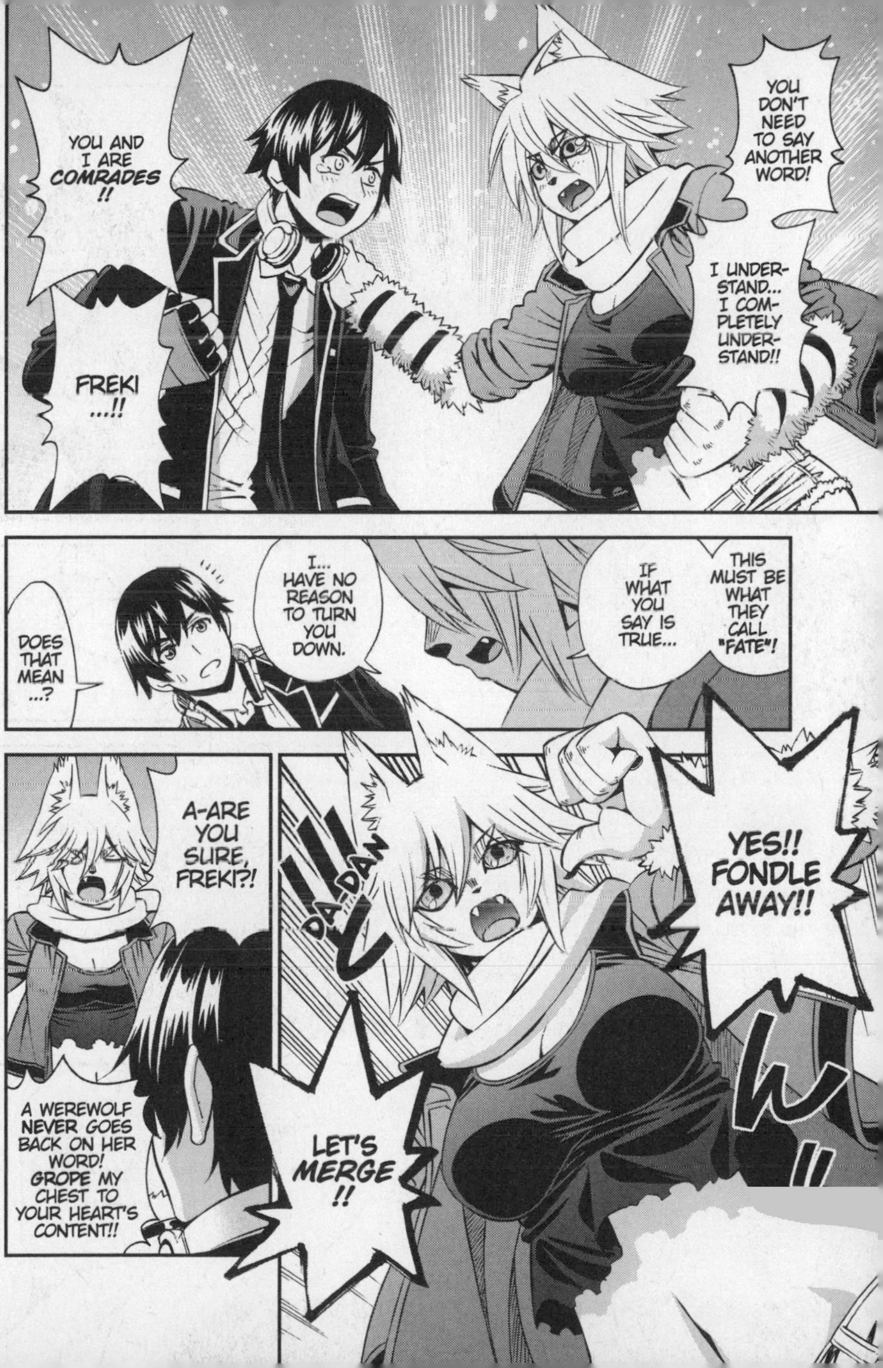
YOU DON'T NEED TO SAY ANOTHER WORD!
I UNDER-STAND... I COM-PLETELY UNDER-STAND!!
YOU AND I ARE COMRADES!!
FREKI ...!!
THIS MUST BE WHAT THEY CALL "FATE"!
IF WHAT YOU SAY IS TRUE...
I... HAVE NO REASON TO TURN YOU DOWN.
DOES THAT MEAN ...?
YES!! FONDLE AWAY!!
DA-DAN
LET'S MERGE!!
A-ARE YOU SURE, FREKI?!
A WEREWOLF NEVER GOES BACK ON HER WORD! GROPE MY CHEST TO YOUR HEART'S CONTENT!!

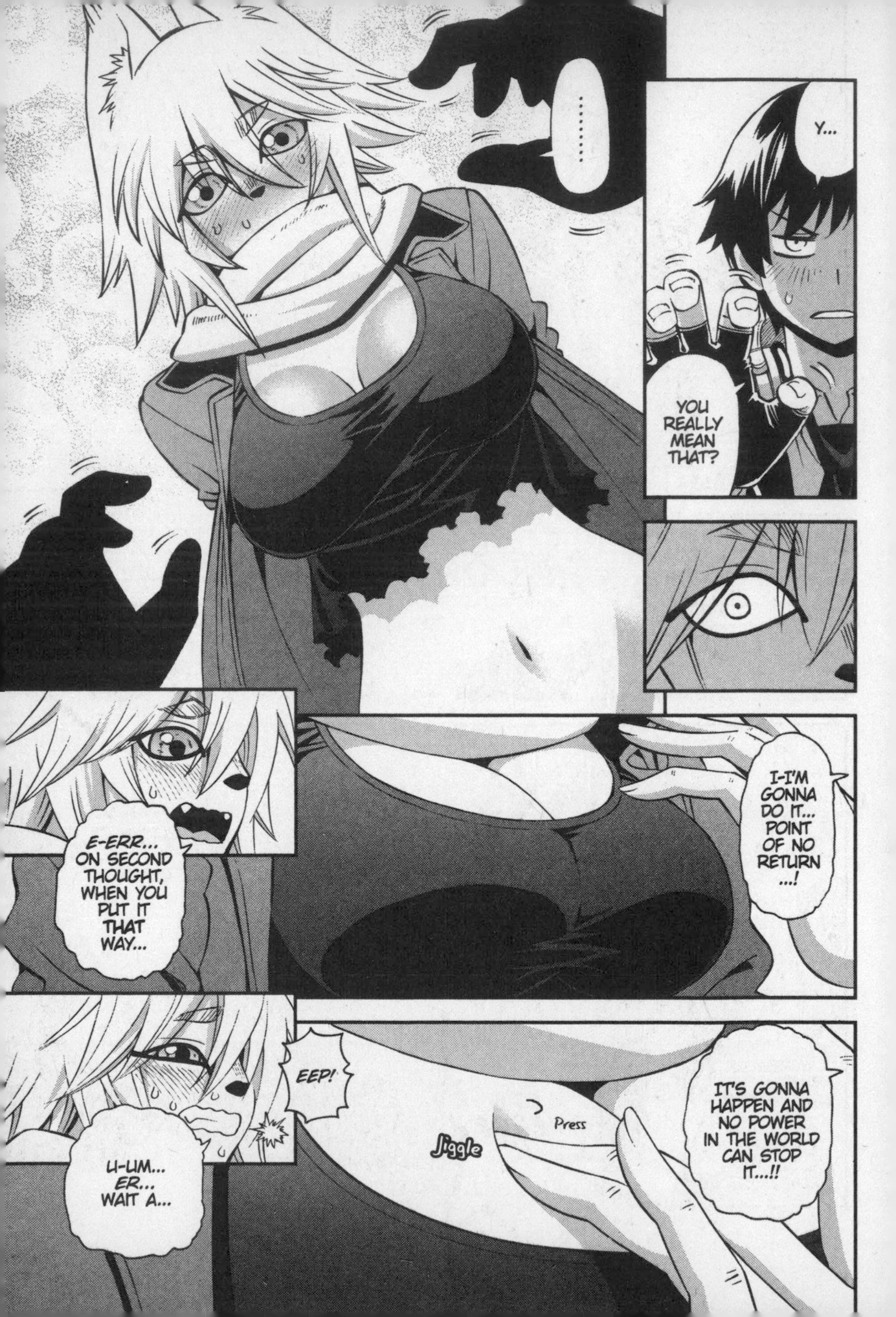
Y...
YOU REALLY MEAN THAT?
......
I-I'M GONNA DO IT... POINT OF NO RETURN ...!
E-ERR... ON SECOND THOUGHT, WHEN YOU PUT IT THAT WAY...
IT'S GONNA HAPPEN AND NO POWER IN THE WORLD CAN STOP IT...!!
Press
Jiggle
EEP!
U-UM... ER... WAIT A...

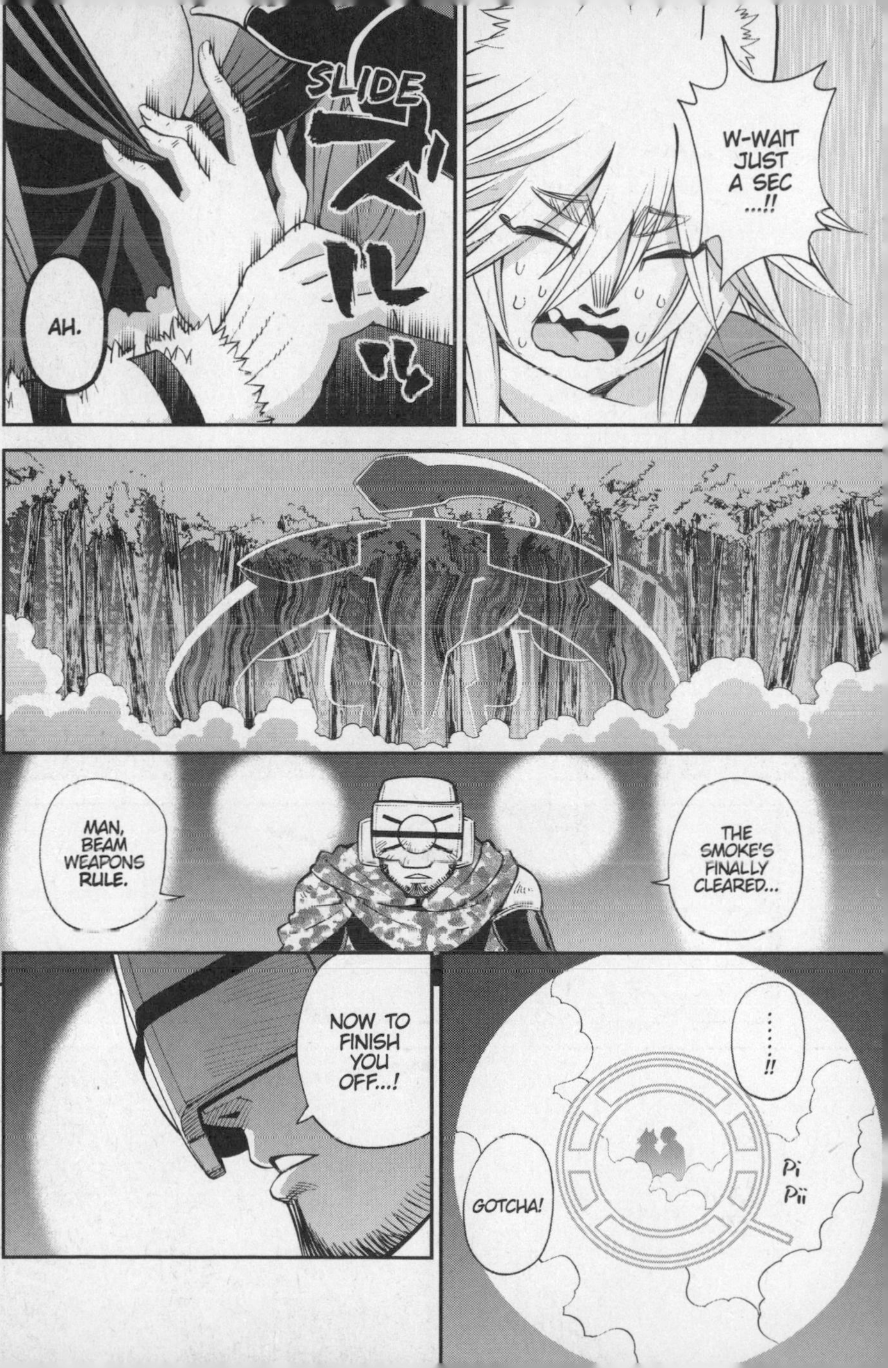
W-WAIT JUST A SEC ...!!
SLIDE
AH.
THE SMOKE'S FINALLY CLEARED...
MAN, BEAM WEAPONS RULE.
.......!!
Pi Pii
GOTCHA!
NOW TO FINISH YOU OFF...!

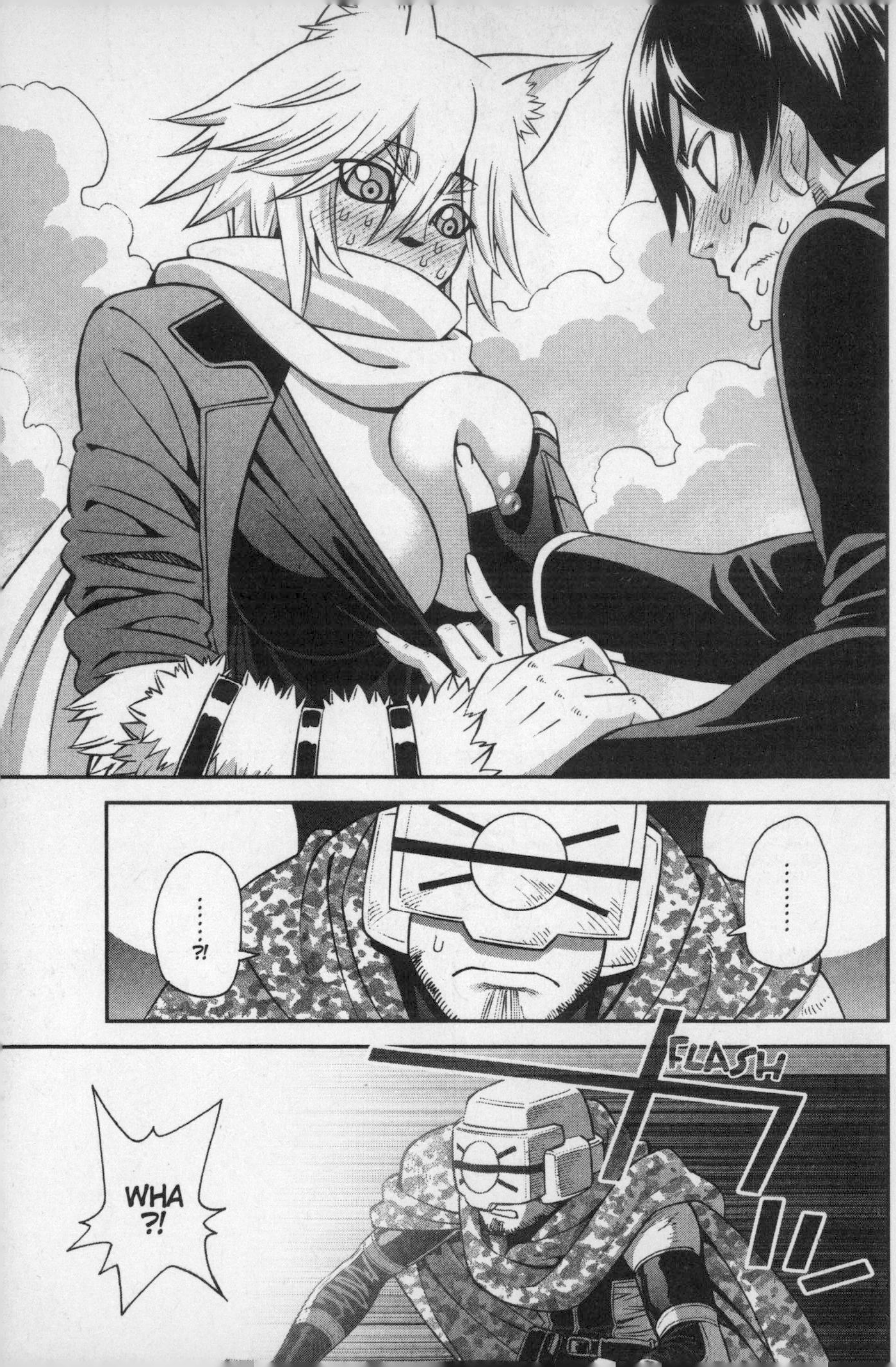
......
......?!
FLASH
WHA ?!

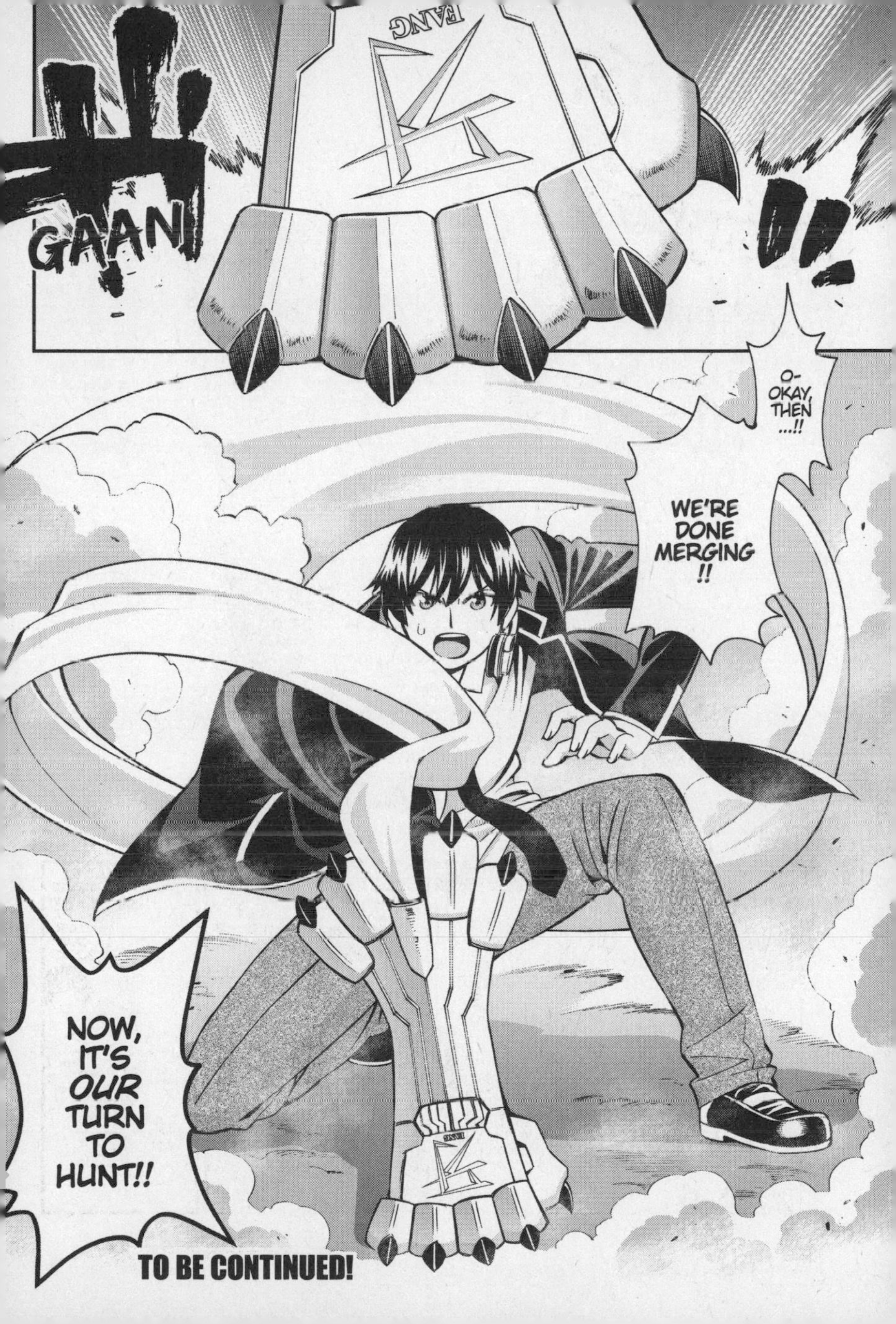
GAAN
O-OKAY, THEN...!!
WE'RE DONE MERGING!!
NOW, IT'S OUR TURN TO HUNT!!
TO BE CONTINUED!

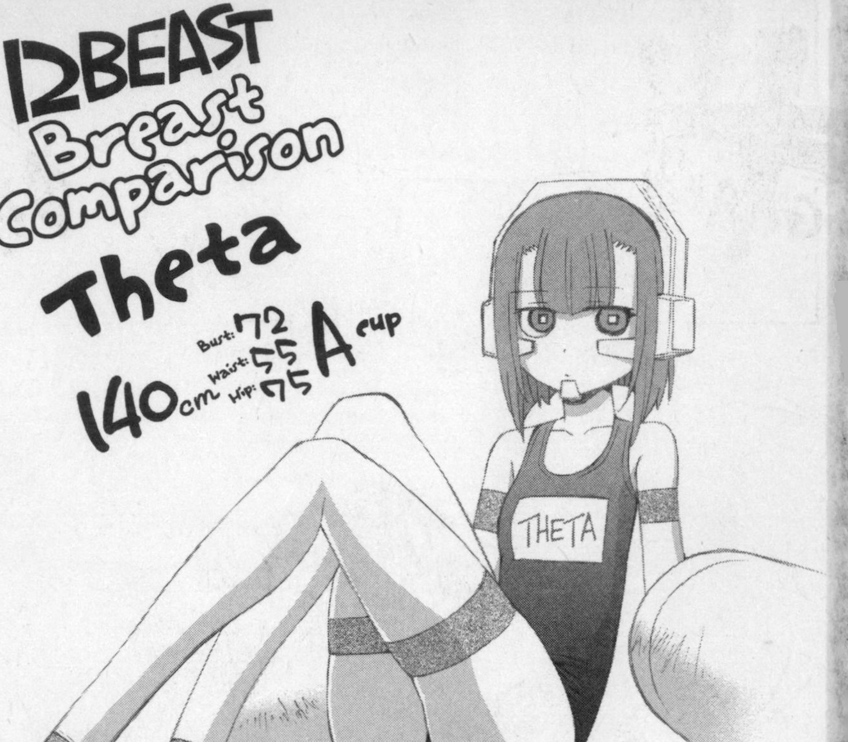
12 BEAST
Breast Comparison
Theta
140cm
Bust: 72
Waist: 55
Hip: 75
A cup
THETA

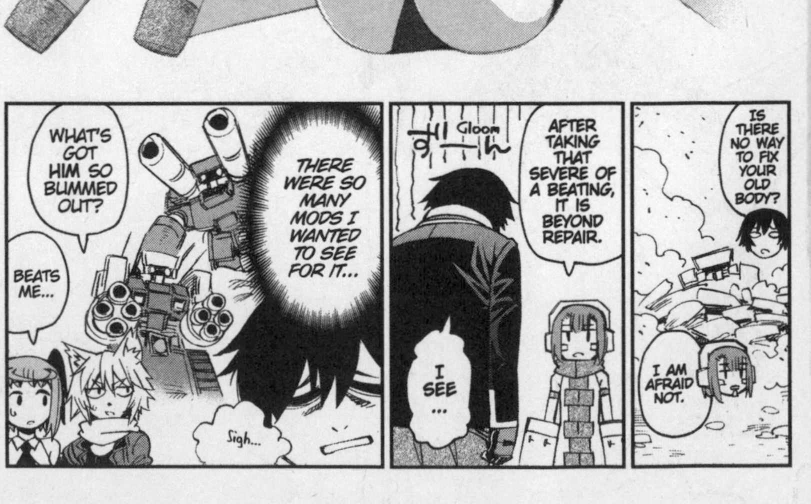
IS THERE NO WAY TO FIX YOUR OLD BODY?
I AM AFRAID NOT.
Gloom
AFTER TAKING THAT SEVERE OF A BEATING, IT IS BEYOND REPAIR.
I SEE ...
THERE WERE SO MANY MODS I WANTED TO SEE FOR IT...
WHAT'S GOT HIM SO BUMMED OUT?
BEATS ME...
Sigh...

SEVEN SEAS ENTERTAINMENT PRESENTS

12BEAST

story and art by OKAYADO   VOLUME 5

TRANSLATION
Ryan Peterson

ADAPTATION
Shanti Whitesides

LETTERING
Ma. Victoria Robado
William Ringrose

COVER DESIGN
Nicky Lim

PROOFREADER
Janet Houck

ASSISTANT EDITOR
Jenn Grunigen

PRODUCTION ASSISTANT
CK Russell

PRODUCTION MANAGER
Lissa Pattillo

EDITOR-IN-CHIEF
Adam Arnold

PUBLISHER
Jason DeAngelis

12BEAST VOLUME 5
© OKAYADO 2017
First published in Japan in 2017 by KADOKAWA CORPORATION,
English translation rights arranged with KADOKAWA CORPORATIO
through TOHAN CORPORATION, Tokyo.

Seven Seas books may be purchased in bulk for promotional, educational, or
business use. Please contact your local bookseller or the Macmillan Corporate
and Premium Sales Department at 1-800-221-7945, extension 5442, or by
e-mail at MacmillanSpecialMarkets@macmillan.com.

Seven Seas and the Seven Seas logo are trademarks of
Seven Seas Entertainment, LLC. All rights reserved.

ISBN: 978-1-626924-45-1

Printed in Canada

First Printing: September 2017

10 9 8 7 6 5 4 3 2 1

FOLLOW US ONLINE: *www.gomanga.com*

READING DIRECTIONS

This book reads from *right to left*, Japanese style.
If this is your first time reading manga, you start
reading from the top right panel on each page and
take it from there. If you get lost, just follow the
numbered diagram here. It may seem backwards at
first, but you'll get the hang of it! Have fun!!

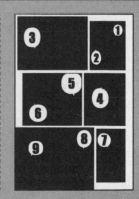